HISTORY OF SPECIAL EDUCATION

ADVANCES IN SPECIAL EDUCATION

Series Editor: Anthony F. Rotatori

Recent Volumes:

ADVANCES IN SPECIAL EDUCATION   VOLUME 21

HISTORY OF SPECIAL EDUCATION

EDITED BY

ANTHONY F. ROTATORI
Saint Xavier University, Chicago, IL, USA

FESTUS E. OBIAKOR
University of Wisconsin-Milwaukee, Milwaukee, WI, USA

JEFFREY P. BAKKEN
Illinois State University, Normal, IL, USA

Emerald

United Kingdom – North America – Japan
India – Malaysia – China

KH

Emerald Group Publishing Limited
Howard House, Wagon Lane, Bingley BD16 1WA, UK

First edition 2011

Copyright © 2011 Emerald Group Publishing Limited

Reprints and permission service
Contact: booksandseries@emeraldinsight.com

British Library Cataloguing in Publication Data
A catalogue record for this book is available from the British Library

ISBN: 978-0-85724-629-5
ISSN: 0270-4013 (Series)

Emerald Group Publishing
Limited, Howard House,
Environmental Management
System has been certified by
ISOQAR to ISO 14001:2004
standards

Awarded in recognition of
Emerald's production
department's adherence to
quality systems and processes
when preparing scholarly
journals for print

INVESTOR IN PEOPLE

2/28/12

CONTENTS

LIST OF CONTRIBUTORS

Betty Y. Ashbaker	Counseling Psychology and Special Education, Brigham Young University, Provo, UT, USA
Jeffrey P. Bakken	Department of Special Education, Illinois State University, Normal, IL, USA
Christine Clark-Bischke	Department of Special Education, Illinois Sate University, Normal, IL, USA
Frederick J. Brigham	Department of Human Development, George Mason University, Fairfax, VA, USA
Sandra Burkhardt	Department of Psychology, Saint Xavier University, Chicago, IL, USA
Carrie Anna Courtad	Department of Special Education, Illinois State University, Normal, IL, USA
Julie A. Deisinger	Department of Psychology, Saint Xavier University, Chicago, IL, USA
Sharon Doubet	Department of Special Education, Illinois State University, Normal, IL, USA
Laurel M. Garrick Duhaney	Department of Educational Studies, State University of New York at New Paltz, New Paltz, NY, USA
Fabiola P. Ehlers-Zavala	Department of English, Colorado State University, Fort Collins, CO, USA
C. Jonah Eleweke	Department of Communication Sciences & Disorders, Texas Woman's University, Denton, TX, USA
Barbara M. Fulk	Department of Special Education, Illinois State University, Normal, IL, USA

Satasha L. Green	Exceptional Education Department, State University of New York College at Buffalo, Buffalo, NY, USA
Brittany L. Hott	Department of Human Development, George Mason University, Fairfax, VA, USA
Stacy M. Kelly	Department of Special Education, Illinois State University, Normal, IL, USA
Michelle J. McCollin	Department of Special Education, Slippery Rock University, Slippery, PA, USA
Kagendo Mutua	Department of Special Education and Multiple Abilities, University of Alabama, Tuscaloosa, AL, USA
Festus E. Obiakor	Department of Exceptional Education, University of Wisconsin-Milwaukee, Milwaukee, WI, USA
Amanda C. Quesenberry	Department of Curriculum and Instruction, Illinois State University, Normal, IL, USA
Anthony F. Rotatori	Department of Psychology, Saint Xavier University, Chicago, IL, USA
Spencer J. Salend	Department of Educational Studies, State University of New York at New Paltz, New Paltz, NY, USA
Christine M. Scott	Speech-Language Pathology Department, State University of New York College at Buffalo, Buffalo, NY, USA
James Siders	Department of Special Education and Multiple Abilities, University of Alabama, Tuscaloosa, AL, USA
Emily Watts	Department of Special Education Illinois State University Normal, IL, USA

PREFACE

Individuals with exceptionalities have been present in society for thousands of years, especially those with sensory and physical characteristics. However, the way society has reacted to individuals with exceptionalities has changed dramatically. The change has been positive, as society initially viewed such individuals as burdens, worthless, demons and buffoons, then exhibited more protective and humanitarian attitudes related to their welfare and finally to the present day in which individuals with exceptionalities are considered part of an inclusive society where all citizens have value and merit and can make meaningful contributions. This journey has not been easy for individuals with exceptionalities, their families or those who have educated them; however, it has been colourful, innovative and intriguing.

This volume in Advances in Special Education focuses on the *History of Special Education*. The volume examines the historical journey of special education by categorical areas (e.g. Learning Disabilities, Autism Spectrum Disorders, Intellectual Impairment, Emotional and Behavioural Disorders, Giftedness and Talent Development). Each categorical chapter includes an examination of early foundations and conceptualizations, pioneers in the field, evolving definitions, impact of legislative acts on the field, educational and intervention practices, assessment parameters, working with families, and technology innovations for practice and education.

The volume also includes chapters on the changing philosophy related to educating students with exceptionalities as well as a detailed history of legal and legislative acts that have influenced the development of special education. The book concludes with an insightful chapter entitled *Historical and Contemporary Contexts, Challenges, and Prospects in the Education of Students with Exceptionalities*.

The volume is composed of 15 chapters written by university professors who are actively involved in teaching special education courses and engaged in research in their prospective fields. It should be used as a supplementary text for advanced undergraduate special education majors and graduate students who are looking for detailed and comprehensive historical information for their research papers or theses.

Anthony F. Rotatori
Festus E. Obiakor
Jeffrey P. Bakken
Editors

CHAPTER 1

HISTORICAL AND PHILOSOPHICAL CHANGES IN THE EDUCATION OF STUDENTS WITH EXCEPTIONALITIES

Spencer J. Salend and Laurel M. Garrick Duhaney

Although the first public use of the term *special education* appears to have occurred at a presentation by Alexander Graham Bell at a National Education Association meeting in 1884 (Winzer, 1998), the historical and philosophical underpinnings of the field of special education emerged long before that event. Forged by a mixture of philosophical, political, economic, legal, and sociocultural factors (Fleischer & Zames, 2001; Giordano, 2007; Osgood, 2007; Reynolds, 1989), the history of special education is characterized by ongoing challenges, successes, and debates related to: (a) What are the goals and desired outcomes of special education? (b) Who should be served by special education? (c) How can a specially designed research-based pedagogy be best provided? and (d) Where should students with exceptionalities be educated? Although different from the history of people with disabilities, the field of special education has been inextricably linked to the treatment of individuals with exceptionalities and the societal perceptions and cultural and philosophical views of disability (Smith, 1998; Winzer, 1993).

History of Special Education
Advances in Special Education, Volume 21, 1–20
Copyright © 2011 by Emerald Group Publishing Limited
All rights of reproduction in any form reserved
ISSN: 0270-4013/doi:10.1108/S0270-4013(2011)0000021004

THE EARLY ROOTS OF SPECIAL EDUCATION

The history of special education has been influenced by changing societal and philosophical beliefs about the extent to which individuals with disabilities should be feared, segregated, categorized, and educated. Prior to the 1700s, individuals with exceptionalities were largely ignored or subjected to inhumane treatment, ridicule, isolation, and at times put to death (D'Antonio, 2004; Winzer, 1993, 1998). However, the sixteenth and seventeenth centuries ushered in rational philosophical beliefs about human dignity, which led to changes in the treatment and societal perceptions of individuals with exceptionalities (Winzer, 1998). These changes also were supported by efforts of pioneering special educators and advocates who began to experiment with various individually designed approaches to educating individuals with exceptionalities and to disseminate their work to others (Winzer, 1993).

In the 1500s and 1600s, the education of individuals with exceptionalities was influenced by European intellectuals seeking philosophical knowledge and a more egalitarian society (Winzer, 1993). In France, the Enlightenment led to changes in core beliefs about human nature, human reason, human rights and dignity, and self-sufficiency. These philosophical changes led to calls for the questioning of long held views and established socio-political structures and a society that recognized the rights of all of its citizens (Knight, 1968; Safford & Safford, 1996; Winzer, 1986, 1993).

In England, developing philosophical beliefs combined with the emerging research on language development conducted by scholars at the Royal Society of London, contributed to the movement to provide educational opportunities to individuals with exceptionalities (Winzer, 1993, 1998). For instance, John Wallis published a book examining the origins of language which served as an important guide that fostered the provision of educational opportunities to deaf individuals (Hoolihan, 1985; Winzer, 1993).

Initial Focus on the Sensory Disabilities

The initial efforts to deliver special education and to develop specially designed instruction were focused on individuals with sensory disabilities (Best, 1930; Winzer, 1998). During the mid-sixteenth century, Pedro Ponce de Leon, a Spanish Benedictine monk, created oralism, an alternative to sign language that involved the teaching of lip-reading and speech, to teach wealthy deaf individuals to speak in order to obtain their inheritance (Buchanan, 1999; Burch & Sutherland, 2006; Lane, 1989; Winzer, 1998). The work of Pedro Ponce de Leon was enhanced by the pedagogical efforts of Jacob Rodrigue Péreire, who was considered one of the first educators of the deaf. Subsequently, the use of oralism grew and became the dominant mode of communication taught in schools for the deaf from the 1890s to the 1920s (Burch & Sutherland, 2006; Winzer, 1998). However, Michel Charles de l'Épée, a French priest, challenged the use of oralism and fostered the belief that the use of written characters and sign language was the most effective way to educate the deaf, which resulted in the use of sign language as the prevailing deaf education pedagogy during the first half of the 1800s (Winzer, 1998).

Successful instructional practices for the deaf led to efforts to develop effective specially designed approaches and techniques for blind individuals (Winzer, 1998). In 1784, Valentin Haüy, the founder of a school for the blind in Paris, devised a system of raised print and embossed books to educate blind students (see Winzer, 1998). In 1829, Louis Braille, a former student at the Paris Blind School, created a raised dot method for reading and a stylus for writing, which led to the creation of a tactile alphabet that provided blind individuals with access to reading materials and allowed them to be more fully included in French society (Koestler, 1976).

As word of the successes of these efforts to educate individuals with sensory disabilities spread outside of Europe, educators traveled to learn about these effective special education practices and to implement and expand on them in their countries (Winzer, 1993). For instance, in 1817, after studying in Europe, Thomas Gallaudet established the first institution for the deaf in Hartford, Connecticut, USA (Osgood, 2005). Similarly, building on his studies in Paris, Dr. John D. Fischer, created the New England Asylum for the Blind in 1829, which was later renamed the Perkins Institute for the Blind and is now called the Perkins School for the Blind (Fleischer & Zames, 2001; Winzer, 1993).

At the Perkins institute, Samuel Gridley Howe worked with Laura Bridgman, a deaf–blind student. Employing an individually designed approach based on her ability to identify letters by distinguishing shapes, Howe showed that Laura Bridgman could be educated. The groundbreaking work of Howe and Bridgman challenged accepted beliefs that deaf–blind individuals could not learn and served as a forerunner for the ensuing accomplishments of Helen Keller and her teacher Anne Mansfield Sullivan (Osgood, 2005; Smith, 1998).

THE EMERGENCE OF SPECIALIZED INTERVENTIONS, PROGRAMS, SCHOOLS, AND INSTITUTIONS

Whereas initial efforts to design and provide specially designed instruction were focused on individuals with sensory exceptionalities, the provision of a special education began to be expanded to include individuals with cognitive disabilities. Although this period in the history of special education saw the development of specialized interventions for this group of individuals, it also was characterized by the rise of institutions and specialized schools.

Institutional Settings

Influenced by negative stereotypes and perceptions and fears of individuals with disabilities, especially toward those with cognitive and emotional and behavioral challenges, the mid-nineteenth century saw the growth of institutions and asylums for individuals with disabilities (Armstrong, 2002). Although some institutions viewed their purpose as providing educational and vocational programs and fostering moral and religious development (Giordano, 2007), many of them saw their role as delivering medical, vocational, and custodial care and serving as a vehicle to separate, mend, and control disabled and "defective" individuals who were perceived as deviant and threatening (Armstrong, 2002; Humphries & Gordon, 1992; Winzer, 1998). As a result of the humanitarian, legal, and economic issues associated with institutional settings, community-based day care and occupation centers that offered custodial care and limited levels of vocational preparation also began to emerge (Giordano, 2007; Read & Walmsley, 2006).

Specialized Interventions for Individuals with Cognitive Disabilities

In the early 1800s, the work of Jean-Marc-Gaspard Itard with Victor, who was referred to as the wild boy of Aveyron, served as a seminal event in the field of special education (Safford & Safford, 1996). Itard developed a specially designed pedagogy that enhanced Victor's language and cognitive development, which showed that individuals previously considerable uneducable could learn (Safford & Safford, 1996). Itard's work served as a springboard for other European scholars and educators (Hinshelwood, 1900; Ireland, 1877; Morgan, 1896) to disseminate their efforts to study and validate a collection of effective special education instructional practices. The most prominent of these efforts was Édouard Seguin's publication, *Treatise on Idiocy*, which presented a set of specialized instructional principles, techniques, and devices that provided others with a pedagogical model for teaching individuals with cognitive disabilities (Giordano, 2007).

Specialized Programs, Schools, and Classes

The success of and attention received by the specialized pedagogies of Itard, Seguin, and other European educators helped to change societal viewpoints with respect to whether individuals with cognitive disabilities could learn and gave rise to laws and efforts to educate these students in specialized schools and classes (Giordano, 2007; Read & Walmsley, 2006). In the early 1900s, France established a law that created special improvement classes for students with learning difficulties that were associated with schools that educated students without disabilities (Armstrong, 2002). In 1913, Great Britain passed the Mental Deficiency Act which promulgated policies for defining and educating students with exceptionalities and mandated that educational and governmental agencies be responsible for administering them (Giordano, 2007).

Advocacy Groups

The rise of specialized schools and classes and the legislation in Europe led families and professionals to form advocacy groups that called for greater inclusion of individuals with exceptionalities into all aspects of society including providing them with increased educational opportunities (Yell, Rodgers, & Rodgers, 1998). These groups included the Council for Exceptional Children, a professional organization that was founded in 1922, and the Cuyahoga County Ohio Council for the Retarded Child, one of the initial groups of families who banded together to advocate for their children in 1933.

THE IMPACT OF INTELLIGENCE TESTING AND EDUCATIONAL RESEARCH

Intelligence Testing

While initially designed to help identify individuals who needed special assistance to learn, the advent of intelligence testing in the early twentieth century hindered efforts to deliver a special education to students with exceptionalities (Armstrong, 2002; Safford & Safford, 1998). The movement toward universal intelligence testing resulted in intelligence being seen as a fixed, inherited, and highly desired scientific concept that guided schools in planning, delivering, and evaluating their instruction. The emphasis on intelligence testing also prompted rigid societal beliefs of normality and aptitude which led to individuals with lower IQs being viewed as "feeble-minded," "mentally defective," "ineducable," and the cause of societal problems, and therefore segregated from society via placement in institutions and exempted from compulsory education laws (Read & Walmsley, 2006; Yell et al., 1998).

These fixed and genetic notions of intelligence also were used to establish a cultural and racial basis for the learning potential of different groups and fostered the promulgation of the Eugenics movement in the early twentieth century (Bursztyn, 2007; Humphries & Gordon, 1992). A social movement which called for the selective reproduction of humans with the purported goal of enhancing the species, the Eugenics movement led to limits on immigration and the sterilization of individuals viewed as "defective" (Gould, 1981). Furthermore, the Eugenics movement coupled with the misuse of intelligence testing led to the segregation of "feebleminded" individuals in institutions and state schools where they were subjected to forced labor, abuse, and experimental surgical procedures (D'Antonio, 2004). Eventually, the Eugenics movement fell out of favor and was abandoned by the end of World War II (Black, 2003).

Educational Research

The setbacks of the intelligence testing movement started to be countered by groundbreaking educational research showing that the learning of students with exceptionalities was enhanced when they were provided with a stimulating environment (Skeels & Dye, 1939). Starting in the 1930s, scholars and researchers such as Orton, Monroe, Kirk, and Myklebust experimented with and applied clinical teaching practices to examine and document effective instructional practices that contributed to the field's legacy of empiricism (Fuchs, Fuchs, & Stecker, 2010). These studies helped alter the purpose of special education from providing custodial care to educating students. These pioneering educational research studies also demonstrated the benefits of early intervention and helped establish the commitment of the field of special education to the development and dissemination of research-based interventions (Morse, 2000).

THE LEGALIZATION AND INTEGRATION OF SPECIAL EDUCATION

Since the 1960s and 1970s, special education has undergone significant growth and changes that has been marked by the legalization of the field. In addition, special education has gone from being a separate system to being integrated into the general education system and serving an important role in advocating for and ensuring the inclusion of individual with disabilities into the larger society.

The Civil Rights Movement and Brown v. Topeka Board of Education

The growth, purpose, and legal precedents for the field of special education were established in the early 1950s by the civil rights movement and the 1954 Supreme court decision in the case of *Brown v. Topeka Board of Education* (Blanchett, Brantlinger, & Shealey, 2005). This landmark civil rights case, establishing that "separate but equal is not equal," became the foundation for legal actions brought by families of children with disabilities to guarantee that their children had the right to a free appropriate public education (FAPE). The Supreme Court decision also contributed to the inclusive education movement, which sought to educate students with disabilities in general education classrooms (Blanchett, Mumford, & Beachum, 2005; Morse, 2000; Salend, 2011).

Special Education-Related Court Cases

Following *Brown v. Topeka Board of Education,* court decisions have upheld and expanded on the educational rights of student with exceptionalities. Table 1 provides a brief summary of court decisions that impacted special

Table 1. Historical Court Decisions that Impacted Special Education (Litton et al., 1989; Schwenn, 1991).

1919	*Beattie v. State Board of Education* – Court ruled that students with physical impairments could be excluded from school if their presence was deemed depressing and nauseating to other students.
1967	*Hobson v. Hansen* – Court ruled that the track system of placing students based upon standardized test scores was unconstitutional because it discriminated against African-Americans and poor children.
1970	*Diana v. State of California* – Court ruled that students must be assessed in their primary language to avoid overrepresentation of minorities in special education.
1972	*Pennsylvania Association for Retarded Children v. Pennsylvania* – Court ruled that a free appropriate education must be provided for all children with exceptionalities regardless of severity of their disability.
1972	*Maryland Association for Retarded Citizens v. Maryland* – Court ruled that all children with intellectual disabilities have a right for a free and appropriate education.
1972	*Frederick v. Thomas* – Court ruled that children with learning disabilities are not receiving an appropriate education if their teachers are not qualified.
1972	*Mills v. Board of Education in the District of Columbia* – Court ruled that the district must provide a free and appropriate education for children with exceptionalities regardless of the severity. Recommended timely reevaluations. Listed rights of parents to appeal, be notified of testing and placement, and have access to child's records.
1972	*Guadlaupe v. Tempe Elementary District* – Delineated standards for placing students with mild cognitive impairments into special education classes such as: scores two standard deviations below the mean; the need to assess adaptive functioning of students; and the testing of students in their primary language.
1972	*Larry v. Riles* – Court ruled that some IQ tests discriminated against African-American children as they were not validated procedures to accurately assess these children's cognitive abilities resulting in their misplacement into special education classes.
1973	*LeBanks v. Spears* – Court ruled that Louisiana schools must educate its students with exceptionalities appropriately, and these students have the right to be educated with their peers without disabilities, if appropriate.
1975	*Lora v. Board of Education of City for New York* – Court ruled that students with emotional impairments must be educated with their peers without disabilities.
1982	*Rowley v. Hendrik Hudson School District* – Court ruled that each child with a disability has a right to an individualized instructional plan and necessary supports.
1984	*Irving Independent School District v. Tatro* – Court ruled that the school must pay for catherization which was necessary for a student with a physical impairment.
1984	*Smith v. Robinson* – Court ruled that the state had to pay for a student with a disability for placement in a residential school.
1988	*Honig v. Doe* – Restricted suspension for students with disabilities even for violent and disruptive behavior to ten days. Schools had to prove why these students should not be in school.
1989	*Timothy v. Rochester School District* – Court ruled that schools must provide an educational program and services that meet the needs of the child regardless of the extent of the disability and even if the child appears unable to profit from existing programs.

education prior to and after the passage of Education for All Handicapped Children Act in 1975.The historic outcomes in *Pennsylvania Association for Retarded Children (PARC) v. Commonwealth of Pennsylvania* in 1972 established the right of students with exceptionalities and their families regarding the delivery of an appropriate education that included special education services (Hulett, 2009; Yell, 2006).

Several court cases focused on the inclusion of students with exceptionalities in general education settings including *Daniel R. R. v. State Board of Education* (1989), *Sacramento City Unified School District v. Rachel H.* (1994), and *Oberti v. Board of Education of the Borough of Clementon School District* (1993) (Hulett, 2009; Murdick, Gartin, & Crabtree, 2007; Yell, 2006). In addition to encouraging school districts to educate all students in general education settings, these cases provided guidelines for placing students in the least restrictive environment (LRE). These guidelines involved: (a) comparing the anticipated educational, behavioral, social, and self-concept outcomes of being taught in inclusive classrooms to the anticipated outcomes associated with special education classrooms; (b) examining the impact of students with disabilities on the education of their general education peers and on teachers; and (c) considering the costs of educating students in inclusive classrooms and the effect of these costs on the district's resources for educating all students.

Advocacy and the Disability Rights Movement

In addition to the Brown decision, the triumphs of the civil rights movement ushered in a time of greater acceptance and possibilities, which strengthened efforts by groups of individuals with disabilities, family members, and professionals to form coalitions to advocate against discrimination, segregation, and marginalization, and to seek equity, opportunity, and greater inclusion into all aspects of society (Giordano, 2007). Guided by the principle of *normalization*, which originated in Scandinavia, these advocacy groups lobbied for educational, housing, employment, social, and leisure opportunities for individuals with disabilities that paralleled those available to people without disabilities (Wolfensberger, 1972). The actions of these advocacy groups also provided the underpinnings of the disability rights movement and the creation of a disability culture and disabilities studies, which affirmed and celebrated disability, and challenged society's traditional beliefs about disability and whether, where, and how to educate students with exceptionalities (Fleischer & Zames, 2001; Burch & Sutherland, 2006).

Special Education-Related Legislation

Advocacy groups succeeded in lobbying for legislative actions that ensured and directed the delivery of special education services and gave students with exceptionalities increased access to society and educational opportunities (Giordano, 2007; Yell et al., 1998). The passage of the 1970 Education (Handicapped Children) Act in England, the Loi d'Orientation en Faveur des Personnes Handicapées in France in 1975, and the Education for All Handicapped Children Act in the United States in 1975 (which was renamed the Individuals with Disabilities Education Act (IDEA) and reauthorized numerous times) provided students with exceptionalities with access to public schools (Armstrong, 2002). The IDEA also mandated that students with exceptionalities be taught in the LRE and have an individualized educational program (IEP) that guides the delivery of special education services, addresses academic and functional goals, and fosters students' education, postsecondary options, employment, and independent living (Ferretti & Eisenman, 2010; McLaughlin, 2010).

As a result of research starting in the 1960s and continuing today that demonstrates the effectiveness of early intervention for infants and young children with exceptionalities, programs, services, and interventions for infants, toddlers, and preschoolers have become an integral part of special education with the passage of P.L. 99-457, Infants and Toddlers with Disabilities Act of 1986 (Bruder, 2010). P.L. 99-457 extended many of the rights and safeguards of the IDEA to children with exceptionalities from birth to 5 years of age and encouraged the delivery of early intervention services and the development of an individualized family service plan.

THE RISE OF SOCIALLY CONSTRUCTED DISABILITY CATEGORIES

The mandates and movements to educate students with exceptionalities contributed to a concomitant increase in the numbers of students identified, and changes in the types of students with exceptionalities served by special education. Whereas special education initially focused on serving students with sensory disabilities and then cognitive disabilities, students with socially constructed disabilities now make up the vast majority of students served by special education. These changes were fostered by the creation of such socially constructed disability categories as *emotionally disturbed* and *learning disabilities* (Armstrong, 2002). In particular, the category of learning disabilities, a term that was initially used by Kirk and Bateman (1962) that related to students who performed poorly but did not have sensory, physical, or severe cognitive disabilities, led to a significant growth in the number of students served by special education and the thrust toward a noncategorical approach to structuring the delivery of special education services (Brownell, Sindelar, Kiely, & Danielson, 2010). There also has been a surge in the number of students receiving special education services who are identified as having an autism spectrum disorder, or an attention deficit disorder (Salend, 2011).

THE PERSISTENT PROBLEM OF DISPROPORTIONATE REPRESENTATION

The creation of socially constructed disabilities and the use of unreliable and invalid procedures to identify students with exceptionalities, as well as the intersection of issues of class, gender, age, language background, and geography contributed to growing concerns about the overidentification of students in special education, and the persistent problem of disproportionate representation of students from culturally and linguistically diverse backgrounds (Artiles, Kozleski, Trent, Osher, & Ortiz, 2010; Black, 2010; Dyches & Prater, 2010; McCall & Skrtic, 2009; Obiakor, 2007). The ongoing overrepresentation of students of color in special education as well as their underrepresentation in programs for gifted and talented students have raised concerns about the racialization of disability, and special education as a program that resegregates students, lowers expectations for students and denies them access to the general education curriculum, and undermines the 1954 Brown decision (Artiles, 2009; Ferri & Connor, 2005; McCall & Skrtic, 2009; Waitoller, Artiles, & Cheney, 2010).

Response-to-Intervention (RtI)

The overidentification of students in socially constructed disability categories and the disproportionate representation of students from culturally and linguistically diverse backgrounds has led to the creation of new models for identifying students in need of special education such as Response-to-Intervention (RtI) (Fuchs & Fuchs, 2006; Wheeler & Mayton, 2010). The RtI process seeks to lessen the number of students identified in need of special education by ruling out poor instruction or lack of instruction as causes of their poor school performance by using a multitiered instructional model for examining the extent to which students respond to and need more intensive and individualized research-based interventions to learn. Although a relatively new methodology, RtI has the potential to dramatically alter the field of special education (Brownell et al., 2010; Fuchs et al., 2010).

THE MOVEMENT TO INCLUSIVE EDUCATION

Concerns about the growth and segregated nature of special education initially expressed by Lloyd Dunn (1968) and supported by the ongoing research questioning the efficacy of special education programs (McLeskey, 2007), legislative and judicial actions, the persistent problem of disproportionate representation of students of color, and the work of advocacy groups led the field of special education to initially focus on mainstreaming during the 1970s and early 1980s. Litton, Rotatori, and Day (1989) stressed that mainstreaming was concerned with the integration of students with disabilities into the general education schools and classes, however, for mainstreaming to work successfully, the student's program needed to be individualized, and supportive services were necessary. Litton et al. stated that while mainstreaming greatly impacted and increased the number of students with disabilities receiving education in general education classrooms, the following problems arose: the special education programs were poorly designed; the students were confronted with competing sets of instructional goals; there was a lack of coordination between general and special education personnel; negative attitudes of general education teachers and peers toward students with disabilities sometimes developed, leading to students with disabilities being poorly accepted; the curriculum for the students with disabilities was too difficult; and the students with disabilities began having problems with their self-concept and self-image.

Due to problems with mainstreaming, the Regular Education Initiative (REI) movement started in the late 1980s and continued into the 1990s (see Rotatori, Schwenn, & Litton, 1994). The REI, which was attributed to Madeline Will, assistant secretary for the Office of Special Education and Rehabilitation Services (Will, 1986), advocated that general education should assume unequivocal and primary responsibility for all students including those with disabilities and other special needs (Rotatori et al., 1994). Proponents of the REI emphasized that the dual system of education should be dissolved because it was cost inefficient and ineffective, and it discriminated against students with disabilities (Schwenn, 1991). In contrast, opponents of REI stressed a more cautious approach in which evaluative research would be conducted to assure that regulating classroom education is appropriate for all students (Schwenn, 1991). A prime emphasis of the REI was the reduction in *pull-out or resource room classes* in which students with disabilities were given instruction in small groups outside their classroom.

The REI movement was the major special education controversy of the 1990s and led to the implementation of *Inclusive* education programs that educate *all students* together in the general education classroom (Obiakor, Harris, Rotatori, & Algozzine, 2010; Osgood, 2005; Salend, 2011; Valle & Connor, 2010). In general, the research findings suggest that inclusive education can benefit students with and without exceptionalities when their teachers use differentiated instruction and assessment as well as curricular and teaching accommodations within the general education setting (Black-Hawkins, Florian, & Rouse, 2007; Cushing, Carter, Clark, Wallis, & Kennedy, 2009; Salend & Garrick Duhaney, 2007). Because inclusive education is a relatively new philosophy and inclusion programs are multifaceted and varied in their implementation and the services provided (Ainscow, 2008; Idol, 2006), research and models that enhance its implementation, effectiveness, and long-term impact continues to be a focus for the field (Sindelar, Shearer, Yendol-Hoppey, & Liebert, 2006).

THE INTERNATIONALIZATION OF SPECIAL EDUCATION

The work of advocacy groups, the passage of special education-related legislation, and the movement toward inclusion also served as a framework for an increased global commitment to disability rights, and the education of students with exceptionalities and inclusive education (Bui, Fletcher, & Keller, 2010; Forlin, 2008). In 1994, the Salamanca statement was adopted by 92 countries and 25 international organizations. This groundbreaking statement called upon all countries to educate all of their students together in inclusive classrooms. As a result, nations throughout the world have established inclusive education initiatives tailored to their country's educational philosophy and history as well as a range of social, political, cultural, and economic factors (Alur & Bach, 2008; Brown, 2005; Fletcher & Artiles, 2005; Heng & Tam, 2006; Mitchell, 2005; Mitchell & Desai, 2005). The implementation of inclusive education in many countries has expanded beyond disability to also address individual differences related to race, linguistic ability, economic status, gender, learning style, ethnicity, cultural and religious background, family structure, and sexual orientation (Mitchell, 2005; Slee, 2005; Verma, Bagley, & Jha, 2007). In 2008, the United Nations expanded on the Salamanca statement and adopted a groundbreaking international agreement that called upon nations throughout the world to take efforts to provide individuals with disabilities with equal access to educational, employment, and social opportunities.

THE ONGOING COMMITMENT
TO RESEARCH-BASED PRACTICES

Consistent with the field's inception and continuing efforts to develop and disseminate empirically based interventions, the commitment to create and use research-based practices that fosters equality, quality instruction, and educational opportunities for all students continues to be a hallmark of the field of special education (Anderson, Marchant, & Somarriba, 2010; Crockett, Gerber, Gersten, & Harris, 2010). The 1960s and 1970s was characterized by debates over effective models (e.g., the medical model, diagnostic-prescriptive teaching model, and the behavioral model), pedagogical approaches (e.g., perceptual and modality training, dietary changes, motor patterning, and aptitude-by-treatment interaction (ATI) approach) (Mostert & Crockett, 2000; Van Acker, 2006), and the emergence of the precision teaching model that was predicated on examining teaching effectiveness by collecting data related to students' mastery of specific behavioral objectives (Brownell et al., 2010).

The inclusive education movement has led researchers to continue to conduct and share research regarding the efficacy of general education placements for students with exceptionalities (McLeskey, 2007; Salend, 2011). The growing body of research has resulted in the development and validation of innovative practices that have become integral parts of general education such as universal design for learning, collaborative teaching arrangements, cooperative learning, family involvement and empowerment techniques, learning strategy instruction, positive behavioral supports, self-management strategies, and culturally responsive teaching (Salend, 2011). The technological advances of the late twentieth and early twenty-first centuries have also led to widespread use of a range of assistive and instructional technologies that enhance student learning and socialization, foster individualized instruction, expand access to all aspects of society, and transform views of exceptionality (Beard, Bowden Carpenter, & Johnston, 2011; Blackhurst, 2005; Bouck, 2010; Brownell et al., 2010; Parette & Peterson-Karlan, 2010).

SUMMARY

This chapter presented some of the important historical and philosophical events, factors, and movements that have influenced the development of special education. Linked to the treatment of individuals with disabilities and marked by ongoing debates about purposes, groups served, effective practices and programmatic models, and desired outcomes, special education today has become an integral part of the educational system that is based on providing and monitoring the effectiveness of a set of specially designed, coordinated, comprehensive, and research-based instructional, social, behavioral, curricular, and assessment practices and related services (Heward, 2009). From its initial focus on providing custodial care in segregated settings to students with sensory and cognitive exceptionalities, special education today has been transformed into a program that seeks to educate students with learning, behavioral, emotional, physical, health, and sensory disabilities in inclusive settings with their peers. Consistent with its empirical legacy, special education today strives to identify a distinctive research base that shapes its policies, practices, and procedures and addresses where, when, and how students with exceptionalities should be educated. While special education also has evolved into a program that seeks to foster equity and access to all aspects of schooling, the community and society, challenges remain. Eliminating disproportionate representation, expanding postsecondary options, closing achievement gaps, helping all students access and succeed in the general education curriculum, improving the implementation of inclusive education, and becoming a cohesive international movement continue to exist and have future implications for enriching the vibrant and dynamic field of special education.

REFERENCES

Ainscow, M. (2008). Making sure that every child matters: Towards a methodology for enhancing equity within educational systems. In: C. Forlin (Ed.), *Catering for learners with diverse needs: An Asia-Pacific focus* (pp. 11–29). Hong Kong: Hong Kong Institute of Education.

Alur, M., & Bach, M. (2008). *The journey for inclusive education in the Indian sub-continent.* London: Routledge.

Anderson, D. H., Marchant, M., & Somarriba, N. Y. (2010). Behaviorism works in special education. In: F. O. Obiakor, J. P. Bakken & A. F. Rotatori (Eds), *Current issues in special education: Identification, assessment and instruction* (Vol. 19, pp. 157–174). Bingley, UK: Emerald Group Publishing Limited.

Armstrong, F. (2002). The historical development of special education: Humanitarian rationality or 'wild profusion of entangled events'? *History of Education, 31*(5), 437–456.

Artiles, A. J. (2009). Re-framing disproportionality research: Outline of a cultural-historical paradigm. *Multiple Voices, 11*(2), 24–37.

Artiles, A. J., Kozleski, E. B., Trent, S. C., Osher, D., & Ortiz, A. (2010). Justifying and explaining disproportionality, 1968–2008: A critique of underlying views of culture. *Exceptional Children, 76*, 279–299.

Beard, L. A., Bowden Carpenter, L., & Johnston, L. (2011). *Assistive technology: Access for all students* (2nd ed.). Columbus, OH: Pearson Education.

Beattie v. Board of Education, 172 N.W. 153 (Wisc. 1919).

Best, H. (1930). Educational provisions for the deaf, the blind, and feeble-minded compared. *American Annals of the Deaf, 75*, 239–240.

Black, E. (2003). *War against the weak: Eugenics and America's campaign to create a master race*. Thunder's Mouth Press: Avalon Publishing Group Inc.

Black, R. S. (2010). Can underidentification affect exceptional learners? In: F. E. Obiakor, J. P. Bakken & A. F. Rotatori (Eds), *Current issues and trends in special education: Identification, assessment, and instruction* (Vol. 19, pp. 37–52). Bingley, UK: Emerald Group Publishing Limited.

Black-Hawkins, K., Florian, L., & Rouse, M. (2007). *Achievement and inclusion in schools*. London: Routledge.

Blackhurst, A. E. (2005). Historical perspective about technology applications for people with disabilities. In: D. Edyburn, K. Higgins & R. Boone (Eds), *Handbook on special education technology research and practice* (pp. 3–29). Whitefish Bay, WI: Knowledge by Design.

Blanchett, W. J., Brantlinger, E., & Shealey, M. W. (2005). Brown 50 years later – Exclusion, segregation and inclusion. *Remedial and Special Education, 26*, 66–69.

Blanchett, W. J., Mumford, V., & Beachum, F. (2005). Urban school failure and disproportionality in a post-Brown era: Benign neglect of the constitutional rights of students of color. *Remedial and Special Education, 26*, 70–81.

Bouck, E. C. (2010). Technology and students with disabilities: Does it solve all problems? In: F. O. Obiakor, J. P. Bakken & A. F. Rotatori (Eds), *Current issues and trends in special education: Research, technology, and teacher preparation* (Vol. 20, pp. 91–106). Bingley, UK: Emerald Group Publishing Limited.

Brown, R. C. (2005). Inclusive education in Middle Eastern cultures: The challenge of tradition. In: D. Mitchell (Ed.), *Contextualizing inclusive education: Evaluating old and new international paradigms* (pp. 253–278). London: Routledge.

Brownell, M. T., Sindelar, P. T., Kiely, M. T., & Danielson, L. C. (2010). Special education teacher quality and preparation: Exposing foundations, constructing a new model. *Exceptional Children, 76*, 357–377.

Bruder, M. (2010). Early childhood intervention: A promise to children and families for their future. *Exceptional Children, 76*, 339–356.

Buchanan, R. (1999). *Illusions of equality*. Washington, DC: Gallaudet University Press.

Bui, Y., Fletcher, T., & Keller, C. (2010, April). *Becoming international.* Presentation at the annual meeting of the Council for Exceptional Children, Nashville, TN.

Burch, S., & Sutherland, I. (2006). Who's not here yet? American disability history. *Radical History Review, 94,* 127–147.

Bursztyn, A. M. (2007). A brief history of intelligence testing. In: A. M. Bursztyn (Ed.), *The Praeger handbook of special education* (pp. 3–5). Westport, CT: Praeger.

Crockett, J., Gerber, M., Gersten, R., & Harris, K. (2010, April). *The contributions of research to special education's past, current, and future identity.* Presentation at the annual meeting of the Council for Exceptional Children, Nashville, TN.

Cushing, L. S., Carter, E. W., Clark, N., Wallis, T., & Kennedy, C. H. (2009). Evaluating inclusive educational practices for students with severe disabilities using the program quality measurement tool. *The Journal of Special Education, 42,* 195–208.

Daniel R. R. v. State Board of Education, 874 F. 2d 1036, 5th Circuit 1989.

D'Antonio, M. (2004). *The state boys rebellion.* New York: Simon & Schuster.

Diana v. California State Board of Education, No. C-7037 RFP, District Court of California (February 1970).

Dunn, L. (1968). Special education for the mildly retarded: Is much of it justifiable? *Exceptional Children, 35,* 5–22.

Dyches, T. T., & Prater, M. A. (2010). Disproportionate representation in special education: Overrepresentation of selected subgroups. In: F. E. Obiakor, J. P. Bakken & A. F. Rotatori (Eds), *Current issues and trends in special education: Identification, assessment and instruction* (Vol. 19, pp. 53–74). Bingley, UK: Emerald Group Publishing Limited.

Ferretti, R. P., & Eisenman, L. T. (2010). Delivering educational services that meet the needs of all students. *Exceptional Children, 76,* 378–383.

Ferri, B. A., & Connor, D. J. (2005). In the shadow of Brown: Special education and overrepresentation of students of color. *Remedial and Special Education, 26,* 93–100.

Fleischer, D. Z., & Zumou, F. (2001). *The disability rights movement: From charity to confrontation.* Philadelphia: Temple University Press.

Fletcher, T., & Artiles, A. J. (2005). Inclusive and equity in Latin America. In: D. Mitchell (Ed.), *Contextualizing inclusive education: Evaluating old and new international paradigms* (pp. 166–201). London: Routledge.

Forlin, C. (2008). Educational reform to include all learners in the Asia-Pacific region. In: C. Forlin (Ed.), *Catering for learners with diverse needs: An Asia-Pacific focus* (pp. 3–10). Hong Kong: Hong Kong Institute of Education.

Frederick, L v. Thomas, No. 71-2897 (1972).

Fuchs, D., & Fuchs, L. S. (2006). Introduction to response to intervention: What, why and how valid is it? *Reading Research Quarterly, 41*(1), 92–99.

Fuchs, D., Fuchs, L. S., & Stecker, P. M. (2010). The "blurring" of special education in a new continuum of general education placement and services. *Exceptional Children, 76,* 301–323.

Giordano, G. (2007). *American special education: A history of early political advocacy.* New York: P. Lang.

Gould, S. J. (1981). *The mismeasure of man.* New York: W.W. Norton.

Guadalupe Organization Inc. v. Tempe Elementary School District, No. CIV 71-453, Phoenix (D. Arizona, January 24, 1972).

Heng, M. A., & Tam, K. Y. (2006). Special education in general teacher education programs in Singapore. *Teacher Education and Special Education, 29,* 149–156.

Heward, W. L. (2009). *Exceptional children: An introduction to special education* (9th ed.). Upper Saddle River, NJ: Merrill/Prentice Hall.

Hobsen v. Hansen, 269 F. Supp. 401 (1967).

Honig v. Doe, 484 U.S. 304 (1988).

Hoolihan, C. (1985). Too little, too soon: The literature of deaf education in 17th century Britain. *Volta Review, 87*, 28–44.

Hinshelwood, J. (1900). Congenital word – Blindness. *Lancet, 1*, 1506–1508.

Hulett, K. E. (2009). *Legal aspects of special education*. Upper Saddle River, NJ: Pearson Education.

Humphries, S., & Gordon, P. (1992). *Out of sight: The experience of disability, 1900–1950*. Plymouth, England: Northcote House Publishers Ltd.

Individuals with Disabilities Education Improvement Act (IDEA) 2004, Pub. L. No. 108-446.

Idol, L. (2006). Toward inclusion of special education students in general education: A program evaluation of eight schools. *Remedial and Special Education, 27*, 77–94.

Ireland, W. W. (1877). *On idiocy and imbecility*. London: Churchill.

Irving Independent School District v. Tatro, 468, U.S. 883 (1984).

Kirk, S., & Bateman, B. (1962). Diagnosis and remediation of learning disabilities. *Exceptional Children, 29*, 73–78.

Knight, I. (1968). *The geometric spirit: The Abbé Condillac and the French Enlightenment*. New Haven, CT: Yale University Press.

Koestler, F. A. (1976). *The unseen minority: A social history of blindness in America*. New York: David McKay Co..

Lane, H. (1989). *When the mind hears: A history of the deaf*. New York: Vintage.

Larry v. Riles, 343 F. Supp. 1306 (1972).

LeBanks v. Spears, No. 71-2897 (1973).

Litton, F. W., Rotatori, A. F., & Day, G. (1989). Individuals with low incidence handicaps: An introduction. In: A. F. Rotatori & R. A. Fox (Eds), *Understanding individuals with low incidence handicaps: Categorical and noncategorical perspectives* (pp. 5–40). Springfield, IL: Charles C. Thomas.

Lora v. Board of Education of City of New York, 623 F. 2d 248, 251 (1975).

Maryland Association for Retarded Citizens v. State of Maryland, Civil Action No. 72–73 (1972).

McCall, Z., & Skrtic, T. M. (2009). Intersectional needs politics: A policy frame for the wicked problem of disproportionality. *Multiple Voices, 11*(2), 3–23.

McLaughlin, M. J. (2010). Evolving interpretations of educational equity and students with disabilities. *Exceptional Children, 76*, 265–278.

McLeskey, J. (2007). *Reflections on inclusion: Classic articles that shaped our thinking*. Arlington, VA: Council for Exceptional Children.

Mills v. Board of Education of the District of Columbia, 508 F. Supp. 866 (1972).

Mitchell, D. (Ed.) (2005). *Contextualizing inclusive education: Evaluating old and new international paradigms*. London: Routledge.

Mitchell, D., & Desai, I. (2005). Diverse socio-cultural contexts for inclusive education in Asia. In: D. Mitchell (Ed.), *Contextualizing inclusive education: Evaluating old and new international paradigms* (pp. 202–232). London: Routledge.

Morgan, W. P. (1896). A case of congenital word blindness. *British Medical Journal, 2*, 1378.

Morse, T. E. (2000). Ten events that shaped special education's century of dramatic change. *International Journal of Educational Reform, 9*(1), 32–38.

Mostert, M. P., & Crockett, J. B. (2000). Reclaiming the history of special education for more effective practice. *Exceptionality, 8,* 133–143.

Murdick, N. L., Gartin, B. C., & Crabtree, T. L. (2007). *Special education law* (2nd ed.). Upper Saddle River, NJ: Merrill/Prentice Hall.

Oberti v. Board of Education of the Borough of Clementon School District, 995 F.2d, 1009, 3rd Circuit (1993).

Obiakor, F. E. (2007). *Multicultural special education: Culturally responsive teaching.* Columbus, OH: Merrill/Prentice Hall.

Obiakor, F. E., Harris, M. K., Rotatori, A. F., & Algozzine, B. (2010). Beyond traditional placement: Making inclusion work in the general education classroom. In: F. E. Obiakor, J. P. Bakken & A. F. Rotatori (Eds), *Current issues and trends in special education: Identification, assessment and instruction* (Vol. 19, pp. 141–156). Bingley, UK: Emerald Group Publishing Limited.

Osgood, R. L. (2005). *The history of inclusion in the United States.* Washington, DC: Gallaudet University Press.

Osgood, R. L. (2007). *The history of special education: A struggle for equality in American public schools (Growing up: History of children and youth).* Westport, CT: Praeger Publishers.

Parette, H. P., & Peterson-Karlan, G. R. (2010). Using assistive technology to support the instructional process of students with disabilities. In: F. E. Obiakor, J. P. Bakken & A. F. Rotatori (Eds), *Current issues and trends in special education: Research, technology and teacher preparation* (Vol. 20, pp. 73–90). Bingley, UK: Emerald Group Publishing Limited.

Pennsylvania Association for Retarded Children v. Commonwealth of Pennsylvania, 343 F. Supp. 279 (E.D. Pa., 1972).

Read, J., & Walmsley, J. (2006). Historical perspectives on special education, 1890–1970. *Disability & Society, 21*(5), 455–469.

Reynolds, M. C. (1989). An historical perspective: The delivery of special education to mildly disabled and at-risk students. *Remedial and Special Education, 10,* 7–11.

Rotatori, A. F., Schwenn, J. O., & Litton, F. W. (1994). *Perspectives on the regular education initiative and transitional programs.* Stamford, CT: JAI Press Inc..

Rowley v. Hendrik Hudson School District, 458 U.S. 176 (1982).

Sacramento City Unified School District, Board of Education v. Rachel H., 14F.3d, 1398, 9th Circuit (1994).

Safford, P. S., & Safford, E. J. (1996). *A history of childhood and disability.* New York: Teachers College Press.

Safford, P. S., & Safford, E. J. (1998). Visions of the special class. *Remedial and Special Education, 19,* 229–238.

Salend, S. J. (2011). *Creating inclusive classrooms: Effective and reflective practices* (7th ed.). Columbus, OH: Pearson Education.

Salend, S. J., & Garrick Duhaney, L. M. (2007). Research related to inclusion and program effectiveness: Yesterday, today, and tomorrow. In: J. McLeskey (Ed.), *Reflections on inclusion: Classic articles that shaped our thinking.* Arlington, VA: Council for Exceptional Children, pp. 127–129, 147–159.

Schwenn, J. O. (1991). Students with high incidence handicaps. In: J. O. Schwenn, A. F. Rotatori & R. A. Fox (Eds), *Understanding students with high incidence handicaps: Categorical and noncategorical perspectives* (pp. 3–28). Springfield, IL: Charles C. Thomas.

Sindelar, P. T., Shearer, D. K., Yendol-Hoppey, D., & Liebert, T. W. (2006). The sustainability of inclusive school reform. *Exceptional Children, 72*, 317–331.

Skeels, H., & Dye, H. A. (1939). A study of the effects of differential stimulation on mentally retarded children. *Proceedings of the American Association on Mental Deficiency, 44*, 114–136.

Slee, R. (2005). Education and the politics of recognition: Inclusive education – An Australian snapshot. In: D. Mitchell (Ed.), *Contextualizing inclusive education: Evaluating old and new international paradigms* (pp. 139–165). London: Routledge.

Smith v. Robinson, 468 U.S. 992 (1984).

Smith, J. D. (1998). Histories of special education: Stories from our past, insights for our future introduction to the special series. *Remedial and Special Education, 19*(4), 196–200.

Timothy v. Rochester School District, No. 875 F. 2d 954 (1989).

Valle, J., & Connor, D. (2010). *Rethinking disability: A disabilities studies approach to inclusive practices*. New York: McGraw-Hill.

Van Acker, R. (2006). Outlook on special education practice. *Focus on Exceptional Children, 38*(6), 8–18.

Verma, G. K., Bagley, C., & Jha, M. (Eds). (2007). *International perspectives on educational diversity and inclusion*. London: Routledge.

Waitoller, F. R., Artiles, A. J., & Cheney, D. A. (2010). The miner's canary: A review of overrepresentation research and explanations. *Journal of Special Education, 44*(1), 29–49.

Wheeler, J. J., & Mayton, M. R. (2010). Other innovative techniques: Positive behavior supports and response to intervention. In: F. E. Obiakor, J. P. Bakken & A. F. Rotatori (Eds), *Current issues and trends in special education: Identification, assessment and instruction* (Vol. 19, pp. 175–198). Bingley, UK: Emerald Group Publishing Limited.

Will, M. (1986). Educating children with learning problems: A shared responsibility. *Exceptional Children, 52*, 411–415.

Winzer, M. A. (1986). Early developments in special education: Some aspects of Enlightenment thought. *Remedial and Special Education, 7*(5), 42–49.

Winzer, M. A. (1993). *The history of special education: From isolation to integration*. Washington, DC: Gallaudet University Press.

Winzer, M. A. (1998). A tale often told: The early progression of special education. *Remedial and Special Education, 19*(4), 212–218.

Wolfensberger, W. (1972). *The principle of normalization in human services*. Toronto: National Institute on Mental Health.

Yell, M. L. (2006). *The law and special education* (2nd ed.). Upper Saddle River, NJ: Merrill/ Prentice Hall.

Yell, M. L., Rodgers, D., & Rodgers, E. L. (1998). The legal history of special education. *Remedial and Special Education, 19*, 219–229.

CHAPTER 2

HISTORY OF LEGAL
AND LEGISLATIVE ACTS
CONCERNED WITH SPECIAL
EDUCATION

Betty Y. Ashbaker

This chapter addresses the history of legal procedures and legislation content concerned with special education. It reviews relevant aspects of the governing structure of the United States of America and leads the reader through the legal processes concerning civil rights, human rights, and rights of education for individuals with disabilities. Examining the U.S. Constitution, it discusses the amendments which lead to federal involvement in providing education, especially to students with disabilities in the Individuals with Disabilities Education Act (IDEA) (34 C.F.R. § 104.36 (2005)).

Other statutory measures have also affected special education, such as Section 504 of the Rehabilitation Act (RA) of 1973 (29 U.S.C. § 794(a)), the 1974 Families Educational Rights and Privacy Act (FERPA) (20 U.S.C. § 1232g), and the Americans with Disabilities Act of 1990 (ADA) (42 U.S.C. § 12101 et seq.). These are discussed along with the well known No Child Left Behind (NCLB) legislation (20 U.S.C. § 6301 et seq. (2002)).

History of Special Education
Advances in Special Education, Volume 21, 21–45
Copyright © 2011 by Emerald Group Publishing Limited
All rights of reproduction in any form reserved
ISSN: 0270-4013/doi:10.1108/S0270-4013(2011)0000021005

SOCIAL AND POLITICAL MOVEMENTS: BACKGROUND AND PROGRESSION

Promise and Hope

We hold these truths to be self-evident, that all men are created equal, that they are endowed by their Creator with certain unalienable Rights, that among these are Life, Liberty and the pursuit of Happiness. (Declaration of Independence, 1776)

A century after the Declaration of Independence affirmed that all men are equal, people with disabilities still had exceedingly poor treatment and few rights. Through the 1800s and early 1900s, physicians usually advised parents who gave birth to a child with a disability to let the child die or place him/her in an institution (Chesterton, 2000). Those children allowed to live were usually committed to institutions so that the disfigured and "different" children were rarely seen in public. The 1880 U.S. Federal Census offers an example of the social context of the time as it refers to a category of people as "insane, idiots, deaf-mutes, blind persons, homeless children, prisoners, paupers, and the indigent" (Ancestry. Com, p. 1). These records, called the *1880 Schedules of Defective, Dependent, and Delinquent Classes*, include the person's name and residence and in the cases of "insane, deaf-mute, blind, and idiotic persons" lists details about their affliction. For those on the insane schedules, information has been recorded about the onset of the disability, when the difficulty first occurred, and the number of "attacks of insanity." This census noted if restraints were necessary; whether the person was suicidal, homicidal, or epileptic; and whether or not he had been an inmate in an asylum (Ancestry.com, n.d.). Institutions were custodial – dealing only with basic needs – and crowded, with the main purpose to control people with disabilities in order to protect the public. Education was not an option for the disabled, and attendance in public schools was prohibited.

Social Advocacy Movement

Public awareness of the potential of education for individuals with disabilities was raised by the highly publicized story of Helen Keller, which began in March 1887 when Anne Mansfield Sullivan refused to give up on a deaf–blind five-year-old and found success in teaching Helen to communicate. Miss Keller later called her breakthrough "the most important day I can remember in my life" (American Federation for the Blind, Helen Keller Biography, para. 4). Building on successes in teaching the deaf–blind, a few

Table 1. Synopsis of Events as Human Rights Began to Evolve for People with Disabilities: Those Who Are Deaf, Blind, Intellectually Disabled, or Have Learning Disabilities.

1817	The Connecticut Asylum at Hartford for the Instruction of Deaf and Dumb Persons opens. It is the first permanent school for the deaf in the United States
1829	The Perkins School for the Blind (then called the New England Asylum for the Blind) opened in Massachusetts – the first school in the United States for children with visual disabilities
1840	Rhode Island became the first American state to mandate compulsory education for children
1848	Dr. Samuel Howe secured funding for the "Massachusetts School for Idiotic and Feebleminded Youth," the first school of its kind in the United States
1864	Edward Miner Gallaudet helped to start Gallaudet University, the first college specifically for deaf students
1876	Edouard Seguin became the first president of the organization that eventually would evolve into the American Association on Mental Retardation
1905	Alfred Binet published an article with Theodore Simon describing the development of a measurement instrument that would identify students with intellectual disabilities: the Binet-Simon scale
1916	Louis M. Terman and a team of Stanford graduate students completed an American version of the Binet-Simon scale. This development initiated the widespread use of intelligence testing used over the course of the next century as part of the procedure for identifying students with learning and intellectual disabilities
1918	By this time, all states in the United States had established compulsory education for children. However, education for all children was not actually an option: Children with disabilities were not included in public schools

Sources: Adapted from McConnell (2007) and Philpot (n.d.).

social reformers began to advocate for people with other types of disabilities. Dr. Samuel Howe was noted for his lobbying efforts to deinstitutionalize people with mental retardation and provide training for them. In 1848, he persuaded the legislature of Massachusetts to appropriate public funds to establish the first state school in the United States to educate persons with mental retardation. Incidentally, Julia Ward Howe, the anti-slavery social reformer who penned the "Battle Hymn of the Republic," did so while on a trip to Washington with her husband, Samuel Howe (Schwartz, 1956). Table 1 summarizes many of the important events occurring during the social advocacy movement, which advanced the recognition of and rights for people with disabilities.

The social advocacy agenda for people with disabilities received impetus when politically and financially influential people such as the Kennedy family became involved. In 1946, Ambassador and Mrs. Joseph P. Kennedy (parents of U.S. President John F. Kennedy) established the Joseph P. Kennedy, Jr., Foundation in honor of their eldest son and in public recognition of the mental disabilities of one of their daughters. This public acknowledgment was a surprise to the American people which led many to rethink their biases concerning people with disabilities. The foundation continues today, working with and on behalf of individuals with intellectual and developmental disabilities and their families (Joseph P. Kennedy, Jr., Foundation, n.d.).

In 1961, when John F. Kennedy became the U.S. President, he organized the President's Panel on Mental Retardation; he formally established the panel in 1966 and directed the members to review and report on mental retardation. The panel found (1) the quality of care given to people with mental retardation varied widely among state institutions and (2) institutions were overcrowded and had inadequate budgets and staff shortages.

Based on these results, the panel identified a need for change in the staff's attitudes toward patients at the facilities. They also recommended changes in the administrative practices that were leading to widespread abuse, along with improvement in the programs available to people with mental disabilities. In response to the Panel's findings, President Kennedy signed into law the Mental Retardation Facilities Construction Act. This Public Law specified that the federal government (1) make federal monies available for the construction of mental health centers and (2) provide grants to assist in the construction of public or nonprofit clinical facilities with the purpose of working with individuals with mental retardation (Public Law 88-164, MR Facilities Act 1963). This lead to a positive system change building on the capacity of local and state services with several goals: (a) make institutions safe, (b) train professionals across disciplines, (c) use expertise found in universities, (d) build interdisciplinary services, and (e) support research in mental retardation (now called intellectual disabilities). Although it was not until later that education was mandated for persons with disabilities, the social advocacy movements made progress in providing better services for them.

Civil Rights Movement

The social advocacy movement slowly morphed into the civil rights movement, which was a hard-fought struggle to bring civil rights and equality to all Americans. The term *civil rights* refers to the efforts to end racial segregation and discrimination against African Americans. The movement increased the public's acceptance of people's civil rights by exposing the prevalence of discrimination. The results of the fight for civil rights had a lasting, positive effect on U.S. African Americans, and through their struggles they opened the avenues of social change for other subgroups – such as women and people with disabilities – to obtain their rights under the law. "Long before the civil rights movement ever crystallized the plight of African Americans, Negro lawyers had identified the inequities in the legal order and begun to lay the foundation for social change" (Thurgood Marshall in McNeil, 1983, p. iv).

Post-Civil War Legislation
After the Civil War of 1865, Vice President Andrew Johnson became U.S. President when Abraham Lincoln was assassinated. Loyal to the South, Johnson was reported to have said, "This is a country for white men and by God, as long as I am president, it shall be a government for white men" (PBS: American Experience, n.d.). During his tenure as President, a bill was introduced to grant citizenship with the same rights enjoyed by white citizens to "all male persons in the United States ... without distinction of race or color, or previous condition of slavery or involuntary servitude" (http://www.ourdocuments.gov). President Johnson vetoed the bill, but a two-thirds majority in both houses of Congress, passed it into law as the Civil Rights Act of 1866. This law reflected the movement favoring increased intervention in the South and providing aid to former slaves (PBS: American Experience, n.d.). The Civil Rights Act of 1871 was a continuation of the Civil Rights Act of 1866, including more information on nondiscrimination toward persons of minority race and color.

Even though earlier discrimination laws had passed, discrimination was still prevalent involving housing, land ownership, education, voting, and other aspects of life. The civil rights movement affected only males of different races, but had little effect on women or persons with disabilities. It was not until the Civil Rights Act of 1964 that the right of education was granted. This law prohibited discrimination in public places, provided for the integration of schools and other public facilities, and made employment discrimination illegal. The needs and equality of persons with different racial backgrounds and color were addressed sooner than the needs and equality of persons with disabilities. The civil right movements had a significant indirect impact on persons with disabilities, even though the Civil Right Acts did not specifically address funding or provide education equality for persons with disabilities (Congress and the Civil Rights Act, 1964).

Although laws were passed, appropriate actions did not always happen. For example, equality regardless of race was part of the Constitution and was rewritten in laws numerous times through different civil rights acts, but even by the 1960s, *separate but equal* procedures were still practiced. Moreover, even though discrimination was officially unlawful and the Fourteenth Amendment addressed freedom of life, liberty, and the pursuit of happiness, persons with disabilities were still institutionalized and provided only minimum amounts of food, water, and assistance (Latham, Latham, & Mandlawitz, 2008).

Charles Hamilton Houston
A lawyer often unrecognized as a leader of the civil rights movement, Charles Hamilton Houston is credited with defeating the *separate but equal* doctrine from the Supreme Court's decision in the *Plessy v. Ferguson* case. Houston's brilliant plan was to attack and defeat segregation by demonstrating the inequality in the "separate but equal" status for African Americans. Houston's target was broad, but the evidence was overwhelmingly obvious: facilities, education, treatment, and accommodations were inferior to those provided for white Americans (McNeil, 1983). Public schools, public places, and public transportation, such as trains and buses, had separate (and inferior) facilities. Southern states spent less than half the amount allotted for White students on education for Blacks. Even greater disparities were found in individual school districts. Black schools were equipped with castoff supplies from white schools, built with inferior materials, and taught by instructors paid disparagingly less than teachers of white students (NAACP, Legal History, n.p.).

Houston's legacy was as the "man who killed Jim Crow" because he had a role in nearly every civil rights case that went before the Supreme Court between 1930 and 1954. Houston was the mastermind who brought about the landmark *Brown* decision, demonstrating the failure of states to even try to provide an equal education as required by the 1896 rule of "separate but equal." Houston hoped to finally overturn the *Plessy v. Ferguson* ruling that had given birth to that phrase (NAACP, Legal History, n.p.).

Plessey v. Ferguson. In 1892, Homer Plessy, who was only one-eighth Black, boarded a car of the East Louisiana Railroad designated for white patrons only. When he refused to leave the white car, he was arrested and jailed. Why? Because under Louisiana law he was still considered an African American and therefore required to ride only in cars for African Americans. The case upheld the practice of separating the two races as a matter of social policy, establishing the *separate but equal* policy for another half-century. On appeal, Plessy's team argued that he had been denied his constitutional rights under the Thirteenth and Fourteenth Constitutional Amendments (Lofgren, 1987).

However, the state supreme court upheld Ferguson's ruling. Plessy's team took the case to the U.S. Supreme Court, where *Plessy v. Ferguson* became one of the most famous court cases in American history (Medley, 2003).

Brown v. Board of Education of Topeka, Kansas. In the mid-1940s, Americans danced to the mellow tones of Nat King Cole, the first African American to host a radio variety show, and cheered Jackie Robinson, who joined the Brooklyn Dodgers to become the first African American to play major league baseball in the twentieth century. These high-profile men helped to raise public awareness of African Americans and the challenges they faced. Meanwhile, Charles Hamilton Houston and his legal team – that included Thurgood Marshall and the NAACP – worked to expose the effects of the separate but equal laws on education by bringing legal challenges to school segregation. They took the landmark of all school cases before the U.S. Supreme Court. A new milestone was reached when the "separate but equal" racial segregation case of *Plessy v. Ferguson* (163 U.S. 537 1896) was overturned.

The Supreme Court decision in the *Brown v. the Board of Education (1954)* initiated reform in educational practices. Through this case the legal team dismantled the legal basis for racial segregation in schools and other public facilities, handing down a 9-0 decision that "separate educational facilities are inherently unequal" (347 U.S. 483 1954). By declaring that the discriminatory nature of racial segregation violates the Fourteenth Amendment to the U.S. Constitution, which guarantees all citizens equal protection of the laws, *Brown v. Board of Education* shaped future national and international policies regarding human rights and education. Recognizing the need for every citizen to receive an education, Chief Justice Earl Warren wrote,

> Today, education is perhaps the most important function of state and local governments. Compulsory school attendance laws and the great expenditures for education both demonstrate our recognition of the importance of education to our democratic society. It is required in the performance of our most basic public responsibilities, even service in the armed forces. It is the very foundation of good citizenship. Today it is a principal instrument in awakening the child to cultural values, in preparing him for later professional training, and in helping him to adjust normally to his environment. In these days, it is doubtful that any child may reasonably be expected to succeed in life if he is denied the opportunity of an education. Such an opportunity, where the state has undertaken to provide it, is a right that must be made available to all on equal terms. (Chief Justice Earl Warren. *Decision on Brown v. Board of Education of Topeka*, 1954, Document 29.3.1; para. 8)

The *Brown* case not only banned segregation in schools, but also helped pave the way for the gradual end of segregation in other aspects of

American society (Branch, 2007). The concept of educating children with disabilities in regular public schools is an extension of the civil rights movement, which was strongly influenced by social developments and court decisions in the 1950s and 1960s. Following *Brown v. Board of Education* were several new cases that addressed the rights of children with disabilities to be educated in regular public schools. The cases continue to define the rights of schoolchildren with disabilities.

Rights for People with Disabilities

I made up my mind that I would never get caught again without knowing something about my rights; that if luck was with me, and I got through this war, I would study law and use my time fighting for men who could not strike back. (Charles Hamilton Houston in the Pittsburg Courier, 24 August 1940, n.p.)

Perhaps those least able to strike back were children with disabilities, who at this time were not afforded their rights to an education, receiving different (and inferior) treatment from their nondisabled peers. The *Brown* decision, which extended public school education to black and white children on equal terms, initiated a period of intense concern and questioning among parents of children with disabilities. Parents asked, "Why do the same principles of equal access to education not apply to our children?" They pressed legal cases, showing their growing dissatisfaction with school procedures that denied access or promoted segregation of students with disabilities. States and federal agencies took notice and passed a series of laws granting rights and supports to the disabled.

Free Public Education and Due Process Rights

Court cases challenged the actions of school districts and states in denying the due process rights of children with disabilities to receive a free appropriate public education in the least restrictive environment, along with their due process rights. Before these cases, they had been excluded from certain education programs or been given what was called a "special" education in segregated settings. In basic terms, the courts examined whether or not such treatment was rational and whether or not it was necessary. One of the most important cases to examine these questions concerning children with disabilities is *Pennsylvania Association for Retarded Children v. Commonwealth of Pennsylvania* (1972).

The Pennsylvania Association for Retarded Children (PARC) brought a lawsuit on behalf of children with retardation against the state of Pennsylvania. In their case, the *Pennsylvania Association for Retarded Children v. Commonwealth of Pennsylvania* (1972), the Association challenged a state law that denied public school education to certain children who were at that time considered unable to profit from public school attendance. The lawyers and parents supporting PARC argued that, though the children had intellectual disabilities, it was neither rational nor necessary to assume that they were ineducable and untrainable. The state could not demonstrate a rational basis for excluding these children from public school programs. The court decided that the children were entitled to receive free public education, that the children's parents had the right to be notified before any change was made in their child's educational program, and that certain procedures known as due process of law must be followed to ensure that parents were fully and fairly informed (*Pennsylvania Association for Retarded Children v. Commonwealth*, 1972).

At about this time a 12-year-old Black student named Peter Mills was excluded from the fourth grade because he allegedly was a "behavior problem." The principal approved his exclusion from school. This precipitated the case of *Mills v. Board of Education* (1972), in which the school district contended that it did not have enough money to provide special education programs for such students. The court ruled that lack of funds is no excuse for failing to educate children, and the court ordered the school to readmit Peter and serve such students appropriately. Even if funds are limited – as is often the case today – children with disabilities may not be denied access to the public schools (*Mills v. Board of Educ.* 348 F. Supp. 866 (1972)). Among other things, the *PARC* and *Mills* cases ruled that children with disabilities have a right to a free public education, and due process, especially in support of parent rights.

In 27 states, an additional 36 court decisions affirmed the right to education for students with disabilities, demonstrating the need for a federal standard. A bill was introduced in the U.S. Senate in 1972 that emerged in 1975 as Public Law 94-142, the Education for All Handicapped Children Act. From the beginning, the law provided hope for people with disabilities and their families, as it included the important concepts of free access to public education and equal rights to due process procedures to ensure equal protection under the law. In addition to a free and appropriate public education and due process, the law provides for education in the least restrictive environment. Table 2 identifies laws affecting the education of children with disabilities.

Table 2.   Laws Supporting People with Disabilities.

1943	Barden-LaFollette Vocational Rehabilitation Act made persons with cognitive impairments or mental illness eligible for vocational rehabilitation services (P.L. 78-113)
1958	National Defense Education Act provided funds for training professionals to train teachers of students with cognitive impairment (P.L. 85-926)
1965	The Elementary and Secondary Education Act (ESEA) provides a detailed plan for redressing some of the unequal conditions in the nation's schools. Several amendments to this law authorize the federal government to provide grants to states to operate schools devoted to the education of children with disabilities (P.L. 89-10 and 89-313)
1966	Congress approves several amendments to the ESEA. These include the creation of a federal grant program for the education of children with disabilities at local schools and the formation of the Bureau of Education of the Handicapped (BEH) and the National Advisory Council (P.L. 89-750)
1973	Section 504 of the Rehabilitation Act is enacted. It requires any recipient of federal financial assistance (such as school districts and state education agencies) to provide accommodations to eligible students with disabilities (Rehabilitation Act 34 C.F.R. § 104.5)
1974	The Family Educational Rights and Privacy Act (FERPA) is enacted. Among other provisions, it allows parents access to all personally identifiable information collected, maintained, or used by their school district concerning their children (P.L. 93-280)
1975	The Education for All Handicapped Children Act (EAHCA) ensures the due process rights of children with disabilities and their parents or guardians. This law also mandates individual education programs for students with disabilities and establishes in law that all children must receive services in the least restrictive environment (LRE) in which it is possible for them to attend school (P.L. 94-142)
1983	The EAHCA is amended. Among other provisions are (a) services to facilitate school-to-work transition through research and demonstration projects, (b) parent training and information centers, and (c) funding for demonstration projects and research in early intervention and early childhood special education (P.L. 98-199)
1986	The EAHCA is amended with the addition of the Handicapped Children's Protection Act. The amendment makes clear that students and parents have rights under the IDEA and Section 504 at the same time; previously, some school districts had treated the two laws as mutually exclusive (P.L. 99-457)
1990	The EAHCA is reauthorized and renamed the Individual with Disabilities Education Act. It expands funding of programs for students with disabilities, mandates transition services, defines assistive technology devices and services, and adds autism and traumatic brain injury to the list of categories of children and youth eligible for special education and related services (P.L. 101-476)
1997	The IDEA is amended with changes to strengthen the role of parents, ensure parent access to the curricula of schools, and encourage parents and educators to resolve differences through mediation or other nonadversarial means (P.L. 105-17)
2001	The 1965 Elementary and Secondary Education Act is updated and renamed the No Child Left Behind Act of 2001. Among its many provisions, this law requires school districts to demonstrate that students are achieving "adequate yearly progress" through their performance on standardized tests. Students with disabilities are generally required to take these tests; if their performance is not adequate, changes may be mandatory for individual schools and districts (20 USC § 6301) (2002)
2004	IDEA of 2004 eliminates the need for students to display a discrepancy between intelligence, typically measured by IQ tests, and achievement, generally measured by standardized tests in areas such as reading and math (U.S.C. § 1400 et seq.) (2005)

Sources: Adapted from McConnell (2007) and Philpot (n.d.).

INDIVIDUALS WITH DISABILITIES EDUCATION ACT (IDEA)

PARC, Mills, and other cases lead to a legislative bill, signed into law as the Education for All Handicapped Children Act of 1975, which has had a major influence on education. Reauthorized numerous times it is known today as the Individuals with Disabilities Education Improvement Act (IDEIA) and shortened to Individuals with Disabilities Education Act '04 (IDEA). This law is classified as an *entitlement law*, meaning that everyone who meets the eligibility requirements for the program is entitled to the program's services. The new name recognized the social importance of acknowledging people first and considering their disability afterward.

Public Law 94-142 had been the basis for assuring that all children with disabilities have available a free appropriate public education, assuring that rights of parents and their children are protected, providing financial assistance to states, and assessing the effectiveness of those efforts. Before the enactment of this law, the education needs of millions of children with disabilities were not being fully met (especially those with mental retardation and mental illnesses, who were excluded from schools). Because of this law, all students are now entitled to a free and appropriate public education; they cannot be excluded from school solely because of disability. Students must receive the special education and related services that they need, but for a child to get a free appropriate public education (FAPE), several provisions must be in place. The following are basic principles: (a) child find and zero reject, (b) nondiscriminatory identification and assessment, (c) individualized education program (IEP), (d) least restrictive environment, (e) procedural safeguards – such as due process, parents' rights to participate in the educational decision-making process for their child, and mediation when there are disagreements, (f) parental participation, and (g) transition. Subsequent reauthorizations of the Act brought greater clarification and enhancements to these significant principles.

Central Concepts of the IDEA

Child Find and Zero Reject
The first action of IDEA includes both child find and zero reject. *Child find* means that the school district must locate, identify, and evaluate unserved and underserved children with disabilities. IDEA 2004 amendments expanded the requirements to find children with special needs in private schools as well as among homeless students and students who are wards of

the state. All teachers are obligated to watch for disabilities among their students and make every effort to ensure the students are receiving a free appropriate public education.

Zero reject means a school district cannot exclude a child with a disability (regardless of the severity of the disability) from receiving a free appropriate public education. In the past, children with disabilities received different treatment than their nondisabled peers: being excluded from certain education programs or given a "special" education in segregated settings. This type of "special" was often less than adequate, with low teacher standards and low or no goals for the students.

Child find and zero reject also apply to children with serious behavior problems. IDEA did not address discipline problems until the 1997 reauthorization. Then in 2004 Congress simplified the complex procedures for dealing with discipline. In general terms, administrators may suspend students with disabilities for up to 10 school days – although instances must be reviewed on a case-by-case basis. However, procedures are in place to assure that students with disabilities receive an FAPE, even if they have been expelled from school as a disciplinary action.

Nondiscriminatory Identification and Assessment
Each student suspected of having a disability will have nondiscriminatory evaluation in all areas of suspected disability. It must be conducted by a team of evaluators who are knowledgeable and trained in the use of the tests and other evaluation materials and capable of gathering relevant information from a variety of sources. The evaluation materials and procedures selected must be administered in ways that are not racially or culturally discriminatory. The child cannot be subjected to unnecessary tests and assessments.

Nondiscriminatory identification and assessment are requirements put into place by EAHCA, but some of the procedures have been refined over the years by court rulings. The *Larry P. v. Riles* (1979) case highlighted unfair placement based on identification, assessment, and evaluation methods. A federal district court in California banned the use of standardized IQ instruments to evaluate African-American students for placement in classes for students with educable mental retardation (EMR). The court ruled that such tests contained racial and cultural bias and discriminated against students from racial minorities. Now local education agencies must conduct a full individual evaluation before beginning to provide special education and related services to a child with a disability (IDEA, 20 U.S.C. 1414(a) (1)).

IDEA requires that assessment materials be administered in the child's native language or mode of communication (such as sign language) and that the tests are validated for the specific purpose for which they are used. Tests must be administered and interpreted by trained personnel, and more than one test must be used to make a determination. *Nondiscriminatory evaluation* means that students must be evaluated in ways that do not discriminate based on language, culture, or race. This evaluation provides information to be used to determine the child's eligibility for special education and related services, and the team must identify information that is instructionally useful in planning for the child's education needs. This program is documented in the child's written individualized education program.

The Individualized Education Program (IEP)

Every child who receives special education services must have an individualized education program (IEP). The IEP is a written document that details the student's strengths and needs in any area affected by the disability and identifies the goals for improvement in those areas. The emphasis of the IEP is on progress in the general curriculum, addressing special factors that may influence a student's ability to learn (e.g., behavior or communication needs, or limited English proficiency). The IEP is the documentation that shows that a student is receiving a free appropriate education.

The IEP is developed by a collaborative team including the regular and special educators, a parent of the student, a representative of the school administration (representative of the local education agency), and any related service providers who may contribute to the process by knowing about the student or about educational services for the student. In addition, because the classroom teacher knows the curriculum and ways to help a student access it, the teacher should participate in developing the IEP. This team considers the student's present levels of educational performance and makes plans for improvement during the year. They then decide what special education and related services are required to help the student achieve the goals and objectives. The IEP team must also determine how to measure progress and how to inform parents about the student's progress toward accomplishing the IEP goals. The team must meet at least annually to update the IEP.

Board of Education of the Hendrick Hudson Central School District v. Rowley (1982) was a landmark case in which parents challenged school officials who refused to provide their hearing-impaired child with a sign language interpreter. This case, which went to the Supreme Court, established a standard for evaluation of an "appropriate education." First, all of the procedures (required under IDEA) must be followed. Second, an appropriate education must be "sufficient to confer some education benefit" (*Board of Ed. of the Hendrick Hudson Central School District v. Rowley* 458 U.S. 176 (1982)).

Least Restrictive Environment
Students with disabilities are educated in the least restrictive environment, in order to prevent them from being secluded because of their disability. The least restrictive environment (LRE) requirement is often referred to as "mainstreaming." Each case must be determined based on the individual needs of the student, but the least restrictive environment is the one that, to the greatest extent possible, satisfactorily educates disabled children together with children who are not disabled, in the same school the disabled child would attend if the child were not disabled. This mandate has been interpreted to require that a disabled child be placed in the LRE that will provide him with a meaningful educational benefit. Decisions about placement are to be made after the child's IEP is developed. Parents are members of any team that develops the IEP and decides on placement. Courts have held that schools may not predetermine placement. Placement decision must be made by the team.

Procedural Safeguards
Due process is among the procedural safeguards specifying that parents must be notified and given an opportunity to participate in developing their child's education program. Congress realized that grievances might occur over the appropriate placement and special education services for students with disabilities, so IDEA describes ways to address these grievances. Either the parents or the school can initiate a grievance process if either feels the needs of the student are not being met. States have adopted procedures for resolving complaints. The complaint must be in writing to the appropriate local education agent (LEA) (usually the district superintendent), and it must both specify the alleged violation of IDEA and give the facts on which the statement is based. A copy of the complaint is also sent to the State Director of Special Education.

IDEA has designed the IEP as a means to afford parents and school personnel the opportunity to work together to develop the plan for student success. In case of disputation, procedures have been designated for resolving differences. The law identifies procedures that allow the parent(s) or the school district to resolve disputes over any matter relating to the identification, evaluation, or educational placement of a child, or the provision of a free appropriate public education. This process is referred to as *mediation*. It is available whenever the parent(s) or school district requests a hearing.

Parent and Student Participation in Decision-Making

Parents and students (when appropriate) are required to participate in the special education process. They must be notified of all meetings and included in the decision-making process.

Fundamental to the safeguards is the right of parents to participate in decisions made about their child's education. This section of IDEA describes ways that the rights of students with disabilities and their parents are protected. The law requires that parents and, when applicable, students are to be notified and allowed to participate in any decision regarding the special education of students with disabilities.

This important aspect of the legislation helps guard against past practices of placing students in programs – or removing them from programs – without the knowledge or involvement of parents. The law recognizes that schools should involve parents as important partners in the special education process. Thus the law requires not only that parents be notified, but also that they give informed consent when the school proposes to evaluate, place, or change any aspect of a student's special educational program. In addition, parents are members of the IEP team with the right to challenge or appeal decisions about their child's identification, evaluation, or education placement.

Students who reach the age of majority and are still in public schools have rights similar to those of parents for making decisions about their program.

The following procedural safeguards are included in IDEA '04:

- Schools must obtain written consent from parents prior to conducting an evaluation or placement of their child.
- Parents must be given written prior notice so they can be involved in proposed changes.
- Parents may obtain an independent educational evaluation of their child – to be paid for by the school district – if the district cannot or will not provide an appropriate evaluation.
- Parents may inspect and review their child's educational records.
- Parents may give – or refuse to give – consent for initial evaluation or placement in special education.
- Students may remain in their current placement while decisions are made about future changes.

Several key provisions in Public Law 105-17 (1997), the Individuals with Disabilities Education Act Amendments of 1997, were added to those previously listed under the purposes of the act, including a new provision in the identification of learning disabilities. The reauthorized version of the law allows local education agencies to eliminate a criterion previously used for students with learning disabilities to qualify for special education and related services: the requirement that students display a discrepancy between intelligence, typically measured by IQ tests, and achievement, generally measured by standardized tests in areas such as reading and math (Klotz & Nealis, 2005) – often referred to as the "ability–achievement" gap.

Transition Services
The current IDEA requires that by the time a student reaches the age of 16, his or her IEP must address transition planning. This means the parent, the student (if appropriate), and the rest of the IEP team collaborate to decide what the student needs in order to prepare for the transition from school to adult life. Transition planning includes any community agencies and work experiences that will be part of the student's school day. To be effective the planning certainly should begin prior to the student's 16th birthday.

Evolution of a New IDEA

Subsequent reauthorizations and amendments to EAHCA in 1978, 1983, and again in 1986 have expanded or clarified procedural safeguards, provided for awarding of attorneys' fees, and expanded services to include children with disabilities ages 3 through 5 (Part C). They have also provided funding for early intervention programs for young children with special needs.

Today referred to as the Individuals with Disabilities Education Act (IDEA), this act provides funding for education and services to children with disabilities, age 3 to 21. These funds must be used to provide a free appropriate public education (FAPE). IDEA provides for and expects schools to involve parents in the process. Schools and their local and state education authorities (LEA and SEA) must make every possible effort to include parents in each step of the process from identification through transition to graduation.

Reauthorized in 1990, amended in 1991, and again reauthorized in 1997 – the act was amended and renamed the Individuals with Disabilities Education Act (IDEA). The new name recognized the social importance of acknowledging people first and considering their disability afterward. Each amendment added or refined new areas within the law, which are discussed briefly.

Individuals with Disabilities Education Act of 1990 and 1997
In 1990, IDEA (Public Law 101-476) confirmed the focus on the individual and expanded services to children with disabilities ages 18 through 21. It also added transition services, assistive technology, and related services such as rehabilitation counseling and social work services. However, according to the 1997 IDEA, a student was to have a transition IEP by age 14. The reauthorization moved the minimum age to 16. IDEA 90 expanded eligibility for services to include children with autism and traumatic brain injury. Moreover, the 1997 amendments made modification to improve educational results and promote school safety. This amendment protected students with disabilities who are violent or dangerous, while enabling educators to more easily remove these students from their current educational placement. The 1997 amendment also addressed the cost of special education and revamped the way schools receive funding.

Individuals with Disabilities Education Improvement Act of 2004
President George W. Bush signed the reauthorized Individuals with Disabilities Education Improvement Act (IDEIA) into law on December 3, 2004. The provisions of the Act became effective on July 1, 2005, with the exception of some of the elements pertaining to the definition of a "highly qualified teacher" that took effect upon the signing of the Act. The final regulations were published on August 2006. The statute allows for a short title: "This Act may be cited as the 'Individuals with Disabilities Education Act'" (Section 601). The new IDEA maintained the basic principles of IDEA and its civil rights guarantees.

Identified Children

Each state that receives federal special education funding is required to have policies and practical methods to ensure that children with disabilities are identified, located, evaluated, and, if eligible, receive special education or related services. This includes groups of children who are

- suspected of having a disability, regardless of whether they are advancing from grade to grade, 3–9 years old and have a developmental delay (or a subset of this age range, depending on state definitions), homeless, wards of the State, migrant or highly mobile, living on Native American reservations, or attending private schools where they have been placed by their parents (34 CFR § 300.111).

Procedures for Identifying Specific Learning Disabilities
IDEA (2005) added procedures for identifying specific learning disabilities. The law required states to adopt criteria for determining whether a child has a specific learning disability. Specifically, states could not require the use of a severe discrepancy between intellectual ability and achievement for determining whether a child has a specific learning disability. The law specifies that Local Education Agencies

- Must permit the use of a process based on the child's response to scientific, research-based intervention and
- May permit the use of other alternative research-based procedures for determining whether a child has a specific learning disability [34 CFR 300.307] [20 U.S.C. 1221e-3; 1401(30); 1414(b)(6)].

IDEA Aligning with No Child Left Behind (NCLB)

New Definitions
IDEA (2005) added new definitions in an effort to align with the definitions and requirements of NCLB. Two discussed here are *academic core subjects* and *limited English proficient*. IDEA defined academic core subjects to mean "English, reading or language arts; mathematics; science; foreign languages; civics and government; economics; the arts; history; and geography" ([9101] of ESEA); (602(4)] of IDEA). The IDEA specifically defines limited English proficient. Please see the textbox.

IDEA defined limited English proficient as

- a child who is aged 3 through 21;
- who is enrolled or preparing to enroll in an elementary school or secondary school;
- who was not born in the United States or whose native language is a language other than English;

- who is a Native American or Alaska Native, or a native resident of the outlying areas; and
- who comes from an environment where a language other than English has had a significant impact on the individual's level of English language proficiency; or
- who is migratory,
- whose native language is a language other than English, and
- who comes from an environment where a language other than English is dominant; and
- whose difficulties in speaking, reading, writing, or understanding the English language may be sufficient to deny the individual; and the ability to meet the state's proficient level of achievement on state assessments (Section 1111(b)(3) of ESEA).

Use of Funds

IDEA aligned more closely with NCLB and established provisions for the use of funds at the state and local levels. For example, it provided use of funds to support the development and provision of appropriate accommodations for children with disabilities, or the development and provision of alternate assessments that are valid and reliable for assessing the performance of children with disabilities (Sections 1111(b) and 6111 of ESEA) and (611(e)(2)(C)(x)] of IDEA).

Performance Goals and Indicators

IDEA also required states to established goals for the performance of children with disabilities in the state that support adequate yearly progress (AYP), including the state's objectives for progress by children with disabilities (Section 1111(b)(2)(C) of ESEA).

It further requires states to address graduation rates and dropout rates. Standards are to be consistent, to the extent appropriate, with any other goals and standards for children established by the state, and IDEA requires state to establish performance indicators it will use to assess progress toward achieving the goals ... including measurable annual objectives for progress (Section 612(a)(15)(A and B) of IDEA and Section 1111(b)(2)(C)(v)(II)(c) of the ESEA).

ADDITIONAL LAWS AFFECTING
SPECIAL EDUCATION

Rehabilitation Act and Section 504

Background on the Rehabilitation Act (RA)
The Rehabilitation Act (RA) was a major victory for the disability rights movement. It expressed Congress's broad vision for remedying discrimination because of disability. It originated in 1918 when the American government sought to provide rehabilitation services for World War I military veterans. This was the first federal civil rights law to protect the rights of the disabled. Having studied the living conditions and challenges facing Americans with disabilities, Congress expressed its finding that these individuals were a severely disadvantaged group within U.S. society; however, Congress also determined that citizens with disabilities have the potential to live independently and pursue careers. Ultimately, federal employment programs, such as the Workforce Investment Act of 1998, would include provisions for training people with disabilities (Rehabilitation Act, 1973).

In amending the RA, Congress stated that the federal government would take a leadership position in creating opportunities for individuals with disabilities to receive training, secure employment, and live independently, and that it would establish partnerships with state governments to develop programs that fulfill those needs.

Section 504
Educators often refer to the Section 504th section of the Rehabilitation Act today. This section defines an individual with a disability. It reads:

> [N]o otherwise qualified individual with a disability in the United States ... shall, solely by reason of his or her disability, be excluded from the participation in, be denied the benefits of, or be subjected to discrimination under any program or activity receiving Federal financial assistance. [29 U.S.C.A. § 794(a)]

Under federal law, prospective employers could not discriminate against qualified applicants based on their disability. This law provided the outline for the future Americans with Disabilities Act. Section 504 defined an individual with a disability:

> [One] who (i) has a physical or mental impairment which substantially limits one or more of such person's major life activities, (ii) has a record of such an impairment, or (iii) is regarded as having such an impairment. [29 U.S.C.A. § 706(7)(B)]

Major life activities in general means functions such as caring for one's self, performing manual tasks, seeing, hearing, eating, sleeping, walking, standing, lifting, bending, speaking, breathing, learning, reading, concentrating, thinking, communicating, and working (45 C.F.R. § 84.3(j)(2)(i)). Major bodily functions are in this category, including (but not limited to) functions of the immune system, normal cell growth, as well as digestive, bowel, bladder, neurological, brain, respiratory, circulatory, endocrine, and reproductive functions.

The law also gives information about specific assistance available to people with disabilities including: the use of assistive technology, reasonable accommodations or auxiliary aids or services, and learned behavioral or adaptive neurological modifications and auxiliary aids and services. The term "auxiliary aids and services" includes the following:

1. Qualified interpreters or other effective means of making aurally delivered materials available to individuals with hearing impairments.
2. Qualified readers, taped texts, or other effective methods of making visually delivered materials available to individuals with visual impairments.
3. Acquisition or modification of equipment or devices.
4. Other similar services and actions (Section 12103).

When a student is identified as having a disability under Section 504, the next step is to determine whether he or she is "otherwise qualified." In order to be "otherwise qualified," the student must be (a) of an age during which nonhandicapped persons are provided such services, (b) of any age during which state law mandates that such services be provided to persons with disabilities, or (c) [a student] to whom a state is required to provide a free appropriate public education (under the IDEA) [45 C.F.R. § 84.3(k)(2)].

Being otherwise qualified means that a student is eligible to participate in a program or activity despite having an impairment; such an individual must be permitted to participate in the program or activity as long as it is possible to do so by means of a "reasonable accommodation."

The key concepts in Section 504 are

- otherwise qualified (noted above),
- disability,
- excluded from the participation in,
- be denied the benefits of,
- be subjected to discrimination, and
- program or activity receiving federal financial assistance.

Americans with Disabilities Act in 1990: Civil Rights Protection

The Americans with Disabilities Act (ADA), signed by President George H. W. Bush in 1990, closely followed the pattern of Section 504 of the Rehabilitation Act. The ADA provides civil rights protection to disabled Americans. This legislation established equal opportunity for employment, transportation, telecommunications, public accommodations, and state and federal government services. This act is considered the most wide-sweeping civil rights bill for individuals with disabilities.

Like Section 504, the ADA is a civil rights law. It works from the definition of disability written in Section 504, but additionally it provides a clear and comprehensive national mandate to eliminate discrimination against individuals with disabilities. It applies to private-sector employment, public services, public transportation, and telecommunications. It requires that employers do not discriminate solely because a person has a disability. If the person with a disability can perform the activities required for the job as well as a nondisabled person, then the employer may not eliminate the person who has a disability as a candidate for employment without making reasonable accommodations.

Effects of the ADA can be seen in many aspects of daily life: sidewalk cutouts, closed captioning on television screens, telecommunications devises in malls and airports, and sign-language translators at public meetings. These accommodations have supported Americans with disabilities in their right to fully participate in all aspects of society: to communicate, to access public information, and to travel by public transportation. In addition, these protections benefit many who do not have disabilities (e.g., a parent pushing a baby stroller more smoothly over the cutouts).

No Child Left Behind (NCLB)

The No Child Left Behind (NCLB) Act (2001) has focused on outcomes for all students, including those who have disabilities. Aspects of particular concern to special educators include stronger accountability for results, requirements for highly qualified personnel, and dependence on high-stakes testing.

The No Child Left Behind Act began as the Elementary and Secondary Education Act of 1965, also called the Eisenhower Education Act, and has since undergone several revisions and reauthorizations. The most recent reauthorization, revision, and renaming of this law has received a good deal of attention in the schools and in the media.

No Child Left Behind is a statute that proposes to increase educational performance for all students in the United States, especially low socio-economic, low-achieving minority students. The act seeks to enhance educational performance from three directions: (1) employment of highly qualified professionals and paraprofessionals, (2) use of research-based, empirically proven curriculum, and (3) assessment through high-stakes testing of student achievement.

When testing shows that students are not achieving adequately, parent and students are given choices to change to better schools, with vouchers to support additional costs. The *No Child Left Behind* Act of 2001 has emphasized the principles of accountability, choice, and flexibility in its reauthorization of other major ESEA programs. For example, the new law combines the Eisenhower Professional Development and Class Size Reduction programs into a new Improving Teacher Quality State Grants program focused on using practices grounded in scientific research to prepare, train, and recruit high-quality teachers (NCLB Executive Summary, 2004).

High-stakes testing has been a controversial aspect of NCLB that is of particular concern for special educators as laws and interpretations of the laws are put into place. Special educators must keep current with professional literature and memberships to know the high-stakes testing policies apply to their teaching areas.

The Family Education Rights and Privacy Act (FERPA)

FERPA is a federal statute with a twofold purpose: (1) to ensure that parents have access to their children's educational records and (2) to protect the privacy rights of parents and children by limiting access to these records without parental consent. FERPA applies to: (a) access to educational records, (b) parental right to inspect and review records, (c) amendment of records, and (d) destruction of records.

FERPA is applicable to all agencies and institutions that receive federal funds, including elementary and secondary schools, colleges, and universities (20 U.S.C. 1232g and 1232h and 34 C.F.R Part 99). In addition to affording parents access to their children's records control over the disclosure of information from the records, FERPA allows parents to have records amended when they are inaccurate or misleading. Schools must comply with a parent's request for access to the student's records within 45 days of the receipt of a request. Generally, a school is required to provide copies of education records to a parent if the failure to do so would prevent the parent from exercising the right to inspect and review the records. FERPA protects the student's privacy interests in "education records." Education records are broadly defined as "those records, files, documents, and other materials, which (a) contain information directly related to a student and (b) are maintained by an educational agency or institution or by a person acting for such agency or institution" [20 U.S.C. § 1232g (a) (4) (A)].

SUMMARY

The people of the United States began to recognize need for human rights and the protection of minority groups, including people with disabilities. Schools and training programs were started, and as public awareness grew legislators passed laws to support these individual rights. The 1960s and 1970s hailed the societal changes, which protected the rights of the disabled and passed statutes to provide funding and a system for compliance. Special education today relies on the framework of these laws to meet the learning needs of children with disabilities.

REFERENCES

American Federation for the Blind. (n.d.). Helen Keller biography. Available at http://www. afb.org/Section.asp?SectionID = 1&TopicID = 129 (para. 4). Accessed on April 15, 2010.
American with Disabilities Act of 1990. (Pub. L. 104 Stat. 327). 42 U.S.C. sections 12101 et seq.
Ancestry.com. (n.d.). *1800 U.S. Federal Census Newsletter*. 1880 schedules of defective, dependent, and delinquent classes. Available at http://www.ancestry.com
Board of Education of the Hendrick Hudson Central School District v. Rowley, 458 U.S. 176 (1982).
Branch, T. (2007). *Parting the waters: America in the King years 1954–1963*. New York: Simon & Schuster.
Brown v. Board of Education, Topeka, 347 U.S.483. (1954). Chief Justice Earl Warren; Decision on *Brown v. Board of Education of Topeka*. Available at https://www.faulkner.edu/ academics/artsandsciences/socialandbehavioral/readings/hy/warren.asp
Chesterton, G. K. (2000). *Eugenics and other evils: An argument against the Scientifically organized state*. Seattle, WA: Inkling Books.
Civil Rights Act of 1964. Retrieved from the U.S. National Archives and Records. Available at http://www.ourdocuments.gov/doc.php?doc = 97
Declaration of Independence (1776). Available at http://www.ushistory.org/declaration/ document/index.htm
Educational of All Handicapped Children Education Act (P.L. 94-142) (1975).
Family Educational Rights and Privacy Act of 1974, 20 U.S.C. § 1232 (g). (1974).

Individuals with Disabilities Education Act of 1990 (Pub. L. No. 101-476, 104 Stat. 1142).

Individuals with Disabilities Education Act of 1997, Pub. L. No. 105-17, § 111, Stat. 37.

Individuals with Disabilities Education Act of 2004, 20 U.S.C. § 1400 et seq. (2005).

Joseph, P. Kennedy, Jr. Foundation. (n.d.). Available at http://www.jpkf.org/index.html

Klotz, M. B., & Nealis, L. (2005). The new IDEA: A summary of significant reforms. Retrieved from the National Association of School Psychologists website. Available at http://www.nasponline.org/advocacy/IDEAfinalsummary.pdf

Larry P. v. Riles. United States Court of Appeals, 1984. 793 F.2d 969 (9th Cir.).

Latham, P. H., Latham, P. S., & Mandlawitz, M. (2008). *Special education law.* Boston, MA: Pearson Education, Inc.

Lofgren, C. A. (1987). *The Plessy case: A legal-historical interpretation.* New York: Oxford University Press.

McConnell, T. (2007). History of special education. Available at http://www.xtimeline.com/timeline/Timeline-for-Special-Education.

McNeil, G. R. (1983). *Groundwork: Charles Hamilton Houston and the struggle for civil rights.* Philadelphia: University of Pennsylvania Press.

Medley, K. W. (2003). *We as Freemen: Plessy v. Ferguson.* Gretna, LA: Pelican.

Mental Retardation Facilities and Community Mental Health Construction Act (P.L. 88-164). Available at http://www.archives.nysed.gov/edpolicy/research/res_digitized.shtml-

Mills v. Board of Education of the District of Columbia, 348 F. Supp. 866. (D.D.C. 1972).

NAACP Legal History. (n.p.). Retrieved from http://www.naacp.org/

No Child Left Behind Act, 20 U.S.C. § 6301 et seq. (2002).

Pennsylvania Association for Retarded Children v. Commonwealth 334 F. Supp. 1257 (E.D. Pa. 1971) and 343 F. Supp. 279 (E.D. Pa. 1972).

Philpot, D. J. (n.d.). History of federal statutes affecting special education. Available at http://www.dphilpotlaw.com/html/history_of_federal_statutes.html. Retrieved on April 5, 2010.

Pittsburg Courier. (1940). Charles Hamilton Houston saving the world for democracy, August 24. Available at http://www.nascp.org/about/history/chhouston/index.htm

Plessy v. Ferguson 163 U.S. 537 (1896).

PSB: American Experience. (n.d.). Available at http://www.pbs.org/wgbh/americanexperience.

Rehabilitation Act (P.L. 93-112) § 504. (1973).

Schwartz, H. (1956). *Samuel Gridley Howe: Social reformer 1801–1876.* Cambridge, MA: Harvard University Press.

U.S. Department of Education. (2004). No child left behind. Overview: Executive summary. Available at http://www2.ed.gov/nclb/overview/intro/execsumm.hmtl

CHAPTER 3

HISTORY OF EARLY CHILDHOOD SPECIAL EDUCATION

Sharon Doubet and Amanda C. Quesenberry

Lisa was born in 1969 into a family that included her parents and four siblings. She grew and thrived in a rural setting experiencing typical developmental milestones until the age of 2 when she began experiencing seizures. For the next few years, the seizure episodes were severe, and as a result, Lisa had cognitive disabilities and language delays.

Twenty-eight years later, Leslie was born prematurely in 1997. Her family consisted of her parents and a brother who was one year older. She spent two months in the Neonatal Intensive Care Unit (NICU). During this time, she and her family were referred for early intervention (birth to three) services. Leslie experienced developmental delays in cognition, speech, and motor areas.

The stories of Lisa and Leslie will be used throughout this chapter to illustrate the history of early childhood special education. The first legislation requiring states to provide comprehensive and coordinated services to young children under the age of three was not passed until 1997 (the year Leslie was born). Over time, services for young children with disabilities have continued to evolve and change as research reveals evidence-based practices to most adequately meet the needs of our nation's youngest and most vulnerable children. This chapter provides a historical perspective on services for young children with disabilities in the United States.

History of Special Education
Advances in Special Education, Volume 21, 47–60
Copyright © 2011 by Emerald Group Publishing Limited
ISSN: 0270-4013/doi:10.1108/S0270-4013(2011)0000021006

1900–1960: LITTLE SUPPORT FOR YOUNG CHILDREN WITH DISABILITIES

Early in the 20th century, many began to voice growing concern over such issues as infant mortality, childhood diseases, and child labor (Anastasiow & Nucci, 1994). At this time, physicians, child advocates, and the general public began to speak out about social concerns regarding children, including those living in orphanages and those with mental illness or intellectual disabilities. These concerns came about at a time when psychologists studying young children began to accept that a child's intelligence was impacted by both genetic and environmental factors (Hunt, 1961). Prior to this point, experts believed a child's IQ was set at birth with little that could be done to influence it over time. Although we were beginning to better understand the importance of environmental influences on young children, at this point, most children with disabilities such as intellectual disabilities, cerebral palsy, and epilepsy were institutionalized rather than treated. On the other hand, children who were deaf or blind were more likely to be treated, but were typically sent away to "schools" and were segregated from their families and peers while receiving treatment and education.

In the mid-20th century, and largely due to the two world wars, the general public began to develop a more positive view of persons with disabilities. As many soldiers returned home from World War I and II with missing limbs and other disabilities, the public began to become more accepting of those with disabilities. With growing public acceptance and concern about those with disabilities, the International Council for Exceptional Children was formed in 1922. This group, which still exists today, worked tirelessly in support of young children with disabilities (Cook, Tessier, & Klein, 1992). In 1930, at a White House Conference on Child Health and Protection, early childhood special education received national attention for the first time in the United States. In the 1940s and 1950s, more and more prominent individuals such as Pearl Buck, Dale Evans, and the Kennedy family began to speak out in support of persons with disabilities. At this time, parents of children with disabilities also began to advocate for their children; and as a result, organizations such as the United Cerebral Palsy Association, the National Association for Retarded Citizens, and the American Foundation for the Blind were formed (Cook et al., 1992).

1960s: GROWING SUPPORT FOR YOUNG CHILDREN WITH DISABILITIES

During the 1960s, much of what we know and understand about early intervention was born from an era of optimism, creativity, and broad public support for social services (Meisels & Shonkoff, 2000). At this time, Presidents Kennedy and Johnson undertook several major social issues, including movements to prevent intellectual disabilities, wipe out poverty, and to promote Civil Rights (Meisels & Shonkoff). As a result of experiences with intellectual disabilities in his family, John F. Kennedy formed a commission to study issues surrounding intellectual disabilities including prevention and research. Consequently, in 1963, P.L. 88-156 was passed to provide funding through Title V of the Social Security Act for special projects for children with mental retardation. When President Johnson took office, he began working on a series of social reform issues called the *Great Society* that were intended to eliminate poverty and racial injustice. As a part of Johnson's *War on Poverty*, he worked with Sargent Shriver, who was the director of the Office of Economic Opportunity to develop the Economic Opportunity Act, which was passed by congress in 1964.

One part of the Economic Opportunity Act included Head Start, a preschool program for young children who were from low-income families. When Project Head Start began in 1965, it was an eight-week summer pilot program directed toward the nation's poorest preschoolers. It served approximately 550,000 four- and five-year-olds throughout the country (Garguilo & Kilgo, 2000). Unlike any program developed before, Head Start was a federally funded program designed to offer children multifaceted services including education, two meals a day, psychological, social, medical, and dental care. Parents were highly involved in the program and were encouraged to volunteer, create goals, and learn about child development and nutrition. Parents were also encouraged to continue their education and/or obtain employment with Head Start programs. Although one of the founding principles for Head Start was to prevent intellectual disabilities and raise IQ scores, in the early days of Head Start, no special efforts were made to serve children with disabilities (Zigler & Muenchow, 1992). These children were not served in the beginning largely because there were very few teachers or other professionals with experience in serving them. As a response to parents and other advocacy groups who were pushing for services for young children with disabilities, the Handicapped Children's Early Education Assistance Act (P.L. 90-538) was passed in 1968. This Act provided funding for university education programs to train professionals to work with young children with disabilities (Garguilo & Kilgo, 2000). Before long, over 200 model programs were developed across the country building on work done by early pioneers such as Samuel Kirk, Louise Phillips, Ruth Jackson, Barbara Smiley, Setsu Furuno, and Merle Karnes (Anastasiow & Nucci, 1994). Many university programs offered training and courses in home visiting, parent support, and quality early childhood education for children in underprivileged areas (Martin, 1989).

1970s: FEDERAL SUPPORT FOR
CHILDREN WITH DISABILITIES

As more and more research was done to support the importance of early intervention with young children with disabilities, parents and other advocacy groups began to challenge public officials and legislators to support public funding for treatment and education for these young children. Strong parental advocacy played a vital role in the passage of the landmark legislation, P.L. 94-142, the Education for All Handicapped Children Act (EHA) in 1975. For the first time, this law required that all children, including those with disabilities, over the age of six years be provided with a free and appropriate public education (FAPE) (Wright & Wright, 2003). Although states were not required to serve children under the age of six years, financial incentives were given to states to serve children with disabilities from three to five years old (McCollum, 2000).

During the 1970s, other federal legislation in support of persons with disabilities was passed, including P.L. 93-112, the Section 504 Vocational Rehabilitation Act. This Act, passed in 1973, established many rights for persons with disabilities including access to public facilities, admission into institutions of higher education, nondiscriminatory employment opportunities, and equal access to federally funded programs for children with disabilities (Meisels & Shonkoff, 2000). The passage of key legislation helped to heighten public awareness of the injustices often faced by persons with disabilities.

> In the introductory case, Lisa and her family lived in an area where early childhood special education and Head Start services were not available. For her this meant there were no educational or therapeutic services provided until she entered the public school system at the age of six years which coincided with the passage of EHA in 1975. The first grade classroom she attended was in a segregated special education building 30 miles from her home. Up until this point in her life, interventions were focused solely on medical needs (reducing seizures), with no speech, physical or occupational therapies offered. At the end of the 1970's, at the age of 10 years, Lisa continued her education at the same school for children with disabilities. Her Individualized Education Plan (IEP) goals focused on life skills activities. Each week, she spent approximately eight hours on a bus traveling to and from school; ironically, this was much less time than the amount of therapies provided to her through her IEP.

1980s: SLASHING SOCIAL SERVICES

The 1980s were dismal years for federally funded social service programs. President Reagan campaigned and carried through with promises to reduce the number of programs supported by the federal government. Basically, the belief was that state and local governments should be providing services to children and families rather than the federal government (Ginsberg & Miller-Cribbs, 2005). Therefore, federal funding for many social service programs were drastically cut or programs were totally dismantled. A few early childhood programs, such as Head Start, survived this era due to overwhelming bipartisan support.

Despite the deep cuts made to many programs for children during the 1980s, the most significant legislation for young children with disabilities since P.L. 94-142 was passed in 1986. Although not mandated, the amendments to the EHA included more comprehensive and coordinated efforts for children under the age of five and their families. Even though full implementation of this law did not come about until after the passage of amendments to the Education of All Handicapped Children Act (EHA) in 1990, it did provide further incentives for states to serve children ages three through five years. It also established a foundation for services to be provided to children under the age of three years (i.e., at this time called Part H). However, at this time providing services for children ages birth to three with disabilities, and their families, was still at each state's discretion.

Looking back at Lisa's case, during the 1980s, at ages 11 through 19 years, she remained in the same distant self-contained school for children with disabilities. If she had been born in this decade, she could have benefited from receiving services and therapies (i.e., speech, motor, social/emotional) in an early childhood special education preschool classroom. An earlier start in supporting Lisa's development may have reduced her delays and increased her skills.

1990s: CAUTIOUS GROWTH: PUBLIC SUPPORT VERSUS INDIVIDUAL RESPONSIBILITY

During the 1990s, a number of key pieces of legislation passed that impacted the lives of children with disabilities and their families. In 1990, the Americans with Disabilities (ADA) Act was passed, which prohibited discrimination against individuals with disabilities. Six years later in 1996, President Clinton signed the Personal Responsibility and Work Opportunity Act into law. Additionally, federal legislation for the provision of services to children with disabilities was amended twice. After years of protest from the disability community and their advocates, in 1990, President George W. Bush signed into law the Americans with Disabilities Act (ADA). This was the most broad-sweeping legislation to ever impact those with disabilities, including young children. Provisions of the law included equal rights for individuals with disabilities in regards to employment, state and public services, and public accommodations. Public accommodations ensured that public schools and other programs receiving federal monies, including Head Start and child care programs, were accessible for children with special needs and also for family members of children who may have special needs.

The Personal Responsibility and Work Opportunity Act passed in 1996, dramatically changing the United States' welfare system. This new law eliminated the entitlement of federal aid to impoverished children and families by converting the system to welfare to work format. As a part of this law, the Aid to Families with Dependent Children (AFDC) program was changed and was now called, Temporary Assistance to Needy Families (TANF), which offered time-limited assistance to families over a two-year period as parents found training and work. Although this law was meant to act as an incentive to some, it created more of a hardship to parents of children with disabilities. These parents were now forced to find jobs and also struggled to find, and pay for, care for their children, especially after benefits ran out. Those impacted most were parents who themselves had disabilities and/or parents of children with disabilities. Ohlson (1998) explained that the new system imposed harsh sanctions on families from low-income backgrounds who were often already stressed by their current situations. Welfare reform also meant that thousands of parents who had been staying at home with their children were now required to go to work or school. For many families, child care became a patchwork of options that did not always include high-quality programs.

The welfare reform act further affected care for young children through the development of two new programs meant to provide additional support for the increased numbers of children now in nonparental care (Raver, 2009). Early Head Start was developed in 1995 to serve qualified children ages birth to three years and their families. The second new program was the Child Care Bureau, developed in 1995, to meet increasing needs for child care as a result of welfare reform. Amendments made to the EHA in 1990 were significant because terminology in the law was changed to reflect increasing respect for persons with disabilities. Throughout the law, the word "handicapped" was replaced with the word "disabled." The name of the law was revised to reflect these changes. Instead of Education for All Handicapped Children Act (EHA), the title was changed to the Individuals with Disabilities Education Act (IDEA). The importance of early intervention was recognized in the 1997 reauthorization of IDEA (P.L. 105-17). Now, for the first time ever, states were mandated to develop comprehensive and coordinated services for infants and toddlers with developmental delays through Part C (formerly known as Part H of IDEA). Additionally, states were also required to provide free and appropriate services (FAPE) to children ages three to five years (Part B of the law) in the least restrictive environment (LRE). At this time, states were granted considerable freedom in program design and implementation, which led to a myriad of service delivery systems across the 50 states and territories.

Looking back at Leslie and Lisa's cases, Leslie was born at the end of this decade. The same year, 1997, amendments were passed to IDEA which mandated early intervention services for infants and toddlers with developmental delays. As a result of her premature birth, Leslie had a number of developmental delays, which ensured her eligibility for early intervention (EI). Through EI, an Individualized Family Service Plan (IFSP) was developed with her parents that outlined goals for her and her family. The comprehensive services provided through the IFSP included a case manager, family-centered plan, and therapies provided in a natural setting (i.e., her home). When EI therapists visited her home to provide services, her family members learned engaging activities that promoted Leslie's growth and development.

At the beginning of this decade, in 1990, Lisa graduated from high school at the age of 21 years. She had attended the same segregated special education school building for 16 years. Her teachers were very proud of her accomplishments as they applauded her graduation class of 8 students. She had developed friendships with other special education students that she was with each day. However, due to the distance to her school (eighty miles round trip), she was not involved in social activities with peers outside of the typical school day. The opportunities for Lisa to develop friendships with peers in her home community were limited due to the amount of time she spent outside of her community.

After graduation from high school, Lisa continued to live at home with her parents. Her transition plan included the opportunity for her to attend a sheltered work place located in a nearby town. This transition was very difficult for her. Many days she stayed at home due to her discomfort with a new environment, new people, and different expectations.

2000s: DECREASED FUNDING; INCREASED ACCOUNTABILITY

The new millennium began with massive reforms to the American education system through the No Child Left Behind (NCLB) Act of 2001. NCLB impacted every level of education, including early childhood special education. As a part of NCLB, in 2002, President Bush formally announced his plans regarding the early childhood programs in a program called Good Start, Grow Smart (GSGS). GSGS outlined three major goals for early childhood programs including: (a) strengthening Head Start, (b) partnering with states to improve early childhood education, and (c) providing information to teachers, caregivers, and parents (Department of Health and Human Service (DHHS) and Department of Education (DOE), 2006). In response to GSGS, states were required to develop early learning standards for educating young children in the areas of language, literacy, and mathematics (National Association for the Education of Young Children (NAEYC), 2009). These standards were intended to create a framework of indicators by which programs could judge the quality of their curriculum, with the goal of implementing evidence-based practices to narrow achievement gaps often found among young preschool-aged children (DHHS and DOE, 2006). For many, these mandates have caused a great deal of stress as they have come with no funding increases and in some cases, even funding cuts.

During the 2000s, changes were also made to federal legislation for persons with disabilities. In 2004, IDEA was reauthorized to become the Individuals with Disabilities Education Improvement Act (IDEIA, Public Law 108-446). This Act aligned IDEA and NCLB, and provided guidance for educators to appropriately identify students in need of special education services. The process, named Response-to-Intervention (RTI), is a systematic decision-making process for early and effective responses to children's learning and behavioral difficulties, provide children with the appropriate level of instruction, and then provide data-based methods for evaluating the effectiveness of instructional approaches (Fox, Carta, Strain, Dunlap, & Hemmeter, 2009). The other area of P.L. 108-446 that affected services for young children with disabilities is the option for parents of children who were eligible to continue early intervention services from birth through age six years, or when their child enters kindergarten (Turnbull, Huerta, Stowe, Weldon, & Schrandt, 2006).

Clearly, legislative efforts by the government have been instrumental in the education of young children (see Table 1 for historical landmarks).

Looking back at Leslie's story, when she was 2.5 years old, her parents, the EI program staff, and the Local Education Agency (LEA) representative met to develop a transition plan for her to move from Part C (ages B-3 years) services to Part B (ages 3–21 years). After visiting a variety of preschools, her parents chose a full day local community collaborative classroom housed at the YWCA. In this service model, the school district (LEA) provides an early childhood special education teacher and therapies, and the YWCA provides a general education teacher and the physical space. The transition team determined that this community program would provide quality services for Leslie in the LRE. The transition plan included an opportunity for Leslie and her family to visit the new setting, meet the teachers, and share information that would be helpful when Leslie entered to the new program.

Table 1. Historical Landmarks for Young Children at Risk.

1963	P.L. 88-156, Provided funding for projects for children with mental retardation through Title V of the Social Security Act
1964	P.L. 88-452, The Economic Opportunity Act, out of which Head Start and other programs were developed
1965	Head Start was established to provide preschool for low income 3- to 5-year-olds
1968	P.L. 90-538, Handicapped Children's Early Education Assistance Act was established to fund model preschool programs for children with disabilities
1972	P.L. 424, Economic Opportunity Amendments passed that required all Head Start programs to serve children with identified disabilities
1975	P.L. 94-142, Education for All Handicapped Children Act required states to provide a free and appropriate public education for students over six years of age
	Head Start Performance Standards are first issued to guide program implementation and evaluation
1986	P.L. 99-457, Education for All Handicapped Children Act was amended to include a statewide, comprehensive, coordinated, multidisciplinary interagency program of early interventions services for all handicapped infants and their families
1996	Personal Responsibility and Work Opportunity Act was passed, which dramatically changed our nation's welfare system
1990	The Americans with Disabilities Education Act was passed to ensure equal rights to all individuals with disabilities
	The EHA was amended, changing the name to the Individuals with Disabilities Education Act (IDEA)
1997	P.L. 105-17, IDEA is amended to include mandates for services to children with disabilities under the age of six
2001	P.L. 107-110, No Child Left Behind (NCLB) was enacted, ushering in a new era of accountability and education reform
2002	Good Start, Grow Smart (GSGS), President George W. Bush's early childhood initiative
2004	P.L. 108-446, IDEA is amended to place a stronger emphasis on highly qualified teachers and the use of a Response to Intervention (RTI) model
2007	P.L. 110-134, Improving Head Start for School Readiness Act was passed, reauthorizing the Head Start program
2009	P.L. 111-5, American Recovery and Reinvestment Act (ARRA) passed, providing billions of dollars to early care and education programs

In the fall after Leslie turned 3 years old, she transitioned into the new classroom where she was fully included with typically developing peers. The teaching team, therapists, and her parents worked together to provide comprehensive, coordinated services for her. The therapies were embedded into the natural classroom routines and activities with her same-age peers (i.e., gross motor development during music and movement).

Remember Lisa? She turned 31 in 2000. She moved to a group home (20 miles from her hometown) and continued to be involved in the sheltered work place where she enjoyed many friendships with other adults with disabilities and the on-site coaches. Lisa has earned awards that acknowledge her efforts at the work place; and she has also been involved with Special Olympics in bowling competitions.

THE EVOLVING ROLE OF THE
FAMILIES IN SERVICE PROVISION

A significant historical shift in early childhood special education was the move from focusing on the child to focusing on the child within the family system (Turnbull & Turnbull, 1997). This model recognized family members and their affects on the family system, ultimately leading to a better understanding of the role each person plays in the life of the young child with disabilities. Definitions of family vary and are strongly influenced by culture, politics, economics, and religion (Howard, Williams, & Lepper, 2005). A more narrow and traditional definition of family (e.g., blood relative who live in the same house as the child) reduces the scope of possible positive benefits for the child. The broader or more complex definition of family (e.g., parents, siblings, grandparents, child-care providers, involved relatives, and close friends of the family) requires more energy placed in engaging the larger group of people in the development of a family service plan in the end, this typically results in greater outcomes for the child with disabilities (Howard et al., 2005).

Family configurations have evolved over the history of early childhood special education to include foster and adoptive families, nuclear biological families, single-parent families, extended families, and same gender–parents families. Along with the ongoing and evolving challenge of defining families comes the dilemma of how best to involve all of these individuals in developing and implementing a plan of support for a young child. This challenge includes the need for professionals to expand their traditional approach of focusing their work on only mothers without engaging fathers in decision making and child-care experiences (Davis & May, 1991; McBride & McBride, 1993). Over time, family-centered services have advanced from the original concept of parent involvement in which the parent was encouraged to be involved in a plan of services and activities that were driven by experts and were centered solely on the child with disabilities (McWilliam, Tocci, & Harbin, 1998). The concept of parents as teachers of their own children began with legislation passed in the 1960s and 1970s, and expanded in the 1980s and 1990s with policies to establish the family unit, rather than the child, as the focus of services (Wehman, 1998). Although practices are constantly redefining terminology, a current broad definition of family-centered practices includes the willingness to orient services to the whole family, rather than just to the child (McWilliam et al., 1998).

FUTURE DIRECTIONS

Attempting to predict future directions is rather challenging given the uncertain times in which we are living. In an address to the joint sessions of Congress on February 24, 2009, President Barack Obama stated, "I know that for many Americans watching right now, the state of our economy is a concern that rises above all others. And rightly so ... The impact of this recession is real, and it is everywhere." As a result of the economic crisis, many state and local programs have been forced to slash budgets, which in turn have impacted services to everyone, including young children with disabilities. However, at the same time that many local and state budgets are diminishing, federal money has been flowing out to programs by way of the American Recovery and Reinvestment Act (ARRA).

After years of budget cuts or static funding in many federal social service programs, President Obama signed P.L. 111-5, the American Recovery and Reinvestment Act (ARRA) into law on February 17, 2009. Many early childhood programs benefited from these funds, including an increase of $11.7 billion for those receiving services under Part B (ages 3–21 years) of IDEA, with $400 million of that going for children ages 3–5 years. An additional $500 million was allotted for infants and toddlers receiving services under Part C (ages birth – 3) of IDEA. This funding is spread over two years. Although funding increases have undoubtedly ameliorated what could have been disastrous consequences for local, state, and federal early childhood programs, funding will continue to be a problem. Every day, there is news about social service programs that are disappearing because of budget cuts. Unfortunately, many state and local governments are using the ARRA funds as a stopgap as other issues loom in the distance. An article in *Education Weekly* on the impact of the stimulus on early childhood programs states that, "the U.S. Department of Education has cautioned that stimulus money should be invested in ways that do not result in unsustainable continuing commitments after the funding expires" (Samuels, 2009, p. 8). We know that unfortunately when the nation suffers, the people suffer. While everyone may feel the weight of tough economic times, it is undeniable that children and families with multiple risk factors are those who suffer the most.

As this decade comes to an end, many uncertainties lay ahead on the horizon for early childhood programs. Although record funding increases were born with the economic stimulus package, many states still face major budget challenges, which could cause cuts to critical early care and education programs. Debates on the reauthorization of the Individuals with

Disabilities Education Act (IDEA) and No Child Left Behind (NCLB) are sure to continue in the near future as well. While all of these issues continue to churn in the background, it is important to not forget what is known about child growth and development and the importance of providing high-quality environments to support this growth.

> Remember Lisa and Leslie? In 2010, Lisa is 42 years old and Leslie is 13 years old. Lisa has continued to enjoy her schedule with daily activities at the sheltered work place and the group home. Leslie still attends the local public school where she no longer needs an IEP to support her development. She has supports in place, such as a study group and extra time to take some exams that are also offered to her peers. Leslie's parents are very involved in her school experiences and she is in the school band. She enjoys typical middle school social activities with a wide range of friends. Leslie is interested in attending the community college to study art.

CONCLUSION

As noted in the differences in experiences for the two children in the vignettes, the field of early childhood special education has come a long way over the past 40 years. The supports accessible to Lisa and Leslie and their families were very different and would seem to have launched them both into unlike life experiences. Through research, we are learning more and more about evidence-based strategies to use when working with young children with disabilities and their families. Even though we know more now than ever, we still face challenging tasks, such as bringing together multiple systems at the local, state, and federal levels to coordinate services and provide services in a timely manner. Moving forward, we must reflect on where we have been and take the lessons we have learned with us as we create supportive environments for young children and their families. While early childhood special education is shaped by its past – what each of us does today influences the future.

REFERENCES

Anastasiow, N., & Nucci, C. (1994). Social, historical, and theoretical foundations of early childhood special education and early intervention. In: P. L. Safford, B. Spodek & O. N. Saracho (Eds), *Early childhood special education* (pp. 7–25). New York: Teachers College Press.

Cook, R. E., Tessier, A., & Klein, M. D. (1992). *Adapting early childhood curricula for children with special needs* (3rd ed.). Upper Saddle River, NJ: Merrill/Prentice Hall.

Davis, P. B., & May, J. E. (1991). Involving fathers in early intervention and family support programs: Issues and strategies. *CHC, 20*(2), 87–92.

Department of Health and Human Services and Department of Education. (2006). *Good Start, Grow Smart: A guide to Good Start, Grow Smart and other federal early learning initiatives* (Retrieved from http://www.acf.hhs.gov/programs/ccb/initiatives/gsgs/fedpubs/GSGSBooklet.pdf).

Fox, L., Carta, J., Strain, P., Dunlap, G., & Hemmeter, M. L. (2009). *Response to intervention and the pyramid model* (Retrieved from http://www.challengingbehavior.org). Tampa, FL: University of South Florida, Technical Assistance Center on Social Emotional Intervention for Young Children.

Garguilo, R. M., & Kilgo, J. L. (2000). *Young children with special needs.* Albany, NY: Delmar.

Ginsberg, L., & Miller-Cribbs, J. (2005). *Understanding social problems, policies, and programs* (4th ed.). Columbia, SC: University of South Carolina Press.

Howard, V. F., Williams, B. F., & Lepper, C. (2005). *Very young children with special needs: A formative approach for today's children* (3rd ed.). Upper Saddle River, NJ: Pearson Education, Inc.

Hunt, J. M. (1961). *Intelligence and experience.* New York: Ronald Press.

Martin, E. W. (1989). Lessons from implementing P.L. 99-142. In: J. Gallagher, P. L. Trohanis & R. M. Clifford (Eds), *Policy implementation & P.L. 99-457* (pp. 19–32). Baltimore: Paul H. Brookes.

McBride, B. A., & McBride, R. J. (1993). Parent education and support programs for fathers. *Childhood Education, 70,* 4–8.

McCollum, J. A. (2000). Taking the past along: Reflecting on our identity as a discipline. *Topics in Early Childhood Special Education, 2*(2), 79–86.

McWilliam, R. A., Tocci, L., & Harbin, G. L. (1998). Family-centered services: Service providers' discourse and behavior. *Topics in Early Childhood Special Education, 18*(4), 206–232.

Meisels, S. J., & Shonkoff, J. P. (2000). Early childhood intervention: A continuing evolution. In: J. P. Shonkoff & S. J. Meisels (Eds), *Handbook of early childhood intervention* (2nd ed., pp. 3–31). Cambridge, UK: Cambridge University Press.

National Association for the Education of Young Children. (2009). NAEYC position statement: Developmentally appropriate practice in early childhood programs serving children from birth through age 8. In: C. Copple & S. Bredekamp (Eds), *Developmentally appropriate practice in early childhood programs* (3rd ed., pp. 1–31). Washington, DC: Author.

Obama, B. (2009). Remarks of President Barack Obama – As prepared for delivery address to joint session of congress, Tuesday, February 24, 2009. Retrieved on August 15, 2009, from http://www.whitehouse.gov/the_press_office/remarks-of-president-barack-obama-address-to-joint-session-of-congress/

Ohlson, C. (1998). Welfare reform: Implications for young children with disabilities, their families, and service providers. *Journal of Early Intervention, 21,* 191–206.

Raver, S. A. (2009). *Early childhood special education, 0–8: Strategies for positive outcomes.* Upper Saddle River, NJ: Merrill/Pearson.

Samuels, C. A. (2009). Infant–toddler special education program gets new life from stimulus. *Education Week,* August. Retrieved from http://www.edweek.org/ew/articles/2009/06/29/36preschool.h28.html?tkn=YMVF8Ys9FVmEkE59EqqPbg6m5EL%2BSqbk39HP

Turnbull, A., & Turnbull, R. (1997). *Parents, professionals, and exceptionality: A special partnership.* Upper Saddle River, NJ: Merrill/Prentice Hall.

Turnbull, H. R., Huerta, N., Stowe, M., Weldon, L., & Schrandt, S. (2006). *The Individuals with Disabilities Education Act as amended in 2004.* Upper Saddle River, NJ: Pearson/Merrill/ Prentice Hall.

Wehman, T. (1998). Family-centered early intervention services: Factors contributing to increased parent involvement. *Focus on Autism & Other Developmental Disabilities, 98*(13), 80–87.

Wright, W. D., & Wright, P. D. (2003). *Wrightslaw: Special education law.* Hartfield, VA: Harbor House Law Press.

Zigler, E. F., & Muenchow, S. (1992). *Head Start: The inside story of America's most successful educational experiment.* New York: Basic Books.

CHAPTER 4

HISTORY OF LEARNING DISABILITIES

Carrie Anna Courtad and Jeffrey P. Bakken

The term "learning disabilities" (LD) is very common today, however, prior to 1965 LD was not referred to in special-education textbooks (Myers & Hammill, 1990) nor did local, state, and federal education agencies recognize LD as a category of exceptionality that necessitated specialized instruction aspects (Sorrel, 2000). LD refers to a variety of disorders that affect the acquisition, retention, understanding, organization, or use of verbal and/or nonverbal information. They range in severity (can be very mild, very severe, or anywhere in the middle) and invariably interfere with the acquisition and use of one or more of the following important skills: (a) *oral language* (e.g., listening, speaking, understanding), (b) *reading* (e.g., decoding, comprehension), (c) *written language* (e.g., spelling, written expression), and (d) *mathematics* (e.g., computation, problem solving) (http://www.adcet. edu.au/Oao/What_is_LD.chpx). People with LD may also have difficulties with organizational skills, social perception, and social interaction.

EARLY BEGINNINGS: NAMING LD

In other words, LD can affect the way in which a person takes in, remembers, understands, and expresses information. Typically, a person with LD is of average intelligence, based on his/her intelligence quotient

History of Special Education
Advances in Special Education, Volume 21, 61–87
Copyright © 2011 by Emerald Group Publishing Limited
ISSN: 0270-4013/doi:10.1108/S0270-4013(2011)0000021007

(IQ); however his/her academic performance is different from how they should be able to perform. People with LD are intelligent and have abilities to learn despite difficulties in processing information; however, they require specialized interventions in home, school, community, and workplace settings, appropriate to their individual strengths and needs, including but not limited to (a) specific skill instruction, (b) the development of compensatory strategies, (c) the development of self-advocacy skills, and (d) appropriate accommodation. Typically, a student with mild LD, who is identified and provided learning-disabilities instruction, can enhance his/her academic achievement, however, a student with undetected LD can struggle with low grades, low self-esteem, a loss of interest in higher education, and later reduced employment opportunities as an adult (Burkhardt, Obiakor, & Rotatori, 2004).

LD was formerly known as "mental handicap." It all began in 1877 with the term "word blindness" that was coined by a German neurologist named Adolf Kussamaul. He used this term to describe "complete text blindness … although the power of sight, the intellect and the powers of speech are intact" (http://www.ldonline.org/article/Timeline_of_Learning_Disabilities). In 1877, a German physician named Rudolf Berlin developed the term "dyslexia" to describe a "very great difficulty in interpreting written or printed symbols" (http://www.ldonline.org/article/Timeline_of_Learning_Disabilities). In the late 1890s, Dr. W. Pringle Morgan wrote about a 14-year-old boy who seemed to have language problems from birth. He was described as bright, intelligent, and quick, but had great difficulty reading and spelling despite the efforts of his teachers. Jump forward to 1905 and Cleveland ophthalmologist Dr. W. E. Bruner publishes the first U.S. report of childhood reading difficulties (http://www.ldonline.org/article/Timeline_of_Learning_Disabilities).

During the early 1900s up into the early 1960s, many different names were used for students who had difficulty learning. These include organic brain damage, primary reading retardation, slow learner, clumsy child syndrome, educational "handicap," brain injury, and minimal brain dysfunction. Then in 1963, the term "learning disability" was first used by Samuel A. Kirk (1963) in a speech to the group in Chicago that would become the Association for Children with Learning Disabilities (and, ultimately, the Learning Disabilities Association of America). The term itself was already used by Kirk and Bateman (1962–1963) in a paper published half a year earlier. That meeting was the beginning of what one might be called the LD movement in the United States and now the world. The Congress then passed the Children with Specific Learning Disabilities Act in 1969 which defined

LD and provided funds for state-level programs for students who were learning disabled (Schwenn, 1991). This act is included in the Education of the Handicapped Act of 1970 (PL 91-230). This is the first time federal law mandated support services for students with learning disabilities. In 1975, the Education for All Handicapped Children Act (P.L. 94-142), which mandated a free, appropriate public education for all students was then established. During the 1980s, the concept of normalization (Wolfensberger, 1972) began to influence the delivery of care for people with LD. Normalization theory began to have an influence on service provision and it emphasized the unique value of the individual, his/her right to choice and opportunity, and the right to any extra support he/she needed to fulfill his/her potential. In 1990, the Individuals with Disabilities Education Act (IDEA) was renamed and changed P.L. 94-142. The term "disability" replaced "handicap," and the new law began to require transition services for students as well as the addition of the disabilities of autism and traumatic brain injury. In 1997, IDEA was reauthorized and now regular education teachers were included in the individualized education program (IEP) process; students began to have more access to the general curriculum and became included in state-wide assessments; and ADHD was added to the list of conditions that could make a child eligible for services under the category "other health impairment." Another reauthorization of IDEA took place in 2004. School personnel now have more authority in special-education placement decisions and the new law is better aligned with the No Child Left Behind act (NCLB) (see Baker & Gulley, 2004).

EARLY PIONEERS AND MAJOR CONTRIBUTORS IN THE FIELD OF LEARNING DISABILITIES

In 1802, *Franz Joseph Gall*, a German/French anatomist and physiologist and Napoleon's surgeon, is recognized as being involved with the earliest believed recognized case of LD. Through his investigations of brain injuries to aphasia, he was able to recognize an association between brain injury in soldiers and subsequent expressive language disorders (Schwenn, 1991). In 1822, he published a book entitled, *Sur les Fonctions*, in which he outlined his belief that the brain was divided into 27 separate "organs," each corresponding to a discrete human responsibility (Who Named It, 2005). He believed one of those separate organs controlled educability, perfectibility, the memory of things, and the memory of facts. His conclusion was that any imperfection in those processes was due to a cranial fault (Who Named It, 2005).

Toward the end of the century, a German physician named *Adolph Kassmaul* coined the phrase, *word blindness* in 1877 for the loss of the ability to read (Hagw & Silver, 1990). The phrase referred to a neurological disorder characterized by the loss of the ability to read or understand the written word, either totally or partially. Partial word blindness permits the individual to recognize letters, but read only certain types of words.

The 1900s

In the early 1900s, *Dr. Kurt Goldstein* first noted the phenomenon of LD, which was called the invisible "handicap" (Gelb & Goldstein, 1918; Goldstein, 1937). Somewhat later, *Samuel Orton, Grace Fernard*, and *Samuel Kirk* were researchers during that era that made substantial headway on understanding some of the more common forms of LD. For example, Samuel Orton teamed with his wife, June Orton, to study the field of LD. Together; they conducted research, trained educators and therapists, and treated individuals with reading and writing difficulties. Educational historians stated they were two of the most important individuals in the history of dyslexia (Columbia, 2003). Samuel Orton (1925, 1929, 1937, 1939) initiated a successful remedial reading training system program based on visual–auditory–kinesthetic linkages and in 1925 he published a paper detailing his version of word blindness (Lloyd, 2005).

Anna Gillingham was a psychologist and educator who did remedial work with bright children who were failing academically. She read much of Orton's work and was influenced by it. In 1928, she brought cases to Dr. Orton after he moved to New York City. By 1931, Dr. Orton and Miss Gillingham began a professional collaboration. Gillingham worked to create a sequential system of reading that built on itself. The approach was to be a multisensory approach that involves all senses (i.e., visual, auditory, tactile, and kinesthetic) (Gillingham & Stillman, 1936). The approach was to show how sounds and letters are related and how they act in words as well as how to attack a word and break it into smaller sounds (see Gillingham & Stillman, 1960). The Orton–Gillingham method was developed (Ritchney & Goeke, 2006). The method is used first to teach students phonemic awareness – how to listen to a single word or syllable and break it into individual sounds. Next, the letters that represented the sounds learned in phonemic awareness were taught. Students were then taught the six types of syllables that determine what sound the vowel will make in the English language. Students would then be taught language rules and probabilities. Finally, roots and affixes and morphology were taught. The Orton–Gillingham method pioneered the multisensory approach to instruction (see Ritchney & Goeke, 2006), for a comprehensive review of the literature). This approach was so successful that, subsequently, the Orton–Gillingham method became the standard for developing additional programs for students with disabilities (http://www.dyslexiaanswers.com/og.html).

Grace Fernald (1943) developed her own kinesthetic method of teaching spelling and reading. She used her finger to trace in the air words that gave her students difficulty; thus incorporating a visual aid into the learning process. She became famous for her teaching methods and students having difficulties were frequently referred to her by academic diagnosticians (Barchas, 1998). She maintained extensive records on the progress of her students, and in 1921, Fernald and Keller published a paper on her style of kinesthetic method's effects on word recognition in nonreaders (Lloyd, 2005).

Another related scholar, *Marion Monroe* was a former research assistant of Orton, prior to moving to Chicago where she worked at the Institute for Juvenile Research. In her work, Monroe (1928, 1932) stressed the phonetic approach to reading and the importance of providing students exhibiting reading difficulties with intensive instruction. Utilizing the experimental research method, she analyzed groups and students and instituted new educational techniques. She also introduced the discrepancy concept as a way of identifying students with reading disabilities (Hallahan & Mercer, 2001).

Samuel Kirk worked with Monroe at the University of Chicago, where he earned his master's degree, and was very much influenced by her work in phonics. During this time, he became acquainted with a young boy, labeled by the establishment as word blind. After working with the lad for some time, he developed and refined an assessment approach for pinpointing a specific LD in children. He was directly responsible for the creation of the Illinois Test of Psycholinguistic Abilities (ITPA) (Kirk, McCarthy, & Kirk, 1968) which assesses specific psycholinguistic abilities and disabilities in young children (Hallahan & Mercer, 2001). This test also facilitates an assessment of a child's abilities for purposes of remediation, and evaluates his/her cognitive and perceptual abilities in communication (Lloyd, 2005).

During this same time frame, several European researchers immigrated to the United States to continue their work because of political unrest in their homelands. They conducted research into the perceptual, perceptual-motor, and attention disabilities of adults with brain injuries (Hallahan & Mercer, 2001). *Kurt Goldstein, Alfred Strauss, Laura Lehtinen,* and *Newell Kephart* were just a few of the immigrants playing major roles in those areas of study. Strauss, Lehtinen, and Kephart worked closely together; ultimately, they recommended a distraction-free environment, thus placing a heavy emphasis on the remediation of perceptional disturbances which they believed would aid students with LD.

Kurt Goldstein, native of what is now Poland, was educated at Breslau and Heidelberg; he became interested in aphasia when he studied under Carl Wernicke. He collaborated with Adhemar Gelb on visual agnosia – which they called mind blindness (Gelb & Goldstein, 1918). Goldstein (1939) had a holistic theory of the human organism, one that challenged reductivist concepts and approaches that deal with localized symptoms. He greatly influenced many researchers in the field of Gestalt psychology (Duchan, 2001).

Strauss, along with Lehtinen and Kephart created the diagnostic category of minimal brain damage in children (Strauss & Lehtinen, 1947; Strauss & Kephart, 1955). He presumed that children with LD, who were not mentally retarded, hearing impaired, or emotionally disturbed, had minimal brain damage (see Duchan, 2001). In 1949, he founded the Cove School in Racine, Wisconsin which was established as a residential school for brain-injured children. He remained the school's president until his death in 1957. *Laura Lechtinen*, a teacher originally from Germany, worked with Strauss at the Wayne County School at Northville Michigan during the mid 1940s (Audiblox, 2000). They believed a student's academic learning skills would be improved if his/her perceptual skills could be developed. Lehtinen believed factors such as bulletin board displays and teacher jewelry were distractions that interfered with the children's ability to think and learn (Friend, 2005)). She also recommended avoiding references to the letters *b* and *d*, because a contiguous use of those letters was confusing to the student (Friend, 2005).

Kephart worked with Strauss at the Cove School during the late 1940s and 1950s. At this time, he expanded the study of brain injury to include children of normal intelligence. Kephart's (1960) research was based upon his focus that "motor development precedes perceptual development and these form the basis of all learning" (Schwenn, 1991, p. 30). They argued that perceptual-motor, cognitive, and behavior problems found among children with mental deficiencies were also found in children with normal intelligence. Thus, they concluded that children of normal intelligence exhibiting those problems were also brain damaged; this led them off track because of an error in deductive reasoning, and that error would influence their work for some time (Hallahan & Mercer, 2001). They were greatly criticized for their deductions, because there was no scientific evidence that brain damage existed, and their reasoning was based only on children's behaviors. Nonetheless, their path of study was followed by many others. Kephart continued research into stages of perceptual development that evolved into a perceptual-motor development theory named after him (Perception, 1995). He believed that the development of motor behaviors arose from a hierarchy of motor achievements. The central idea of the theory concluded that motoric responses to a child's environment are the central core to all behaviors. He was one of the first researchers to incorporate neurological networks into his theory of development, and he concluded that discovery by a child of how certain movements can affect their environment; such as eye–hand coordination, substantiated his theory (see Roach & Kephart, 1966). Because he believed all perceptual development rises from a hierarchy of motor skills, he deduced that learning disabilities must arise from a general slowdown of achievement in motor development and cause a breakdown of that achievement at some point (Perception, 1995).

In spite of the inability of researchers to prove LD was caused by neurological dysfunction, middle-class parents during this zeitgeist welcomed the explanation of why their child was experiencing such difficulty in school. Prior to the 1960s, those children were frequently described as *dumb* – even though they were smart in other ways; they often tried very hard and the parents believed they would learn, if only they could. Those same children were often labeled *mentally retarded* – a label they would wear for the rest of their lives (Duchan, 2001). In the 1960s, the term "minimal brain dysfunction" was used to describe children with LD type learning difficulties (Silver & Hagin, 2002). According to Deisinger (2004), this term implied problems in the central nervous system; however, it was later abandoned because it lacked clarity. In addition, conceptualizing LD as minimal brain dysfunction did not result in any pertinent educational guidance for specific instructional planning (Hallahan & Kauffman, 1997). Interestingly, parents of those affected children during the 1960s and early 1970s clung to the concept of a neurological dysfunction being the cause of their child's problems just as a drowning person would cling to a lifeline thrown from a sinking ship. Many changes took place between 1960 and 1975; not only in research that changed the scientific views of LD, but the general public's awareness of LD improved dramatically. It was during this time period that the term *LD* was first introduced; the federal government included learning disabilities on its agenda, parents and professionals founded organizations for LD, and educational programming for students with learning disabilities blossomed – with a particular focus on psychological processing and perceptual training (Hallahan & Mercer, 2001).

Samuel Kirk continued to be heavily involved in research aimed at understanding the conflicting variables that continually arose with individual students (see Kirk & Chalfant, 1984; Kirk & Kirk, 1971). He was officially credited with coining the term *LD*; and in 1963, he used it as a means to identify groups of what he called perceptually "handicapped" children. This term became the most frequently used label in special education. Parents and advocates used the term as a central theme in their efforts to organize and gain services for students with LD. As a result, major organizations began to surface. For example, in 1968, the Division for Children with Learning Disabilities of the Council for Exceptional Children was formed (Schwenn, 1991).

DEFINITION OF LD

Historically, defining LD has been an ongoing and controversial process since the field's inception in the 1960s (Rotatori & Wahlberg, 2004). An array of definitions have been proposed with each emphasizing important aspects of what LD is. Unfortunately, this process has generated considerable ambiguity and inconsistence. For instance, in 1990, Hammill discussed 11 definitions that were considered significant in their conceptual development. However, when Hallahan and Kauffman (1997) examined these definitions, it was apparent that none of them were comprehensive enough to cover the diverse aspects of LD. These researchers pointed that that the definitions examined covered the following factors: "(a) IQ achievement-discrepancy; (b) presumption of central nervous system dysfunction; (c) psychological processing disorders; and (d) learning problems not due to mental retardation or emotional disturbance," however, none of them covered all four (Hallahan & Kauffman, 1997).

Today, most school districts in the United States follow the federal government's definition of LD to establish student eligibility for government-funded support services. In general, the federal code states that LD is "a disorder in which one or more of the basic psychological processes involved in understanding or in using language, spoken or written, that may manifest itself in an imperfect ability to think, speak, read, write, spell, or to do mathematical calculations, including conditions such as perception disabilities, brain injury, minimal brain dysfunction, dyslexia, and developmental aphasia. The term LD does not include learning problems that primarily are the result of vision, hearing, motor disabilities, mental retardation, emotional disturbance, or environmental, cultural, or economic disadvantages" (Lloyd, 2005). Although the federal government had good intentions when it established the above guidelines, it left interpretation of the code up to individual states. This created inconsistencies and at times misinterpretations regarding which students qualified for special assistance (see Obiakor & Utley, 2004), and the result has frustrated parents and students across the United States.

IDENTIFICATION AND SERVICES

Identification

When the concept of LD was first coined in the 1960s, work began on how to identify the phenomena that educators saw on a regular basis. In order to "diagnose" the learning disability, professional educators concluded that students who were not performing to their academic ability but had the intelligence (IQ) to do so were those with LD. This became known as the *discrepancy* formula (see Bender, 2007; Deisinger, 2004; Flanagan, Ortiz, & Mascolo, 2002; Sorrel, 2000; Rotatori & Wahlberg, 2004). The student performance in general academics were discrepant in terms of the IQ. Individual states were left to decide how much of a discrepancy was needed for a student to qualify as learning disabled; and in a number of states discrepancy formulas were left to the district resulting in 40 plus different discrepancy models in one state. Theoretically, a student could qualify for special-education services in one district, move to a different district and no longer qualify for special-education services. However, in 2004, IDEA regulations mandated that individual states, "must not require the use of a severe discrepancy between intellectual ability and achievement for determining whether a child has a specific LD, as defined in 34 CFR 300.8(c) (10)." These regulations also indicated a different method may be used to determine if a student qualifies as LD. The clause denotes that local education agencies, "must permit the use of a process based on the child's response to scientific, research-based intervention; and may permit the use of other alternative research-based procedures for determining whether a child has a specific learning disability, as defined in 34 CFR 300.8(c)(10)." This section is often referred to as response to intervention (RTI) and is another way to identify students with LD.

RTI has been written about extensively (see Wheeler & Mayton, 2010). The overall idea of RTI is that students who are not performing at successful academic benchmarks are remediated based on tiers of intervention levels before students are identified as having LD (see Gresham 2002). RTI is commonly viewed as having three levels of intervention services and each level increases in intensity (Johnson & Smith, 2008). The first level is the general-education classroom, the second level is usually a small group or individual students receiving intensive instruction in the area of weakness and the third level is often more intensive intervention with special services such as special education. If students respond to a given tier of intervention then they would not qualify as LD, if they do not respond they move up the next tier. If a student moves up to the last tier because he is not making progress he would qualify for special-education services.

There has been a lot of debate between these two methods to identify students with LD (see Berninger, 2001; Deisinger, 2004; Torgesen, 2001; Wilson & Reynolds, 2002). The discrepancy model is based on the idea that an average IQ is the marker of a student with LD who is not performing academic tasks at the average level. RTI, however, assumes that a student who has LD is not making the necessary gains in the curriculum and fails to respond to a second level of more intensive instruction (see Fuchs & Fuchs, 2007). The traditional discrepancy model has been viewed as a "wait to fail" method because often the IQ discrepancy versus class performance does not show up until later elementary (Wright, 2007). Concern for the RTI model, however, is that all underachievers have the potential to not perform at local academic benchmarks and that perhaps those who do not have an average IQ would be identified as LD. This brings the debate back to how do we conceptualize the construct of LD. Those who feel strongly about using a discrepancy model feel that this identification process allows for fair and objective evaluations (see Scruggs & Mastropieri, 2002). Those in favor of the discrepancy model also believe it removes the responsibility from the classroom teacher for the diagnosis of LD and places it on the school psychologist or diagnostician (Deisinger, 2004). However, those who disagree with this identification process feel that IQ tests themselves are biased and ability and achievement not always closely correlated (Tanner, 2001). Others stress that culture and ethnicity, age, poverty, and the stability of discrepancy scores over time may be variables that confound the use of discrepancy formulas (Dean & Burns, 2002; Gunderson & Siegel, 2001; Obiakor & Utley, 2004; Warner, Dede, Garvan, & Conway, 2002). Those in favor of using an RTI model believe a school has to wait too long for a student to fail before identification when using the discrepancy model and that RTI ensures that all who struggle will receive remediation and access to evidence-based instruction (see Johnson & Smith, 2008; Torgesen, 2009).

Where are Students with LD Served?

Prior to the label of LD, students with LD were still present in either general-education classrooms or institutions. Indeed, the LD label was conceived in order to describe a certain population that educators saw in their classrooms. Students with LD were in the general-education classroom struggling to learn like their peers until they might become so far behind that they would eventually drop out. In some cases, these students were herded to "special schools" or institutions and labeled mentally retarded. It was not until 1969 when Congress passed the Children with Specific Learning Disabilities Act, included in the Education of the Handicapped Act of 1970 (PL 91-230) that funding for support services for students with LD was finally mandated. In 1975, with the Education for All Handicapped Children Act (PL 94-142), reauthorization that included a free and appropriate education for all did direct support become available for students with LD.

Students with LD are served in a variety of settings. Between the mid-1970s and 1990s, students with LD were served in a resource room sometimes referred to as a pull-out model with modified or different curriculum (see Mitchem & Richards, 2003). These students would leave their classroom and go to the special-education teacher to receive the education away from their peers. If students received all their education in a room away from the general-education classroom, it was considered a self-contained classroom, meaning they were not integrated with peers in the general-education classroom. As time progressed, less and less reliance on adapted curriculum occurred and access to the general-education curriculum was considered. This began the push for students with LD to be included in the general-education classroom with their peers (see Rotatori, Schwenn, & Litton, 1994). In the late 1990s, the United States began to view students with LD as not only needing access to the general-education classroom but their curriculum as well (see Richards & Dooley, 2004).

EDUCATIONAL PRACTICES
FOR STUDENTS WITH LD

Typically, students with LD have normal or better intelligence, but they also have severe "information-processing deficits" that make them perform significantly worse in one or more academic areas (reading, writing, and math) than might be expected, given their intelligence and performance in other academic areas (see Burkhardt et al., 2004; Deisinger, 2004; Lerner,

2005; Stefani, 2004; Swanson, 2000). Though each student with LD is different, students with LD report some common problems, including slow and inefficient reading; slow essay writing, with problems in organization and the mechanics of writing; display of developmental discrepancies in ability, difficulty in acquiring and using information requisite to problem solving, behavioral difficulties such as impulsivity and distractibility, perceptual difficulties, and frequent errors in math calculation (Sorrel, 2000). Swanson (1999) and his colleagues found two major intervention practices that produced large outcomes. One is *direct instruction* that uses highly structured materials, advanced organizers, mnemonics and a specified assessment process that is built into the instructional process (see Deshler, 1998; Deshler & Ellis, & Lenz, 1996). The other is *learning strategy instruction* which encompasses a definitive process that is strategically organized and preparatory such that students are instructed to prepare for the next step via reviewing prior learning steps and answering test items by starting with the easy ones first (see Greene, 1994; Winnery & Fuchs, 1993). Something else that seems to make a real difference is the practice of scaffolding. The teacher starts out with heavily teacher-mediated instruction – explicit instruction – then as students begins to acquire the skill, moving down the continuum to more student-mediated instruction.

Whether the student is learning in a general-education classroom or pulled out into a special-education resource setting, the teacher should be sure that activities are focused on assessing individual students to monitor their progress through the curriculum. Concerns for the individual must take precedence over concerns for the group, and over concerns about the organization and management of the general-education classroom. Success for the student with LD requires a focus on individual achievement, individual progress, and individual learning. This requires specific, directed, individualized, intensive remedial instruction of students who are struggling. Research (Gersten, 1998; Swanson, 2009; Vaughn, Gersten, & Chard, 2000) confirms that these students can be taught how to learn. They can be put in a position to compete by implementing strategies that focus on their unique needs. These include (a) break learning into small steps, (b) administer probes (short little assessments/quizzes on progress), (c) supply immediate feedback, (d) use diagrams, graphics and pictures to augment what they are saying in words, (e) provide ample independent, well-designed, intensive practice, (f) model instructional practices that they want students to follow, (g) provide prompts of strategies to use, and (h) engage students in process type questions such as "How is that strategy working? Where else might you apply it?" Clearly, most instructions at home or in school can be adapted to

Table 1. Strategies for Success in the Classroom.

- Set the stage for learning by telling children why the material is important, what the learning goals are, and what the expectations are for quality performance.
- Use specific language. Instead of saying, "do quality work," state the specific expectations. For example, in a writing assignment, a teacher might grade based on correct punctuation, spelling, and inclusion of specific points.
- Develop a scoring guide, share it with students, and provide models of examples of each level of performance.
- Never use a student's work as a public example of poor work for the class to see. This is humiliating, and it has no place in any classroom or home.
- Have the student repeat back the instructions for a task to ensure he/she understands.
- Correct any miscommunication before he/she begins the actual work. Check back on the student as he/she works to ensure he/she is doing the work correctly. Prompt him/her as necessary to ensure that he/she corrects any mistakes before he/she finishes.
- Clearly define classroom expectations for work and behavior. Post them, and use them for a basis of all interactions and class projects. Make requirements a part of the classroom or homework routine to help the student meet expectations.
- Use graphic organizers to help students understand the relationships between ideas.
- Include specific, step-by-step instructions that are explicitly stated and modeled for the student.
- Create models of quality work that students can see and analyze. Include both spoken and written explanations of how the work fulfills academic expectations.

---

accommodate the needs of a student with LD. These strategies and others can be used to modify instruction in most subject areas to improve students' comprehension of tasks and the quality of their work. See Table 1 for a listing of strategies that are frequently employed with student with LD. Other suggestions include (a) extended time on assignments or exams, (b) assigned due dates for all assignments/exams/activities, (c) frequent opportunities for feedback (i.e., weekly quizzes on assigned reading, instructor review of early drafts of essays, and error-analysis of tests), (d) encourage contacts to clarify assignments, (e) be sensitive to students who, for disability-related reasons, may be unable to read aloud or answer questions when called on, and (f) compose exams in a way that makes them accessible for students with LD.

ASSESSMENT OF LD

Rotatori and Wahlberg (2004) stressed that assessment of LD needs to be comprehensive to meet the diverse evaluation purposes that can include the following: screening; academic, social-emotional and vocational evaluation; eligibility and diagnosis; IEP development; and instructional planning. These researchers indicate that professionals working with individuals with LD have a variety of approaches to collect assessment data such as using: norm-referenced; criterion-referenced; curriculum-based; portfolio assessment; and authentic assessment. These approaches can be used to gather comprehensive assessment data on areas such as: preacademic skills; cognitive assessment; academic (readiness levels, grade levels in specific subject areas, mastery levels); learning style; social–emotional–behavioral characteristics; and career vocational aspects. A comprehensive listing of specific devices and instruments for the above areas is provided in Rotatori and Wahlberg.

WORKING WITH FAMILIES

Just like students with LD, families also present themselves in a wide range of types and degrees of involvement. If a student has just recently been labeled as having LD or rather you are the teacher that needs to inform the parents of that diagnosis, you should be informative, positive, and realistic (see Goor, McKnab, & Davidson-Aviles, 1995). Studies indicate that professionals struggle with providing a false hope when informing families about the outcomes of students with LD (Harnet, Tierney, & Guerin, 2009). It is important that professionals present a wide range of possible outcomes for these students to the families (see Rosenthal, 1992). Parents often have conflicting feelings about their child being identified as having LD (see Gerber, 1986). Many parents might have suspected that something was not "quite" right but were unable to communicate this to other professionals (see Schwenn, 1991). In this situation, they often feel relieved that someone understands their feelings and feels like they are in a position to advocate for their child now that there is a name associated with what they already suspected or knew. Sometimes parents feel guilty that their child has been labeled with LD (see Waggoner & Wilgosh, 1990). The guilt might stem from the parent feeling like he/she should have done more to prevent this (e.g., if only I read to my student more, if only I ate better during the pregnancy). Then again, there are other parents who might feel very frightened about the outcomes their child might face when needing special services. Or, there are the parents who feel that they did not do well in school or might even have a disability themselves and that if they overcame it surely their child can too, without the help of special education (Atkins & Litton, 1995).

There are wide ranges of emotions that parents feel at any given time toward their child with LD. The professional in this situation, should be sure to bring information on family and child support groups in your local area, present the wide range of outcomes for students with LD, not focusing on the worst-case scenario and understand that this new information can present a new source of stress in the family relations (Trotter, 1993). Even though students with LD have an increased risk of academic problems, social issues, and dropping out of school, it is important to remember that there are many cases where students with LD are very resilient, attend and complete college and are very successful in life (see Castellanos & Septeowski, 2004; Obi, 2004). It is important as professionals to provide the hope and wide range of possibilities for students with LD (see O'Shea, O'Shea, & Hammitte, 1994). This is especially important knowing that people with LD tend to live with their parents into early middle age (U.S. Department of Health and Human Services Public Health Service National Institutes of Health & National Institute of Mental Health, 1993). When speaking with parents, it is important to remember that disability brings an amount of stress into the family (see Dyson, 1996). Assuring parents that professionals are there to help and that a wide range of outcomes are possible for their student eases the stress.

REDUCING RISKS FOR STUDENTS WITH LD

As mentioned earlier, it is important to present upbeat and positive outcomes for student with LD; but it is important not to ignore the risks for these students. Risks factors are generally regarded as a situation or condition in which possible outcomes are negative in one's life (Raskind, n.d.). Students with LD have increased risks for being unsuccessful in academics and social situations, an increased possibility of having depression and behavior problems. These students traditionally underperform in areas of reading, writing, and math and have difficulties with memory, metacognition, and social skills. Two thirds of these students read at two to three grade levels behind their peers who do not have LD and about 25% of these students are reading more than five grade levels behind their peers (Wagner et al., 2003). Reading especially after 3rd grade is often how students are expected to gain information. Reading to learn as opposed for enjoyment begins with expository text traditionally at grade three in the American school systems so that when they struggle with reading it does run the risk of jeopardizing their school career. Students with LD are more likely to drop out of high school (nearly 39%) compared to students who do not have a LD (11%) (U.S. Department of Education, 2003). Part of the reason students with LD drop out is due to their struggle with reading.

Students with LD frequently struggle with social skills (Burkhardt et al., 2004; Gerber, 1986; Goor et al., 1995). "Effective social skills involve the ability to initiate and respond appropriately to others" (Vaughn, Elbaum, & Boardman, 2001, p. 49). Research has shown that as many as 75% of students with LD receive lower rating than their non-LD peers (Kavale & Forness, 1996). Poor social skills affect personal relationships with families, peers, and teachers. This can lead to possible rejection by peers and teachers because of the inability to read social cues, and react in a prosocial way (Vaughn et al., 2001). Since students with LD have poor academic performance and social skills, they often suffer from lower self-esteem (see Sorrel, 2000; Rotatori & Wahlberg, 2004). Low self-esteem can be a symptom of depression. When measuring depression by self-evaluation, depression in students with LD was higher than nondisabled peers. It is not known at this time if these students have more clinical depression than nondisabled peers (Maag & Reid, 2006). It is critical to note that these students do not have to suffer nor are they doomed to always inherit these risks. Professionals and parents can lower the potential risks for students who have LD. By working closely with the student, family, and other supports, a student with LD has many options open to them.

TECHNOLOGY FOR STUDENTS WITH LD

In today's world, we are very fortunate to have a large number of assistive technologies available for students with LD (see Bakken & Wojcik, 2004). Mandates requiring IEP committees to consider assistive technology (AT) for these students ares fairly new. The Technology-Related Assistance for Individuals with Disabilities Act of 1988 otherwise know at the "Tech Act" was the first time a federal act defined assistive technology and services and promoted the use of AT for all people with disabilities (P.L. 100-407). IDEA 1990 and then IDEA 1997 brought AT to students with disabilities. These amendments strengthened the definition of AT, outlined that districts were responsible for providing AT to students with disabilities as part of FAPE, and improved lives of students with disabilities beyond the classroom. Clearly, since 1990, technology devices, software, and support have multiplied (see Bakken & Wojcik, 2004; Bouck, 2010; Parette & Peterson-Karlan, 2010). Prior the laws defining AT and supports, assistive technology was traditionally viewed for only individuals with several, multiple, or physical disabilities. Many of the technology devices used today were originally developed for students with visual impairments (see Banks & Coombs, 2005; Freitas & Kouroupetroglou, 2008); however, as technology became readily available, it was apparent that those with LD could benefit from the same technology that improved the capabilities of many students with disabilities (see Alper & Raharinirina, 2006; Nkabinde, 2008).

There are a wide variety of technology supports for students with LD and a large number of these supports can be accessed for free and used with regular computer or an MP3 player and even smart phones (see Bakken & Wojcik, 2004; Bouck, 2010). A computer and word processor have many features that can immediately improve the learning and production of students with LD (see Montgomery, Karlan, & Coutinho, 2001). Digital text has made way to the mainstream market. With access to digital text and a computer, these students can be highly productive. A student with LD often struggles in areas of language processing (see Kerchner & Kistinger, 1984). As mentioned earlier, students are often reading behind grade level of their peers. A free assistive technology that is built into computers running either Mac OS 10 or Window 7 operating system are screen readers or text-to-speech accessibilities. These items allow digital text to be read aloud to the student enabling him/her access material that is above reading grade level. There are a number of free programs along with some that are available for purchase. Word processors have standard features such as grammar and spelling checks that are helpful to students with LD who are in the editing phase of their writing.

Technology is changing at a rapid pace, therefore there should be reluctance to recommend any one product or website. However, there are common academic areas that students with LD encounter problems with, in which technology can provide a workaround for them. For example, text readers allow the text that appears on the computer screen to be read aloud often using computer-generated voices that are already included in the operating system of computers. Text readers sometimes allow text to be imported into MP3 files which allow the text to be read aloud on players such as iPods. Some text readers also have features that allow a student to speak what he/she would like to write and they will convert it to text, this is called either voice recognition or speech to text. Speech to text or voice recognition allows a student to turn words that they speak into text. When a student with LD is writing, there is a lot of executive function running in the background to remember all the items he/she needs to complete. Voice recognition frees up the mind to allow a student to concentrate in creating

Table 2.   Sample of Technology Studies with Students with LD.

Author Content	Area
Ashton (2000)	Reading
Crealock and Sitko (1990)	Handwriting
De La Pas (1999)	Composing
Gerlach, Johnson, and Ouyang (1999)	Spelling
Glaser and Curry (1988)	Writing
Deong (1992)	Reading Comprehension
Kerchner and Kistinger (1984)	Language Processing
Lundberg and Olofsson (1993)	Reading Comprehension
MacArthur, Graham, Hayes, and De La Pas (1996)	Spelling
Montgomery et al. (2001)	Spelling
Olson and Wise (1992)	Reading
Outhred (1989)	Writing

the content of the text as opposed to the mechanics involved in writing. Table 2 provides a sample of articles about technology that has been implemented with students with LD in different academic areas.

More than the majority of students with an academic label of learning disabled need some type of remediation in reading. The National Reading Panel (n.d.) also indicated that reading is perhaps the most important academic skill one can have. Often, before relying on assistive technology to compensate for weak reading skills, remediation should be attempted. Direct instruction, a general term for explicit teaching in reading, has shown to improve weak reading skills for students with LD. In addition to the general term of direct instruction, there is also the Direct Instruction that is a prescriptive, scripted method intended to accelerate students learning. Direct Instruction was developed out of the University of Oregon in the 1960s. Scripted lesson plans, ability grouping, and frequent assessment characterize Direct Instruction; and it has been shown to have success with a variety of populations including those students with LD (Engelmann & Carmine, 1982). Another frequently used method is a multisensory approach, such as Orton–Gillingham. Samuel Orton was at Columbia University and combined his background of remediation and neuroscience to develop his program. Anna Gillingham worked with Dr. Orton and added her knowledge of the structure of the English language to create Orton–Gillingham program, and Stillman published the first teaching manual in 1936. The   Orton–Gillingham method is characterized by multisensory, language-based, structured, sequential, and cumulative delivery of reading instruction. It has been in existence for almost a century, however, there are inconclusive research results (see Ritchney & Goeke, 2006). The studies that are available are usually flawed in some methodical manner.

CONCLUSION

In the past five and a half decades, a lot of progress has been made in the identification, education, and instructional and treatment outcomes of students with LD. This has been a critical development as students with LD "comprise the single largest category of students who receive special education services" today (Deisinger, 2004, p. 1). Since Kirk stood in front of a group of researchers, educators, and parents in 1963, the topic of learning disabilities has traveled far. Prior to that time, there was little hope that students with LD could attain meaningful academic achievement or develop their full career potential. Since the passage of IDEA in 1975, schools have earnestly modified curriculums and added technology components to enhance the learning of students with LD (see Bakken & Wojcik, 2004; Richards & Dooley, 2004). Also, federal laws such as the NCLB has placed performance demands upon schools (see Baker & Gulley, 2004). Because of this, many students with LD today go to college and are successful especially when sophisticated higher education support services are made available to them (see Obi, 2004). Furthermore, high school and postsecondary education career counseling and vocational assessment aspects have allowed persons with LD to choose work careers that are meaningful while positioning them financially to live independently from their parents (see Castellanos & Septeowski, 2004). This journey toward independence for persons with LD has not been easy but federal legislation such as the American Disabilities Act (ADA)(PL-101-336) has leveled the employment playing field for persons with LD such that it is more equal than ever before in terms of services for work training and employability provisions (see Grant, Barger-Anderson, & Fulcher, 2004).

While there has been considerable progress, concerns still exist such as the current debate over the best procedures to identify students with LD (ability–achievement discrepancy vs. response to intervention) and a definition of LD that is representational of diverse aspects of LD. In addition, there needs to be more work and emphasis on the needs of multicultural learners with LD (Obiakor & Utley, 2004). Further, there are some areas of LD that do not receive enough attention such as: nonverbal learning disabilities (see Burkhardt et al., 2004); innovative trends in teacher preparation for teaching students with LD (see Carrol, 2004); creating charter schools for students who experience learning difficulties (see LaPorte & Leather, 2004), the development of innovate counseling services for students with LD and their families (Goor et al., 1995); recognizing the comorbidity of learning disabilities and social skill deficits, depression, and juvenile delinquency (Crawford, 1982; Dunivant, 1982; Gilbert, 2000; Karr & Davis, 1996; Kosier-Leonard, 1996); gifted students with learning disabilities (Vail, 1989; Vaugh, 1989); and the emerging area of neurological and neuropsychological aspects of learning problems (Stefani, 2004).

While shortcomings exist in the field of LD, the future is bright. As a community working with students with LD, we know more about the type of instruction that will benefit these students, better ways to assess their strengths and deficits, and how to include them with the advances in technology. As a community, we are well aware of the potential risks revolving around school and potential lifelong outcomes; however, we are also more aware of how to help students with LD to overcome those obstacles.

REFERENCES

Alper, B. C., & Raharinirina, S. (2006). Assistive technology for individuals with disabilities: A review and synthesis of the literature. *Journal of Special Education Technology*, *21*(2), 47–64.

Ashton, T. M. (2000). Technology for students with learning disabilities in reading. *Journal of Special Education*, *15*(2), 47–48.

Atkins, K., & Litton, F. W. (1995). Counseling factors and strategies for working with families of children with learning disabilities. In: A. F. Rotatori, J. O. Schwenn & F. W. Litton (Eds), *Counseling special education populations: Research and practice perspectives* (Vol. 9, pp. 65–98). Greenwich, CT: JAI Press Inc.

Audiblox. (2000). History of learning disabilities. Chapter 2: Birth of a syndrome. Available at http://www.audiblox2000.com/book2.htm

Baker, C., & Gulley, B. (2004). The impact of the No Child Left Behind Act. In: S. Burkhardt, F. E. Obiakor & A. F. Rotatori (Eds), *Current perspectives on learning disabilities* (Vol. 16, pp. 193–206). London: Elsevier Ltd.

Bakken, J. P., & Wojcik, B. W. (2004). Technology resources for persons with learning disabilities. In: S. Burkhardt, F. E. Obiakor & A. F. Rotatori (Eds), *Current perspectives on learning disabilities* (Vol. 16, pp. 113–132). London: Elsevier Ltd.

Banks, R., & Coombs, N. (2005). Accessible information technology and persons with visual impairments. In: D. Edyburn & R. Boone (Eds), *Handbook of special education technology research and practice* (pp. 379–391). Whitefish Bay, WI: Knowledge by Design.

Barchas, C. (1998). History of literacy. Grace Fernald as remembered by Cecile Barchas 55 years later. Available at http://www.historyliteracy.org/scripts/search_+display. php?Article)ID = 136

Bender, W. N. (2007). *Learning disabilities: Characteristics, identification, and teaching strategies* (6th ed.). Boston: Allyn & Bacon.

Berninger, V. W. (2001). Understanding the "lexia" in dyslexia: A multidisciplinary team approach to learning disabilities. *Annuals of Dyslexia, 51,* 23–48.

Bouck, E. C. (2010). Technology and students with disabilities: Does it solve all the problems. In: F. E. Obiakor, J. B. Bakken & A. F. Rotatori (Eds), *Current issues and trends in special education: Research, technology and teacher preparation* (Vol. 20, pp. 91–104). United Kingdom: Emerald Group Publishing Limited.

Burkhardt, S., Obiakor, F. E., & Rotatori, A. F. (2004). *Current perspectives in learning disabilities* (Vol. 16). London: Elsevier Ltd.

Carrol, M. (2004). Trends in teacher preparation for teaching students with learning disabilities. In: S. Burkhardt, F. E. Obiakor & A. F. Rotatori (Eds), *Current perspectives on learning disabilities* (Vol. 16, pp. 207–228). London: Elsevier Ltd.

Castellanos, P., & Septeowski, D. (2004). Career development for persons with learning disabilities. In: S. Burkhardt, F. E. Obiakor & A. F. Rotatori (Eds), *Current perspectives on learning disabilities* (Vol. 16, pp. 157–181). London: Elsevier Ltd.

Columbia University. (2003). *Samuel Torrey Orton.* Available at http://cpmcnet.columbia.edu/ library/archives/findingaids/ortonpapers.html

Crawford, D. (1982). *The ACLD-R&D project: A study investigating the link between learning disabilities and juvenile delinquency: Executive summary.* Phoenix, AZ: ACLD-R&D Project.

Crealock, C., & Sitko, M. (1990). Comparison between computer and handwriting technologies in writing training with learning disabled students. *International Journal of Special Education, 5,* 173–183.

Dean, V. J., & Burns, M. K. (2002). Inclusion of intrinsic processing difficulties in LD diagnostic models: A critical review. *Learning Disabilities Quarterly, 25*(3), 170–176.

Deisinger, J. (2004). Conceptualizations of learning disabilities: Beyond the ability–achievement discrepancy. In: S. Burkhardt, F. E. Obiakor & A. F. Rotatori (Eds), *Current perspectives on learning disabilities* (Vol. 16, pp. 1–20). London: Elsevier Ltd.

De La Pas, S. (1999). Composing via dictation and speech recognition system: Compensatory technology for students with learning disabilities. *Learning Disability Quarterly, 22*(3), 173–182.

Deong, C. K. (1992). Enhancing reading comprehension with text-to-speech (DECtalk) computer system. *Reading and Writing: An Interdisciplinary Journal, 4,* 205–217.

Deshler, D. D. (1998). Grounding intervention for students with learning disabilities in "powerful ideas". *Learning Disabilities Research and Practice, 13*(1), 29–34.

Deshler, D. D., Ellis, E. S., & Lenz, B. K. (1996). *Teaching adolescents with learning disabilities: Strategies and methods* (2nd ed.). Denver, CO: Love Publishing.

Duchan, J. (2001). History of speech-pathology in America: Kurt Goldstein. Available at http:// www.ascu.buffalo.edu/~duchan/history_subpages/

Dunivant, N. (1982). *The relationship between learning disabilities and juvenile delinquency: Executive summary.* Williamsburg, VA: National Center for State Courts.

Dyson, L. L. (1996). The experiences of families of children with learning disabilities: Parental stress, family functioning, and sibling self-concept. *Journal of Learning Disabilities, 29,* 280–286.

Engelmann, S., & Carmine, D. W. (1982). *Theory of instruction: Principles and application.* New York: Irvington.

Fernald, G. M. (1943). *Remedial techniques in basic school subjects.* New York: McGraw-Hill.

Fernald, G. M., & Keller, H. (1921). The effects of kinesthetic factors in the development of word recognition in the case of non-readers. *Journal of Educational Research, 4,* 355–377.

Flanagan, D. P., Ortiz, S. O., & Mascolo, J. T. (2002). *The achievement test desk reference: Comprehensive assessment and learning disabilities.* Boston: Allyn & Bacon.

Freitas, D., & Kouroupetroglou, G. (2008). Speech technologies for blind and low vision persons. *Technology and Disability, 20,* 135–156.

Friend, M. (2005). *Special education: Contemporary perspectives for school professionals.* Boston: Allyn & Bacon.

Fuchs, L. S., & Fuchs, D. (2007). A model for implementing response to intervention. *Teaching Exceptional Children, 37*(4), 14–20.

Gelb, A., & Goldstein, K. (1918). Analysis of a case of figural blindness. In: W. D. Ellis (Ed.), *A source book of Gestalt psychology* (pp. 315–325). New York: Harcourt, Brace.

Gerber, P. J. (1986). Counseling the learning disabled. In: A. F. Rotatori, P. J. Gerber, F. W. Litton & R. A. Fox (Eds), *Counseling exceptional students* (pp. 99–122). New York: Human Sciences Press, Inc.

Gerlach, G. J., Johnson, J. R., & Ouyang, R. (1999). Using an electronic speller to correct misspelled words and verify correctly spelled words. *Reading Improvement, 28,* 188–194.

Gersten, R. (1998). Recent advances in instructional research for students with learning disabilities: An overview. *Learning Disabilities Research and Practice, 11,* 214–229.

Gilbert, C. (2000). The comorbidity of learning disabilities and social skills deficits: Implications for school intervention. In: F. E. Obiakor, S. Burkhardt, A. F. Rotatori & T. Wahlberg (Eds), *Interventions for individuals with exceptionalities* (Vol. 13, pp. 299–346). Stamford, CT: JAI Press, Inc.

Gillingham, A., & Stillman, B. (1936). *Remedial work for reading, spelling, and penmanship.* New York: Hackett & Wilhelms.

Gillingham, A., & Stillman, B. (1960). *Remedial training for children with specific reading disability in reading, spelling, and penmanship.* Cambridge, MA: Educators Publishing Service.

Glaser, S. M., & Curry, D. (1988). Word processing programs: Survival tools for children with writing problems. *Reading, Writing and Learning Disabilities, 4,* 291–306.

Goldstein, K. (1937). The problem of the meaning of words based on observations of aphasia patients. *Journal of Psychology, 2,* 302–316.

Goldstein, K. (1939). *The organism.* New York: American Book.

Goor, M. B., McKnab, P. A., & Davidson-Aviles, R. (1995). Counseling individuals with learning disabilities. In: A. F. Rotatori, J. O. Schwenn & F. W. Litton (Eds), *Counseling special populations: Research and practice perspectives* (Vol. 9, pp. 99–118). Greenwich, CT: JAI Press Inc.

Grant, P. A., Barger-Anderson, R., & Fulcher, P. A. (2004). Impact of the American Disabilities Act on services for persons with learning disabilities. In: S. Burkhardt,

F. E. Obiakor & A. F. Rotatori (Eds), *Current perspectives on learning disabilities* (Vol. 16, pp. 183–192). London: Elsevier Ltd.

Greene, G. (1994). The magic of mnemonics. *LD Forum, 19*, 34–37.

Gresham, F. M. (2002). Response to intervention: An alternative approach to the identification of learning disabilities. In: R. Bradley, L. Danielson & D. P. Hallahan (Eds), *Identification of learning disabilities: Research to practice* (pp. 467–519). Mahwah, NY: Erlbaum.

Gunderson, L., & Siegel, L. S. (2001). The evils of the use of IQ tests to define learning disabilities in first- and second-language learners. *Reading Teacher, 55*(1), 48–55.

Hagw, R. A., & Silver, A. A. (1990). *Disorders of learning in childhood.* New York: Wiley.

Hallahan, D. P., & Kauffman, JM. (1997). *Exceptional learners: Introduction to special education* (7th ed.). Boston: Allyn & Bacon.

Hallahan, D. P., & Mercer, C. D. (2001). Learning disabilities, historical perceptions. Executive summary. Available at http://www.air.org;/ldsummit/

Hammill, D. D. (1990). On defining learning disabilities: An emerging consensus. *Journal of Learning Disabilities, 23*, 74–84.

Harnet, A., Tierney, E., & Guerin, S. (2009). Convention of hope – Communicating positive, realistic messages to families at the time of a child's diagnosis with disabilities. *British Journal of Learning Disabilities, 37*(4), 257–264.

Johnson, E. S., & Smith, L. (2008). Implementation of response to intervention at a middle school. *Teaching Exceptional Children, 40*(3), 46–52.

Karr, S. K., & Davis, K. (1996). Assessment of depression in special populations. In: A. F. Rotatori, J. O. Schwenn & S. Burkhardt (Eds), *Assessment and psychopathology issues in special populations* (Vol. 10, pp. 201–230). Greenwich, CT: JAI Press, Inc.

Kavale, K. A., & Forness, S. R. (1996). Social skill deficits and learning disabilities: A meta-analysis. *Journal of Learning Disabilities, 29*(3), 226–237.

Kephart, N. C. (1960). *The slow learning in the classroom.* Columbus, OH: Charles E. Merrill.

Kerchner, L. B., & Kistinger, B. J. (1984). Language processing/word processing: Written expression, computers, and learning disabled students. *Learning Disability Quarterly, 7*, 329–335.

Kirk, S. (1963). *Proceedings of the conference on exploration into the perceptually handicapped child.* Fund for Perceptually Handicapped Children, Inc., Evanston, IL.

Kirk, S., & Bateman, B. (1962–1963). Diagnosis and remediation of learning disabilities. *Exceptional Children, 29*, 73–87.

Kirk, S., & Chalfant, J. (1984). *Academic developmental learning disabilities.* Denver, CO: Love Publishers.

Kirk, S., & Kirk, W. D. (1971). *Psycholinguistic learning disabilities: Diagnosis and remediation.* Champaign, IL: University of Illinois Press.

Kirk, S. A., McCarthy, J. J., & Kirk, W. D. (1968). *Illinois test of psycholinguistic abilities* (Rev. ed.). Urbana, IL: University of Illinois Press.

Kosier-Leonard, J. A. (1996). The assessment of depression and suicide in juvenile delinquents. In: A. F. Rotatori, J. O. Schwenn & S. Burkhardt (Eds), *Assessment and psychopathology issues in special populations* (Vol. 10, pp. 231–244). Greenwich, CT: JAI Press, Inc.

LaPorte, D., & Leather, N. (2004). Wings Academy: A new charter school for students who learn differently. In: S. Burkhardt, F. E. Obiakor & A. F. Rotatori (Eds), *Current perspectives on learning disabilities* (Vol. 16, pp. 247–264). London: Elsevier Ltd.

Lerner, J. (2005). *Learning disabilities and related disorders: Characteristics and teaching strategies*. Belmont, CA: Wadsworth Publishing.

Lloyd, J. W. (2005). Chronology of some important events in the history of learning disabilities. Available at http://curry.edschool.virginia.edu

Lundberg, L., & Olofsson, A. (1993). Can computer speech support reading comprehension? *Computers in Human Behavior*, *9*, 282–293.

Maag, J. W., & Reid, R. (2006). Depression among students with learning disabilities. *Journal of Learning Disabilities*, *39*, 3–10.

MacArthur, C. A., Graham, S., Hayes, J. B., & De La Pas, S. (1996). Spell checkers and students with learning disabilities: Performance comparison and impact on spelling. *Journal of Special Education*, *30*, 35–57.

Mitchem, K. J., & Richards, A. (2003). Students with learning disabilities. In: F. E. Obiakor, C. A. Utley & A. F. Rotatori (Eds), *Effective education for learners with exceptionalities* (Vol. 15, pp. 99–117). London: Elsevier Science Ltd.

Monroe, M. (1928). Methods for diagnosis and treatment of cases of reading disorders. *Genetic Psychology Monographs*, *4*, 341–356.

Monroe, M. (1932). *Children who cannot read*. Chicago: The University of Chicago Press.

Montgomery, D. J., Karlan, G. R., & Coutinho, M. J. (2001). The effectiveness of word processor spell checker programs to produce target words for misspellings generated by students with learning disabilities. *Journal of Special Education Technology*, *16*(2), 27–41.

Myers, P., & Hammill, D. D. (1990). *Learning disabilities: Basic concepts, assessment, practices and instructional strategies*. Austin, TX: RRO-ED.

National Reading Panel. (n.d.). Available at http://www.nationalreadingpanel.org/

Nkabinde, Z. (2008). Using assistive technology to educate students with developmental disabilities and autism. In: A. F. Rotatori, F. E. Obiakor & S. Burkhardt (Eds), *Autism and developmental disabilities: Current practices and issues* (Vol. 18, pp. 273–285). United Kingdom: Emerald Group Publishing Limited.

Obi, S. O. (2004). Support services for college students with learning disabilities. In: S. Burkhardt, F. E. Obiakor & A. F. Rotatori (Eds), *Current perspectives on learning disabilities* (Vol. 16, pp. 229–245). London: Elsevier Ltd.

Obiakor, F. E., & Utley, C. A. (2004). Multicultural learners with learning disabilities: Beyond Eurocentric perspectives. In: S. Burkhardt, F. E. Obiakor & A. F. Rotatori (Eds), *Current perspectives on learning disabilities* (Vol. 16, pp. 35–64). London: Elsevier Ltd.

Olson, R. K., & Wise, B. W. (1992). Reading on the computer with orthographic and speech feedback. *Reading and Writing: An Interdisciplinary Journal*, *4*, 107–144.

Orton, S. (1925). Word blindness in school children. *Archives of Neurology and Psychiatry*, *14*, 581–615.

Orton, S. (1929). The sight reading method of teaching reading as a source of reading disability. *Journal of Educational Psychology*, *20*, 135–143.

Orton, S. (1937). *Reading, writing and speech problems in children: A presentation of certain types of disorders in the development of the language faculty*. New York: W.W. Norton.

Orton, S. (1939). A neurological explanation of the reading disability. *Education Record*, *12*, 58–68.

O'Shea, D. J., O'Shea, L. J., & Hammitte, D. J. (1994). Expanding roles for teachers of students with learning disabilities. *LD Forum*, *19*, 28–30.

Outhred, L. (1989). Word processing: Its impact on children's writing. *Journal of Learning Disabilities, 22*, 262–264.

Parette, H. P., & Peterson-Karlan, G. R. (2010). Using assistive technology to support the instructional process of students with disabilities. In: F. E. Obiakor, J. P. Bakken & A. F. Rotatori (Eds), *Current issues and trends in special education: Research, technology and teacher preparation* (Vol. 20, pp. 73–89). United Kingdom: Emerald Group Publishing Limited.

Perception. (1995). Perceptual motor models. Available at http://www.umsl.edu/~optrgarz/perceptual_motor_models.htm

Raskind, M. (n.d.) Success attributes among individuals with learning disabilities. GreatSchools Inc. Available at http://www.greatschools.net/LD/managing/success-attributes-among-individuals-with-learning-disabilities.gs?content — 851&page — all

Richards, A., & Dooley, E. (2004). Curriculum modifications for students with learning disabilities. In: S. Burkhardt, F. E. Obiakor & A. F. Rotatori (Eds), *Current perspectives in learning disabilities* (Vol. 16, pp. 95–111). London: Elsevier Ltd.

Ritchney, K. D., & Goeke, J. L. (2006). Orton–Gillingham and Orton–Gillingham based reading instruction: A review of the literature. *Journal of Special Education, 40*, 171–183.

Roach, E. F., & Kephart, N. C. (1966). *The Purdue perceptual-motor survey*. Columbus, OH: Merrill.

Rosenthal, I. (1992). Counseling the learning disabled late adolescent and adult: A self study perspective. *Learning Disabilities Quarterly, 7*, 217–225.

Rotatori, A. F., Schwenn, J. O., & Litton, F. W. (1994). *Perspectives on the regular education initiative and transitional programs* (Vol. 9). Greenwich, CT: JAI Press Inc.

Rotatori, A. F., & Wahlberg, T. (2004). Comprehensive assessment of students with learning disabilities. In: S. Burkhardt, F. E. Obiakor & A. F. Rotatori (Eds), *Current perspectives on learning disabilities* (Vol. 16, pp. 133–155). London: Elsevier Ltd.

Schwenn, J. O. (1991). Students with high incidence handicaps. In: J. O. Schwenn, A. F. Rotatori & R. A. Fox (Eds), *Understanding students with high incidence exceptionalities* (pp. 3–27). Springfield, IL: Charles C. Thomas.

Scruggs, T. E., & Mastropieri, M. A. (2002). On babies and bathwater: Addressing the problems of identification of learning disabilities. *Learning Disabilities Quarterly, 25*(3), 155–169.

Silver, A. A., & Hagin, R. A. (2002). *Disorders of learning in children* (2nd ed.). New York: Wiley.

Sorrel, A. L. (2000). Learning disabilities: From understanding to intervention. In: F. E. Obiakor, S. A. Burkhardt, A. F. Rotatori & T. Walhberg (Eds), *Intervention techniques for individuals with exceptionalities in inclusive settings* (Vol. 13, pp. 53–77). Stamford, CT: JAI Press, Inc.

Stefani, R. (2004). Neurological and neuropsychological aspects of learning and attention problems. In: S. Burkhardt, F. E. Obiakor & A. F. Rotatori (Eds), *Current perspectives on learning disabilities* (Vol. 16, pp. 95–111). London: Elsevier Ltd.

Strauss, A. A., & Kephart, N. (1955). *Psychopathology and education of the brain injured child* (Vol. 2). New York: Grune & Stratton.

Strauss, A. A., & Lehtinen, L. E. (1947). *Psychopathology and education of the brain injured child*. New York: Grune & Stratton.

Swanson, H. L. (1999). *Interventions for students with learning disabilities: A meta-analysis of treatment outcomes.* New York: Guilford.

Swanson, H. L. (2000). Issues facing the field of learning disabilities. *Learning Disability Quarterly, 23*(1), 37–50.

Swanson, H. L. (2009). Intervention research for students with LD, LD.org. Available at http://www.ncld.org/at-school/especially-for-teachers/effective-teaching-practices/intervention-research-for-students-with-ld

Tanner, D. E. (2001). The learning disabled: A distinct population of students. *Education, 121*(4), 795–798.

Technology-Related Assistance for Individuals with Disabilities Act. (1988). PL100-407 (August 19, 1988). Title 29, U.S.C. 2201 et seq. U.S. *Statutes at Large, 102,* 1044–1065.

Torgesen, J. K. (2001). Learning disabilities as a working memory deficit: The important next questions. *Issues in Education, 7*(1), 93–102.

Torgesen, J. K. (2009). The response to intervention instructional model: Some outcomes from a large-scale implementation in reading first schools. *Child Development Perspectives, 3*(1), 38–40.

Trotter, T. V. (1993). Counseling with exceptional children. In: A. Vernon (Ed.), *Counseling children and adolescents* (pp. 119–135). Denver, CO: Love Publishing.

U.S. Department of Education. (2003). *25th annual report to Congress on the implementation of the Individuals with Disabilities Education Act.* Washington, DC: Author.

U.S. Department of Health and Human Services Public Health Service National Institutes of Health & National Institute of Mental Health. (1993). Learning disabilities. NIH Publication No. 93-3611.

Vail, P. (1989). The gifted learning disabled student. In: S. Silver (Ed.), *The assessment of learning disabilities: Preschool through adulthood* (pp. 135–160). Boston: Little, Brown.

Vaughn, S. (1989). Gifted learning disabilities: Is it such a bright idea? *Learning Disability Focus, 4,* 123–128.

Vaughn, S., Elbaum, B., & Boardman, A. (2001). The social functioning of students with learning disabilities: Implications for inclusion. *Exceptionality: A Special Education Journal, 9*(1), 47–65. 10.1207/S15327035EX091&2_5

Vaughn, S., Gersten, R., & Chard, D. (2000). The underlying message in intervention research: Findings from research syntheses. *Exceptional Children, 67,* 99–114.

Waggoner, K., & Wilgosh, L. (1990). Concerns of families with learning disabilities. *Journal of Learning Disabilities, 23,* 97–113.

Wagner, M., Marder, C., Blackorby, J., Cameto, R., Newman, L., Levine, P., & Sumi, C. (2003). *The achievements of youth with disabilities during secondary school. A report from the National Longitudinal Transition Study-2 (NLTS2).* Menlo Park, CA: SRI International. Available at www.nlts2.org/reports/2003_11/nlts2_report_2003_11_complete.pdf

Warner, T. D., Dede, D. E., Garvan, C. W., & Conway, T. W. (2002). One size does not fit all in specific learning disabilities assessment across ethnic groups. *Journal of Learning Disabilities, 35*(6), 501–509.

Wheeler, J. J., & Mayton, M. R. (2010). Other innovative techniques: Positive behavioral supports and response to intervention. In: F. E. Obiakor, J. P. Bakken & A. F. Rotatori (Eds), *Current issues and trends in special education: Identification, assessment and instruction* (Vol. 19, pp. 175–195). United Kingdom: Emerald Group Publishing Limited.

Wilson, V. L., & Reynolds, C. R. (2002). Misconceptions in Van den Broeck's representation of misrepresentations about learning disability research. *Journal of Learning Disabilities*, *35*(3), 205–208.

Winnery, K. W., & Fuchs, L. S. (1993). Effects of goal and test-taking strategies on the computation performance of students with learning disabilities. *Learning Disabilities Research and Practice*, *8*, 204–214.

Wolfensberger, W. (1972). *The principle of normalization in human services.* Toronto: National Institute of Mental Retardation.

Wright, J. (2007). *Response to intervention toolkit. A practical guide for schools.* New York: Dude.

Who Named It? (2005). Biographics: Franz Joseph Gall. Available at http://www.whonamedit. com/doctor.cfm/1018.html

http://www.adcet.edu.au/Oao/What_is_LD.chpx

http://www.ldonline.org/article/Timeline_of_Learning_Disabilities

CHAPTER 5

HISTORY OF INTELLECTUAL DISABILITIES

Kagendo Mutua, James Siders and
Jeffrey P. Bakken

OVERVIEW

This chapter traces the history of intellectual disabilities by exploring significant historical periods and personalities who impacted the disability field and specifically the area of intellectual disability. Like other documented histories, the purpose of this chapter is to instruct and inform readers about the historical underpinnings of the labels, practices, and programs related to intellectual disability that are in effect today. While this chapter is not intended to be prescriptive in how the information presented here is to be interpreted, we are acutely aware that historical accounts are often interpreted based upon contemporary ideologies, knowledge, and practices. As such, as a historical account, this chapter is no exception. Current belief and practices about intellectual disabilities indeed influence the choices that, we as the chapter authors, made about the relative importance of the events that we select to highlight in this chapter. Nonetheless, this account reflects the events and personalities who, in our estimation, transformed and/or advanced the field of intellectual disability. We open with a brief prologue of the representations of the intellectual disability in popular culture and its potential impact on perceptions of persons with intellectual disability.

History of Special Education
Advances in Special Education, Volume 21, 89–117
Copyright © 2011 by Emerald Group Publishing Limited
All rights of reproduction in any form reserved
ISSN: 0270-4013/doi:10.1108/S0270-4013(2011)0000021008

INTRODUCTION: THE LAY OF THE LAND

Throughout civilization, human tendency has been to exercise superiority over one another and to ultimately subjugate and control the one found wanting. Outside of war and conquest, this tendency was evidenced in the treatment of persons with physical, sensory, and/or mental impairments, particularly those with readily visible markers of difference. The visibility of such disabling conditions rendered the persons identifiably different from the rest of humanity, and therefore more likely to be slotted as inferior. Writing about disability, Leonard Davis (1995) in *Enforcing Normalcy* argues that disability is constructed not by attending to the differences engendered in the impairment itself, but rather by attending to what's culturally constituted as normal and adhered to as the average, hence the imperative. All other bodies outside of that normative imperative are then considered deviant. This idea of the average man was popularized by the French statistician Adolphe Quetelet (1796–1847), cited in Davis (1995), who postulated that the average man was the aggregate measure of all ordinary human attributes within specific cultures. Therefore, average became accepted as the yardstick against which all bodies were measured throughout the 19th century. The bodies that differed significantly from the average were therefore considered deviant, such as persons with disabilities in general and intellectual disabilities in particular. This idea of the average that Quetelet advanced has been studied in recent times as the notion of prototyping. According to McCaughey and Strohmer (2005), a prototype is a cognitive representation of characteristics that define an object or person. These scholars found that the ideas about the prototype of intellectual disability, for instance, were largely negative, stereotypical, and emphasized significant functional limitations as the prototypical descriptor of the average person with intellectual disabilities, regardless of the severity of the condition. Therefore, the notion of the prototype impacted how nondisabled persons behaved toward and treated those with intellectual disabilities.

As society advanced and humane treatment was demanded by individuals capable of standing up for themselves or by their advocates, treatment began to positively shift toward respect for persons with disabilities. However, even then, there were clear lines drawn that demarcated the separation of the normal bodies from those with disabilities. Acceptable variations of the normal body existed along a continuum from the ideal and humanly unachievable bodies (such as the ideal female embodiment in mythologized figures like Venus or Helen of Troy) to the grotesque. As a visual human form, the grotesque was inversely related to the ideal, and yet at the same time, the grotesque did not epitomize disability. Davis (1995) argues that "...the grotesque were on the facades of cathedrals throughout Europe. The grotesque, therefore, permeated culture and signified the norm, whereas the disabled body, a later concept, was formulated as by definition excluded from culture, society, the norm" (p. 25). Therefore, the deviance embodied in the disabled body placed it out of the realm of normalcy (in other words, it did not fall on the continuum of normalcy), but rather it was viewed as an aberration thereby placing the disabled person's body on a continuum all of its own. This made possible the exclusion, and often the mistreatment of persons with disabilities because disability rendered one a nonperson.

THE MEDIEVAL PERIOD: PERSONS WITH INTELLECTUAL DISABILITY AS THE SCOURGE OF THE EARTH

In European history, the medieval period or the Middle Ages is the period spanning 5th century to the 15th century. Historians consider it the period that was a deviation from the path of classical learning, a path supposedly reconnected by Renaissance scholarship. Although practices related to the treatment of persons with intellectual disabilities differed within countries, during medieval times, persons with intellectual disabilities were valued due to high demand for manual labor as well as a high mortality rate that rendered all children desirable (Scheerenberger, 1983). Women were encouraged to drop off their disabled children at church doors where they would be taken in and provided care, but many died because of the low quality of care provided. Therefore, those children with intellectual disabilities were served in church or state-sponsored foundling homes, orphanages, and hospitals. However, according to Scheerenberger (1983), this benevolence toward persons with intellectual disabilities changed significantly during that period spurred by three major events. First, during the Dark Ages impoverished inhabitants of Britain, Germany, and Gaul sold thousands of children into slavery, including those with intellectual disabilities who appeared capable of working. Some of the misery of the Dark Ages was alleviated by the purchase of those children by holy men of the church. At the time, the church in some western European countries held that such children were of God and were innocent. Second, during the Middle Ages, some of the changes that took place in the Catholic church included a basic change in the belief that children with intellectual disabilities were children of God to those children being products of sin and the devil. This stemmed from the basic Catholic belief in the original sin: that all persons are born with the original sin and are predisposed to impiety and death. Scheerenberger notes that the preaching of this doctrine led to many medieval Christians feeling a deep sense of depravity, shame, and inborn guilt, in particular, mothers of children with intellectual disabilities who believed that their actions resulted in the birth of the impure child. This doctrine came to even greater emphasis during the Reformation. Third, the inquisition that resulted in the burning of heretics and witch-hunting correlated also with suspicion of persons with intellectual disabilities therefore being unmercifully treated.

During this period some other practices that related to persons with mental disabilities included using them for amusement as buffoons and jesters to provide comedic relief. According to Scheerenberger (1983), during the Middle Ages, a variety of institutions sprung up catering to persons with intellectual disabilities as well as those with mental illnesses. These institutions provided residential facilities in monasteries, pesthouses, workhouses, warehouses, and other buildings that had lost their utility. This historian of intellectual disabilities also noted that while conditions of care of persons with intellectual disabilities were deplorable in most institutions in western European countries, there existed an exemplary institution in Cairo called the Mansur Hospital where residents were treated with superior care and provided all manner of comfort and habilitation. However, this superior model of care was not replicated in the West, favoring rather the warehousing of persons with disabilities as dispensable and not unworthy of optimal care.

The tendency to conflate mental illness with intellectual disability was prevalent even during the medieval times. People with these conditions were treated as in similarly inhumane manner, with the exception noted in the Mansur Hospital model in Cairo. An ordinance passed by King Edward I of England and reconfirmed by King Edward II in 1324 (Zilboorg, 1941, cited in Scheerenberger, 1983) brought about notable change in the proprietary rights of persons labeled as idiots or mentally ill. This is one of the more notable contributions of the period. The ordinance required that the lands of "natural fools" (p. 36) be placed in the custody of the crown to assure that such a natural fool nor his heirs were not swindled of their property. The reference made of natural fools as "idiots" in the ordinance heralded the second major contribution of this period to the understanding of intellectual disability. Specifically, a definition of intellectual disabilities that drew a distinction between intellectual disability and mental illness came to be seen as another significant contribution of the Middle Ages to the understanding of intellectual disability. Idiots were distinguished from lunatics. "Idiocy was defined as a congenital condition (*idiota a nativitate*) with a continuing lack of mental capacity, while a lunatic was potentially able to regain his faculties" (Scheerenberger, 1983, p. 36). This distinction, while useful, did not necessarily end the conflation of intellectual disability with mental illness: a tendency that has endured for years well into the 21st century. For instance, to this day, many state agencies are named Department of Mental Retardation/Mental Health (MR/MH) which is an index of the vestiges of the conflation of these two distinctly different conditions of the mind.

With a legal definition of intellectual disability in place, the next natural progression was an attempt to provide an objective measure or some index for assessing it. In an article published in *Natura Brevium* in 1534, Sir Anthony Fitzherbert (cited in Scheerenberger, 1983) offered the first published test of intellectual ability:

> ...he who shall be said to be a sot or idiot from his birth is such a person who cannot account or number twenty pence, nor can tell who was his father or mother nor how old he is so as it may appear he hath no understanding of reason what shall be for his profit nor what be his loss. But if he has such understanding that he knoweth and understand his letters, and do read by teaching or information of another man, then he seemeth he is not a sot nor a natural idiot. (p. 36)

This definition was later extended by other scientists to include specific functional abilities that such an individual must show deficits in, including measuring a yard of cloth or naming the days of the week.

THE RENAISSANCE PERIOD

The period that followed was the renaissance period that spanned between the 17th and 18th centuries. As a cultural movement, the renaissance encompassed a resurgence of learning based on classical sources, the development of linear perspective in painting, and gradual but widespread educational reform. The Renaissance is viewed as a bridge between the Middle Ages and the Modern era or the Enlightenment period. During this period, there was an increased awareness of intellectual disability as its own entity. It was a period in which the elegance of Mozart, the salons of Paris, and baroque design stood in stark contrast with the abject deprivation and cruelty that was meted against the less fortunate, those with intellectual disability included. To sustain the life of opulence of the wealthy, international trade increased, territorial expansionism through wars and colonization, and the desire for luxury goods for the consumption by the powerful and the wealthy increased in fashion value and costliness, leading to significant increases in taxation. These events further increased the depravity of the poor due to increased and constant demand for money. Consequently, during this period, begging increased substantially, especially in cities all across Europe. This ideological change in the view of begging as a lucrative practice that yielded an income led to a transformation in the accepted societal sensibility toward poor children in general and those with disabilities in particular who lived in poor houses, fondling homes, and alms houses. The rise in begging as a bona fide and lucrative business resulted in professional beggars purchasing children, with and without intellectual disabilities, and breaking their legs or maiming them in some way and putting them back on the streets to beg. This marked the evolution of the construct of cap-in-hand (handicap). Ostensibly, the more "disabled" the child appeared to be, the greater response in pity they elicited, thereby resulting in receiving more alms. As such, children with intellectual disabilities became perversely valued, but paradoxically also even more easily dispensable when they were of no more economic value.

During this period, there emerged several personalities who made many notable contributions to science and philosophy. In this section, we focus on some of those contributions that had a bearing on intellectual disability. The greatest contribution of the renaissance period insofar as intellectual disabilities are concerned was the rise in scientific knowledge and under-standing. Specifically, the understanding of the brain anatomy was spurred by the work of Francis Sylvius (1614–1672) by whose name many regions of the brain are named. In a famous text, he attributed intellectual disability to repeated seizures or epilepsy. Another notable contribution came from William Harvey (1616) whose work contributed to the understanding of the circulatory system by proving that blood circulates through the body. Yet another worthwhile development in science came from a physician and lecturer, Francis Clisson, who was granted permission by Queen Elizabeth to perform dissection and was able to accurately identify the true cause of hydrocephaly. Occurring alongside these advances in science were scientific assertions which, though questionable today, back then linked intellectual disability with witchcraft (Scheerenberger, 1983). Misinformation notwithstanding, perhaps the contributions of this period can be encapsulated as the expansion in science of the understanding of the brain, epilepsy, and the hydrocephalus. Though some attention was drawn to the role of heredity in the causation of intellectual disability, for the most of its proponents, that link between heredity and epilepsy and hydrocephalous was at best tenuous.

THE ENLIGHTENMENT PERIOD

The Age of Enlightenment (or simply the Enlightenment) is the era in Western philosophy and intellectual, scientific, and cultural life that centered upon the 18th century, in which reason was advocated as the primary source for legitimacy and authority. The period produced many intellectual giants who had profound impact on education and the understanding of humans, including the revival of the ideas of Roger Bacon, a respected Oxford teacher, who believed strongly that all philosophical teachings and claims to authority must be verified by experiential facts and experiment. During the Enlightenment period, Francis Bacon extended Roger Bacon's ideas that knowledge about the world must be acquired sensorily (Scheerenberger, 1983). Therefore, such knowledge could be acquired through controlled experimentation, investigation, and explanations drawn from the experimentation.

The same period produced other philosophers like Rene Descartes who proclaimed that the true understanding of the natural world was only possible through the application of mathematical principles and deductive reasoning. While Descartes' ideas were highly influential in philosophical thinking, the real tour de force in the advancement of knowledge within the Enlightenment period was John Locke. His theory of knowledge was central to the development of psychology and the training and treatment of persons with intellectual disabilities (Scheerenberger, 1983). Locke believed that no one is born with innate ideas, but rather at birth one's mind was *tabula rasa* (a blank slate). He theorized that experience, either from sensation or reflection, provided one with ideas of simple substances and qualities. On the other hand, reflection enabled one to acquire such abstract concepts as thinking, willing, and doubting. Locke also firmly believed that human beings were rational; therefore, a humane social order was possible. Further, Locke distinguished between "idiots" and "lunatics," that is, between intellectual disability and mental illness which, though previously distinguished during the Middle Ages by King Edward II, continued to be conflated and to be thought of as one and the same.

Another important contributor to the Enlightenment period thinking was Jean Jacques Rousseau (1712–1778). Jean Jacques Rousseau ideas had profound impact on the future course of intellectual disabilities. His two most famous works *The Social Contract* and *Emile* continue to be cited even to this day. In *Emile*, he argued for the unfolding of the man according to natural rather than social laws. Consistent with Locke's earlier ideas, Rousseau affirmed the centrality of the senses in the formation of the mind. His ideas on the natural child, self-direction, and the sensory training and experiences directly influenced Pestalozzi and Froebel, Montessori, Seguin, and Itard.

Other important personalities of that period included Vincent de Paul who established service organizations for the poor and the disabled. Along with de Paul, was a French physician named Pillipe Pinel who in 1793 was appalled at the deplorable conditions at a residential treatment center for persons with intellectual disabilities and mental illness. Similarly, another key reformer, an English merchant named William Tuke, spurred by the mysterious death of a Quaker woman who was confined to an asylum in York England, urged the Society of Friends to establish a mental hospital where a kinder gentler more appropriate treatment would be adopted.

Other key personalities of the period include Johann Pestalozzi (1746–1827) whose vital concern for education was spurred by an intense desire to change the life conditions of the less fortunate, of whom many had disabilities. Alongside him was Fredrich Froebel (1782–1852) whose philosophical ideas emphasized the importance of properly raising children. The ideas of these three philosophers and personalities greatly influenced educational thought, including the education of children with intellectual disabilities.

THE AGE OF PROGRESS (1800–1899)

During this period, a number of personalities emerged who had direct and significantly profound impact on the understanding and programming for individuals with intellectual disability in Europe and ultimately later into the United States. The individuals whom we focus on here are Edouard Seguin, John Langdon Down, Johann J. Guggenbuhl, and Jean-Marc-Gaspard Itard. Overall, as an era, the Age of Progress brought with it an innovative and provocative theory that had a profound effect on the treatment of intellectual disability. This was the theory of phrenology. Also known as craniology, as a theory, phrenology was conceived by brain anatomist Franz Joseph Gall (1758–1828). Phrenology had six overarching principles: (a) the brain was the organ of the mind; (b) the mind was comprised of faculties that were autonomous, innate, and independent; (c) fragment brain tissues connected each faculty; (d) the faculties, though independent, were extensions of and interacted with the lower nervous system; (e) the size of each fragment correlated with the strength of the associated faculty; and (f) the skull contour correlated with the hypothesized variation in the size of the underlying faculty of the brain. Phrenology led to "scientific" rankings of intellectual functioning that were both racialized and genderized (Gould, 1981). At the heyday of phrenology, it was unquestionably "proven," through many repeated measures that white men ranked at the top in intellectual functioning with black women being at the bottom of those scientific measures of cognitive functioning. Tomlinson (2005) argues that phrenology sought to provide a theoretical basis to reconcile the body and the mind and to provide a theorized rationale for general and special education. While today phrenology exists on the same questionable plane as attempts at foretelling the future as palmistry, phrenology had a noble origin. Noble beginnings notwithstanding, the effects and consequences of phrenology have been resoundingly felt for generations where it has been used for providing an evidentiary basis for justifying social Darwinism or eugenics. As we discuss later in this chapter, eugenics was practiced in the United States, justified by works of scientists like Goddard in the early 1900s, and even as recently as 1990s a sanitized version of the principles underlying eugenics is the basis for the rankings proposed by Herrnstein and Murray (1994), authors of *Bell Curve: Intelligence and Class Structure in American Life.*

Edouard Seguin (1812–1880)

In 1846, Seguin offered his definitional perspective on idiocy. He defined idiocy as an infirmity of the nervous system and divided it into four broad categories, namely:

a. Idiocy which today would encompass the severe and profound intellectually disabled.
b. Imbecility which would today equate to mild and moderate intellectually disabled.
c. Backwardness or feeble-mindedness.
d. Simpleness and superficial retardation which might today equate to developmentally delayed.

This classification was significant in that it acknowledged the variations within the category of intellectual disability: an idea that is still upheld today.

While Seguin is known as the father of special education, his life's work aligned more with Pillipe Pinel and William Tuke whose work was in creating better institutions or conditions in institutions that served persons with intellectual disability rather than spearheading efforts to refine or develop systematic direct instructional services (Scheerenberger, 1983). He founded a number of schools in France for individuals with intellectual disabilities.

However, fearing that the French Revolution would fail, he migrated to the United States with his son and wife in 1848. While in the United States, he helped with the development of a number of early institutions serving individuals with intellectual disability, including Samuel Grindley Howe's experimental Institution for Feeble-Minded Youth in Barre Massachusetts. A final and major contribution of Seguin was his encouragement in the formation of the first association dedicated solely to intellectual disability. In 1866, he called together fellow superintendents to meet annually to share their experiences serving and working with persons with intellectual disabilities. This call was realized and ultimately led to the formation of the American Association of Mental Deficiency (AAMD), later changing its name to the American Association on Mental Retardation (AAMR) and now to its current name, the American Association on Intellectual and Developmental Disabilities (AAIDD).

John Langdon Down (1826–1896)

Down was the medical superintendent of the Asylum for Idiots in Earlswood, England. Down made several important contributions to the field of intellectual disability. First, he provided the first comprehensive description of a mongoloid individual (later named Down's syndrome). Secondly, he proposed the first comprehensive classification of intellectual disability by equating the differences to ethnicity. His classification system was violently opposed by other scientists of the time, so it did not take root. In his comprehensive text titled *Mental Affections of Children and Youth* (Down, 1887), he classified idiocy into three etiological categories: (a) congenital (idiots); (b) accidental (idiots and feeble-minded); and (c) developmental (feeble-minded). This classification led to the realization and acknowledgment that idiocy was not a simple, single phenomenon, thereby ushering in the idea of classification of intellectual disability by degrees of severity.

Johann Jakob Guggenbuhl (1816–1863)

Guggenbuhl was a Swiss doctor who was gravely concerned about children with cretinism. At the time, cretinism was associated with some environmental factor related to low-lying lands. So in 1842, after receiving a parcel of land from a forester benefactor, Guggenbuhl opened the first residential facility for persons with intellectual disabilities on a mountain summit in

Adendberg, Switzerland. Scheerenberger (1983) wrote that Guggenbuhl believed that cretinism was curable with fresh mountain air, good nutrition, baths, massage, and exercise. He tried various forms of medications, established routines and set activities, sensory and memory training, and various language training programs. Among the many visitors to Adendberg was Samuel Grindley Howe. Guggenbuhl is credited with starting systematic instruction for persons with intellectual disabilities. Also, his efforts were emulated in many contexts across Europe and the United States.

Jean-Marc-Gaspard Itard (1774–1838)

Without a doubt, Itard and Seguin were the foremost leaders in education of persons with intellectual disabilities in the 19th century. Before Itard ever encountered Victor, the latter was somewhat of well-known celebrity in France. Victor was captured from the woods and escaped back into the woods many times before he was finally brought to National Institute for the Deaf-Mutes where Itard worked. While all his colleagues believed otherwise, Itard did not believe that Victor was born an idiot. Rather, he believed that Victor's deficiencies were the result of a lack of appropriate sensory stimulating experiences in a socialized environment. Thus, Itard believed that with adequate systematic instruction, Victor would show substantial intellectual development. Itard's instructional program for Victor comprised of developing three faculties: functional use of senses (sensory), intellectual functions (cognitive), and emotions (affective). While Victor's progress was disappointingly slow and almost nonexistent, Itard nonetheless laid the blueprint for individualized systematic instruction which is still the gold standard in special education today.

THE UNITED STATES: THE COLONIAL YEARS

Right from the beginning at the formation of new citizen groups in the America, there was recognition and acknowledgment of intellectual disabilities. Scheerenberger (1983) notes that the *Body of Liberties*, the country's first code of laws that was adopted by the Massachusetts General Court in 1961, explicitly mentioned intellectual disabilities vis-á-vis holding public office. The code prohibited anyone from holding a public office if such a person had intellectual disabilities. In terms of early care for persons with intellectual disabilities, the first hospital to establish a section for the mentally ill and those with intellectual disabilities was the Pennsylvania Hospital in Philadelphia. However, conditions in the hospital were deplorable. Later in 1769 the legislature of the Virginia Colony passed an act "to make provision for the support and maintenance of idiots, lunatics, and other persons of unsound minds" (Scheerenberger, 1983, p. 83). During that era, several personalities emerged who championed the cause of those with intellectual disabilities. These personalities dedicated themselves to providing medical care to the poor and challenged the inhumane approaches to treating unruly patients. The two personalities who changed the cause of intellectual disabilities during this period were Samuel Grindley Howe and Dorothea Dix.

Samuel Grindley Howe (1801–1876)

Howe was Harvard Medical School graduate whose interest and genuine concern for the less fortunate began by accident. Upon his return from a six-year stint in Greece, he was requested by a college friend, Dr. John D. Fisher, to finalize plans for an asylum of the blind in Boston and to become its first director. He toured Europe extensively and visited various schools for the blind and intellectually impaired. One tour took him to Guggenbuhl's mountain residential summit school for persons with intellectual disabilities in Adendberg, Switzerland. Howe was extremely impressed with the facility. When he returned to the United States, Howe petitioned the Massachusetts legislature to fund the care and education of 30 blind students. The legislature provided funds for educational and food costs but not funds to house the students. Howe decided to use his own home to house the students. He conducted extensive child-find all over Massachusetts, and soon he had more children than he could serve in his home. A benefactor, Colonel Perkins, offered his estate and gardens on the condition that his gift would be matched with $50,000 toward its support. This estate became the Perkins Institute and Massachusetts School for the Blind (Scheerenberger, 1983). In 1839, Howe accepted a student who was blind and cognitively impaired. Based upon Howe's training success with this student, the Massachusetts's legislature in 1848 approved to spend $2500.00 of public funds to support a 3-year experimental school for 10 idiot children. This marked the first publicly funded program serving individuals with intellectual disabilities. Happening almost concurrently was the opening of the first private facility for individuals with intellectual disabilities in Barre Massachusetts called the Institution at Barre by Hervey Wilbur (1820–1883).

Dorothea Lynde Dix (1802–1877)

Dix started her work as an advocate for persons with intellectual disabilities and other "unfortunates" who needed care and protection of the state. She traveled extensively across several north-eastern states visiting almshouses, asylums, and jailhouses documenting, with meticulous detail, the deplorable conditions of those facilities. Here crusade led her to address many legislative bodies, including Massachusetts, New York, New Jersey, and a number of others. She addressed the 30th Congress of the United States and made an impassioned plea on behalf of the "Wards of the Nation" (Scheerenberger, 1983, p. 106) to pass an act to set aside land for their care and provision. The act was passed by both houses, but was vetoed by President Pierce in 1845. Interestingly, Dix blamed parent's overindulgences and depravity as being the root cause of the intellectual disabilities in children. Additionally, she blamed immigrants for the increase in the incidence of intellectual disabilities in the northern states where their proportion was higher than in the south. Undoubtedly, the contributions of Dix and Howe and other reformers started a new era of programming for persons with intellectual disabilities.

INTELLECTUAL DISABILITY AS THE ULTIMATE COOTIE BUG: THE PROGRESSIVE ERA OF EUGENICS

This period brought much "progress" with it, including the development of an objective and standardized tool for measuring intellect for the purpose of devising appropriate instruction. Hence, the partnership of Alfred Binet and Theodore Simon yielded the Binet–Simon Intelligence Scale. The test was used to determine intellectual functioning. Later in 1916, Lewis Madison Terman revised Binet's test, renamed it the Stanford–Binet test, and introduced the concept of Intelligence Quotient (IQ) as the standard operational interpretation of intelligence tests. Following the introduction of IQ, he devised a new classification system of intellectual functioning.

One of the strongest admirers of Binet's work was Henry Herbert Goddard (1866–1957). He translated the Binet–Simon into English and became one of the greatest advocates of IQ testing. He published extensively and one of his in/famous publications, *The Kallikaks* (Goddard, 1912), linked idiocy with heredity and argued that there was a direct correlation between feeble-mindedness and immorality and a host of other socially undesirable traits and behaviors. In a similar vein, Dugdale's (1910) study of the Jukes' family linked them with poverty, criminality, and retardation.

Advances in mental testing soon resulted in systematic evaluation of inmates in various jailhouses, reformatories, and other correctional facilities. The findings of these evaluations led to the overwhelming conclusion that prostitutes, criminals, and perverts were mentally defective as they had lacked the cognitive ability necessary for self-control in order to exercise common decency. Women, who had children outside of wed-lock, were also viewed as mentally defective. Terman (1916) offered empirical evidence to explain the proclivity of those individuals toward socially undesirable behaviors. Given the overwhelming evidence provided especially by the genealogical students (the Jukes and Kallikaks) that linked intellectual disability with a host of social ills, proponents of eugenics, racism, sterilization, deportation, and stronger immigration control often cited those studies as justification for their positions. Unfortunately, these positions led to the formation of the American Breeders Association in 1904 which held that persons with intellectual functioning deficits were a real threat to a purity of the white race (Selden, 1999). Shortly after, massive sterilization of persons with intellectual disabilities was instituted to assure a pure race was sustained.

The work of Edgar Doll in the early 1900s offered the voice of reason. Doll (1953) illustrated the fact that social behavior contributed to the determination of intellectual disability. Doll, affiliated with the Vineland Institution in Vineland, New Jersey, authored *Vineland Social Maturity Scale* (Doll, 1936). A common thread of wisdom wove through his prolific works on the subject of intellectual disability. Doll (1953) frequently reminded his readers that "...., we have deliberately avoided over-refinement of definition for the simple reason that as a definition becomes more and more meticulously explicit, its application becomes correspondingly impractical" (p. 61), particularly with regard to defining intellectual disability. He cautioned his readers to view definitions of intellectual disability as less than absolute. Correspondingly, therefore, measures of an imprecise construct of intelligence are to be viewed as approximations rather than absolutes (Brody, 1992).

The 1954 high court ruling that ended segregation in schools on the basis of race in the landmark case *Brown v. Board of Education of Topeka*, Kansas, catapulted disability advocacy efforts to the foreground. Additionally, disability advocacy movements found traction in the civil rights era of the 1960s that coincided with several events. First was the election of John F. Kennedy as the president of the United States in 1960. His election provided a national stage for parents to realize that any family was just as likely as another to experience the impact of intellectual disability when the First Family announced that Kennedy's sister was born with intellectual disability and that she was favored just as much as any other member of the family. In a later election, Vice-President Hubert H. Humphrey followed suit with the acknowledgment that he had fathered a child with intellectual disability. His acknowledgment was broadcasted via television to the entire nation. It served as a significant impetus for families to lift their chins and stand by their offspring. Telephone and instantaneous communications facilitated the organization of parent groups and efforts to educate children with cognitive impairments in private facilities. At the same time, Blatt and Kaplan (1966) wrote *Christmas in Purgatory* that chronicled the deplorable conditions in institutions for persons with intellectual disabilities in the United States, along with the rising popularity of reformists ideals like Nirje's (1969) concept of normalization and Wolfensberger's (1972) social role valorization further fueled advocacy movement.

As the family movement gained ground and advocates for services began to surface, the role of parents morphed from subservient to enabled citizens. Parents began to tire of schools' stonewalling and denying children with intellectual disability a public education. Ultimately, the Pennsylvania Association for Retarded Children (PARC) filed a class-action suit against the Commonwealth of Pennsylvania. *PARC v Pennsylvania* (1972) ruled that tax dollars supporting public schools should benefit all citizens and that to deny access to public education for a child with intellectual disability was discriminatory, in much the same way as *Brown v. Board of Education* in 1954 about discriminating against African Americans. This litigation placed the burden of proof on the schools rather than the family. Also, it outlined key conditions to be provided to these families (e.g., child-find efforts, individualized education programs, right to access records of eligibility and placement meetings, right to counsel, etc.). Five years later, the Education of All Handicapped Children's Act was passed in 1975 that guaranteed access to education of all children, regardless of severity or nature of disabling conditions.

DEFINING INTELLECTUAL DISABILITIES

Defining intellectual disabilities is a complex process due to the many conditions which it is associated with (Rinardo, St. Peter, Rotatori, Day, & Carlson, 1991). Numerous definitions have been proposed over the past

70 years using a variety of focuses such as Tredgold's (1937) social incompetence; Doll's (1941) mental age; Kirk and Johnson's (1951) education; Benoit's (1959) physiology; Heber's (1961) emphasis on IQ score and/or adaptive behavior; Kolstoe's (1971) developmental aspects; Kidd's (1979) general functioning; Grossman's (1973, 1983) IQ score and adaptive functioning; Luckasson et al.'s (1992) less reliance on IQ and emphasis on adaptive behavior; Luckasson et al.'s (2002) systems of support; and Schalock et al.'s (2010) systems of support and name change from mental retardation to intellectual disability. Readers interested in the numerous debates, disagreements, agreements, confusion, societal influences, and diagnostic difficulty related to definitions of persons with intellectual disabilities should consult the following: Greenspan (1994); Heber (1970); Jacobson and Mulick (1992); Litton (1986); MacMillan, Gresham, and Siperstein (1993); Snell and Luckasson (2009); Switzky, Greenspan, and Granfield (1996); Utley and Obiakor (2003); and Zigler, Balla, and Hodapp (1984).

The most widely used definition has been developed by the AAIDD over the past 50 years. The early definitions (i.e., Heber, 1959, 1961) were described as being too inclusive due to cut-off scores being relatively high (IQ below 84) which resulted in many persons, especially minority individuals, being classified as intellectually disabled. This problem was eliminated by making the cut-off score to be classified as intellectually disabled much lower (IQ below 70) (Grossman, 1973, 1983). Then in 1992, the AAIDD emphasized the need for providing systems for supports for persons with intellectual disabilities and classified persons based on an IQ and adaptive behavior cut-off scores that are approximately two standard deviations from the normal mean of 100 (Luckasson et al., 1992, 2002). This systems approach emphasized the needs of individuals with intellectual disability rather their deficits (Utley & Obiakor, 2003). The current definition is similar to the 2002 AAIDD definition but it changed the term mental retardation to intellectual disability. In addition, the current definition is more operational as it includes three key components, namely "(a) the actual definition and the assumptions underlying it; (b) the use of cut-off scores to establish the construct's boundaries; and (c) the use of the assessment instrument's standard scores to establish a statistical confidence interval within which the person's true score falls" (AAIDD, 2009, p. 2). The 2010 AAIDD definition follows:

Intellectual disability is characterized by significant limitations both in intellectual functioning and adaptive behavior as expressed in conceptual, social, and practical skills. This disability originates before age 18. (p. 1)

Readers interested in a more comprehensive discussion of the AAIDD's systems of supports may wish to consult the following resources: Schalock, Luckasson, and Shogren (2007) and Thompson et al. (2009).

STRATEGIC EDUCATIONAL PROGRAMMING FOR STUDENTS WITH INTELLECTUAL DISABILITIES

Educational programming for persons with intellectual disabilities has made great strides in the last 25 years. Specifically, systematic instruction of students with severe intellectual disabilities has provided empirical data to illustrate that learning actually occurs (Snell, 1993). Optimal educational programs are generally community referenced or related to actual incidents that naturally occur in the environment. Clearly, the most useful learning activities are both functional and age appropriate. Because education is designed to enhance the student's ability to function successfully in a world inhabited largely by people without disabilities, it is important that instruction be delivered in integrated settings. Consider the following example. There is a difference between a person from Wisconsin who took a class in Spanish as a high school sophomore and a person from Wisconsin who spent his sophomore year as an exchange student in Spain. Although it is possible to learn about another culture without experiencing it firsthand, opportunities for learning are greatly enhanced through direct experience. There are four reasons that all school-aged children should be educated in the same settings (Brown et al., 1989). First, students without disabilities who are educated alongside students with disabilities are more likely to function as responsible adults in a pluralistic society. Second, integrated schools provide more meaningful instructional environments. Third, families have greater access to activities in neighborhood schools. Finally, integrated schools offer more opportunities to develop a wide range of social relationships. Integrated learning settings are as important for adults as they are for children. When teaching a person who has pronounced difficulties learning new information, it is very important to give the person every advantage. For adults, this means that job skills are better taught on the job and domestic skills are better taught in the person's home.

The determination of a curriculum is overwhelmingly important for learners with intellectual disabilities. Skills are typically found in the domains of communication, domestic, leisure, self-help, social/friendship, and voca-tional. Recently, self-determination skills have been added to best-practice curricula. The need to teach self-determination was first documented in the literature related to employment (Moon, Inge, Wehman, Brooke, & Barcus, 1990). Although persons with intellectual disabilities are able to complete requisite job skills, they are frequently dependent on their job coaches to "cue" them to begin and end tasks. The development of self-determination competencies challenges students to become actively involved in their learning and decision-making. Ultimately, self-determination and overall student empowerment improve the quality of students' adult lives. Increasing students' self-determination may increase their success in transitioning from high school to adult living.

THE USE OF ASSISTIVE TECHNOLOGY

"Assistive technology" is defined by the Technology-Related Assistance Act (Tech Act) of 1988 (P.L.100-407) and the Individuals with Disabilities Act (IDEA) of 1990 (P.L.101-476) as "any item, piece of equipment, or product system, whether acquired commercially off-the-shelf, modified, or customized, that is used to increase, maintain or improve the functional capabilities of individuals with disabilities." It can describe both devices and services that aid an individual. Assistive technology allows a person with disabilities (in this case, a person with intellectual disabilities) to become an integral part of the school or community (Hasselbring, 1998). Examples of commonly used assistive technology devices that illustrate the formal definition include positioning equipment, computer applications, adaptive toys and games, adaptive environments, mobility devices, home-made battery-powered toys, medical equipment, prostheses, electronic interfaces, and alternative and augmentative communication aids (Parette, Brotherson, Hourcade, & Bradley, 1996). There are two purposes of assistive technology. First, technology can augment an individual's strengths by counterbalancing the effects of a disability; and second, it can provide alternative methods for performing a task so that disabilities can be compensated for or bypassed entirely (Lewis, 1998). For example, an individual with difficulties in reading who possesses good listening skills can listen to books on tape rather than reading the print version. Persons with poor computational skills but with good fine-motor skills may use a handheld calculator. Those with poor spelling abilities but with a measure of computer literacy may write with a word processor that offers assistance in spelling.

To determine the type of technology or support a particular student may need, it is critical to address the issues of individual needs and differences. Applying technology involves matching the individual's exhibited needs with the potential benefits possible through the rise of the technology (Parette & Murdick, 1998). In addition, less emphasis should be placed on the categorization of the devices as being low or high tech. By considering that students with disabilities possess individual interests, strengths, and weaknesses, one may conclude that a device appropriate for one person may be inappropriate for another. In a similar way, a device that may assist in one setting may be inappropriate in a different situation or environment (Bryant, Erin, Lock, Allan, & Resta, 1998). Once individual needs have been targeted and appropriate technology has been applied, then the technology has the potential to provide a variety of needs for a person with a disability, such as intellectual disabilities.

Instructional modifications include changes to teaching procedures, curricula, management materials and technology, and the physical environment to facilitate learning (Bryant & Bryant, 1998). Specifically, assistive technology may require simple, low-tech modifications. Off-the-shelf technologies can become adaptive when they are used to enhance the learning of a student with an intellectual disability (Lewis, 1998). For example, an audiotape becomes assistive when it is used to compensate for an individual's memory or note-taking problems. In addition, low-tech modifications, such as sticky notes, flags, and highlighters, can enhance a student's organizational skills. Such modifications require minimal time and training to be implemented in the classroom. Simple and uncomplicated modifications are sometimes all that are needed to allow a student to use a computer software program (Olson & Platt, 2000). Standard computer keyboards pose a number of problems for some students with intellectual disabilities (Kincaid, 1999). Various modifications may need to be considered so that students with limited hand and finger mobility can access computer technology. Before a student can use computer technology for a given task, an appropriate method for inputting information must be available.

To a large measure, word processing has the capability of helping individuals improve their writing skills (MacArthur, 1996). Students with intellectual disabilities often possess limited conceptualization of editing and revising; thus such students limit their revision to minor errors that fail to strengthen a written document as a whole. Therefore, using word processor may not only teach students who are intellectually delayed to edit their writing better, but also can help them to make frequent revisions without labored rewriting. Word processing reduces resistance to revising as a whole and eliminates errors due to transcription (MacArthur, Graham, & Schwartz, 1991). In addition, it has the potential to facilitate other operational revisions such as moving content and deleting material.

It has been proven that computers can help young children with intellectual disabilities develop language (MacArthur, 1996). The goal of any language development program is to provide young children with the tools for independent communication. Some children will learn to speak, some will learn sign language, and others will need the assistance of augmentative communication. Augmentative communication refers to a set of approaches used to improve the communication skills of persons who do not speak or whose speech is not intelligible (Olson & Platt, 2000). Aided systems require the use of a picture or word board, a notebook, or a computerized aid. An unaided system requires the individual to use only hand or body motions to communicate (e.g., sign language). Augmentative communication options can range from high- to low-tech devices, including aids such as a symbol system, electronic communication devices, speech synthesizers, and communication enhancement software. Communication boards, a low-tech alternative to augmentative communication, assist young children in language expression. Communication boards are usually made of cardboard or another material used to display choices for children who cannot speak (Ysseldyke & Algozzine, 1990). A more comprehensive discussion of assistive technology utilization for individuals with intellectual disability appears in the following sources: Nkabinde (2008); Romanski and Sevcik (1997); and St. Peter, Morris, and Murdock (1987).

ASSESSMENT

According to the latest edition of *Diagnostic and Statistical Manual of Mental Disorders* (DSM-IV) (American Psychiatric Association, 2000), three criteria must be met for a diagnosis of intellectual disabilities: an IQ below 70, significant limitations in two or more areas of adaptive behavior as measured by an adaptive behavior rating scale (i.e., communication, self-help skills, interpersonal skills, and more), and evidence that the limitations became apparent before the age of 18 years.

The first English-language IQ test, the Terman–Binet, was adapted from an instrument used to measure potential to achieve developed by Binet in France. Terman translated the test and employed it as a means to measure intellectual capacity based on oral language, vocabulary, numerical

Table 1. Categories Based on IQ.

Class	IQ
Profound mental retardation	Below 20
Severe mental retardation	20–34
Moderate mental retardation	35–49
Mild mental retardation	50–69
Borderline intellectual functioning	70–84

Source: http://en.wikipedia.org/wiki/Mental_retardation

reasoning, memory, motor speed, and analysis skills. The mean score on the currently available IQ tests is 100, with a standard deviation of 15 (WAIS/WISC-IV) or 16 (Stanford–Binet). Subaverage intelligence is generally considered to be present when an individual scores two standard deviations below the test mean. Factors other than intellectual ability (depression, anxiety, etc.) can contribute to low IQ scores. It is very important for the evaluator to rule other factors out prior to concluding that measured IQ is "significantly below average." See Table 1 for categories based on IQ.

Because the diagnosis also includes a person's adaptive functioning and not only based on IQ scores, the diagnosis based on IQ is not made rigidly. It encompasses intellectual scores (from an IQ test), adaptive functioning scores (from an adaptive behavior rating scale based on descriptions of known abilities provided by someone familiar with the person), and also the observations of the assessment examiner who is able to find out directly from the person what he or she can understand, communicate, and the like. In regards to adaptive behavior to be classified with intellectual disabilities, one must have significant limitations in two or more areas of adaptive behavior (i.e., communication, self-care, home living, social skills, community use, self-direction, health and safety, functional academics, leisure, and work).

Adaptive behaviors are everyday living skills, such as walking, talking, getting dressed and going to school, going to work, preparing a meal, and cleaning the house. They are skills that a person learns in the process of adapting to his/her surroundings. Since adaptive behaviors are for the most part developmental, it is possible to describe a person's adaptive behavior as an age-equivalent score. An average 5-year-old, for example, would be expected to have adaptive behavior similar to that of other 5 year olds.

Behavior problems, often called maladaptive behaviors, are behaviors that interfere with everyday activities. Good adaptive behavior and a lack of behavior problems promote independence at home, at school, and in the community. Behavior problems are much more difficult to quantify than adaptive behaviors are, because they are not very developmental and because their expression varies more from day to day and from setting to setting. Behavior problems do not increase or decrease steadily with age. Nevertheless they can be measured reliably. To be diagnosed with an intellectual disability, it is necessary to have significant below-average deficits in both IQ and adaptive functioning.

FAMILIES

The family plays a large role in regards to a child with an intellectual disability. Whether it is social, care, or support, the family is essential and needed for those with intellectual disabilities. The family also can go through a lot when they have a child with an intellectual disability. Families often get mixed messages. Many people expect families live their lives by pretending that their child's significant intellectual disability does not exist. On the one hand, there are the messages about normalization, independence, community inclusion, and self-determination. Families of individuals with a significant intellectual disability do not have the same "punctuation marks" nudging them along to recognize their child's increasing competence as their son or daughter moves from being a child to an adult. This section will address the family and some of the issues.

Family Care

Research has shown that family care-taking accounts for over 80% of the support provided people with intellectual disability and that family care remains the predominant type of support until middle age (Hassall, Rose, & McDonald, 2005). There needs to be a greater depth of understanding and empathy for the needs of family care-givers than they have at present. Accounts of families' experiences frequently contain examples of unsympathetic and unhelpful interventions from professionals, which may add further to family stress. Families vary enormously both from one another and over time; the emphasis should therefore be on understanding processes rather than categorical facts and generalizations. Families need support and should be helped to understand what their son or daughter with an intellectual disability is capable of doing socially and academically. Knowing the correct information is half the battle.

Historical Perspectives

Until the 1950s, the focus was mainly on maternal reactions to the birth of a child with an intellectual impairment. The birth of a child with a disability was seen as a tragedy for the family, without hope of resolution or adaptation, a view that stigmatized the child, the mother, and the family. Within this context, institutional care was seen as a way of preventing the child disabling the family. Putting the child into an institution was accepted and viewed positively. Such views are unacceptable now, but they illustrate that the early research into family functioning was based on a pathological model of adaptation, and that inferred maternal psychological reactions were equated to family functioning. Mitigating or mediating factors within the family or society were not felt to be relevant, given the tragic nature of the birth, thus ignoring the positive adaptations that families made. Families were not even given the chance to bond nor were they invited to. Many parents missed out on raising their son or daughter because society dictated that having the child at home or going to public school was not a viable option for them.

Family Systems Theory

In the 1970s, family research moved away from models of individual pathology with the development of family systems theory. The family was seen as an interacting set of relationships, both between the members of the family and with the wider society. This changed the focus to an interactional, and subsequently more complex, model of family functioning. It also allowed for the development of ideas about family life cycle in relation to disability and changes over time as opposed to the static individual pathology model. Research developed into areas, such as stress, coping mechanisms, support networks, effects on siblings, other family members, and the families of adults with a disability. Today, children with intellectual disabilities unusually stay with their parents and there are structures in place so that they may grow and develop to the best of their abilities within the family structure.

CONCLUSION

Throughout cross-cultural history, social disregard for persons with intellectual limitations has often stripped them of human dignity and reduced them to beg for resources ("handouts in their cap") to sustain themselves. Other times in history, they were used as cheap street entertainers with little to no agency and as human beings were defined entirely by their handicap. The complexity of the lives of such individuals was completely blurred through the act of single-mindedly focusing on their cognitive deficits. However, as a society today, we distinguish between disabilities and handicaps, with disability being the presence of an impairment that makes life accomplishments more challenging in contexts that are devoid of accommodations, and handicaps being the perception of functional limitations of the persons with disabilities. Also, society recognizes the importance of the emerging field of infant mental health for children with intellectual disability (Holtz & Fox, 2008); the psychiatric needs of persons with intellectual disability (Poindexter, Bihm, & Litton, 1996); the emotional counseling needs of the individuals and their families (Litton, 1986; Rotatori, Schwenn, & Litton, 1995); the health benefits that result from designing weight-reduction programs for those individuals who suffer from obesity (Rotatori & Fox, 1981, 1989); the importance of assisting them with issues related to death and dying (Miller & Rotatori, 1986); the necessity to educate them to avoid sexual abuse (Rappaport, Burkhardt, & Rotatori, 1997); the value related to enhancing their self-determinism in the academic curriculum (Bakken & Parette, 2008); critical need to develop post-secondary training programs (Obi & Obi, 2008); and the essence in preparing them for retirement (Dykema-Engblade & Stawiski, 2008). The historical reduction of the individual with intellectual difference to "a comedic fool" for pleasure and entertainment is perhaps best illustrated in the longest-running Warner Brothers creation of the cartoon character, Elmer Fudd. Elmer Fudd's cartoon character demonstrated an ineptitude, which portrayed him as being disabled, although his condition was a speech impediment. Under the façade of impaired language, Fudd displayed poor mental judgment and perpetuated the belief that all disabilities were rooted in mental deficiency. More to the point of historical events and influences on intellectual disability, the Three Stooges' advent on the big screen in theaters then gravitated into individual homes through television. Their media presence relied on demeaning commentary and juvenile humor. One could argue that these comedians provided the catalyst to bring about changes in professional terminology as it related to persons with intellectual disability. However, we use these contemporary examples from popular culture as a prologue that point to how closely history mirrored unexamined and often unsubstantiated beliefs about persons with intellectual disabilities. Additionally, it ushers the issue of language and terminology that has evolved over the years regarding intellectual disabilities that has ranged from imbecile, idiot, feeble-minded, and/or moron and the ebb and flow of that history has also similarly carried with it specific attitudes about people with intellectual disability at particular points in history.

REFERENCES

AAIDD. (2009). *Frequently asked questions on the AAIDD 11th edition of intellectual disability: Definitions, classification, and systems of supports.* Washington, DC: American Association on Intellectual and Developmental Disability.

American Psychiatric Association. (2000). *Diagnostic and statistical manual of mental disorders* (4th ed.). Arlington, VA: Author.

Bakken, J. P., & Parette, H. P. (2008). Self-determination and persons with developmental disabilities. In: A. F. Rotatori, F. E. Obiakor & S. Burkhardt (Eds), *Autism and developmental disabilities: Current practices and issues* (Vol. 18, pp. 21–234). Bingley, UK: Emerald Group Publishing Limited.

Benoit, E. P. (1959). Toward a new definition of mental retardation. *American Journal of Mental Deficiency, 67*, 56.

Blatt, B., & Kaplan, F. (1966). *Christmas in purgatory.* Boston: Allyn and Bacon.

Brody, N. (1992). *Intelligence.* San Diego, CA: Academic Press.

Brown v. Board of Education. (1954). 347 U.S. Supreme Court 485.

Brown, L. E., Udavari-Solner, A., Davis, L., Van Devon, P., Ahlgren, C., Johnson, F., Gruenewald, L., & Jorgensen, J. (1989). The home school: Why students with severe intellectual disabilities must attend the schools of their brothers, sisters, friends and neighbors. *Journal for the Association of Persons with Severe Handicaps, 14*(1), 1–7.

Bryant, D. P., & Bryant, B. R. (1998). Using assistive technology to enhance the skills of student with learning disabilities. *Intervention in School and Clinic, 34*(1), 53.

Bryant, D. P., Erin, J., Lock, R., Allan, J. M., & Resta, P. E. (1998). Infusing a teacher preparation program in learning disabilities with assistive technology. *Journal of Learning Disabilities, 31*, 55–66.

Davis, L. J. (1995). *Enforcing normalcy: Disability, deafness and the body.* London: Verso.

Doll, E. A. (1936). *The Vineland Social Maturity Scale.* Minneapolis, MN: American Guidance Service, Inc.

Doll, E. A. (1941). Definitions of mental retardation. *Training School Bulletin, 37*, 163–164.

Doll, E. A. (1953). *The measurement of social competence.* Educational Test Bureau, Educational Publishers.

Down, L. (1887). *Mental affections of children and youth.* London: J & A Churchill.

Dugdale, R. (1910). *The Jukes: A study in crime, pauperism, disease, and heredity.* New York: G.P. Putnam.

Dykema-Engblade, A., & Stawiski, S. (2008). Employment and retirement concerns for persons with developmental disabilities. In: A. F. Rotatori, F. E. Obiakor & S. Burkhardt (Eds), *Autism and developmental disabilities: Current practices and issues* (Vol. 18, pp. 253–272). Bingley, UK: Emerald Group Publishing Limited.

Goddard, H. H. (1912). *The Kallikak family: A study in the hereditary of feeble mindedness.* New York: MacMillan.

Gould, S. J. (1981). *The mismeasure of man.* New York: Norton & Company.

Greenspan, S. (1994). Review of Luckasson et al. effort to redefine mental retardation. *Journal of Mental Retardation, 98,* 544–549.

Grossman, H. J. (Ed.) (1973). *Manual on terminology and classification on mental retardation* (Rev. ed.). Washington, DC: American Association on Mental Deficiency.

Grossman, H. J. (Ed.) (1983). *Classification in mental retardation.* Washington, DC: American Association on Mental Deficiency.

Hassall, R., Rose, J., & McDonald, J. (2005). Parenting stress in mothers of children with an intellectual disability: The effects of parental cognitions in relation to child characteristics and family support. *Journal of Intellectual Disability Research, 49,* 405–418.

Hasselbring, T. S. (1998). *The future of special education and the role of technology* [Outline]. Available at http://peabody.vanderbilt.edu/ltc/hasselbringt/future.html

Heber, R. (1959). A manual on terminology and classification in mental retardation. *American Journal on Mental Deficiency,* Monograph Supplement 64.

Heber, R. (1961). A manual on terminology and classification in mental retardation (Rev. ed.). *American Journal on Mental Retardation,* Monograph Supplement 64.

Heber, R. (1970). *Epidemiology of mental retardation.* Springfield, IL: Charles C. Thomas.

Herrnstein, R. J., & Murray, C. (1994). *The bell curve: Intelligence and class structure in American life.* New York: Free Press.

Holtz, C. A., & Fox, R. A. (2008). Infant mental health: An emerging field for children with developmental disabilities. In: A. F. Rotatori, F. E. Obiakor & S. Burkhardt (Eds), *Autism and developmental disabilities: Current practices and issues* (Vol. 18, pp. 163–219). Bingley, UK: Emerald Group Publishing Limited.

Individuals with Disabilities Education Act Amendments of 1990 (P.L. 104-476). Washington, DC: U.S. Government Printing Office.

Jacobson, J. W., & Mulick, J. A. (1992). A new definition of MR or a new definition of practice?. *Psychology in Mental Retardation and Developmental Disabilities, 18,* 9–14.

Kidd, J. W. (1979). An open letter to the committee on terminology and classification of AAMD from the committee on definition and terminology of CEC-MR. *Education and Training of the Mentally Retarded, 14,* 74–76.

Kincaid, C. (1999). Alternative keyboards. *Exceptional Parent, 29*(2), 34–37.

Kirk, S. A., & Johnson, G. O. (1951). *Educating the retarded child.* Boston: Houghton Mifflin.

Kolstoe, O. P. (1971). Defining mental retardation. In: E. H. Williams, J. F. Magary & F. A. Moored (Eds), *Ninth annual distinguished lecture series in special education and rehabilitation.* Los Angeles: University of Southern California.

Lewis, R. B. (1998). Assistive technology and learning disabilities: Today's realities and tomorrow's promises. *Journal of Learning Disabilities, 31*(1), 16–26.

Litton, F. (1986). Counseling the mentally retarded. In: A. F. Rotatori, P. J. Gerber, F. W. Litton & R. A. Fox (Eds), *Counseling exceptional students* (pp. 78–98). New York: Human Sciences Press, Inc.

Luckasson, R., Coulter, D. L., Polloway, E. A., Reiss, S., Schalock, R. I., Snell, M. E., Spitalnik, D. M., & Stark, J. A. (1992). *Mental retardation: Definition, classification, and systems of support* (9th ed.). Washington, DC: American Association on Mental Deficiency.

Luckasson, R., Schalock, R. I., Spitalnik, D. M., Spreat, S., Tass, M., Snell, M. E., Coulter, D. I., Borthwick-Duffy, S. A., Reeve, A. A., Buntinx, W., & Craig, P. (2002). *Mental retardation: Definitions, classifications and systems of support* (10th ed.). Washington, DC: American Association on Intellectual and Developmental Disabilities.

MacArthur, C. A. (1996). Using technology to enhance the writing processes of student with learning disabilities. *Journal of Learning Disabilities, 29*(4), 344–354.

MacArthur, C. A., Graham, S., & Schwartz, S. (1991). Knowledge of revision and revising behaviors among students with learning disabilities. *Learning Disability Quarterly, 14*, 61–73.

MacMillan, D. L., Gresham, F. M., & Siperstein, G. N. (1993). Conceptual and psychometric concerns over the 1992 AAMR definition of mental retardation. *American Journal of Mental Retardation, 98*, 325–335.

McCaughey, T. J., & Strohmer, D. C. (2005). Prototypes as an indirect measure of attitudes towards disability groups. *Rehabilitation Counseling Bulletin, 44*, 3–9.

Miller, J., & Rotatori, A. F. (1986). *Death education and the educator.* Springfield, IL: Charles C. Thomas.

Moon, M. S., Inge, K. J., Wehman, P., Brooke, V., & Barcus, J. M. (1990). *Helping persons with severe mental retardation get and keep employment. Supported employment issues and strategies.* Baltimore: Paul H. Brookes.

Nirje, B. (1969). The normalization principle and its human management implications. In: R. B. Kugel & W. Wolfensberger (Eds), *Changing patterns in residential services for the mentally retarded* (pp. 179–195). Washington, DC: President's Committee on Mental Retardation.

Nkabinde, Z. (2008). Using assistive technology to educate students with developmental disabilities and autism. In: A. F. Rotatori, F. E. Obiakor & S. Burkhardt (Eds), *Autism and developmental disabilities: Current practices and issues* (Vol. 18, pp. 273–285). Bingley, UK: Emerald Group Publishing Limited.

Obi, S. O., & Obi, S. L. (2008). Post-secondary planning for students with developmental disabilities. In: A. F. Rotatori, F. E. Obiakor & S. Burkhardt (Eds), *Autism and developmental disabilities: Current practices and issues* (Vol. 18, pp. 235–251). Bingley, UK: Emerald Group Publishing Limited.

Olson, J. L., & Platt, J. M. (2000). *Teaching children and adolescents with special needs.* Upper Saddle River, NJ: Merrill.

Parette, H. P., Brotherson, M. J., Hourcade, J. J., & Bradley, R. H. (1996). Family-centered assistive technology assessment. *Interventions in School & Clinic, 32*, 104–112.

Parette, H. P., & Murdick, N. L. (1998). Assistive technology and IEP's for young children with disabilities. *Early Childhood Education Journal, 25*(30), 193–197.

Pennsylvania Association for Retarded Children v Commonwealth of Pennsylvania 334 F. Supp. 279 (E.D. PA 1972).

Poindexter, A. R., Bihm, E. M., & Litton, F. W. (1996). Dual diagnosis and severe behavior problems. In: A. F. Rotatori, J. O. Schwenn & S. Burkhardt (Eds), *Assessment and psychopathology issues in special education* (Vol. 10, pp. 87–96). London: JAI Press Ltd.

Rappaport, S., Burkhardt, S., & Rotatori, A. F. (1997). *Child sexual abuse curriculum for the developmentally disabled*. Springfield, IL: Charles C. Thomas.

Rinardo, J., St. Peter, S., Rotatori, A. F., Day, G., & Carlson, J. (1991). Mental retardation. In: J. O. Schwenn, A. F. Rotatori & R. A. fox (Eds), *Understanding students with high incidence exceptionalities: Categorical and noncategorical perspectives* (pp. 102–152). Springfield, IL: Charles C. Thomas.

Romanski, M. A., & Sevcik, R. A. (1997). Augmentative and alternative communication for children with developmental disabilities. *Mental Retardation and Developmental Disabilities Research Reviews, 3*, 363–368.

Rotatori, A. F., & Fox, R. A. (1981). *Behavioral weight reduction program for mentally handicapped persons: A self-control approach*. Baltimore: University Park Press.

Rotatori, A. F., & Fox, A. R. (1989). *Obesity in children and youth*. Springfield, IL: Charles C. Thomas.

Rotatori, A. F., Schwenn, J. O., & Litton, F. W. (1995). *Counseling special populations: Research and practice perspectives* (Vol. 10). Greenwich, CT: JAI Press Ltd.

Schalock, R. L., Luckasson, R. A., & Shogren, K. A. (2007). The renaming of mental retardation: Understanding the change to the term intellectual disability. *Intellectual and Developmental Disabilities, 45*(2), 116–124.

Schalock, R. L., Borthwick-Duffy, S. A., Buntinx, W. H. E., Coulter, D. L., & Craig, E. M. (2010). *Intellectual disability: Definition, classification, and systems of supports* (11th ed.). Washington, DC: American Association on Intellectual and Developmental Disabilities.

Scheerenberger, R. C. (1983). *A history of mental retardation*. Baltimore: Paul H. Brookes.

Selden, S. (1999). *Inheriting shame: The story of eugenics and racism in America*. New York: Teachers College Press.

Snell, M. E. (1993). *Instruction of students with severe disabilities* (4th ed.). New York: Macmillan.

Snell, M. E., & Luckasson, R. A. (2009). Characteristics and needs of people with intellectual disability who have higher IQs. *Intellectual and Developmental Disabilities, 47*(3), 220–233.

St. Peter, S., Morris, P., & Murdock, J. (1987). Computer applications in special education. In: A. F. Rotatori, M. M. Banbury & R. A. Fox (Eds), *Issues in special education* (pp. 187–203). Mountain View, CA: Mayfield Publishing Company.

Switzky, H., Greenspan, S., & Granfield, J. (1996). Adaptive behavior, everyday intelligence and the constitutive definition of mental retardation. In: A. F. Rotatori, J. O. Schwenn & S. Burkhardt (Eds), *Assessment and psychopathology issues in special education* (pp. 1–24). London: JAI Press Inc.

Technology-Related Assistance Act of 1988 (P.L. 100-407). Washington, DC: U.S. Government Printing Office.

Terman, L. (1916). *The measurement of intelligence*. Boston: Houghton Mifflin.

Thompson, J., Bradley, V. I., Buntinx, W. H. E., Schalock, R. L., Shogren, K. A., Snell, M. E., & Wehmeyer, M. I. (2009). Conceptualizing supports and the support needs of people with intellectual disability. *Intellectual and Developmental Disabilities, 47*(2), 135–146.

Tomlinson, T. (2005). *Head masters: Phrenology, secular education, and nineteenth-century social thought*. Tuscaloosa, AL: University of Alabama Press.

Tredgold, A. F. (1937). *A textbook on mental deficiency*. Baltimore: William Wood.

Utley, C. A., & Obiakor, F. E. (2003). Educating students with cognitive disabilities. In: F. E. Obiakor, C. A. Utley & A. F. Rotatori (Eds), *Effective education for learners with exceptionalities* (Vol. 15, pp. 77–98). London: Elsevier Science Ltd.

Wolfensberger, W. (1972). *The principle of normalization in human services.* Toronto: National Institute on Mental Retardation.

Ysseldyke, J. E., & Algozzine, B. (1990). *Introduction to special education.* Boston: Houghton Mifflin.

Zigler, E., Balla, D., & Hodapp, R. (1984). On the definition and classification of mental retardation. *American Journal of Mental Retardation, 89,* 215–230.

CHAPTER 6

THE HISTORY OF SPEECH AND LANGUAGE IMPAIRMENTS

Satasha L. Green and Christine M. Scott

EARLY BEGINNINGS

Writings about language and speech impairments (SLI) have been present for many centuries (Smith, 2004). Unfortunately, early historical accounts tended to reflect negatively upon individuals with SLI. For example, Van Riper and Erickson (1996) related that during the Roman times, an individual who stuttered was placed into a cage for entertainment purposes. According to these authors, citizens passing would throw coins into the person's cage to get him to talk. During the late 1800s, the profession of speech-language pathology began as an avocation of certain professionals, notably doctors, educators, and elocutionists (public speakers), who were interested in helping others improve their speech. American doctors studied under the auspices of European doctors who treated people with communication disorders. The two most common disorders that were treated then were dysfluency (stuttering) and speech sound errors (articulation) (Duchan, 2002). Treatment was available for the above disorders, however, the programs were not in public schools and the results of intervention were mixed (Smith, 2004).

History of Special Education
Advances in Special Education, Volume 21, 119–149
Copyright © 2011 by Emerald Group Publishing Limited
All rights of reproduction in any form reserved
ISSN: 0270-4013/doi:10.1108/S0270-4013(2011)0000021009

U.S. public school classes were first organized in 1896 and children who were typical residents of asylums were now placed into the public school system. A few years later, public schools started services for students with mild SLI. Historically, students with mild/moderate SLI in the elementary grades received intervention from a variety of service providers (i.e., speech correctionists, speech specialists, or speech teachers) (Whitmire, Spinello, & Clausen, 2002). For example, the Chicago public schools provided SLI services via an itinerant teacher for students with fluency problems in 1910 (see Moore & Kester, 1953). Then in 1913, the New York public schools initiated a speech intervention program for students with moderate to mild speech impairments (Smith, 2004). Unfortunately, societal barriers became obstacles for students with more severe SLI which prevented them from receiving equal public school intervention services. This population of students received services in private schools, institutions, or clinics. (Whitmire et al., 2002).

Organizations, societies, and associations dedicated to the advocacy of students with SLI began as early as the late 18th century and special clinics for students with speech, language, and voice disorders were initiated in the early 19th century. During this era, organizations and scientists began to focus their studies on speech, hearing, and language disorders. For example, the first professional American journal regarding speech disorders, *The Voice*, was published from 1879 to 1892 by Edgar Werner, who was a stutterer (Duchan, 2002).

In 1891, Freud wrote his first book on aphasia. Aphasia is an acquired communication disorder, usually from a stroke or head injury, that impairs a person's ability to process language. It impairs the ability to speak and/or understand others (National Aphasia Association, 2010). Freud's book which was a study of speech and language disorders led to a series of studies on this topic (Gay, 1988).

MODERN TIMES

By the early 1900s, self-proclaimed speech correctionists began to form their own organizations (Duchan, 2002) as no certifying organization existed for the profession at that time. In 1918, teachers who were members of the National Education Association (NEA) formed the National Society for the Study and Correction of Speech Disorders, a subgroup of the NEA. Seven years later, the American Academy of Speech Correction (AASC) (currently the American Speech-Language-Hearing Association – ASHA) was established by scholars, doctors, and school administrators. The formation of the AASC was headed by Robert West, a professor at the University of Wisconsin who is considered to be the "father of the field" (see Van Riper, 1981). West received his doctoral degree at the University of Wisconsin in the newly established speech pathology department. In addition to his work in establishing AASC, West and his colleagues wrote a classic textbook on speech pathology, titled *The Rehabilitation of Speech: A Textbook of Diagnostic and Corrective Procedures* (West, Kennedy, & Carr, 1937).

West was greatly influenced to study in this field by Smiley Blanton who was the director of the first U.S. speech clinic at the University of Wisconsin. The clinic, which was established in 1914, was called the "Speech and Mental Hygiene Clinic." Blanton combined his medical and psychoanalytic training to create counseling and family therapy interventions for children and adults with stuttering, voice, and articulation disorders. With his wife, Margaret, he wrote a number of influential books on speech training such as *Speech Training for Children: The Hygiene of Speech* (Blanton & Blanton, 1919) and *For Stutterers* (Blanton & Blanton, 1936).

Many organizations, agencies, and institutions developed treatment and rehabilitation services for individuals with hearing impairments and speech and language disorders. These entities were direct service providers, information resource centers, and advocates for individuals with speech and language disorders (Maryland Speech-Language-Hearing Association, 2010). For example, the Department of Otolaryngology at The University of Iowa was founded in 1922. The department's Head and Neck Surgery Center develops and delivers treatment and rehabilitation for individuals with SLI and diseases of the head and neck. The department is among the oldest in the country and one of the most comprehensive in the world (University of Iowa Health Care, 2010). Similarly, the Hearing and Speech Agency (2010), founded in 1926, is a private, nonprofit organization in Maryland dedicated to meeting the speech, language, and hearing needs of children and adults of the state. The agency provides direct services and serves as an information resource for its clients (Hearing and Speech Agency, 2010).

Lee Travis and Wendell Johnson were other significant founders in SLI who engaged in extensive research on stuttering at the University of Iowa starting in the early 1930s. Travis carried out research that supported his cerebral dominance theory of stuttering which hypothesized that a lack of brain dominance resulted in stuttering symptoms (see Travis, 1931,

1934, 1946). In contrast, Johnson examined the importance of a stutterer's thoughts, attitudes, beliefs, and feelings. His work led to considerable information on the nature of stuttering especially why stuttering starts. An excellent example of his ideas can be found in *People in Quandaries: The Semantics of Personal Adjustment* (Johnson, 1946).

Another factor in the growth of SLI services was the development of screening procedures by the federal government to identity military recruits with speech and hearing problems during World War II (Smith, 2004). These efforts led to successful clinical and research programs that demonstrated the effectiveness of therapy (Smith, 2004). When World War II ended, the knowledge base gained from these clinical and research programs was incorporated into the training of speech-language pathologists (SLPs) at universities across the country. Soon after, SPL were employed in greater numbers to provide services to students with mild SLI to correct problems such as stuttering, voice, and articulation problems. This service increased and the training of SLPs continued throughout the 1950s and 1960s. Some of the cost for these services and training were supported by federal and state personnel training and assistance grants (i.e., Training of Professional Personnel Act of 1959 – Public Law 86-158, Elementary and Secondary Education Act of 1965 – Public Law 89-10; State Schools Act of 1965 – Public Law 89-313, Handicapped Children's Early Education Assistance Act – Public law 90-538) (see Carpenter, Hutchings, MacFarlane, & Richard, 2010; Nisbet, 1994).

A historical analysis of educating individuals with SLI reveals that while there were many advocates for this population, they were often not ardent proponents of a quality education for this population of students. These advocates believed that students with SLI especially those with more severe SLI were intellectually inferior and would not benefit from formal schooling. Instead, they placed a greater emphasis on education for this population that involved learning basic fundamentals of daily living and survival skills. Therefore, a large percentage of individuals with SLI remained unidentified and/or inadequately educated (Whitmire et al., 2002) prior to the 1950s. In spite of the slow response and effort by federal and state agencies to adequately educate students with SLI, these students gradually gained access to rudimentary education in the 1950s and 1960s. These gains were due to the communal efforts by SLI organizations, parents, and adult individuals with disabilities to educate their children and to fight for equal educational opportunities for them.

DEFINING SPEECH AND LANGUAGE IMPAIRMENTS

Special education personnel consider a communication disorder as "a disorder in speech, hearing, and/or language" (Kirk, Gallagher, Anastasiow, & Coleman, 2006, p. 260). St. Peter and Rotatori (1991) indicated that historically language impairments have been divided into two groups, namely, speech disorders and language disorders. However, each group is further broken into more specific deficits. Traditionally, speech disorders encompass the following problems: articulation (i.e., substitutions, distortion, omissions, additions); fluency (i.e., stuttering); and voice (i.e., vocal quality, pitch, intonation). Language disorders, however, encompass problems in the following areas: form (phonology, morphology, syntax); content (semantics); and function (pragmatics).

The Individuals with Disability Education Act (IDEA, 1990) states that "individuals with speech and language disorders exhibit problems in communication and related areas such as oral motor functioning that adversely affect educational performance. A speech disorder is the impairment of the articulation of speech sounds, fluency, and/or voice. A language disorder is the impairment of communication and/or use of spoken, written, and/or other symbol systems."

As a means of clarifying and identifying students with speech and language impairments for service delivery purposes, ASHA formed a committee in 1993. This committee published a detailed definition of communication disorder which stated that "A communication disorder is impairment in the ability to receive, send, process, and comprehend concepts of verbal, nonverbal, and graphic symbol systems. A communication disorder may be evident in the processing of hearing, language, and/or speech. A communication disorder may range in severity from mild to profound. It may be developmental or acquired. Individuals may demonstrate one or any combination of communication disorders. A communication disorder may result in a primary disability or it may be secondary to other disabilities" (ASHA, 1993, p. 40). The committee further defined the following: a speech disorder (articulation, fluency, voice); a language disorder (form, content, function); a hearing disorder (deaf, hard of hearing); central auditory processing disorders; and communication variations (communication difference/dialect, augmentative/alternative communication systems) (see ASHA, 1993). In terms of best practice, the ASHA definition has prevailed and is used across the country to identify and classify students with SLI.

LEGISLATIVE ACTS AND SERVICE DELIVERY TO STUDENTS WITH SLI

The service delivery for students with SLI changed with the passage of several legislation (see Tables 1 and 2) and civil rights act for individuals with disabilities starting in the 1970s (see Fleischer & Zames, 2001; Wright & Wright, 2006). Initially, service delivery for students with SLI provided intervention outside of the classroom either in one-to-one sessions or with a small group of students with similar SLI. As stated earlier, most of the students served had mild SLI such as articulation problems. However research revealed that there was a developmental factor that coincided with the occurrence of articulation problems and as the child matured the problems were corrected naturally (Smith, 2004). This factor combined with the right for all handicapped students to receive education in the least restrictive environment resulted in a change in the priority of serving students with SLI. First, SLP began to serve students with more significant SLI problems and students with severe SLI problems who were educated in private schools or institutions could now attend public schools and receive speech and language intervention. These aspects lead to a hierarchy of SLP service delivery which is displayed in Table 3. Since the majority of students with SLI are served in the general classroom, the SLP's role has become much more collaborative and consultative in scope (see Wegner, Grosche, & Edmister, 2003). According to Sparks and Hale (2000), this new role focuses on identifying "how the child's language can influence learning and in

Table 1.   Progression of IDEA Legislation.

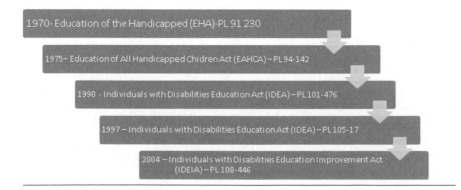

1970- Education of the Handicapped (EHA)-PL 91 230

1975– Education of All Handicapped Chidren Act (EAHCA) – PL 94-142

1990 - Individuals with Disabilities Education Act (IDEA) – PL 101-476

1997 – Individuals with Disabilities Education Act (IDEA) – PL 105-17

2004 – Individuals with Disabilities Education Improvement Act (IDEIA) – PL 108-446

Table 2. Specifics of Education Legislation.

EAHCA
- Provided the minimum requirements to receive federal funds for SPED services and became foundation of today's SPED services
  - Free and appropriate education (FAPE)
  - Least restrictive environment (LRE)
- Individual education plans (IEPs) initiated
- Procedural safeguards for parents established
- Early intervention of preschool

IDEA 1990
- *People first* language introduced
- Inclusion model implemented
- Traumatic brain injury (TBI) & Autism – new categories added
- Assistive technology may be added to the IEP

IDEA 1997 amendments
- Focus changed from access to accountability, due to lack of students' progress
  - IEP goals are to be curriculum-based
  - Special education students are to be included in district- and state-wide assessments
    - Provisions for alternative assessment

IDEA 2004
- Personnel standards issue removed regarding highest requirement for SLPs
- Discrepancy model may no longer be utilized
- Disproportionality of CLD students in special education
- RtI model implemented to address students who do not qualify for special services yet who are still struggling
  - 15% of funds may be applied to early intervening services (different from early intervention) for K-12, but especially for *K-3 Grades (addresses the Wait to Fail* model)
- IEP Team and meeting revisions
- Assessments must be in the student's native language

Table 3. SLP Service Delivery Hierarchy for Students with SLI.

- Full Inclusion – SLP'S service is brought to student in his/her general classroom
- SLP coteaches with general education teacher in the same classroom for entire day
- SLP provides consultation to general education teacher (indirect service)
- Resource room – SLI students are pull out of class for part of day and receive SLP service (either individually or in a small group)
- Students with serve SLI are in a self contained class within the regular school and receive SLP service (time in class varies from partial to full day)
- Designated building within a school district are 100% special education classroom and students with SLI receive SLP service

educating the general and special education teacher on strategies to enable him/her to use the language skills he/she possesses in the classroom for educational and social interactions" (p. 104).

In addition to the changes in the service delivery for students with SLI, the 1990s also brought to the forefront of educational discourse the relationship between language and literacy, for example, reading and writing as well as language-based learning disabilities (LLD) (see Bender, 2007; Moore-Brown & Montgomery, 2008; Nelson, 2010). Learning disabilities represent "a heterogeneous group of disorders manifested by significant disabilities in the acquisition and use of listening, speaking, reading, writing, reasoning, or mathematical abilities" (Hammill, Leigh, McNutt, & Larsen, 1981, p. 336). Approximately 80% of all school-aged children with learning disabilities have language impairments that substantially characterize their disorder (Wiig & Secord, 1998). Spoken and written language are reciprocal and build on each other, often affecting both, which results in general language and literacy competence that starts early in childhood and continues through adulthood (Qualls, 2007). Research suggests that language issues in children and adolescents may be caused by and a result of literacy problems (Moore-Brown & Montgomery, 2008). Language and reading problems in children with LLD result largely from impairments in vocabulary and comprehension (McCormick & Becker, 1996; Minskoff, 1982; Wright & Newhoff, 2002). Students with LLD often show average to superior intelligence, but have difficulty in one or more aspects of language such as spelling, reading, and/or writing. For instance, a child with dyslexia has trouble almost exclusively with reading, whereas a child with an expressive language disorder has significant difficulty communicating their thoughts although they understand what has been said. These students also have difficulty with figurative (nonliteral) language such as idioms and metaphors (Qualls, Lantz, Pietrzyk, Blood, & Hammer, 2004). Because of the reciprocal relationship between spoken and written language, SLPs work with children in spelling, reading, and/or writing to ensure that they gain access to appropriate instruction in these areas (ASHA, 2007). SLPs play an important role in early identification, assessment, intervention, and the development of literacy programs (ASHA, 2007).

In 1997, the IDEA of 1990 was amended to IDEA 1997, which was later re-authorized in 2004 as the Individuals with Disabilities Education *Improvement* Act (IDEIA). This reauthorization provides some guidance for SLPs and others in planning and implementing assessment procedures for all students, including culturally and linguistically diverse (CLD) students who may or may not have a disability. IDEA stipulates that testing and evaluation procedures should be nondiscriminatory and requires that all children be fairly assessed in their dominant (native) language (U.S. Department of Education, 2007).

ASSESSMENT PRACTICES

The language-assessment practices for students with SLI have undergone a number of changes since the 1950s. For example, during the 1950s, the assessment of language typically involved either a normative or pathological approach (Bartels, Sexton, & Rotatori, 1990). A normative approach is used to ascertain whether a student has reached typical developmental language milestones (i.e., first two-word combination – 18 months). In contrast, a pathological approach is used to determine whether a student may have a specific speech diagnostic impairment (i.e., dysarthia, dyspraxia, stuttering) and the etiology that caused that impairment. Additionally, SLP were influenced by Milisen's (1957) language-classification system which directed their assessment to be more descriptive and based more upon clinical observation (Bartels et al., 1990).

According to Bartels et al. (1990), language assessment in the 1960s was influenced by two major trends, namely, a focus on formal testing procedures to ascertain whether a student's speech was atypical enough to be classified as disordered and the behavioral model that stressed that deviant language is learned and conditioned in the environment. Formal testing practices in the 1960s were highly standardized and the assessment involved gathering information on the following linguistic categories: phonology, morphology, syntax, and semantics (see Wallace & Larsen, 1978). A large part of language assessment during this period was based upon the work of Chomsky (1957) who stressed that children are born with knowledge of an underlying structure of language (Bartels et al., 1990). This aspect leads to the high importance of syntax assessment because syntax assists one to generate sentences (Owens, 1984). In contrast, the behavioral model led to a language-assessment approach that focused on identifying environmental stimuli and reinforcement aspects that could be manipulated to remediate a student's language impairment (Bartels et al., 1990).

The high emphasis on syntax assessment was challenged in the 1970s by researchers such as Schlesinger (1971) and Brown (1973), who favored assessment that examined "the importance of situational context to possible meaning of word(s) that children produce" (Bartels et al., 1990, p. 210). This led to a semantic focus on language development and assessment during the 1970s. Unfortunately, this emphasis, failed to assess the context of meaning or polysemy which is needed to understand the word meanings in puns, metaphors, and proverbs (see Wiig & Semel, 1984).

Other trends that influenced language assessment in the 1970s were a renewed interest in cognition and language development. The importance of Piaget's (1952) cognitive theory was reexamined in light of its importance in the development of language (see Reed, 1986). Also, researchers (see Bever, 1970; Snyder, 1984) in language development examined the theme that individuals use cognitive strategies to communicate and that certain cognitive skills are precursors to spoken language. Lastly, by the end of the 1970s, researchers and practitioners began voicing objections about the frequent use of standardized tests to measure the language capabilities of students with SLI (see Danartz, 1981; Leonard, Perozzi, Prutting, & Berkeley, 1978). These objections led to supplementing standardized language-assessment devices with informal language-assessment procedures such as sentence modeling, language-sampling techniques (i.e., mean length utterances), teacher made tests, and story-retelling sessions to gain added knowledge about a student's language skills (Bartels et al., 1990; Currie, Rotatori, & Fox, 1985).

Starting in the late 1970s and early 1980s and continuing till today, language assessment has included pragmatic language-assessment practices. Pragmatic language assessment is concerned with the social aspects of language. It allows the SLP to evaluate whether a student understands when and how to use language to communicate socially with others (Sparks & Hale, 2000). Pragmatic language skills assessment of a student with SLI involves six components, namely, turn taking, topic maintaining, presupposition, conversational exchange clusters or units, nonverbal communication, and deixis (Bartels et al., 1990).

The historical changes discussed above have led to language assessment practices today that are both comprehensive and complex. Traditional language-assessment practices today involve "formal and informal, norm-referenced and criterion referenced assessments along with language samples and category inventories" (Wegner et al., 2003, p. 182). Administering traditional assessment practices allows SLP to establish whether a student is eligible for SLI services. However, traditional assessment may only provide a limited profile of a student's abilities and they do not address a student's classroom learning experiences (Wegner et al., 2003). As such, Wegner et al. (2003) recommend that traditional assessment practices be combined with naturalistic, dynamic, and performance assessment, which utilize a team approach, to provide a more comprehensive profile of a student's language capabilities.

With the changing U.S. public schools demographics, SLPs are increasingly working more with culturally, racially, ethnically, and linguistically diverse student bodies with a wide range of abilities. Of the nearly 48.2 million students receiving a public school education in the United States (Lips, 2006), 17% are African-American while 19% are Hispanic-American. Although African-Americans comprise 17% of all students in U.S. public schools, they make up 20% of students receiving special education services. Similarly, a large percentage of Hispanic-American students are in special education programs and encompass 14% of the special education population (23rd Annual Report to Congress, 2001). According to ASHA (1999), the number of students with limited-English-proficiency (LEP) is increasing and a large proportion of CLD students are considered to be LEP or speakers of nonstandard English dialects. These students may not fully benefit from classroom English instruction. Further, some classroom teachers may not be able to distinguish SLI from linguistic differences (Garcia & Dominquez, 1997).

SLPs are trained to distinguish between language differences and language disorders. It is unethical to diagnose someone who exhibits a language difference, for example, dialect speakers or ESL as having a language disorder. IDEA (1997) began to address the issues of CLD students and IDEIA (2004) mandated that all CLD students should be tested in their native language. The effect of this legislation has produced an insurmountable obstacle for SLPs and educators. Many urban and intercity school districts have large immigrant populations with a multitude of different languages spoken. For instance, over 65 different languages are spoken by students within a public school in the Central Mid-west, and the school district has translators for only 20 of these languages. Similarly, a public school in Western New York has students from 50 different languages. Many of these students are from small third-world countries and translators/interpreters that can translate academic language cannot be found to assist in formal assessment of the students. Although IDEIA (2004) does recognize that a CLD student's assessment does not need to be formal given the language differences, it still mandates that the assessment be administered to obtain the most accurate information of the student's academic, developmental, and functional ability.

Therefore, the increase in LEP and CLD student populations require attention to issues of nonbiased assessments and intervention considerations related to these diverse populations (Whitmire et al., 2002). It is important to note that existing special education referral practices primarily consider the culture and language of mainstream English speakers and do not take into account nonstandard dialect speakers and/or non-English speakers. Historically, standardized assessments have been used to determine placement or nonplacement into special education (see Table 4 for a sampling of traditional language-assessment tests). Many if not all standardized assessments show some level of bias in favor of the culture, language, and cognitive learning styles of speakers of mainstream English. Hence, these assessments will disadvantage anyone who does not possess those characteristics of the mainstream population. Therefore, it is important to address that historically African-American students who are speakers of African-American English (AAE) have been overidentified and are disproportionately placed in special education for speech and language services (Hosp & Reschly, 2002). Speakers of AAE perform more poorly on these assessments; additionally, students with cognitive and learning styles that are field dependent and associative have similar outcomes. However, while it is not known to what extent AAE directly affects the placement of African-Americans in special education for speech and language disorders, they are frequently misidentified and misdiagnosed with these communication disorders, for example, language disorders, speech-language impairments (Rickford, Sweetland, & Rickford, 2004).

Researchers assert that AAE is but one of a multitude of variables that can impact the attitudes, expectations, and perceptions which often lead to special education referral for speech and language disorders and placement (Anderson, 1992; Hilliard, 1992). Therefore, in 2000 in an effort to alleviate the number of nonmainstream English speakers' overidentification in the category of SLI, the Dialect Sensitive Language Test (DSLT) (Seymour, Roeper, & de Villiers, 2000) was developed. In 2003, the DSLT became the Diagnostic Evaluation of Language Variation (DELV) (Seymour, Roeper, & de Villiers, 2005). The Diagnostic DELV is a norm-referenced test designed to assess children's language abilities by not penalizing students whose language may differ from mainstream English on test performance. The DELV is responsive to cultural and linguistic differences of many African-American children and is used frequently to assess this population. However, it is an effective assessment tool for children of all races and ethnicities because the DELV examines language structures common to different varieties of English (Seymour et al., 2005).

Table 4. Sampling of Standardized Language Assessment Tests.

Test Name	Age Range	Content Area
Clinical Assessment of Articulation and Phonology (CAAP) (Secord & Donohue, 2002)	2-6 to 8-11 years	Articulation and phonology skills.
Comprehensive Receptive and Expressive Vocabulary (CREVT-2) (Wallace & Hammill, 2002)	4-0 to 89-11	Receptive language skills.
Dynamic Indicators of Basic Early Literacy Skills (DIBELS) (Good & Kaminski, 2003)	Kindergarten through adulthood	Reading skills, phonemic awareness, fluency comprehension.
Fluharty Preschool Speech and Language Test – Second Edition (Fluharty, 2000)	3-0 to 6-11 years	Articulation, repeating sentences, responding to directions, phonemic awareness, phonics, fluency comprehension.
Goldman–Fristoe Test of Articulation – Second Edition (G-FTA-2) (Goldman & Fristoe, 2001)	2-0 to 21-0 years	Articulation skills.
Oral Speech Mechanism Screening Examination – Third Edition (OSMSE-3) (St. Louis & Ruscello, 2000)	5-6 to 78-0 years	Assesses oral speech mechanism.
Pre-Literacy Skills Screening (PLSS) (Crumrine & Lonegan, 1999) Rhyme, naming, blending, sentence repetition and segmentation, letter naming, syllable segmentation, word repetition.		Prekindergarten
Screening Test for Developmental Apraxia of Speech – Second Edition (STDAS-2) (Blakely, 2000)	4-0 to 12-10 years	Apraxia of speech.
Stuttering Severity Instrument – Fourth Edition (SSI-4) (Riley, 2009)	2-0 years and up	Severity of stuttering.
Test of Childhood Stuttering (TOCS) (Gillam, Logan, & Pearson, 2009)	4-0 to 12-10 years	Stuttering, rapid picture naming, modeled sentences, standard sentences, sentence narration.
Test of Language Development-Intermediate (TOLDI-4) (Hammill & Newcomer, 2008)	8–0 to 17–11 years	Sentence combining, picture vocabulary, word ordering, relational vocabulary, morphological comprehension
Test of Narrative Language (TNL) Gillam & Pearson, 2004)	5-0 to 11-11 years	Identifies language impairment.

Table 4. (*Continued*)

Test Name	Age Range	Content Area
Test of Pragmatic Language – Second Edition (TOPL-2) (Phelps-Terasaki & Phelps-Gunn, 2007)	6-0 to 18-11 years	Pragmatic language skills.
Test of Preschool Early Literacy (TOPEL) (Lonigan, Wagner, Torgensen, & Rashotte, 2007)	3-0 to 5-11 years	Print knowledge, definitional vocabulary, phonological awareness.
Test of Reading Comprehension (TORC-4) (Brown, Wiederholt, & Hammill, 2009)	7-0 to 17-11 years	Relational reading, sentence completion, paragraph construction, text completion, contextual fluency.
Token Test for Children – Second Edition (TTFC-2) (McGhee, Ehrler, & DiSimoni, 2007)	3-0 to 12-11 years	Receptive language.

Additionally, 2001 brought about more accountability for school districts to educate all students, those with and without disabilities with the passing of the *No Child Left Behind* (NCLB) Act. NCLB (2001) is an ambitious effort that lends attention to achievement disparities among students in public education. Specifically, the *Reading First Initiative* targets children of color and English Language Learners (ELLs) in kindergarten through Grade 3 (see Lindo, 2006; U.S. Department of Education, 2000) and establishes that instructional decisions in reading will be guided by the best available research for teaching basic reading skills, that is, decoding and comprehension for these grade levels. SLPs were affected by this act because of the reciprocal relationship between spoken and written language. SLPs are an integral factor in providing reading instruction to children, and subsequently are held to the same standards of providing students with evidence-based reading instruction (ASHA, 2010).

ASHA (2010) provides an in-depth professional issues statement that delineates the roles and responsibilities for SLPs working in the schools. These roles were developed according to federal mandates and changing professional practices. It is worth noting that federal mandates, specifically IDEA 1990 and NCLB, require that services be provided to students with disabilities, when the disabilities impact their academic performance. Certain disorders can occur in children that do not influence their academic performance. Examples include students with distorted speech sound errors (producing a lateral /s/distortion or producing *wat* for *rat*), mild attention issues, or vocal nodules, etc. The academic performance of each child becomes the ultimate goal when considering whether specific problems/disorders result in academic failure.

The ASHA (2010) roles and responsibilities for SLPs in the schools detail the following range of responsibilities: prevention of academic failure, assessment to identify disorders, research-based intervention relative to appropriate curriculum, designation of a school-wide program utilizing a continuum of service delivery, collection of student data, and compliance of federal, state, and local regulations that pertain to Medicaid billing and Individualized Education Plan (IEP).

EDUCATIONAL AND TREATMENT PRACTICES

By federal law an IEP is required for all students who have been identified as requiring special education services, including those receiving services for speech and language disorders. A multidisciplinary team (e.g., students, general education teachers, special education teachers, guardians, counselors, principals, social worker, and SLPs and other related disciplines) determines a student's eligibility in one or more of the 13 disability categories and the need for special education and/or related services. Refer to Fig. 1 for a listing of these categories and their percentages.

Clearly, an IEP assists the school staff in meeting the student's learning needs as well as helps plan educational goals for him/her. When a student has been diagnosed as having a SLI only, the SLP would lead the IEP team in setting objectives and educational goals for him/her and helps to determine any adaptations deemed appropriate for services. Prior to 1997, most SLP therapy was conducted as a pull-out model, either in an individual or a small group setting. SLP goals were always speech or language based but may not have reflected the student's curriculum. With IDEA (1997), there was a major change for SLPs to become involved in curriculum-based IEP goals, which required that the goals incorporated content from the student's curriculum (ASHA, 2006). This change required that SLPs and teachers work together to determine how speech-language goals could best reflect the student's curriculum.

The teacher, the SLP, and parents/guardians must work collaboratively to provide necessary services for the student to successfully meet their annual IEP goals. ASHA (2010) specifically addresses collaboration and leadership for SLPs. They are expected to collaborate with all educators, administrators, and staff. This synergistic model becomes evident during child study

■ Emotional Disorders   ■ Other Health Impairments

■ Learning Disability   ■ Mental Retardation

■ Multiple disabilities   ■ Speech and Language Disorders

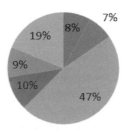

Fig. 1. Six Major Disability Categories. *Note:* Hearing impairments (1.2%), orthopedic impairments (1.1%), visual impairments (0.4%), autism (2.3%), deaf-blindness (0.03%), traumatic brain injury (0.4%), and developmental delay (1.1%). *Source:* U.S. Department of Education, Office of Special Education Programs, Data Analysis System (DANS), OMB #1820-0043: "Children with Disabilities Receiving Special Education Under Part B of the *Individuals with Disabilities Education Act*," 2003. Data updated as of July 31, 2004. Also Tables 1–3 in vol. 2 of this Report. These Data are for the 50 States, District of Columbia, BIA schools, Puerto Rico, and the Outlying Areas.

team meetings when a child is initially referred. SLPs need to obtain information from the general and special education teachers, any aides working with a child, social worker, and the school nurse. Even the parents, who are significant members of the team, are considered equal partners to the school professionals. They should be consulted to help identify the child's needs as well as provide pertinent information to the team about the child's development, including social and medical history, assist with ensuring he/she is practicing strategies at home, and report on his/her progress from the perspective of the home environment. SLPs collaborate with the IEP teams to administer comprehensive language and speech assessments and to evaluate, create, and implement intervention plans and services. There are several models of intervention that SLPs can provide, for example, individual sessions or small group sessions, pull-out or push-in classroom supports, consultative model with teachers and parents (Wegner et al., 2003). Additionally, SLPs can supply information regarding local agencies for social services which can be extended to families in need. To furnish better research-based information, ASHA expects SLPs to form collaborative relationships with researchers at the local universities/colleges to collect pertinent research-driven data (Brackenbury, Burroughs, & Hewitt, 2008; Johnson, 2006).

INDIVIDUALS WITH SPEECH AND LANGUAGE DISORDERS IN THE TWENTIETH CENTURY

The numbers of school-aged children with speech and language disorders in the United States and Canada have continued to rise. In 2001, more than 1 million children, an increase of 10.5% since 1990, received services for speech or language disorders (Whitmire et al., 2002). Advances in medicine, genetics, and technology and recent changes to the laws affecting services to individuals with disabilities contribute to these increasing numbers, particularly as more students with disabilities attend school. According to the ASHA (2010), communication disorders are among the most common disabilities in the United States. A communication disorder can be manifested as a unitary speech, language, or hearing disorder, or maybe a combination with one or more of these aspects of communication. In fact, the most frequently provided services for school-aged children with disabilities are speech-language intervention services (Kirk et al., 2006). The National Information Center for Children and Youth with Disabilities (NICCYD, 2010) reported that one in every 10 people in the United States have a communication disorder, and in the 2002–2003 school year over one million students who received special education services were categorized as having a SLI. In some countries other than the United States and Canada, for example, China and Africa, the numbers may be even greater.

Approximately half of the 135,000 members of ASHA work as SLPs in an educational setting, many of them in the public schools (ASHA, 2010). One misconception that SLPs frequently dispel pertains to their original goal of correcting only speech problems and dysfluency. A SLP receives training on the nature, causes, identification, prevention, assessment, and treatment of SLI. Their current role also includes the assessment and treatment of fluency disorders, in addition to multiple aspects of language, cognition, voice, literacy, and feeding/swallowing deficits. Refer to Table 5 for a sampling of the scopes of practice for SLPs listed (ASHA, 2007).

SLPs' work with a variety of students with learning disabilities, autism, attention deficit disorder, stuttering, hearing loss, traumatic brain injury, specific language impairment, cerebral palsy, medically fragile children, cognitive impairments, rare syndromes, and difficulties with feeding and/or swallowing (Whitmire et al., 2002). They are trained in interviewing

Table 5. ASHA's Scopes of Practice for SLPs.

Speech Sound Production	Resonance	Fluency	Cognition	Feeding/ Swallowing	Language

• Articulation
• Apraxia of speech
• Dysarthria
• Ataxia
• Dyskinesia
	• Hypernasality
	• Hyponasality
	• Mixed Resonance
		• Stuttering
		• Cluttering
			• Attention
			• Memory
			• Critical thinking
				• Oral
				• Pharyngeal
				• Laryngeal
				• Esophageal
				• Orofacial
					• Phonology
					  • Phonemic awareness
					• Morphology
					  • Word structure
					• Syntax
					  • Word order
					• Semantics
					  • Word meaning
					• Pragmatics
					  • Language use
					• Literacy
					  • Reading, Writing, Spelling
					• Prelinguistic
					  • Joint attention
					  • Intentionality
					  • Communicative festuring
					• Paralinguistic communication
					  • Suprasegmental features

and counseling (see Kelly & Rotatori, 1986). Also, SLPs work closely with other educational and health professionals to ensure those individuals with speech and language disorders and their families receive the highest quality services.

The ASHA Code of Ethics involves advocating for the welfare of clients and also for the profession (ASHA, 2010). As this relates to services in the schools, SLPs should advocate for the appropriate services for students from preschool through 12th grade. As the profession is constantly adding new scopes of practice, SLPs frequently need to educate the community and school staff with regard to their changing roles. This has become especially crucial regarding the SLP's role in literacy. With their detailed knowledge of phonology, morphology, and semantics, SLPs are instrumental to teachers regarding instruction in decoding (reading), encoding (spelling), and comprehension. SLPs need to stay up-to-date with research and evidence-based practices to provide the most current and efficacious practice.

MAJOR IMPLICATIONS OF IDEA AND NCLB

Discrepancy Model

IDEIA (2004) finally addressed the problem of the discrepancy model. In the past, local education agencies (LEAs) have applied the discrepancy model to determine if a student qualifies for special education services or not. This model compares a child's overall performance standard score (considered the true IQ) to the child's overall verbal standard score (language ability). If the difference is 15 points or less, no discrepancy is considered to exist. The child is believed to be operating within his/her ability and does not qualify for special education services. According to this model, language disorders can only be determined if the language standard score is more than 15 points *lower* than the performance standard score.

This model has always presented several problems. For example, does a student qualify for language services when the performance standard score is 135, while the language standard score is 115? Both of these scores are in the above average range, yet the language ability is 20 points lower. A second more significant problem for students with cognitive impairments is the fact that their performance standard score will always be low due to their cognitive impairment. Many students with cognitive impairment will exhibit higher language than cognitive scores. In this example, suppose a student with mental retardation receives a 70 performance standard score and a 75 verbal standard score, with only a 5 point difference between the two. As these scores are within 15 points, no discrepancy exists according to the model. Yet both scores are at or near the negative two standard deviation mark that typically qualifies students for special education services; however, this student is believed to be functioning at his/her cognitive ability and would not qualify because no discrepancy exists.

The discrepancy model (also known as cognitive referencing by ASHA) is in clear violation of the ASHA Code of Ethics for SLPs. SLPs cannot apply the discrepancy model when determining whether a student qualifies for special education services. This has placed SLPs in a precarious predicament: either follow the LEA policy or violate their ASHA Code of Ethics.

The 2006 Part B final regulations of IDEIA mandate that the LEAs must not require the use of a severe discrepancy to determine eligibility and must permit the use of a process-based intervention, known as response to intervention (RtI) (see Wheeler & Mayton, 2010).

Response to Intervention

Previously, students were divided into general education and special education, essentially a two-tier instructional system. In contrast, the RtI model has three tiers of instructional intervention (see Fig. 2). Tier I of the RtI model involves students who are performing at grade level and would be taught in the regular education classroom. Teaching methodologies for Tier I include universal screenings, instruction and design, and differentiated instruction. Frequent probes for all students are conducted to catch any problems early. Students who are struggling academically are then placed in Tier II. Teachers and SLPs will often collaborate to determine which research-based teaching methodologies are the most effective to enhance the student's learning. Students will receive targeted instruction during an intensive intervention time frame either individually or in a small group. The intention for Tier II is to provide targeted and intensive instruction, with the hope that the student will not need special education services. If Tier II intervention has not improved the student's academic

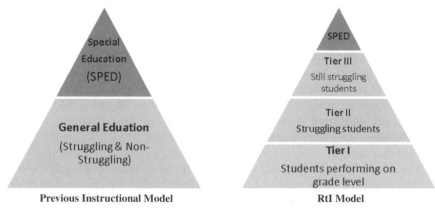

Fig. 2. Comparison of Previous Instructional Model to Response to Intervention Model.

performance and he/she is still struggling, then Tier III will be implemented. Students in Tier III have continued to exhibit difficulties and receive more of the same intervention: individualized or small group setting, increased intensity of targeted intervention. At this point, special education teachers and/or SLPs may provide the interventions. Students who do not improve in Tier III are then referred to special education for assessment. Nelson (2010) noted that the RtI model *should not* be utilized to delay children who have obvious special educations needs from being identified.

Assistive Technology

Assistive technology (AT) has been and still is an integral part of speech and language intervention services. Historically, Wolfgang von Kempelen, in the late 1700s, was the first to attempt using AT for individuals with SLI, by building the "Speaking Machine" (Aaron, Eide, & Pitrelli, 2003). This machine produced basic words by using a complex series of sounds. However, the first creation of modern text-to-speak digital computing technology was in the 1970s when robotic-sounding speech was produced (see Aaron et al., 2003).

In the 1980s, researchers (see McCormick & Haring, 1986; Schwartz, 1984; Sicoli, 1982) began evaluating the practical value of AT for use with students who had SLI (see St. Peter, Morris, & Murdock, 1987). For example, Rushakoff (1984) discussed the use of AT intervention as a supplement to SLPs. This could be set up by using computer-assisted instruction (CAI) for drill and practice and tutorial aspects. In addition, instruction for clients who live in rural areas or at a distance from the clinic could receive instruction via computer modem hook-ups through telephone lines (St. Peter et al., 1987). Other researchers (Behrman, 1984; Meyers, 1984) investigated the utilization of AT in early language intervention for infants and toddlers. Also, Gall et al. (1989) utilized computer technology to develop prosthetic devices that enhanced the communication capabilities of children with SLI.

In the 1990s, more human-sounding synthetic speech was developed using improved technology, faster computers, and inexpensive data storage (see Beukelman & Mirenda,1992; Maugh, 1996; Schery & O'Connor, 1995). In addition, computer technology was developed to serve broader applications for SLI such as articulation (i.e., drill and practice), voice (i.e., biofeedback aspects), fluency (biofeedback and relaxation), syntactic (i.e., drill and practice, games, tutorials), semantic (i.e., language sample analysis and cognitive rehabilitation), and pragmatic (i.e., problem solving and simulations) (see Cochran & Bull, 1993).

AT can be defined as accessories that help alleviate a person's physical and/or communicative inabilities. Many students with severe communication and/or physical limitations are unable to communicate their wants and needs orally or gesturally. AT can provide a means of maintaining or improving functional capabilities through the use of tools, strategies, software, and devices. Typically students who have significant difficulty being understood and/or are unable to communicate over the phone because of speech and/or physical deficits can benefit from AT. AT cannot eliminate an individual's speech and/or physical deficit; however, it can assist with successfully interacting with the environment (Duke University Health System, 2010). AT can help to make educational materials significant and motivating. For example, integrating technology into speech and language interventions can make the process easier and more successful (Speech, 2010).

AT comes in a variety of forms such as, high-technology, mid-technology, and low-technology (see Nkabinde, 2008). Examples of an assistive device include: on/off switch, large keyboard, adaptive computer mouse, pointer, voice-activated computer, etc. Augmentative and alternative communication (AAC) devices function as an output mode for speech and also help students develop language and communication skills (see Bryen & Pecunas, 2004; Ellenson, 2006; Kangas & Lloyd, 2002).

IDEA (1990) provided for the inclusion of AT devices to the IEP. Because of this, AT usage to instruct a student with exceptionalities in the classroom has become widespread (see Bouck, 2010). It has also led to the use of AT to foster speech and language skills at home (see Skau & Cascella, 2006). However, AT devices can cost several thousand dollars and LEAs are reluctant to include AT devices due to their high cost. Also, most families will find it difficult to purchase the devices due to their cost and limited generic applications for other family members (Nkabinde, 2008). In addition, AT presents challenges for families "such as the time and effort required to learn how to use the different devices effectively" (Nkabinde, 2008, p. 280). In spite of the above, the future use of AT with students with SLI will increase because of its many advantages such as: giving them greater control over their lives; allowing for greater participation in their environment; enhancing their social communication with others; and giving them greater access to academic learning opportunities (Bouck, 2010).

WORKING WITH FAMILIES OF STUDENTS WITH SLI

Research on the effects of working with families of students with SLI is an important area due to past findings (Bondurant, Romeo, & Kretshmer, 1983; Hall, Oyer, & Haas, 2001; Hardwood, Warren, & Yoder, 2002; Hart & Risley, 1995; Lombardo, 1999; Shriberg & Kwiatowski, 1988). For example, Bondurant et al. (1983) reported a noticeable difference between the language behaviors of mothers of normal children and the mothers of children with delayed language. These authors noted that mothers of children with delayed language tended to use shorter sentences, asked fewer questions, gave twice as many directions, and made fewer acceptance comments about what their child said. Similarly, Hardwood et al. (2002) reported that the quality and quantity of early language input influenced the vocabulary and language acquisition of children significantly. Also, Shriberg and Kwiatowski (1988) analyzed 43 studies regarding their effectiveness of home language intervention with students that had LLD. They reported that the composite gain of these students went from the 50th percentile to the 85th percentile. Furthermore, Culatta and Goldberg (1995) have stressed that early home intervention for stutters has become so popular that the family is considered a critical factor in prevention. Lastly, Hall et al. (2001) reported that home parent language intervention increased students scores more than students who received clinic-based language intervention. According to St. Peter and Rotatori (1991), research findings have consistently demonstrated the need for early intervention programs to assist parents in "the positive facilitation of positive language interactions with their speech and language-disordered children" (p. 90). This becomes even more critical when parents and SLP realized that the quality of their child's home environment has significant and long-term effects on a child's language acquisition and development (Hart & Risley, 1995).

Also, parents need to acquire a sound understanding and knowledge base of their son/daughter's SLI and the available educational intervention services that are available to their child (Prizant & Tiegerman, 1984). This understanding is critical according to Kelly and Rotatori (1986) due to the fact that parents of students with SLI often have misconceptions about their child's SLI and future learning progress. These authors stress that parents of students with SLI must understand "that their child is deficit in his ability to comprehend or express thoughts presented in a verbal or nonverbal that may affect academic as well as psychosocial progress" (p. 156). One way of gaining knowledge and awareness about school programs for their children is for parents to join parent associations or professional SLI organizations and volunteer to agencies serving children with SLI (Kelly & Rotatori, 1986). The impact that knowledgeable parents of students with SLI can have on other parents who have children with similar impairments can not be stressed enough because these parent–group interactions facilitate personal growth and effective parenting (see Kelly & Rotatori, 1986).

Today's intervention for students with severe SLI needs to be community based. Sparks and Hale (2000) advocate a Community-Based Functional Intervention Model in which all assessment and intervention aspects take place in the environment where the skill is to be utilized. As such, the family becomes a critical partner in these endeavors. SLPs work closely with the family to identify what the student needs to say, how he needs to say it, and when he *needs to say it* (Sparks & Hale). This model places a heavy emphasis on pragmatic elements of communication which should allow the student to be more functionally independent in the home and other environments.

Smith (2004) delineated a number of language-intervention strategies that parents can implement which leads to improvements in their child's speech and language development. These strategies include the following: labeling or naming objects in the home; the frequent use of simple words to describe toys that the child is playing with; encourage repetitions of correct production of sounds to assist the child in correcting an error; asking questions that require additional information; and modeling good language (Smith, 2004). Other strategies that have been used in the classroom but are easily adapted for intervention in the home includes: story retelling, recasting the child's incomplete sentences, capitalizing on the child's natural inclination to talk about what they *are doing*, *plans to do*, *or wants to do* (Kirk et al., 2006).

CONCLUDING REMARKS: SLP AND SERVING STUDENTS WITH SLI

Over the last several decades, the profession of speech-language pathology has seen a burgeoning expansion of new duties along with the progression of disability rights legislations. Although multiple laws have been enacted since the 1960s regarding economically disadvantaged persons and people with disabilities, IDEA and NCLB have had the greatest impact with respect to SLPs and other school personnel (administrators, educators, aides, related services personnel, nursing, counseling). Additionally, IDEA (1997) directives involving CLD students created the need for more substantial programming for these students by SLPs.

The federal government has determined that a high percentage of students of color are placed in special education. LEAs have been mandated to review their ethnic/race data and if a disproportionate number of CLD students have been identified for special education services, then the LEAs must funnel their federal monies into early intervening services for these students. LEAs are also required to publicly report this data. A typical occurrence of a misidentified student often involves African-American students who speak AAE. SLPs can play a key role in reducing the number of these students who are misidentified.

IDEA (2004) included significant changes regarding when students would qualify for specialized services, primarily through issues concerning the discrepancy model and the wait-to-fail model. Because speech-language interventions are the most common service provided for school-aged children with disabilities (Wegner et al., 2003) as well as the changing demographics in public schools, it is imperative that SLPs employ culturally appropriate practices when identifying, referring, assessing, and treating the speech and language skills of CLD students. School-based SLPs are responsible for providing services to children with speech and/or language disorders that are curriculum-based, evidence-based, and that are guided by legal and ethical tenets that include consideration of the student's cultural and linguistic experiences. ASHA continues as the governing body for SLPs and audiologists and provides a code of ethics, standards of practice, credentialing and certification criteria, and roles and responsibilities for this discipline.

REFERENCES

23rd Annual Report to Congress on the Implementation of the Individuals with Disabilities Act. (2001). Available at http://www.ed.gov/offices/OSERS/OSEP/Products/OSEP2001AnlRpt

Aaron, A., Eide, E., & Pitrelli, J. F. (2003). Making computers talk: Say good-bye to stilted electronic chatter. Available at http://www.scientificamerican.com

American Speech-Language-Hearing Association. (1993). Ad hoc committee on service delivery in the schools, definitions: Communication disorders and variations. *ASHA*, *35*(Suppl. 10), 4041.

American Speech-Language-Hearing Association. (1999). *Guidelines for the roles and responsibilities of the school-based speech-language pathologist*. Rockville, MD: American Speech-Language-Hearing Association.

American Speech-Language-Hearing Association. (2006). IDEA: [A supplement to the ASHA Leader]. *The ASHA Leader*, October 17. Available at http://www.asha.org/leaderissue. aspx?year=2006&id=2006-10-17

American Speech-Language-Hearing Association. (2007). Scope of practice in speech-language pathology [scope of practice]. Available at http://www.asha.org

American Speech-Language Hearing Association. (2010). Roles and responsibilities of speech-language pathologists in schools [Professional issues statement]. doi:10.144/policy. PI2010-00317

Anderson, M. G. (1992). The use of selected theatre rehearsal technique activities with African-American adolescents labeled behavior disordered. *Exceptional Children, 59*, 132–140.

Bartels, K., Sexton, D., & Rotatori, A. F. (1990). Assessment of language. In: A. F. Rotatori, R. A. Fox, D. Sexton & J. Miller (Eds), *Comprehensive assessment in special education* (pp. 207–242). Springfield, IL: Charles C. Thomas.

Behrman, M. (1984). A brighter future for early learning through high tech. *Pointer, 28*(2), 23–26.

Bender, W. N. (2007). *Learning disabilities: Characteristics, identification and teaching strategies.* Boston: Allyn and Bacon.

Beukelman, D., & Mirenda, P. (1992). *Augmentative and alternative communication: Management of severe communication disorders in children and adults.* Baltimore, MD: Paul H. Brookes.

Bever, T. G. (1970). *Cognition and the development of language.* New York: Wiley.

Blakely, R. W. (2000). *Screening test for developmental apraxia of speech – Second edition (STDAS-2).* Austin, TX: PRO-ED.

Blanton, S., & Blanton, M. J. (1919). *Speech training for children: The hygiene of speech.* New York: The Century Company.

Blanton, S., & Blanton, M. J. (1936). *For stutterers.* New York: Appleton-Century Company.

Bondurant, J. L., Romeo, D. J., & Kretschmer, R. (1983). Language behaviors of mothers of children with normal and delayed language. *Language, Speech, and Hearing Services in Schools, 14*, 233–242.

Bouck, E. C. (2010). Technology and students with disabilities: Does it solve all the problems. In: F. E. Obiakor, J. P. Bakken & A. F. Rotatori (Eds), *Current issues and trends in special education: Research, technology and teacher preparation* (Vol. 20, pp. 91–104). United Kingdom: Emerald Group Publishing Limited.

Brackenbury, T., Burroughs, E., & Hewitt, L. E. (2008). A qualitative examination of current guidelines for evidence-based practice in child language intervention. *Language, Speech, and Hearing Services in Schools, 39*, 78–88.

Bryen, D. N., & Pecunas, P. (2004). Augmentative and alternative communication and cell phone use: One off-the-shelf solution and some policy considerations. *Assistive Technology, 16*(1), 11–17.

Brown, R. (1973). *A first language: The early stages.* Cambridge, MA: MIT Press.

Brown, V. L., Wiederholt, J. L., & Hammill, D. D. (2009). *Test of reading comprehension – Fourth edition (TORC-4).* Austin, TX: PRO-ED.

Carpenter, J., Hutchings, G., MacFarlane, B., & Richard, H. (2010). Discipline issues: Educators and the law. Available at http://www.educatorsandthelaw.com/speddiscipline.htm

Chomsky, N. (1957). *Syntactic structures.* The Hague: Mouton.

Cochran, P. S., & Bull, G. L. (1993). Computers and individuals with speech and language disorders. In: J. D. Lindsey (Ed.), *Computers and exceptional individuals* (pp. 78–93). Austin, TX: PRO-ED.

Crumrine, L., & Lonegan, H. (1999). *Pre-literacy skills screening (PLSS)*. Austin, TX: PRO-ED.

Culatta, R., & Goldberg, S. A. (1995). *Stuttering therapy: An integrative approach to theory and practice.* Needham, MA: Allyn and Bacon.

Currie, P., Rotatori, A. F., & Fox, R. A. (1985). Language assessment. In: A. F. Rotatori, J. O. Schwenn & R. A. Fox (Eds), *Assessing severely and profoundly handicapped individuals* (pp. 138–156). Springfield, IL: Charles C. Thomas.

Danartz, M. W. (1981). Formal verse informal assessment. Fragmentation versus holism. *Topics in Language Disorders, 3*, 166–173.

Duchan, J. (2002). What do you know about your profession's history: And why is it important? *The ASHA Leader*, December 24. Available at http://www.asha.org

Duke University: Assistive Technology Clinic. (2010). Available at http://www.dukehealth.org

Ellenson, R. (2006). Two who tango! A father, a son, and a new generation of speech generating devices. *Exceptional Parent, June*, 29–31.

Fleischer, D. Z., & Zames, F. (2001). *The disability rights movement: From charity to confrontation.* Philadelphia, PA: Temple University Press.

Fluharty, N. B. (2000). *Fluharty Preschool speech and language screening test* (2nd ed.). Austin, TX: PRO-ED.

Gall, D., Icke, N., Jones, J., Tsantis, L., Vogel, K., & White, L. (1989). School university, IBM partnership helps: Children develop communication skills. *Teaching Exceptional Children, 22*, 54–55.

Garcia, S., & Dominquez, L. (1997). Cultural contexts that influence learning and academic performance. *Child and Adolescent Psychiatric Clinics of North America, 6*, 621–655.

Gay, P. (1988). *Freud: A life for our time.* New York: W.W. Norton.

Gillam, R. B., Logan, K. J., & Pearson, N. A. (2009). *Test of childhood stuttering (TOCS)*. Austin, TX: PRO-ED.

Gillam, R. B., & Pearson, N. A. (2004). *Test of narrative language (TNL)*. Austin, TX: PRO-ED.

Goldman, R., & Fristoe, M. (2001). *Goldman-Fristoe test of articulation – Second edition (G-FTA-2)*. Austin, TX: PRO-ED.

Good, R., & Kaminski, R. (2003). *Dynamic indicators of basic early literacy skills (DIBELS)*. Austin, TX: PRO-ED.

Hall, B., Oyer, H. J., & Haas, W. H. (2001). *Speech, language and hearing disorders: A guide for the teacher.* Boston: Allyn and Bacon.

Hammill, D. D., Leigh, J. E., McNutt, G., & Larsen, S. C. (1981). A new definition of learning disabilities. *Learning Disability Quarterly, 4*, 336–342.

Hammill, D. D., & Newcomer, P. L. (2008). *Test of language development-intermediate – Fourth edition (TOLDI-4)*. Austin, TX: PRO-ED.

Hardwood, L., Warren, S. F., & Yoder, P. (2002). The importance of responsivity in developing contingent exchanges with beginning communication. In: J. Reichle, D. R. Beukelman & J. C. Light (Eds), *Exemplary practices for beginning communication: Implications for ACC* (pp. 59–96). Baltimore, MD: Paul H. Brookes.

Hart, B., & Risley, T. (1995). *Meaningful differences in the everyday lives of American children.* Baltimore, MD: Paul H. Brookes.

Hearing and Speech Agency. (2010). *Mission and history.* Available at http://www.hasa.org/

Hilliard, A. G. (1992). The pitfalls and promise of special education practice. *Exceptional Children, 59*, 168–171.

Hosp, J., & Reschly, D. (2002). Predictors of restrictiveness of placement for African-American and Caucasian students. *Exceptional Children, 68*(2), 225–238.

Individuals with Disabilities Education Act Amendments. (1990). Public Law No. 101-476, 20 U.S.C. (*1400 et seq*).

Individuals with Disabilities Education Act Amendments. (1997). Public Law No. 105-117, 20 U.S.C. (*1400 et seq*).

Individuals with Disabilities Education Improvement Act. (2004). Public Law No. 108-446.

Johnson, C. J. (2006). Getting started in evidence-based practice for childhood speech language disorders. *American Journal of Speech Language Pathology, 15*, 20–35.

Johnson, W. (1946). *People in quandaries: The semantics of personal adjustment*. New York: Harper & Brothers.

Kangas, K. A., & Lloyd, L. (2002). Augmentative and alternative communication. In: G. H. Shames & N. B. Anderson (Eds), *Human communication disorders: An introduction* (pp. 545–593). Boston: Allyn and Bacon.

Kelly, R. H., & Rotatori, A. F. (1986). Counseling the language disordered child. In: A. F. Rotatori, P. J. Gerber, F. W. Litton & R. A. Fox (Eds), *Counseling exceptional students* (pp. 144–161). New York: Human Science Press, Inc.

Kirk, S. A., Gallagher, J. J., Anastasiow, N. J., & Coleman, M. R. (2006). *Educating children with exceptionalities*. Boston: Houghton Mifflin Company.

Leonard, L. B., Perozzi, J. A., Prutting, C. A., & Berkeley, N. K. (1978). Nonstandardized approaches to the assessment of language behavior. *ASHA, 20*, 371–379.

Lindo, E. J. (2006). The African-American presence in reading intervention experiments. *Remedial and Special Education, 27*, 148–153.

Lips, D. (2006). America's opportunity scholarships for kids: School choice for students in underperforming public schools. *Research Education*. Available at http://www.new. heritage.org

Lombardo, L. A. (1999, July). Children score higher on tests when child care meets standards. *Early Childhood Reports, 10*, 4.

Lonigan, C. J., Wagner, R. K., Torgensen, J. K., & Rashotte, C. A. (2007). *Test of preschool early literacy (TOPEL)*. Austin, TX: PRO-ED.

Maryland Speech-Language-Hearing Association. (2010). History of MSLHA. Available at http://www.mdslha.org

Maugh, T. H. H. (1996). New therapy aids pupils with speech problems. *The Los Angeles Times*, January 5, pp. A1, A25.

McCormick, L. P., & Haring, N. (1986). Keeping up with language intervention trends. *Teaching Exceptional Children, 18*, 123–129.

McCormick, S., & Becker, E. Z. (1996). Word recognition and word identification: A review of research on effective instructional practices with learning disabled students. *Reading Research and Instruction, 36*(1), 5–17.

McGhee, R. L., Ehrler, D. J., & DiSimoni, F. D. (2007). *Token test for children – Second edition (TTFC-2)*. Austin, TX: PRO-ED.

Meyers, L. F. (1984). Unique contributions of microcomputers to language interventions with handicapped children. *Seminars in Speech and Language, 5*, 1.

Milisen, R. (1957). Methods of evaluation and diagnosis of speech disorders. In: L. E. Travis (Ed.), *Handbook of speech pathology* (pp. 234–258). New York: Appleton-Century Crofts.

Minskoff, E. H. (1982). Sharpening language skills in secondary LD students. *Academic Therapy, 18*, 53–60.

Moore-Brown, B. J., & Montgomery, J. K. (2008). *Making a difference for America's children: Speech-language pathologists in public schools* (2nd ed.). Greenville, SC: Thinking Publications.

Moore, G. P., & Kester, D. (1953). Historical notes on speech correction in the preassociation era. *Journal of Speech and Hearing Disorders, 18*, 48–53.

National Aphasia Association. (2010). More about aphasia. Available at http://www.aphasia.org.

National Information Center for Children and Youth with Disabilities. (2010). Disabilities: speech and language impairments. Available at http://www.nichcy.org/Disabilities/Specific/Pages/speech-language.aspx

Nelson, N. W. (2010). *Language and literacy disorders: Infancy through adolescence.* Boston, MA: Allyn and Bacon.

Nisbet, J. (1994). *Education reform: Summary and recommendations. The national reform agenda and people with mental retardation: Putting people first.* Washington, DC: U.S. Department of Health and Human Services.

Nkabinde, Z. (2008). Using assistive technology to educate students with developmental disabilities and autism. In: A. F. Rotatori, F. E. Obiakor & S. Burkhardt (Eds), *Autism and developmental disabilities: Current practices and issues* (Vol. 18, pp. 273–285). United Kingdom: Emerald Group Publishing Limited.

No Child Left Behind Act. (2001). Public Law No. 107-110.

Owens, R. E. (1984). *Language development.* Columbus, OH: Charles E. Merrill.

Phelps-Terasaki, D., & Phelps-Gunn, T. (2007). *Test of pragmatic language – Second edition (TOPL-2).* Austin, TX: PRO-ED.

Piaget, J. (1952). *The origins of intelligence in children.* New York: Norton.

Prizant, B. M., & Tiegerman, E. M. (1984). Working with language impaired children: Problems/issues often encountered but (too) rarely discussed. *Journal of National Students Speech Language Hearing Association, 12*(1), 18–32.

Qualls, C. D. (2007). Speech, language, and neuropsychological assessment: Implications for African-Americans. In: B. P. Uzzell, M. Ponton & A. Ardila (Eds), *International handbook of cross-cultural neuropsychology* (p. 127). New York, NY: Routledge.

Qualls, C. D., Lantz, J. M., Pietrzyk, R. M., Blood, G. W., & Hammer, C. S. (2004). Comprehension of idioms in adolescents with language-based learning disabilities compared to their typically developing peers. *Journal of Communication Disorders, 37*(4), 295–311.

Reed, V. A. (1986). *An introduction to children with language disorders.* New York: Macmillan.

Rickford, J. R., Sweetland, J., & Rickford, A. E. (2004). African American English and other vernaculars in education: A topic-coded bibliography. *Journal of English Linguistics, 32*, 230–320.

Riley, G. D. (2009). *Stuttering severity instrument – Fourth edition (SSI-4).* Austin, TX: PRO-ED.

Rushakoff, G. E. (1984). Microcomputer assisted instruction in communication disorders. *Journal of Communication Disorders, 8*, 51–61.

Schery, T., & O'Connor, L. (1995). Computers as a context for language intervention. In: M. Rey, J. Windson & S. Warren (Eds), *Language intervention* (pp. 45–68). Baltimore, MD: Paul H. Brookes.

Schlesinger, L. M. (1971). Production of utterances and language acquisition. In: D. I. Slobin (Ed.), *The ontogenesis of grammar* (pp. 56–71). New York: Academic Press.

Schwartz, A. H. (1984). *The handbook of microcomputer applications in communication disorders.* San Diego, CA: College-Hill Press.

Secord, W., & Donohue, J. (2002). *Clinical assessment of articulation and phonology (CAAP)*. Austin, TX: PRO-ED.

Seymour, H. N., Roeper, T., & de Villiers, J. G. (2000). *Dialect sensitive language test (DSLT)*. San Antonio, TX: The Psychological Corporation.

Seymour, H. N., Roeper, T., & de Villiers, J. G. (2005). *DELV-NR (diagnostic evaluation of language variation) norm-referenced test*. San Antonio, TX: The Psychological Corporation.

Shriberg, L., & Kwiatowski, J. (1988). A follow-up study of children with phonology disorders of unknown origin. *Journal of Speech and Hearing Disorders, 53*(2), 144–145.

Sicoli, T. R. (1982). Computers and the special education classroom. *Byte, 7,* 270–274.

Skau, L., & Cascella, P. W. (2006). Using assistive technology to foster speech and language at home and preschool. *Teaching Exceptional Children, 38*(6), 12–17.

Smith, D. D. (2004). *Introduction to special education: Teaching in an age of opportunity* (5th ed.). Boston: Allyn and Bacon.

Snyder, L. (1984). Communication competence in children with delayed language development. In: R. Schiefelbusch & C. Picar (Eds), *Communication competence: Acquisition and intervention* (pp. 123–142). Baltimore, MD: Paul H. Brookes.

Sparks, S., & Hale, K. E. (2000). Intervention techniques for learners with speech and language impairments. In: F. E. Obiakor, S. Burkhardt & A. F. Rotatori (Eds), *Intervention techniques for individuals with exceptionalities inclusive settings* (Vol. 13, pp. 95–114). Oxford: Elsevier Sciences.

Speech, T. X. (2010). Available at http://www.speechtx.com

St. Louis, K. O., & Ruscello, D. M. (2000). *Oral speech mechanism screening examination – Third edition (OSMSE-3)*. Austin, TX: PRO-ED.

St. Peter, S., Morris, P., & Murdock, J. (1987). Computer applications in special education. In: A. F. Rotatori, M. B. Banbury & R. A. Fox (Eds), *Issues in special education* (pp. 187–203). Mountain View, CA: Mayfield Publishing Company.

St. Peter, S., & Rotatori, A. F. (1991). Speech and language disorders. In: J. O. Schwenn, A. F. Rotatori & R. A. Fox (Eds), *Understanding students with high incidence exceptionalities* (pp. 68–101). Springfield, IL: Charles C. Thomas.

Travis, L. E. (1931). *Speech pathology: A dynamic neurological treatment of speech and speech deviations*. New York: Appleton Century Company.

Travis, L. E. (1934). A neurological consideration of stuttering. *Spoken Word, 1,* 8–11.

Travis, L. E. (1946). My present thinking on stuttering. *Western Speech, 10,* 3–5.

University of Iowa Health Care. (2010). Research. Available at http://www.uihealthcare.com

U.S. Department of Education. (2000). *Twenty-second annual report to Congress on the implementation of the individuals with disabilities education act*. Washington, DC: U.S. Government Printing Office.

U.S. Department of Education. (2007). Building the legacy: IDEIA 2004. Available at http://idea.ed.gov/

Van Riper, C. (1981). An early history of ASHA. *ASHA, 23,* 855–858.

Van Riper, C., & Erickson, R. L. (1996). *Speech correction: An introduction to speech pathology and audiology* (9th ed.). Boston: Allyn and Bacon.

Wallace, G., & Hammill, D. D. (2002). *Comprehensive receptive and expressive vocabulary test – second edition (CREVT-2)*. Austin, TX: PRO-ED.

Wallace, G., & Larsen, S. C. (1978). *Educational assessment of learning problems: Testing for teaching*. Boston: Allyn and Bacon.

Wegner, J. R., Grosche, K., & Edmister, E. (2003). Students with speech and language disorders. In: F. E. Obiakor, C. A. Utley & A. F. Rotatori (Eds), *Effective education for learners with exceptionalities* (Vol. 15, pp. 181–193). Oxford: Elsevier Sciences.

West, R., Kennedy, L., & Carr, A. (1937). *The rehabilitation of speech: A textbook of diagnostic and correction procedures.* New York: Harper & Brothers.

Wheeler, J. J., & Mayton, M. R. (2010). Other innovative techniques: Positive behavior supports and response to intervention. In: F. E. Obiakor, J. P. Bakken & A. F. Rotatori (Eds), *Current issues and trends in special education: Identification, assessment and instruction* (Vol. 19, pp. 175–195). United Kingdom: Emerald Group Publishing Limited.

Whitmire, K., Spinello, E., & Clausen, R. (2002). Speech and education of individuals with language impairment. *Encyclopedia of Education.* Available at http://www.encyclopedia.com

Wiig, E. H., & Secord, W. A. (1998). *Diagnostic speech and language profiler: Experimental edition.* Arlington, TX: Schema Press.

Wiig, E. H., & Semel, E. M. (1984). *Language assessment and intervention for the learning disabled* (2nd ed.). Columbus, OH: Charles E. Merrill.

Wright, H. H., & Newhoff, M. (2002). Inferencing and story retelling abilities of children with and without language learning disabilities. *American Journal of Speech-Language Pathology, 10,* 308–319.

Wright, P., & Wright, P. (2006). *Wrights law: From emotions to advocacy – The special education survival guide.* Hartfield, VA: Harbor House Law Press.

CHAPTER 7

HISTORY OF EMOTIONAL AND BEHAVIORAL DISORDERS

Frederick J. Brigham and Brittany L. Hott

Education of children with emotional and/or behavioral disorders (EBD) is a very emotionally charged topic. Across its short history in the United States, the field has evoked a number of heated debates among advocates and scholars as well as controversial legislative actions and legal decisions. The controversies and strong opinions surrounding the field are unsurprising. Children and youths with EBD evoke strong negative feelings in the people they encounter in their communities and schools (Shores & Wehby, 1999). The ways that society has chosen to respond to those feelings over time have changed a great deal with the interpretations of EBD, the interventions offered, and the supports provided for these children, their families, and their teachers.

One element that has remained constant is the trajectory of development, adoption, disillusionment, and eventual abandonment of ideas in the field. Vonk (1979) named this pattern "the innovation cycle" and described it as the way that many new approaches were oversold and subsequently applied to problems they were never intended to solve or in levels that lacked appropriate fidelity of treatment, thereby undercutting its promised effectiveness.

All societies have rules for acceptable behavior. The rules are not always the same from place to place, but at a fundamental level, societies tend to invest themselves in regulating similar behaviors for similar reasons

History of Special Education
Advances in Special Education, Volume 21, 151–180
Copyright © 2011 by Emerald Group Publishing Limited
All rights of reproduction in any form reserved
ISSN: 0270-4013/doi:10.1108/S0270-4013(2011)0000021010

(Neiman, 2009; Shermer, 2004; Wilson, 1998). Some activities are classified as acceptable and even desirable and others as undesirable or prohibited. Classification is a fundamental human activity that exists in all societies (Bowker & Star, 1999).

EVOLVING CLASSIFICATION SYSTEMS

All societies carry out sorting and classificatory actions, the way they view deviance changes over time for a variety of reasons that are sometimes unrelated to the behavior or its consequences (Moynihan, 1993). Also, some behaviors that were considered to be illnesses or crimes at one time have been redefined in ways that remove them from the medical, psychological, or legal professions' guidelines for interpreting them as deviant behaviors. Homosexuality is one example of such a reclassification (Bowker & Star, 1999).

Some critics of special education have suggested that changes in definition of acceptable and unacceptable behaviors over time undermine the entire enterprise of determining who is and is not appropriately considered to have EBD. Some advocates have proposed that all categories for special-education services be eliminated because of harmful effects of labeling and the time required to identify students according to disability categories (O'Donnell, 2009). However, classificatory systems: (a) allow communication among practitioners, researchers, and policymakers, (b) allow for more clear organization of information regarding students with EBD, (c) help to guide the selection of interventions, and (d) establish a basis for marshalling resources to provide services to students with EBD (Cullinan, 2004). Worse, lack of formal structures for classification and consideration of action often overwhelms individual efforts to make meaning of immediate experience, and encourages low-level convenience classifications rather than well-considered and thought-out systems of classifications (Freeman, 1972).

The classification practices of all sciences change across time as new facts are discovered and paradigms for understanding allow for different questions to be pursued (Kuhn, 1996). Many constructs that were once considered important guideposts for understanding and working in EBD have been discarded or replaced as our understanding of human behavior has changed over time (Kauffman, Brigham, & Mock, 2004). Further, the conditions under which educational activities are carried out have also affected the way we view students with EBD and our goals for intervention (Brigham, Tochterman, & Brigham, 2000).

As our knowledge base evolves and educators respond to continued changes in society, the understanding of EBD as well as its classifications and interventions will need to change as well. Kauffman et al. (2004) suggested that the future holds a rather stark choice between science and antiscience or pseudoscience (see Shermer, 2002). We agree that pursuing scientific understanding is the best way of attaining our goals for individuals with EBD. Bowker and Star (1999) pointed out, however, that even objective systems of classification are influenced by social and political factors. Rather than undermining the scientific enterprise, we suggest that social and political influences are other elements that must be considered in their own right. Social and political influences address different aspects of experience than do scientific inquiries. Science without social concern is cold, politics without scientific verification is unwise. One of the tasks facing people concerned with the field of education for individuals with EBD is finding ways of bringing rapprochement to scientific and sociopolitical elements in the field.

EDUCATIONAL TREATMENT
OF CHILDREN WITH EBD

Individuals with EBD have been a part of society as long as society has existed, and, as in the present, they have drawn strong and negative reactions from the people that they encounter. After all, while it is possible to like an individual with EBD, it is difficult to imagine referring to a person as having EBD *because* their company is enjoyable and others like being with them. Other descriptors apply in those cases. A common thread across the descriptions of each of the historical periods that follow is the strong and often conflicting emotions that this population evokes.

Protection From and For

Early responses to EBD were quite severe, and often included incarceration under very cruel conditions. Supernatural phenomena such as demonic possession were often invoked to explain the behavior of people who would now be called individuals with EBD (Kauffman & Landrum, 2009). The concept of childhood as a developmental period distinct from adulthood had not yet emerged, and the years now considered to be adolescence were part of adult life during these times (Mussen, Conger, & Kagan, 1975). Consequently, interventions for disturbed and disturbing behavior were the same as those applied to adults in the era and included bleeding, incarceration, and even execution. Society viewed these behaviors with great fear, and sought to protect themselves *from* people who exhibited these behaviors. At the same time, some provisions were made to ensure that protections were also provided *for* individuals with such behaviors. Providing protections for individuals with such behaviors was an outgrowth of the enlightenment ideas about human dignity that led to both the American and French revolutions. Rethinking the rights of humanity set the stage for the treatments that followed.

Individual Demonstrations of Moral Treatment

There are no references to emotional disorders of children before the 18th century (Kanner, 1962). This is hardly surprising given the absence of acknowledgment of childhood as a distinct developmental period and the poor understanding of human behavior of the era. No systematic efforts at education and treatment of individuals with EBD were prominent during the latter part of the 18th century and the early parts of the 19th century; however, several notable individuals made substantial contributions through demonstrations that individuals with EBD could, indeed, respond to more appropriate treatment.

Philippe Pinel (1745–1826) is credited with developments in the understanding and treatment of psychiatric conditions known as moral treatment. A painting by Robert-Fleury entitled "Dr. Pinel freeing the insane in the courtyard of the Salpêrière" appears in many introductory special education and psychology textbooks, attesting to the monumental contribution made by this early leader. Pinel noted that people who had been confined and treated with indifference and brutality for years in hospitals and other places that housed disturbed individuals often made dramatic improvements in behavior when treated with kindness and respect (Kauffman, 2001).

Another notable effort in this era involved attempts to treat a boy who was found wandering the countryside without the ability to communicate or interact with others in a manner expected of humans. Estimates at the time suggest that he had existed in the wild for six years (Shattuck, 1994).

Jean Marc Gaspard Itard, a student of Pinel, attempted to educate the boy, Victor, so that he might participate fully in society. Victor, otherwise known as the "wild boy of Aveyron," made dramatic improvement by the standards of the day, but Itard considered the effort to have been a failure because Victor never learned to speak and required substantial care and supervision the rest of his life. Nevertheless, Itard's work spurred others to investigate methods for teaching children who had previously been dismissed as idiots and imbeciles who could be taught very little if anything at all.

Developments in America

In the United States, Benjamin Rush, a professor of chemistry and signer of the Declaration of Independence (Urban & Wagoner, 2009) began writing about the needs of the newly independent country to form its own system of education. Among other contributions, Rush advocated public support for schools for the poor and also education of females. He objected to the harsh treatment that often characterized schooling of the day, and advocated milder forms of punishment such as confining the child after school hours (Kauffman, 2001).

Current ideas of reinforcement and positive behavior management were absent from discussions of child rearing and managing the behavior of children in schools. Early enthusiasm for education of large segments of society in general waned as the hope for results of widespread dissemination of knowledge and literacy proved to be more expensive and also harder to attain than had been previously imagined (Urban & Wagoner, 2009). As enthusiasm for widespread education waned, so did enthusiasm for education of individuals with disabilities, and the latter half of the 19th century was characterized more by regression than the development of ways of teaching individuals with disabilities, including those with EBD. It should be noted that recognition of emotional disorders of childhood as a distinct and legitimate field of study would have to wait until the early 20th century.

Disillusion and Retreat

Throughout the latter half of the 19th century, children were treated as miniature adults (Mussen et al., 1975). With the coming of the industrial revolution, children as well as adults congregated in urban centers around factories and went to work. Child labor laws had yet to be developed and the working as well as the living conditions for many children of this era was quite grim. Further, the period of westward expansion in the United States resulted in many children living in extremely rural areas with few educational resources.

Little progress was made during this period. For most of the era, there was no discrimination among various forms of cognitive and emotional/or behavioral disorders. Rather, all forms of disability were considered as a group. It was not until 1886 that mental retardation and EBD were distinguished from each other (Gargiulo, 2010). Treatment began to resemble the earlier modes of protection from and for individuals with disabilities. Across the last half of the 19th century, most individuals with EBD were either in jails, almshouses, or the currently popular form of treatment for the period, asylums.

The Asylum Movement

The asylum movement was, to a large extent, promoted by efforts of Dorothea Dix. Her vivid accounts of the horrible conditions experienced by most people who were insane prompted legislators to create a more humane alternative to the brutal conditions that most people experienced in prisons (Gollaher, 1995). Favoring the sentiments of popular American philosophers such as Walt Whitman, who viewed the cities as a corrupting influence, the asylums were located in rural areas where the insane could escape the turmoil of urban life. Although not a major focus of the asylums, some systematic efforts at education were reported within these facilities (e.g., Brigham, 1845, 1848).

The early promises of asylums began to fade as they became overcrowded, experienced difficulties in recruiting and maintaining competent staffs, and were the targets of sensational newspaper reports about poor conditions and unacceptable treatment of residents (Luchins, 1988). Another issue facing the asylums was their locations. Located in rural areas but serving populations from primarily urban areas, the asylums found increasing difficulty in obtaining funding from local populations who felt little need to burden themselves with the costs of treating disturbed city dwellers. As the need outstripped society's willingness to support these facilities, they increasingly became the targets of scorn rather than hopeful alternatives for humane treatment.

At the close of the 19th century, textbooks that systematically described the characteristics and treatments for mental disorders began to appear. The first juvenile courts were established in Chicago and Denver in 1899 indicating the beginnings of clear differentiation of childhood and adolescence from adult life. It was not, however, until 1900 that publications began to appear that "announced to an astonished world that children were known to display psychotic phenomena" (Kanner, 1962, p. 99).

Mental Hygiene

By 1909, a number of prominent physicians and early psychologists established the National Committee for Mental Hygiene. It is interesting to note that one of the founders of the mental hygiene movement, Clifford Beers, had been hospitalized after a nervous breakdown in 1900. He recovered and related his experiences in the mental health system of his day in a book entitled *A Mind that Found Itself* (Beers, 1908). Along with Adolph Meyer and William James, Beers sought to revitalize the public health system to include the mental as well as physical well-being with the goal of "attainment of physical and mental health by all U.S. citizens" (Becker & Marecek, 2008, p. 595). The mental hygiene movement is considered by many to be the forerunner of the positive psychology movement (see Seligman & Csikszentmihalyi, 2000).[1]

Preventing Emotional Disturbance

The Committee for Mental Hygiene promoted early diagnosis and intervention as well as the establishment of clinical and guidance programs in schools (Spaulding & Balch, 1983). It is most notable as an early and substantial effort at preventing the development of mental health problems in later life by ensuring that the conditions in childhood were conducive to the development of physical and mental health. The mental hygiene movement is also notable for its union of physical and psychological functioning in mental illness.

Although efforts to provide treatment to children and youth with EBD were increasingly prominent across the early 20th century, it was not until the 1930s that systematic and sustained efforts were made to understand the etiology, diagnosis, treatment, and prognosis of children with severe emotional disturbances (Kanner, 1962).

DEVELOPMENT OF SYSTEMATIC PROGRAMS AND CONCEPTUAL MODELS

The period from the 1930s through the mid-1970s witnessed an explosion of interest in children and youth with EBD. The growth in educational services for children with EBD occurred along with major developments in the field of child psychiatry. Researchers in this period refined descriptions of characteristics and etiological factors before the 1950s, but it was not until 1950 that programs and clear intervention strategies became evident (Yell, Meadows, Drasgow, & Shriner, 2009).

Through the 1940s, 1950s, and the 1960s, educational options for children and youth with EBD appeared in some locales, usually larger cities. The federal government began encouraging educational services for individuals with disabilities when Congress amended the Elementary and Secondary Education Act of 1966 so that states could *elect* to use federal funds to provide educational services to students with disabilities (Egnor, 2003). Schools were not required to provide services for individuals with disabilities until 1975 when Congress passed and Gerald R. Ford signed P.L. 94-142, the Education for All handicapped Children Act (Cross, 2004).

As researchers examined the undifferentiated construct of emotional disturbance and began to notice different features of the various disorders that the term includes, they began to create conceptual models for explaining and treating EBD based on their differing perspectives. Some of the conceptual models developed during this period have fallen into relative disfavor and others have emerged as profitable, albeit incomplete, approaches to identification and treatment of EBD. These conceptual models tell the story of this period of the education and treatment for students with EBD.

Psychodynamic Approach

Bower (1990) referred to the period of the 1930s and 1940s as the resolution of intrapsychic conflict era (RICE). The RICE era was rooted clearly in the psychodynamic theory of Sigmund Freud. Psychodynamic theorists postulate that imbalances in an individual's mental state cause the pathologies that are expressed as emotional disturbances. Interventions based on psychodynamic theory include individual talking therapy and permissive classroom environments with highly accepting teachers (Yell et al., 2009). The child is encouraged to resolve his or her interpsychic conflicts and thereby attain more optimal functioning. Although still found in special-education programs for children with EBD, psychodynamic approaches are increasingly in disfavor in school settings. One reason for this is that they are often incompatible with the high demands imposed upon schools by current federal and state regulations associated with standards-based reforms. Another reason is that counseling interventions in general are "among the *least effective* options to us if the goal is to produce reliable, meaningful changes in student behavior" (Walker, Ramsey, & Gresham, 2004, p. 159).

Psychoeducational Approach

The psychoeducational approach includes many of the psychotherapeutic aspects of the psychodynamic approach, but it adds systematic analysis of behavior in the context where it happens (Yell et al., 2009). The signature treatment of the psychoeducational approach is the "Life Space Interview" (Redl, 1959). The Life Space Interview is now called Life Space Intervention (LSI). LSI is a verbal technique for intervening with children and youth experiencing a behavioral crisis. LSI focuses on the student's immediate experiences (life space) during the crisis to gain understanding of the event. The goal of LSI is to promote self-regulated and adaptive behavior on the part of the individuals with whom it is used (Wood & Long, 1991).

The ideas behind LSI appear to be the basis for another technique that is currently discussed for helping students gain insight and regulation of their behavior, "social skill autopsies" (Lavoie, 2005). While there are a number of other aspects to the psychoeducational model, the LSI component marks the acknowledgement and systematic attempt to deal with learned behaviors.

Ecological Approach

The ecological approach was prompted, to a large extent, by dissatisfaction with hospitalization and psychotherapeutic approaches that were prominent in the 1940s and 1950s. By the early 1960s, a model program called Project Re-Ed was being implemented to treat the child as well as make the child's home and community more supportive of adaptive behavior (Kauffman, 2001).

Hobbs (1966) described the Re-Ed model as being based on the assumption that emotionally disturbed children have learned maladaptive behaviors and therefore can be reeducated to display adaptive behaviors. In doing so, Re-Ed practitioners focus on health rather than illness in the life of the child. Further, a major goal of Re-Ed is teaching children cognitive control strategies to help them manage their own behaviors. "The emotionally disturbed child has fewer degrees of freedom in behavior than the normal child, yet he is not without the ability to shape his own behavior by self-administered verbal instruction" (Hobbs, 1966, p. 1111).

Another important element in Re-Ed is in developing a sense of competence. By competence, Hobbs and colleagues specifically meant mastery of school skills with most attention directed toward the skills of reading and arithmetic. By developing skills that will enable them to function more typically in a classroom situation, the most common ecology shared by children in the United States, children are believed to gain confidence as well as the ability to gain acceptance by other children, teachers, and other community members, including the child's parents. Many examples of programs operating under Re-Ed principles are still in existence today, although few public schools provided the dedicated intensity of service and support necessary for Re-Ed. Nevertheless, the model, like many of the others has much to offer individuals seeking ways to improve educational outcomes for students with EBD.

Humanistic Approach

The humanistic approach also departed dramatically from the psychotherapeutic models that had preceded it. Carl Rogers is probably the best known of the humanists of the 1960s and 1970s. He, along with other influential educators and psychologists of the day, called for an individual, person-centered approach to therapy and development (Rogers, 1954, 1970). In short, abnormal behavior was suggested to be the result of pressures to conform to societal expectations that block the individual's drive toward self-actualization (Yell et al., 2009). Rogers' book, *Freedom to Learn* (1969), was quite influential among humanists of the era. In it, he outlined approaches to nondirective teaching based on assumptions that people, given sufficient freedom, will pursue the learning that they need for their own purposes. The "free schools" and "open education" movements were, to a large part, based on the ideas of Rogers and other educators who espoused similar theories (e.g., Knoblock, 1965; Morse, 1985). The popularity of humanistic approaches diminished as subsequent research consistently supported more directive and structured approaches for most students, including those with EBD. Nevertheless, concepts such as self-determination (e.g., Agran, 1997; Wehmeyer, Agran, & Hughes, 1998) contain many of the humanist ideas blended with ideas from other areas including cognitive and behavioral approaches.

Behavioral Approach

The behavioral approach assumes that behavior is shaped as a function of environmental events. By arranging consistent consequences for behaviors, teachers can encourage the behaviors that they desire and discourage less desirable behaviors. In short, people act the way that they do because they obtain a payoff of some sort for their behavior. The payoff can be something that is obtained (e.g., money for work, or attention) or it may be escaping some noxious stimulus (e.g., giving a child a candy bar to stop whining). Behaviors can also be diminished by punishment (technically, anything that decreases a behavior is a punishment) or extinction (lack of response to the behavior).

Educators such as Haring and Phillips (1962) and Hewett (1968) developed highly structured approaches that included elements such as giving clear directions, maintaining firm expectations, and using follow-through for behavior that exploited behavioral principles, particularly of reinforcement of desirable behavior. Behavioral approaches often employ systematic data-collection procedures to validate the existence of the target problem and the adequacy of response to treatment.

Behavioral principles remain prominent in education programs today because of their effectiveness and clear ability to communicate the actions and results of an intervention to funding agencies and other stakeholders. Federal regulations require functional behavior assessments (FBA) for students who are facing serious disciplinary action (Fox & Gable, 2004). FBA is a set of procedures that are clearly aligned with the behavioral model. While there is some controversy regarding the extent to which FBAs can actually fill the needs to which they are directed, the requirement of this activity in the regulations demonstrates the efficacy that the behavioral model has shown over time.

Cognitive–Behavioral Approach

Cognitive–behavioral psychologists suggest that just like physical movements, cognitions (thoughts) are behaviors. If movements and other behaviors are learned, so must the behaviors that are thoughts be learned. Similar to the thinking found in the ecological and behavioral approaches, cognitive practitioners suggest that learned maladaptive thought patterns can be replaced with more adaptive thoughts.

Cognitive–behavior modification procedures (Meichenbaum, 1977) have been applied to a wide variety of behavioral issues. They appear to have greatest efficacy in areas such as anxiety disorders and depression (Beck, 1976). Additionally, cognitive–behavioral approaches have been used to teach behavioral self-control in a variety of settings to students with EBD (Polsgrove & Smith, 2004).

Biological Approach

Many of the approaches previously described are compatible with ideas that behavioral problems are the result of unfortunate, maladaptive learning or of a mismatch between the individual and his or her environment. Such analyses place the problem in the interaction of the child with the environment. The biological approach, however, places the origins of the problem squarely within the child.

The biological approach is closely tied to developments in the medical profession and, as the name suggests, other life sciences such as biology. As scientists in these fields develop and refine their understanding of neurobiology related to human behavior, the implications for the field of EBD are often quite noticeable. For example, some conditions that were once considered an indicator of emotional imbalance (e.g., epilepsy) are now properly understood as biophysical disorders that can be managed by medication. Medical intervention is increasingly viewed as important in conditions such as attention deficit/hyperactivity disorder, depression, or anxiety disorders (Pennington, 2002). Often, medications are provided in conjunction with behavioral or cognitive–behavioral treatments to boost the effects of each. Educators often serve as data collectors to verify changes in behavior resulting from the medical interventions and also as agents and instructors in behavioral and cognitive interventions that may co-occur with medical treatments.

LEGISLATION AND LITIGATION

It is difficult to believe that anything other than legal intervention through legislation and litigation has been a great influence in the field of EBD during the latter third of the 20th century. Before 1975, no requirement for schools to provide educational services to students with EBD was in place. With the passage of the Education for All Handicapped Children Act in 1975 (later renamed the Individuals with Disabilities Education Act), all of that changed. Schools were required to provide educational and related services that constituted a "free and appropriate education" (FAPE) in the "least restrictive environment" (LRE) to each student with EBD who resided in their catchment areas. Further, the regulations required that each student with EBD receive services under an individual education plan (IEP) that details the individual's present level of performance, instructional needs, necessary supports, and so forth.

Access to the General Education Curriculum

One step in the direction of creating a balance between FAPE and LRE is the requirement that instruction be directed toward access to the general education curriculum in IDEA regulations. Advocates for students with EBD consider the first wave of access to have been obtaining access to the schools. The next step is, therefore, access to the curriculum in place for all other students. Some schools, however, have interpreted the statement to mean that all students should be in the general education curriculum in the general education classroom. Such an interpretation is inappropriate and denies many students opportunities for remedial instruction. This area seems to be another aspect of education of students with EBD that will be the target of litigation in the coming years. As the standards-based instruction movement shrinks the curriculum in breadth (Hess & Brigham, 2001), it is hard to imagine that the unique needs of students with EBD can be met in the general education curriculum.

Discipline Procedures for Students with EBD

Although the arguments surrounding full inclusion of students with EBD into general education settings are controversial, they are often relatively tame compared to the ire that accompanies discussion of the discipline provisions of IDEA. As might be expected of a group of students who are identified by their high levels of problematic behavior, most of the discipline controversies center on students with EBD. Most public policies are intentionally crafted to be somewhat vague, thereby prompting litigation to fine-tune the elements that legislators omitted or about which they were unclear (Stone, 2002). IDEA was no exception to this.

While schools were expected to develop IEPs for each student with a disability, some critics noted that students with EBD were often involved in disciplinary actions in their school that interrupted or even ended their educational careers. Some advocates began to worry that schools were using disciplinary procedures to repeatedly suspend or even expel students who were difficult to teach in an effort to avoid their responsibilities to deliver FAPE (Egnor, 2003).

The 1988 decision by the US Supreme court in the *Honig v. Doe* case established that schools were denied the unilateral authority to remove students with disabilities from schools because of their behavior. Schools were not left powerless to remove students with dangerous behaviors from the general population, but establishing behavior interventions to support them was clearly necessary. Other circuit court cases followed and created various legal procedures for determining LRE for students with EBD (see Yell, 2006 for a thorough discussion of these actions). It is unlikely that legal scrutiny of the field will abate, given the importance of education for life in the 21st century.

ASSESSMENT OF CHILDREN AND YOUTHS WITH EBD

Assessment of children and youths with EBD follows the general trends in all forms of scientific endeavor with the initial recognition and description of the phenomenon continuing through periods of false starts leading to increasing consistency, greater specificity, and the development of more rigorous procedures (Kauffman et al., 2004). As new conceptual models developed and replaced earlier, less productive models, the definitions and procedures employed to identify individuals with EBD became more formal and open to scrutiny.

Establishing an accurate definition of EBD is a very important task because the elements contained in an accepted definition guide the selection of procedures and interpretative frameworks in the field. Although there are a number of definitions of emotional disturbance in the literature, the one that is currently most influential in education is found in IDEA. The federal definition of EDB in IDEA contains the following text.

> The term means a condition exhibiting one or more of the following characteristics over a long period of time and to a marked degree that adversely affects a child's educational performance:
>
> (A) An inability to learn that cannot be explained by intellectual, sensory, or health factors.
> (B) An inability to build or maintain satisfactory interpersonal relationships with peers and teachers.
> (C) Inappropriate types of behavior or feelings under normal circumstances.

(D) A general pervasive mood of unhappiness or depression.

(E) A tendency to develop physical symptoms of fears associated with personal or school problems.

The term includes schizophrenia. The term does not apply to children who are socially maladjusted unless it is determined that they have an emotional disturbance (U.S. Department of Education, 1998, p. II-46).

Each of the points can be the focus of assessment efforts (Cullinan, 2004). The definition insists that the characteristics must be present for a long period of time and to a marked degree. There are many people who exhibit behavior problems that fail to rise to the level of a "marked degree" or that arc without adverse impact on their educations. These individuals are excluded from identification as having EBD under IDEA although they may qualify for special-education services in other disability categories. When individuals are considered to have behavior problems for a long period of time and to a marked degree, further assessment is carried out to identify individuals with EBD.

Ruling out other Factors

It is clear from the definition that intellectual, sensory, or physical conditions that could explain learning problems must be ruled out as the probable causes of the individual's problems in school. Measures of intelligence, visual and auditory acuity, and sometimes, medical examinations are employed to address these issues.

Learning

A variety of measures can be used to measure school learning. For example, classroom grades over the course of a school year provide one indication of academic performance. State achievement test data is another and increasingly prominent form of information regarding the presence or absence of learning problems (Gordon, 2006). Additionally, individual achievement measures of basic skills like reading, mathematics, or written language are also administered. Examples of such measures include the *Kauffman Tests of Educational Achievement* (Kaufman & Kaufman, 2004), or the *Woodcock-Johnson–III, Scales of Achievement* (Woodcock, McGrew, & Mather, 2001). Finally, curriculum-based measurement (CBM) of academic skills is a useful tool for identification, monitoring, and guiding instruction for students with EBD and it is a major part of response to intervention (RTI) initiatives (Brigham & Brigham, 2010).

Behavior and Social Relationships

Although the remaining four aspects of the definition are different from each other, they are generally evaluated with the same kinds of procedures. We will, therefore, describe these procedures as a group rather than repeating them for each element of the definition. Assessment of interpersonal relationships, manifestation of inappropriate behavior, mood disorders such as depression, and manifestation of physical symptoms and fears in association with school situations for students with EBD are frequently conducted by, (a) direct observation of behavior, (b) behavioral rating scales, and (c) self-report measures (Kavale, Mathur, & Mostert, 2004).

Direct observation of behavior is by far the most frequently used tool for evaluating these aspects of EBD (Sasso, Conroy, Stichter, & Fox, 2001). Observations completed according to a predetermined structure including operational definitions of the target behaviors and time parameters are usually more useful than general narrative observations (Merrell, 1994). Frequently, observers will select one or two individual, who are also present in the environment and take data on them for comparison purposes. In that way, the behavior exhibited by the target individuals can be compared to others under the same stimulus conditions. Additionally, the behavior of individuals with EBD within the context of the classroom and relative to the teacher's behaviors in relation to the target child should be considered in direct observation efforts (Slate & Saudargas, 1986).

Behavior Rating Scales

A number of behavior rating scales are available to help evaluate, categorize, and identify problem behaviors. Among these are the *Systematic Screening for Behavior Disorders* (SSBD; Walker & Severson, 1992) and the *Behavioral and Emotional Rating Scale* (BERS; Epstein & Sharma, 1998). Teachers and parents complete such instruments by rating the frequency of a variety of behaviors during a given period of time (e.g., six months). The SSBD is an example of a "multiple gating system" where each level of the assessment becomes progressively more precise and demanding. It moves from a general screening of behavior to actual comparison of the target student's behavior to norms constructed from more than 4,500 cases. The BERS is an example of "strength-based assessment" that examines the presence of social abilities as well as deficits.

Self-Report Measures

Individuals with EBD are also asked to complete self-rating scales in many cases. *The Student Self-Concept Scale* (SSCS; Gresham, Elliott, & Evans-Fernandez, 1992) is once such instrument. The SSCC collects information across three content domains: self-image, academic, and social and creates ratings of the individuals: (a) self-confidence to perform the behaviors, (b) importance placed upon the various behaviors, and (c) confidence that positive outcomes will result from carrying out the behaviors (Gresham, 1995). While such self-report instruments are highly subjective and open to social expectancy effects (people may report in ways that they think are beneficial to them rather than honestly), they may provide insights into the individual's emotional state that would otherwise be unavailable or at least very difficult to obtain (Elliott & Busse, 2004).

FAMILY INVOLVEMENT

As the understanding of EBD changed across the 19th and 20th centuries, so did the understanding of the contribution and roles of the family relative to causal factors, treatment selection, and supports for individuals with EBD. As may be expected, given the psychodynamic orientation of the early part of the century, families, particularly parents, were often considered to be the causes of the observed problems.

Most notably, Bruno Bettelheim, proposed that children developed autism due to cold and emotionally distant mothers, which he called "refrigerator mothers" (Bettelheim, 1967). Mothers of children with schizophrenia were labeled as "schizophrenogenic" and their parenting practices cited as primary factors to the development of mental disorders (Kauffman & Landrum, 2009). Ironically, while parents were often blamed for their children's problems, they bore much of the burden for educating their children during this period (Wehman & Gentry, 2008).

With the rise of behavioral learning approaches to EBD, efforts shifted from blaming parents and families to developing services and supports to meet student needs. Part of this effort was driven by families who initiated litigation to secure public educational services for their children (e.g., *Mills v. Board of Education*, 1972, *Pennsylvania Association for Retarded Children v. Pennsylvania*, 1972). Students slowly began to receive more appropriate intervention services within schools through placement in specialized classes by teachers or administrators of the schools that they attended. Students with EBD were often served in programs designed for the mildly retarded.

With the Education of All Handicapped Children Act, parents were provided with a more prominent role in the education and treatment of their children with EBD through a system of procedural safeguards. Parent education and support programs were offered in some schools and the ecological behavioral movement sought to include parents as active participants in their children's treatment programs.

During the 1980s, a body of research began to emerge specifically addressing the needs of families coping with emotional disabilities. Various advocacy organizations provided a means for parents, social workers, psychologists, teachers, and other professionals to work toward establishing better mental health and special-education legislation, proposing a new definition of EBD, and improving mental health and educational services (Forness & Knitzer, 1992; Kauffman, 2001). By 1986, educational rights were extended to youngsters aged 3–5 years old so that early intervention services may be provided. In 1989, the Federation of Families for Children's Mental Health was established to advocate for students with EBD and offer support to their families (Kauffman, 2001). Additionally, family stressors were acknowledged and found to be compounded as children with disabilities reached adolescence (Gallagher, Beckman, & Cross, 1983).

The nineties were characterized by an increased focus on parental rights and the family unit as thinking shifted from finding causes of stressors to supporting families and students. Genetic, social, and environmental influences were accepted as risk factors for the development of emotional and behavioral disabilities (Mash & Wolfe, 2010; Plomin, 1995) and the concept of wraparound services emerged focusing on providing support for students in the community, within the home and at school. Targets for program development included strengthening school and community capacity as well as collaborating with families with an emphasis on shared decision making. Also, during this time period, research on family stresses demonstrated that children and youth with EBD encounter family stresses such as lower socioeconomic status, poor levels of maternal education, having a biological parent with a psychiatric disorders as well as the experience of physical and/or sexual abuse at rates that far exceed the general population (Mattison, 2004).

During the nineties, fathers were often taking a more active role in parenting and the educational process while in other families, grandparents were serving in the role of parents (Glover & Wehman, 2008). At the same time, focus on the needs of siblings of children with disabilities began to emerge indicating that siblings were often ill-informed of disabilities and often made up stories to explain their siblings problems (Gallagher, Powell, & Rhodes, 2006). At the conclusion of the first decade of the 21st century, focus is increasingly placed on family, school, and community partnerships (Glover & Wehman, 2008). Family-centered practice is viewed as a critical part of providing effective special-education services to individuals with EBD. However, barriers to parent involvement in educational endeavors remain. These barriers include school personnel not allotting adequate time to meet with parents and lack of knowledge regarding how to glean beneficial information from parents (Bos & Vaughn, 2006). The predominant research efforts for family support have focused on parents of students with intellectual and physical disabilities with little attention to students identified as having EBD (Bos & Vaughn, 2006). Therefore, additional research is needed effectively to support students and families of youngsters with EBD.

TECHNOLOGY AND EDUCATION OF INDIVIDUALS WITH EBD

Students with EBD present serious behavior challenges and also experience severe achievement deficits (Reid, Gonzalez, Nordness, Trout, & Epstein, 2004). A number of technological applications are available to support academic learning. Although the research base for individuals with EBD is most focused on technological applications in support of behavioral issues, it seems logical that instructional technologies developed to promote academic achievement, particularly for others with similar achievement deficits, would be beneficial for individual with EBD as well. We suggest that any instructional approach be monitored with CBM to ensure that it is meeting the needs of the students with whom it is used. Current applications of technology with individuals with EBD can be grouped into (a) behavioral observation tools, (b) self-modeling of behaviors, (c) self-recording and self-management tasks.

Technology for Observation

Emerging technology makes it possible for observation data to be directly entered into computers in real time. Kahng and Iwata (2000) suggested that computer-based observation programs allowed observers to collect, graph, and analyze data more accurately and quickly than did older paper and pencil methods. Additionally, computer-based observation systems provide efficiencies in storing, retrieving, and sharing observational data that far exceed other forms of record keeping. Similar applications are being developed for palmtop computers such as Pam Pilots and i-pad tablet computers (Emerson, Reeves, & Felce, 2000). Additionally, small portable bar code scanners can be employed to collect data in a variety of categories associated with pre-established bar codes according to various time parameters. For example, in a time-sampling procedure, an individual would scan the behavior code for whatever behavior that was being observed when prompted by a visual or auditory signal from the bar code reader (Tapp & Wehby, 2000). Such procedures have the potential to make structured observations in natural settings much easier to carry out.

Video Modeling

"Video modeling consists of having an individual watch a video of him/ herself (or someone similar) engage in the behavior targeted for improvement" (Baker, Lang, & O'Reilly, 2009, p. 404). It has several appealing advantages. First, with a modest degree of effort, videotapes of the individual who is the target of the intervention can be created to provide a positive model of the individual him or herself exhibiting the desired behavior. Also, videos demonstrating the desired skills can be created across multiple contexts to promote generalization. Additionally, video modeling interventions are potentially less demanding of teacher time and attention than are other, more typical interventions.

Baker et al. (2009) summarized the literature on the use of video modeling with students with EBD from 1974 through 2005. The studies were classified according to their intervention targets, (a) increasing peer interaction, (b) increasing on-task behavior, and (c) decreasing inappropriate behavior. All of the studies examined reported positive outcomes for the target individuals. Outcomes appear to be consistently greater when video modeling is combined with other forms of instruction such as discussion and behavioral rehearsal and also when the video modeling programs are accompanied with systematic reinforcement of desired behaviors. The research on this technique yields few other firm guidelines.

Self-Recording with Handheld Computers

Self-monitoring and self-recording are well-established interventions that have been demonstrated to yield positive outcomes in a nonintrusive manner (Rock, 2005; Rock & Thead, 2007). Most self-monitoring programs first teach the target student to discriminate the occurrence or nonoccurrence of the target behavior and then to self-record ratings of the behavior such as on-task or off-task (self-monitoring of attention), or in the case of academics, number of tasks completed and accuracy (self-monitoring of performance). A final step, self-graphing the behavior completes the program and reinforces the first two steps. Recent efforts have demonstrated that using handheld computers such as Palm Pilots is a viable approach to implementing self-monitoring with individuals with EBD in a variety of settings (Gulchak, 2008). Gulchak suggested that the handheld computer had the advantages of, (a) social validity in that they are popular devices that are common in business and other natural settings, (b) cost effectiveness (less than 10% of common laptop computers), (c) portability, (d) enhanced recording and transcription accuracy over paper/pencil formats, and (e) ease of use.

ISSUES FACING THE FIELD

As the field of education for students with EBD moves into the next century, a number of issues that have their roots in practices of the 20th century will probably be prominent in considerations of the next steps for the profession. Among these are concerns about who gets identified as having EBD, what services should be provided, and the role of education for students with EBD in the broader mental health community.

Under-Service

Critics of special education point to the increasing numbers of students declared to be eligible for special-education services because of disabilities. There is no doubt that the numbers are rising for the population of all students with disabilities; however, students with EBD are a historically and dramatically underserved group (Walker, Nishioka, Zeller, Severson, & Feil, 2000). Estimates of the proportion of the school-aged population that are likely to qualify as having EBD are as high as 20% but the actual proportion of students served hovers around 1–2% (Walker et al., 2004).

Resistance to identifying students as having EBD seems to focus on two areas, philosophical and fiscal (Walker et al., 2004). Some professionals resist the idea of EBD because of the stereotypes of insanity that characterize the past. Perhaps they read *One Flew Over the Cuckoo's Nest* (Kesey, 1962) and assume that all persons with psychiatric disorders are treated in the same inhumane manner as were the characters in that book. Perhaps they have been hoodwinked by rhetoric that suggests that individuals with serious emotional problems are really more burdened by their society than they are dysfunctional within their society (e.g., Laing, 1999). The evidence is different than these authors suggest.

Individuals with EBD have very painful lives and also make the lives of those around them painful. Rather than society seeking to oppress large numbers of individuals, the evidence is more that society tends to ignore the plight of many people with EBD until they become intolerable. Rhetoric that suggests that the individual's right to freedom is protected more by limiting the chances that they will be provided service is directly contradicted by first-person accounts of the difficulty parents face trying to obtain help for their disturbed adolescent and adult children. Earley's (2006) description of the struggles he and his son faced in obtaining services is an excellent example of how things get worse when we ignore the problems of disturbed individuals.

Services for students with EBD can be very expensive. When local schools are unable to manage students with EBD, they may be compelled to provide costly out-of-district services (Brigham, Blaiklock, & Bon, in press). Some school officials appear to be avoiding the potential costs of such services by failing to identify certain individuals as having EBD, thereby limiting the student's right to an education. If students are not identified, it is more likely that they will be removed from schools for disciplinary reasons. The long-term costs of failing to educate such students to society is, however, dramatically higher than the cost of education.

Disproportionality

Many advocates are concerned that certain groups of students are more likely to be identified as having EBD and placed in special education than are members of other groups of students who demonstrate similar behaviors. It is clear that superficial factors such as race and sex affect the treatment that individuals receive from the schools and also within the legal system. Some groups may be overidentified and others may be under-identified. The major concern regarding disproportionality has been related to "students of color," particularly males (Osher et al., 2004). However, females have traditionally been underidentified in many areas of disability including EBD.

It is clear that schools in different communities identify students who display very different behaviors as having EBD (Wiley, Siperstein, Bountress, Forness, & Brigham, 2009; Wiley, Siperstein, Forness, & Brigham, 2010). Much more work is needed to understand the mechanisms that lead to this phenomenon. Osher and colleagues (2004) provided a thoughtful and provocative summary of many of the concerns facing professionals who wish to confront this issue. A careful reading of their work suggests that disentangling culture, language, and EBD has been a thorny problem in the past and will be very likely continue to be difficult in the future.

Evidence-Based Practices

The NCLB and IDEA regulations require schools to engage in evidence-based practices (EBP). The current evidence-based practices movement is centered on judgments of the adequacy of the research base rather than the emotions of the believer. Summaries of the criteria for determining the adequacy of evidence in various research models (Brantlinger, Jimenez, Klingner, Pugach, & Richardson, 2005; Gersten et al., 2005; Horner et al., 2005; Odom et al., 2005; Thompson, Diamond, McWilliam, Snyder, & Snyder, 2005) were published in a special issue of *Exceptional Children* in 2005. The US Department of Education also provides a "What Works" website in which a variety of educational practices are evaluated in terms of the adequacy of the supporting research, and also the efficacy of the effects that those techniques generate (Brigham, Gustashaw, & Brigham, 2004).

Education and Mental Health Professions

Children and youth with EBD come as a unique package but the service systems that attempt to support them come in fragmentary units (Eber &

Keenan, 2004). Special education, community mental health, medical health, child welfare, and the juvenile justice system all ostensibly work toward the same ends, but there is little if any coordination among these entities. Many advocates suggest that interagency collaboration will bring about far more positive outcomes than is presently the case (Dwyer, 2002; Dwyer & Bernstein, 1998). However, it is unclear from present practice how the sharing of responsibility for outcomes and decisions about primacy of needs will be resolved.

CONCLUSION

Professionals and laypersons concerned with the welfare of individuals with EBD have labored to understand the phenomena associated with the condition, differentiate among different forms of the condition, create effective treatments for individuals with EBD, and demonstrate that they, indeed, make a difference for the better in the lives of the people that they serve. Progress in one aspect of EBD often provokes changes in other areas and, as new treatments are developed in one area, they often change our understanding of the behavior demonstrated by individuals with EBD as well as best practices for intervening on their issues. The importance of the work in this field is underscored by the attention that legislators and litigators have directed toward it in the latter part of the 20th century. As the field enters the second decade of the 21st century, many issues remain to be resolved. One thing seems certain, however individuals with EBD will be with us always, and the needs that these individuals demonstrate will continue to require expert, well-researched, and effective intervention.

NOTE

1. The positive psychology movement has recently been criticized as unrealistic and counterproductive. Critics suggest that by cutting individuals off from normal expression of fear, anger, and grief, many problems are in the long run made more difficult (Ehrenreich, 2009). It is likely that the positive psychology movement has much to offer but will, like other movements in psychology and mental health, succumb to disappointment as people discover that it will not solve all of their problems.

REFERENCES

Agran, M. (1997). *Student-directed learning: Teaching self-determination skills.* Pacific Grove, CA: Brooks/Cole Pub. Co.

Baker, S. D., Lang, R., & O'Reilly, M. (2009). Review of video modeling with students with emotional and behavioral disorders. *Education and Treatment of Children, 32*(3), 403–420.

Beck, A. T. (1976). *Cognitive therapy and the emotional disorders.* New York: International Universities Press.

Becker, D., & Marecek, J. (2008). Positive psychology: History in the remaking? *Theory and Psychology, 18*(5), 591–604.

Beers, C. W. (1908). *A mind that found itself: An autobiography.* New York: Longmans, Green, and Co.

Bettelheim, B. (1967). *The empty fortress: Infantile autism and the birth of the self.* New York: Free Press.

Bos, C. S., & Vaughn, S. (2006). *Strategies for teaching students with learning and behavior problems* (6th ed.). Boston: Pearson/Allyn & Bacon.

Bower, E. M. (1990). A brief history of how we have helped emotionally disturbed children and other fairy tales. *Preventing School Failure, 35*(1), 11–16.

Bowker, G. C., & Star, S. L. (1999). *Sorting things out: Classification and its consequences.* Cambridge, MA: MIT Press.

Brantlinger, E., Jimenez, R., Klingner, J., Pugach, M., & Richardson, V. (2005). Qualitative studies in special education. *Exceptional Children, 71*(2), 195–207.

Brigham, A. (1845). Schools in lunatic asylums. *American Journal of Insanity, 1,* 326–340.

Brigham, A. (1848). Schools and asylums for the idiotic and imbecile. *American Journal of Insanity, 5,* 19–33.

Brigham, F. J., Blaiklock, D., & Bon, S. C. (in press). School choice and specialized settings. In: B. Billingsley, M. L. Boscardin & J. B. Crockett (Eds.), *Handbook of leadership & administration for special education.* New York: Routledge Press.

Brigham, F. J., & Brigham, M. S. P. (2010). Preventive instruction: Response to intervention can catch students before their problems become insurmountable. *The American School Board Journal, 197*(6), 32–33.

Brigham, F. J., Gustashaw, W. E., III., & Brigham, M. S. P. (2004). Scientific practice and the tradition of advocacy in special education. *Journal of Learning Disabilities, 37*(3), 200–206.

Brigham, F. J., Tochterman, S., & Brigham, M. S. P. (2000). Students with emotional and behavioral disorders and their teachers in test-linked systems of accountability. *Assessment for Effective Intervention, 26*(1), 19–27.

Cross, C. T. (2004). *Political education: National policy comes of age.* New York: Teachers College Press.

Cullinan, D. (2004). Classification and definition of emotional and behavioral disorders. In: R. B. Rutherford, M. M. Quinn & S. R. Mathur (Eds), *Handbook of research in emotional and behavioral disorders* (pp. 32–53). New York: Guilford Press.

Dwyer, K. P. (2002). Mental health in the schools. *Journal of Child and Family Studies, 11*(1), 101–111.

Dwyer, K. P., & Bernstein, R. (1998). Mental health in the schools: 'Linking islands of hope in a sea of despair'. *School Psychology Review, 27*(2), 277–286.

Earley, P. (2006). *Crazy: A father's search through America's mental health madness.* New York: G.P. Putnam's Sons.

Eber, L., & Keenan, S. (2004). Collaboration with other agencies: Wraparound and systems of care for children and youths with emotional and behavioral disorders. In: R. B. Rutherford, M. M. Quinn & S. R. Mathur (Eds), *Handbook of research in emotional and behavioral disorders* (pp. 502–516). New York: Guilford Press.

Egnor, D. E. (2003). *IDEA reauthorization and the student discipline controversy*. Denver, CO: Love Publishing Co..

Ehrenreich, B. (2009). *Bright-sided: How the relentless promotion of positive thinking has undermined America*. New York: Metropolitan Books.

Elliott, S. N., & Busse, R. T. (2004). Assessment and evaluation of students' behavior and intervention outcomes: The utility of rating scale methods. In: R. B. Rutherford, M. M. Quinn & S. R. Mathur (Eds), *Handbook of research in emotional and behavioral disorders* (pp. 123–142). New York: Guilford Press.

Emerson, E., Reeves, D. J., & Felce, D. (2000). Palmtop computer technologies for behavioral observation research. In: T. Thompson, D. Felce & F. J. Symons (Eds), *Behavioral observation: Technology and applications in developmental disabilities*. Paul.

Epstein, M. H., & Sharma, H. M. (1998). *Behavioral and emotional rating scale (BERS)*. Austin, TX: PRO-ED.

Forness, S. R., & Knitzer, J. (1992). A new proposed definition and terminology to replace 'serious emotional disturbance' in Individuals with Disabilities Education Act. *School Psychology Review, 21*(1), 12–20.

Fox, J. J., & Gable, R. A. (2004). Functional behavioral assessment. In: R. B. Rutherford, M. M. Quinn & S. R. Mathur (Eds), *Handbook of research in emotional and behavioral disorders* (pp. 143–162). New York: Guilford Press.

Freeman, J. (1972). The tyranny of structurelessness. *Berkeley Journal of Sociology, 17*, 151–164.

Gallagher, J. J., Beckman, P., & Cross, A. H. (1983). Families of handicapped children: Sources of stress and its amelioration. *Exceptional Children, 50*(1), 10–19.

Gallagher, P. A., Powell, T. H., & Rhodes, C. A. (2006). *Brothers & sisters: A special part of exceptional families* (3rd ed.). Baltimore: Paul H. Brookes.

Gargiulo, R. M. (2010). *Special education in contemporary society: An introduction to exceptionality* (4th ed.). Thousand Oaks, CA: SAGE Publications.

Gersten, R., Fuchs, L. S., Compton, D., Coyne, M., Greenwood, C., & Innocenti, M. S. (2005). Quality indicators for group experimental and quasi-experimental research in special education. *Exceptional Children, 71*(2), 149–164.

Glover, B. G., & Wehman, P. (2008). Parents, siblings, and families. In: P. Wehman (Ed.), *Exceptional individuals in school, community, and work* (pp. 39–53). Richmond, VA: Virginia Commonwealth University Rehabilitation Research and Training Center on Workplace Supports and Job Retenion.

Gollaher, D. (1995). *Voice for the mad: The life of Dorothea Dix*. New York: Free Press.

Gordon, S. (2006). Making sense of the inclusion debate under IDEA. *Brigham Young University Education and Law Journal, 189*(1), 176–213.

Gresham, F. M. (1995). Student self-concept scale: Description and relevance to students with emotional and behavioral. *Journal of Emotional and Behavioral Disorders, 3*(1), 19–26.

Gresham, F. M., Elliott, S. N., & Evans-Fernandez, S. (1992). *Student self-concept scale*. Circle Pine, MN: American Guidance Service.

Gulchak, D. J. (2008). Using a mobile handheld computer to teach a student with an emotional and behavioral disorder to self-monitor attention. *Education and Treatment of Children, 31*(4), 567–581.

Haring, N. G., & Phillips, E. L. (1962). *Educating emotionally disturbed children.* New York: McGraw-Hill.

Hess, F. M., & Brigham, F. J. (2001). How federal special education policy affects schooling in Virginia. In: C. E. J. Finn, Jr., A. J. Rotherham & C. R. Hokanson, Jr. (Eds), *Rethinking special education for a new century* (pp. 161–182). Washington, DC: The Thomas B. Fordham Foundation and The Progressive Policy Institute.

Hewett, F. M. (1968). *The emotionally disturbed child in the classroom: A developmental strategy for educating children with maladaptive behavior.* Boston: Allyn & Bacon.

Hobbs, N. (1966). Helping disturbed children: Psychological and ecological strategies. *American Psychologist, 21*(12), 1105–1115.

Horner, R. H., Carr, E. G., Halle, J., McGee, G., Odom, S., & Wolery, M. (2005). The use of single-subject research to identify evidence-based practice in special education. *Exceptional Children, 71*(2), 165–179.

Kahng, S. W., & Iwata, B. A. (2000). Computer systems for collecting real-time observational data. In: T. Thompson, D. Felce & F. J. Symons (Eds), *Behavioral observation: Technology and applications in developmental disabilities* (pp. 35–46). Baltimore: Paul H. Brookes.

Kanner, L. (1962). Emotionally disturbed children: A historical review. *Child Development, 33*(1), 97–102.

Kauffman, J. M. (2001). *Characteristics of emotional and behavioral disorders of children and youth* (7th ed.). Upper Saddle River, NJ: Merrill Prentice-Hall.

Kauffman, J. M., Brigham, F. J., & Mock, D. P. (2004). Historical to contemporary perspectives on the field of emotional and behavioral disorders. In: R. B. Rutherford, M. M. Quinn & S. R. Mathur (Eds), *Handbook of research in emotional and behavioral disorders* (pp. 15–31). New York: Guilford Press.

Kauffman, J. M., & Landrum, T. J. (2009). *Characteristics of emotional and behavioral disorders of children and youth* (9th ed.). Upper Saddle River, NJ: Merrill.

Kaufman, A. S., & Kaufman, N. L. (2004). *Kaufman test of educational achievement second edition (KTEA-II).* Circle Pines, MN: American Guidance Service.

Kavale, K. A., Mathur, S. R., & Mostert, M. P. (2004). Social skills training and teaching social behavior to students with emotional and behavioral disorders. In: R. B. Rutherford, M. M. Quinn & S. R. Mathur (Eds), *Handbook of research in emotional and behavioral disorders* (pp. 446–461). New York: Guilford Press.

Kesey, K. (1962). *One flew over the cuckoo's nest, a novel.* New York: Viking Press.

Knoblock, P. (1965). *Educational programming for emotionally disturbed children: The decade ahead.* Syracuse, NY: Division of Special Education and Rehabilitation, Syracuse University.

Kuhn, T. S. (1996). *The structure of scientific revolutions* (3rd ed.). Chicago: University of Chicago Press.

Laing, R. D. (1999). *Knots.* New York: Routledge.

Lavoie, R. (2005). Social skill autopsies: A strategy to promote and develop social competencies. LD Online Retrieved July 9, 2010, from http://www.ldonline.org/article/Social_Skill_Autopsies%3A_A_Strategy_to_Promote_and_Develop_Social_Competencies

Luchins, A. S. (1988). The rise and decline of the American asylum movement in the 19th century. *Journal of Psychology: Interdisciplinary and Applied, 122*(5), 471–486.

Mash, E. J., & Wolfe, D. A. (2010). *Abnormal child psychology* (4th ed.). Belmont, CA: Wadsworth CENGAGE Learning.

Mattison, R. E. (2004). Psychiatric and psychological assessment of emotional and behavioral disorders during school mental health consultation. In: R. B. Rutherford, M. M. Quinn & S. R. Mathur (Eds), *Handbook of research in emotional and behavioral disorders* (pp. 163–180). New York: Guilford Press.

Meichenbaum, D. (1977). *Cognitive-behavior modification: An integrative approach*. New York: Plenum Press.

Merrell, K. W. (1994). *Assessment of behavioral, social & emotional problems: Direct and objective methods for use with children and adolescents*. New York: Longman.

Mills v. Board of Education of the District of Columbia, 348 F. Supp 866 (D. DC 1972).

Morse, W. C. (1985). *The education and treatment of socioemotionally impaired children and youth*. Syracuse, NY: Syracuse University Press.

Moynihan, D. P. (1993). Defining deviancy down. *American Scholar, 62*(1), 17.

Mussen, P. H., Conger, J. J., & Kagan, J. (1975). *Basic and contemporary issues in developmental psychology*. New York: Harper & Row.

Neiman, S. (2009). *Moral clarity: A guide for grown-up idealists* (Rev. ed). Princeton, NJ: Princeton University Press.

O'Donnell, S. (2009). Learning, not labels, for special-needs students. Edmonton Journal. Retrieved from http://www.edmontonjournal.com/News/Learning + labels + special + needs + students/1677448/story.html

Odom, S. L., Brantlinger, E., Gersten, R., Horner, R. H., Thompson, B., & Harris, K. R. (2005). Research in special education: Scientific methods and evidence-based practices. *Exceptional Children, 71*(2), 137–148.

Osher, D., Cartledge, G., Oswald, D., Sutherland, K. S., Artilles, A., & Coutinho, M. (2004). Cultural and linguistic competency and disproportionate representation. In: R. B. Rutherford, M. M. Quinn & S. R. Mathur (Eds), *Handbook of research in emotional and behavioral disorders* (pp. 54–77). New York: Guilford Press.

Pennington, B. F. (2002). *The development of psychopathology: Nature and nurture*. New York: Guilford Press.

Pennsylvania Association for Retarded Children v. Commonwealth of Pennsylvania, 343 F. Supp. 279 (E.D. Pa., 1972).

Plomin, R. (1995). Genetics and children's experiences in the family. *Journal of Child Psychology and Psychiatry and Allied Disciplines, 36*(1), 33–68.

Polsgrove, L., & Smith, S. W. (2004). Informed practice in teaching self-control to children with emotional and behavioral disorders. In: R. B. Rutherford, M. M. Quinn & S. R. Mathur (Eds), *Handbook of research in emotional and behavioral disorders* (pp. 399–425). New York: Guilford Press.

Redl, F. (1959). The life space interview: Workshop, 1957. I. Strategy and techniques of the life space interview. *American Journal of Orthopsychiatry, 29*, 1–18.

Reid, R., Gonzalez, J. E., Nordness, P. D., Trout, A., & Epstein, M. H. (2004). A meta-analysis of the academic status of students with emotional/behavioral disturbance. *Journal of Special Education, 38*(3), 130–143.

Rock, M. L. (2005). Use of strategic self-monitoring to enhance academic engagement, productivity, and accuracy of students with and without exceptionalities. *Journal of Positive Behavior Interventions, 7*(1), 3–17.

Rock, M. L., & Thead, B. K. (2007). The effects of fading a strategic self-monitoring intervention on students' academic engagement, accuracy, and productivity. *Journal of Behavioral Education, 16*(4), 389–412.

Rogers, C. R. (1954). *Becoming a person ... Pt. 1. Some hypotheses regarding the facilitation of personal growth. Pt. 2. What it means to become a person.* Oberlin, OH: Oberlin College.

Rogers, C. R. (1969). *Freedom to learn: A view of what education might become.* Columbus, OH: C. E. Merrill Publishing Co..

Rogers, C. R. (1970). *Becoming a person: Two lectures.* Austin, TX: University of Texas.

Sasso, G. M., Conroy, M. A., Stichter, J. P., & Fox, J. J. (2001). Slowing down the bandwagon: The misapplication of functional assessment for students with emotional or behavioral disorders. *Behavioral Disorders, 26*(4), 282–296.

Seligman, M. E. P., & Csikszentmihalyi, M. (2000). Positive psychology: An introduction. *American Psychologist, 55*(1), 5–14.

Shattuck, R. (1994). *The forbidden experiment: The story of the wild boy of Aveyron.* New York: Kodansha International.

Shermer, M. (2002). *Why people believe weird things: Pseudoscience, superstition, and other confusions of our time* (Rev. and expanded. ed.). New York: A.W.H. Freeman/Owl Book.

Shermer, M. (2004). *The science of good and evil: Why people cheat, gossip, care, share, and follow the golden rule.* New York: Times Books.

Shores, R. E., & Wehby, J. H. (1999). Analyzing the classroom social behavior of students with EBD. *Journal of Emotional and Behavioral Disorders, 7*(4), 194–199.

Slate, J. R., & Saudargas, R. A. (1986). Differences in the classroom behaviors of behaviorally disordered and regular class children. *Behavioral Disorders, 12*(1), 45–53.

Spaulding, J., & Balch, P. (1983). A brief history of primary prevention in the twentieth century: 1908 to 1980. *American Journal of Community Psychology, 11*(1), 59–80.

Stone, D. A. (2002). *Policy paradox: The art of political decision making* (Rev. ed.). New York: Norton.

Tapp, J., & Wehby, J. H. (2000). Observational software for laptop computers and optical bar code readers. In: T. Thompson, D. Felce & F. J. Symons (Eds), *Behavioral observation: Technology and applications in developmental disabilities* (pp. 71–82). Baltimore: Paul H. Brookes.

Thompson, B., Diamond, K. E., McWilliam, R., Snyder, P., & Snyder, S. W. (2005). Evaluating the quality of evidence from correlational research for evidence-based practice. *Exceptional Children, 71*(2), 181–194.

U. S. Department of Education. (1998). *Twentieth annual report to Congress on the implementation of the Individuals with Disabilities Education Act.* Washington, DC: Author.

Urban, W. J., & Wagoner, J. L. (2009). *American education: A history* (4th ed.). New York: Routledge.

Vonk, H. G. (1979). The innovation cycle. *The Clearing House, 52*(5), 208–210.

Walker, H. M., Nishioka, V. M., Zeller, R., Severson, H. H., & Feil, E. G. (2000). Causal factors and potential solutions for the persistent underidentification of students having emotional or behavioral disorders in the context of schooling. *Assessment for Effective Intervention, 26*(1), 29–39.

Walker, H. M., Ramsey, E., & Gresham, F. M. (2004). *Antisocial behavior in school: Evidence-based practices* (2nd ed.). Belmont, CA: Thomson/Wadsworth.

Walker, H. M., & Severson, H. H. (1992). *Systematic screening for behavior disorders (SSBD) technical manual.* Longmont, CO: Sopris West.

Wehman, P., & Gentry, R. (2008). Education for individuals with disabilities. In: P. Wehman (Ed.), *Exceptional individuals in school, community, and work* (pp. 39–53). Richmond, VA: Virginia Commonwealth University Rehabilitation Research and Training Center on Workplace Supports and Job Retenion.

Wehmeyer, M. L., Agran, M., & Hughes, C. (1998). *Teaching self-determination to students with disabilities: Basic skills for successful transition.* Baltimore: Paul H. Brookes.

Wiley, A., Siperstein, G., Forness, S., & Brigham, F. (2010). School context and the problem behavior and social skills of students with emotional disturbance. *Journal of Child and Family Studies, 19*(4), 451–461.

Wiley, A. L., Siperstein, G. N., Bountress, K. E., Forness, S. R., & Brigham, F. J. (2009). School context and the academic achievement of students with emotional disturbance. *Behavioral Disorders, 33*(4), 198–210.

Wilson, E. O. (1998). *Consilience: The unity of knowledge.* New York: Knopf.

Wood, M. M., & Long, N. J. (1991). *Life space intervention: Talking with children and youth in crisis.* Austin, TX: PRO-ED.

Woodcock, R. W., McGrew, K. S., & Mather, N. (2001). *Woodcock-Johnson-III tests of achievement.* Itasca, IL: Riverside Publishing.

Yell, M. L. (2006). *The law and special education* (2nd ed.). Upper Saddle River, NJ: Prentice Hall.

Yell, M. L., Meadows, N. B., Drasgow, E., & Shriner, J. G. (2009). *Evidence-based practices for educating students with emotional and behavioral disorders.* Upper Saddle River, NJ: Merrill/Pearson.

CHAPTER 8

HISTORY OF DEAFNESS AND HEARING IMPAIRMENTS

C. Jonah Eleweke

EARLIEST HISTORY OF DEAFNESS AND HEARING IMPAIRMENTS

Deafness and hearing impairments have a very interesting and ancient history. The term *hearing impairments* is used here to refer to any dysfunction of the hearing organ, regardless of the etiology, degree of hearing loss, and service provision implications. The history of hearing impairments can be traced back to centuries before Christ (BC). For instance, around 1000 BC a Hebrew law provided those with deafness and hearing impairments limited rights to own property and marry. Nonetheless, although this law protected people with hearing impairments from being cursed and maltreated by others, it did not grant them full participation in rituals of the temple (ASLInfo, 2010). People with hearing impairments were considered to be "subnormal" by great philosophers of that time. For instance, between 427 and 347 BC, Plato's philosophy of innate intelligence was the vogue. It claimed that all intelligence was present at birth. Therefore, all people were born with ideas and languages in their minds and required only time to demonstrate their outward sign of intelligence through speech. People with hearing impairments could not speak and were therefore considered incapable of rational thoughts and ideas. Indeed in 355 BC Aristotle was reported to have claimed that those who were born deaf would

History of Special Education
Advances in Special Education, Volume 21, 181–212
Copyright © 2011 by Emerald Group Publishing Limited
ISSN: 0270-4013/doi:10.1108/S0270-4013(2011)0000021011

become stupid and incapable of reason. According to him, people with hearing impairments could not be educated because without the ability to hear, people could not learn. Greek which was spoken in his society was considered the perfect language and all people who did not speak Greek including people with deafness were considered Barbarians (ASLInfo, 2010).

Hearing impairment was in the past considered a sign of God's anger or punishment for secret sins. For instance, St. Augustine (354–430 AD) in "Guilt Trip" claimed that the sins of parents were visited on their children with hearing impairments. Augustine believed that faith came about by hearing the word of God and that deafness was a hindrance to faith. However, he believed that people with hearing impairments could learn and thus were able to receive faith and salvation. Augustine referred to bodily movements, signs, and gestures used by people with hearing impairments, and believed that these modes of communication were capable of transmitting thought and belief. He implied that it was equal to spoken language in terms of reaching the soul (Bragg, 1997).

According to Bragg (1997), St. Augustine was intrigued how children with hearing impairments could communicate with their hearing parents. Augustine noted that these children would communicate with their parents by learning the gestures, bodily movements, and signs the parents used to communicate with them. It could be the case that Augustine's acceptance that bodily movements, signs, and gestures as capable means of communication influenced monks during the Benedictine Reform in the 10th century. The monks vowed themselves to remaining in silence to avoid annoying fellow monks who could be in deep contemplation or meditation. Monks used gestures, bodily movements, and signs to communicate. Speech was to be used only when absolutely necessary. It is thought that this practice of silence among the monks resulted in the development of the earliest sign language (Bragg). Bragg posited that the gestures and signs used by the monks somehow began to spread to other countries, such as Germany, France, England, and Spain, where they were refined, reinforced, and used in communicating with Deaf[1] people. Nonetheless, evidence indicated that around 529 AD *Corupus Iurus Civilis*, or the Justinian Code, was developed during the reign of Emperor Justinian. It was a result of the Emperor's desire that existing Roman laws should be collected into a simple and clear system of laws or "code." The code denied deaf people the ability to hold and control property, make contracts, or write a valid will (Wikipedia, 2010a).

14th and 15th Centuries

Evidence is consistent from long ago that people with hearing impairments were not considered equals compared to those who were hearing simply because of their inability to use spoken language. However, as time went on, beliefs about the nature of people with hearing impairments gradually began to change. In 1521, Rudolphus Agricolo, a Dutch humanist, believed that people with hearing impairments could communicate via writing. He advocated the theory that the ability to use speech was separate from the ability of thought. He wrote *De Inventione Dialectica* (Wikipedia, 2010b). Similarly, Girolamo Cardano (1501–1576) was the first physician to recognize the ability of people with hearing impairments to reason and the first to challenge Aristotle's belief that hearing was a requirement for understanding. Girdamo Cardano believed that Deaf people learned to read and write by showing them pictures, things, and gestures. He noted that people with hearing impairments could be taught information that was communicated by speech and reading by writing, and use of pictures and figures (Leigh & Power, 2000).

In 1575, Lasso, a Spanish lawyer, argued that people with hearing impairments, who learned to speak, were no longer dumb and therefore had a right to inheritance (ASLInfo, 2010). In 1591, Solomon Alberti, a German physician, published the first book of any kind, specifically regarding deafness, entitled: *Discourse on Deafness and Speechlessness*. He argued that hearing and speech were separate functions. Alberti believed that people with hearing impairments were rational, and capable of thought, even though they lacked speech. He showed that people with hearing impairments could be taught to read lips, understand speech, and read, without the ability to hear (Van Cleve & Crouch, 2002).

Development of Deaf Education

Earliest records of attempts to educate people with hearing impairments could be traced in Spain around 1620. Melchor de Yebra and Juan Pablo de Bonet were prominent during this era. De Yebra was familiar with the hand alphabet used by monks sworn to vows of silence. He published those handshapes and publicized their use for religious purposes among people with hearing impairments to promote understanding of spiritual matters. Bonet reproduced de Yebra's work in 1620 entitled *Simplification of the*

Letters of the Alphabet and Method of Teaching Deaf Mutes to Speak. He supported oralism but used finger spelling to teach speech and literacy. He used this methodology, so the deaf could be integrated into the hearing society (Daniels, 1997).

In England, John Bulwer (1614–1684), a British physician, studied gestures and published *Philocopus*, also known as *Deaf and Dumbe Man's Friend* in 1648 and *Chirologia*, also known as *Natural Language of the Hand* in 1644. These were the first English books on deaf education and language. These books showed the use of manual signs but did not refer directly to the sign language of Deaf people. Bulwer also advocated the establishment of a school for those with hearing impairments (Marschark & Spencer, 2003). In 1680, George Dalgarno, a Scottish tutor, taught students with hearing impairments how to read lips, speak, and use fingerspelling. He published his observations and conclusions about the education of the deaf in *Didascalocophus,* also known as *Deaf and Dumb Man's Tutor,* which supported the use of fingerspelling and gestures in the education of people with hearing impairments (Delgarno, 1971).

The Enlightenment Era: 16th–18th centuries

Enlightenment Era philosophers Locke, Rousseau, and Condillac debated the nature of language, the origin of language and thought, and sign languages (ASLInfo, 2010). The Enlightenment Era was a period of spiritual awakening and intellectual growth. It brought some positive changes to the treatment of people with hearing impairments, especially in those societies that were considered "enlightened" (ASLInfo, 2010). Efforts to provide education to people with hearing impairments continued during this era. For instance, in 1755, Samuel Heinicke established the first oral school for the deaf in Germany (Reynolds & Fletcher-Janzen, 2007). Abbe Charles Michel de l'Epee (1712–1789) established the Royal Institution of Deaf and Mutes in Paris in 1755. The Royal Institution was the first free school for the deaf in the world (Dilka, 2006). Later Abbe de l'Epee published his methods of educating those with hearing impairments in a book entitled *Instruction of Deaf and Dumb by Means of Methodical Signs.* It should be noted that L'Epee supported the school at his own expense until his death. After his death, the French government began to support the school. His successor was the Abbe Roch Concurrou (Curcurran) Sicard (1742–1822). It was Sicard who brought Laurent Clerc and Jean Massieu to London where they met Thomas Hopkins Gallaudet who pioneered education of the deaf in the

United States (New World Encyclopedia, 2010). Thomas Braidwood founded the first British Academy for the deaf in 1760 (Deafhistoryscotland, 2010). Thus, the Enlightenment Era positively influenced efforts to provide education to people with hearing impairments in Europe.

Formal Education for the Deaf in the United States

The development of formal education for people with hearing impairments and American Sign Language (ASL) is credited to the efforts of Thomas Gallaudet (1787–1851). He founded and served as principal of the first institution for the education of the deaf in the United States. Opened in 1817 as the American Asylum for the Instruction of the Deaf and Dumb at Hartford, Connecticut, it is now known as the American School for the Deaf. Gallaudet was also instrumental in the creation of ASL, which was later recognized as a true language, not just a code representing English words. He went to Yale University at the age of 14, earning his Bachelor's degree in 1805, at the top of his class. He then received his Master's degree in 1810. He excelled in all subjects and was well-liked by his classmates. He studied law for one year, studied teaching for two years, and was actively involved in business for three years. He also attended Andover Theological Seminary from 1811 to 1814. In 1814, Gallaudet became a preacher, and his strong Congregationalist faith guided him throughout his life. Although most of his life would not be actively spent preaching, Gallaudet continued to serve in this capacity, giving guest sermons that were said to uplift both congregations and individuals (New World Encyclopedia, 2010).

Gallaudet put his wish to become a preacher aside when he met Alice Cogswell, the nine-year-old deaf daughter of a neighbor Mason Cogswell. He taught her many words by writing them with a stick in the dirt. Cogswell was impressed by Gallaudet's efforts to teach his daughter and asked Gallaudet to travel to Europe to study methods for teaching deaf students. Gallaudet at first went to study the methods of the Braidwood family in London, England, Edinburgh, and Scotland. Gallaudet found that the Braidwoods were only willing to share their methods of teaching the deaf, if he promised to be their assistant for three years and not to share the knowledge he learned with others. Gallaudet felt it expedient to return to America to start teaching the deaf and did not want to wait for three years. Also, he was not convinced that the Braidwood method was the best way to teach the deaf (Van Cleve & Crouch, 2002; New World Encyclopedia, 2010).

While still in Great Britain, Gallaudet met Abbé Sicard, head of the Institution Nationale des Sourds-Muets in Paris, and two of its deaf faculty members, Laurent Clerc and Jean Massieu. Sicard invited Gallaudet to Paris to study the school's method of teaching the Deaf using manual communication. Impressed with the manual method, Gallaudet studied teaching methodology under Sicard and learned sign language from Massieu and Clerc, who were both highly educated Deaf graduates of the school (Zapien, 1998). At the school in Paris, Clerc offered to accompany him back to the United States and teach with Gallaudet, and the two sailed to America. On returning to the United States, they toured New England and successfully raised private and public funds to found a school for deaf students in Hartford, which later became known as the American School for the Deaf (Moores, 2007).

According to New World Encyclopedia (2010), young Alice was one of the first seven students in the new school. Some hearing students came to the school to learn as well. The school became well recognized and was visited by President James Monroe in 1818. Gallaudet served as principal of the school from its opening to 1830, when he retired due to health problems. During most of his time as principal, he also taught on a daily basis. By the time he retired, the school had 140 students and was widely recognized throughout the United States.

Gallaudet was offered other teaching leadership positions at special schools and universities, but declined these offers so he could write children's books and advance education. At this time, there were very few children's books published in America, and Gallaudet felt a strong desire to assist in the training of children in this way. During a period of eight years, he worked mainly as a writer and also devoted himself to other social causes he deemed worthy. Gallaudet wrote several religious-themed children's books, as well as a dictionary and a speller. He also took to caring for those with mental illness and served as chaplain of both an insane asylum and a county jail (New World Encyclopedia, 2010).

Gallaudet's son, Edward Miner Gallaudet (1837–1917), helped found the first college for the deaf in 1857, and was its first superintendent. The college was originally called the Columbia Institution, and in 1864, it became Gallaudet College, named in honor of Thomas Hopkins Gallaudet, and in 1986, it became Gallaudet University. The university also offers education for those in elementary, middle, and high school levels. The primary language used on the Gallaudet University Campus is ASL. Gallaudet's work helped to develop ASL. Like any language, ASL has a complex history with a combination of the informal signs that were already in use by the Deaf in

America, French Sign Language, and efforts by Gallaudet and Clerc to add English grammar to some words (New World Encyclopedia, 2010; Moores, 2007).

While Gallaudet helped to bring ASL and education to the Deaf, it would not be until 1960 that William C. Stokoe, Jr., of then Gallaudet College, proposed to linguists that ASL was indeed a real language, and not just a signed code for English. Stokoe's studies resulted in ASL becoming a respected and recognized language in the academic world (Stokoe, 2005).

PRESENT TIME: IMPACT OF LAWS – INCLUSION AND CLOSING OF DEAF SCHOOLS

Since 1975 when the Individuals with Disabilities Education Act came into force in the United States, other laws, such as the Americans with Disabilities Act (ADA), and No Child Left Behind (NCLB) have affected the education and services provided to learners with hearing impairments or other disabilities. The noble goal of these laws has been to give all children with hearing impairments and other disabilities free appropriate public education in the least restrictive environment and to facilitate their integration into the communities. Since that time, several factors have come to the forefront concerning the rights of students with hearing impairments to be educated in inclusive settings. Students and parents face a conglomeration of situations that require solutions in providing these students with the best education possible in their present inclusive environment. Some of these situations are communication, education and school environment, culture, and social skills (Hall, 2005; Kelman, Azulay, & Uchôa, 2009).

Communication

Communication presents a large barrier in inclusive settings for students with hearing impairments (Kelman et al., 2009). Most often in regular schools, Deaf students find themselves in a world of hearing peers and teachers who do not know sign language, forcing the Deaf student to pick up whatever tidbits of information is possible by trying to lip read. As a result, Deaf students receive inaccurate language input when communication is produced in English and often critical language elements needed for comprehension are left out. These students struggle to achieve academically due to a communication breakdown between the Deaf student and the teacher. Well-meaning hearing teachers may view these students as having learning disabilities simply because of their communication difficulties (Hall, 2005).

Isolation and Anxiety

Another issue Deaf students encounter in the mainstream setting is isolation and anxiety. This is brought about by the extreme amount of effort on both the hearing and the Deaf participants to understand each other. There tends to be a display of impatience between the participants when trying to converse due to the Deaf students' unclear speech, and the inability of the hearing students to sign. Also, when a child has a disability, such as deafness, the general population tends to lower their expectations of the child's abilities to partake in normal social interactions (Hall, 2005).

Prior to the introduction of these laws, most learners with hearing impairments were educated in residential schools for the Deaf. Residential schools for the Deaf play an enormous part in fostering and maintaining Deaf culture (Lane, Hoffmeister, & Bahan, 1996). There, Deaf students form close bonds with each other and remain friends for years after their time in school together. According to these authors, these bonds are quite hard to build in inclusive schools where relationships are strained by the lack of appropriate communication skills. Other factors important to Deaf culture are touching, conversation styles, and physical actions. In the regular educational environment, touching may be considered inappropriate, especially between teachers and students, but in the Deaf world, it is vital (Lane et al., 1996). Touching is important to deaf people and one of the important characteristics of the Deaf culture. Deaf students can use touching to get a person's attention, to indicate taking a turn in speaking, and at times, as acknowledgement of another's presence. While it's alright for hearing people to move about during conversations with others, drop their heads to glance at something, or even rest their eyes for a moment, some Deaf people may consider these actions as offensive and rude. On the other hand, when Deaf people communicate with sign language, full attention and eye contact of both parties must be maintained because it is a very visual language. Maintaining eye contact in this fashion can be mistaken for staring and hearing participants may feel quite uncomfortable to communicate effectively (Takushi, 2000). Given that this situation could cause misunderstanding between the student with hearing impairment and his or her hearing peers, the deaf student may decide to keep to himself or herself in the classroom. The student, in that case, will certainly feel lonely and isolated.

Social Skills

Social skills have a tremendous impact on how well a Deaf student copes in the mainstream setting. Hearing children learn these skills early in life by watching and imitating parents, other family members, and friends. For those children with hearing impairments, the development of social skills is determined by their degree of hearing loss, their age at diagnosis, treatment, and experiences (Patton, 2004). Mainstreaming for Deaf students can be tremendously difficult in so many aspects and for so many reasons. Skills such as getting along with others, making friends, and developing a pleasant personality are lifelong endeavors for many Deaf students. While most hearing students breeze through social situations with minimal instruction, children with hearing impairments typically lack some of these skills, making them a target of intolerant children who taunt, tease, and use poor behavior and manners toward those who are deaf (Patton, 2004).

Cambra (2002) examined the attitudes of some hearing students to their 34 deaf peers in an inclusive program. The results indicated that although most of the hearing students felt the deaf students who attended classes should not be isolated and that their presence would not upset the normal flow of the class routine, they felt that students with deafness-related disabilities would possibly be better off attending a special school more suited for their needs. Further, the data indicated that the hearing students did not feel that their deaf counterparts worked as hard as they did. In a related study, Nunes, Pretzlik, and Olsson (2001) examined peer relationships among 62 hearing students and nine deaf students from two different mainstream schools. The ability to relate well socially is an essential aspect of meaningful peer relationships. The findings indicated that of the nine deaf students involved in the peer review rating scale, three were located at the bottom of the review, four were located in the middle, and two were located at the top. Students were classified as popular, neglected, rejected, or average. Although the sample of deaf students was small, 67% of deaf pupils were classified as neglected, whereas only 27% of the hearing pupils received this rating.

Schirmer (2004) suggested that the social skill challenges of students with hearing impairments may be because personal and social development seems to take the backseat during the early and adolescent years of these children because more attention is focused on their language and academic progress.

It's not surprising then that students with hearing impairments, who have poor social skills, may be unable to interact socially with their hearing peers in inclusive settings. They may therefore experience rejection, neglect, loneliness, and isolation in mainstream settings. Consequently, programs and supports to assist students with hearing impairments to acquire good social skills should be stressed as equally important as other programs focused on their language and academic development.

TOTAL COMMUNICATION AND BILINGUAL–BICULTURAL PHILOSOPHIES

Although ASL has been proved to be a complete natural language, it does not have a writing system. ASL is a visual language different from the syntax, grammar, and structure of the English language. Thus, over the years, there has been a huge shift in language and communication policies in the education of learners with hearing impairments. This is mostly because of the low reading scores of students with hearing impairments. Evidence indicates that children with hearing impairments have a harder time reading and writing in English than their hearing peers (Kuntze, 1998). A majority of students with hearing impairments graduating from high school can only read at fourth grade level. Studies have shown that many Deaf readers do not have the subskills needed for reading. Skills, like word identification, metacognition, morphosyntax, vocabulary, and prior knowledge are not fully developed to make the reading connection by these students (Hermans, 2008; Moores, 2008).

Concerns about the low reading levels and academic achievement of students with hearing impairments brought about the "total communication" philosophy in the education of students with hearing impairments. The term "total communication" was first used by Roy Holcomb in California around the late 1960s. The idea was further developed by David Denton in 1967 and was adopted by his school – the Maryland School for the Deaf – as the official name for their educational philosophy. The philosophy was supposed to enhance the literacy and educational performance of students with hearing impairments by using every method of communication (e.g., manual, oral, aural, pictures, drawings, etc.) possible in educating students with hearing impairments. The philosophy was well received and it soon spread to other countries, such as the United Kingdom, France, China, Malaysia, Singapore, Australia, Scandinavian countries, the Netherlands, France, and Germany. In the United States, total communication was most popular during the 1970s and 1980s, when most schools and programs for children who are deaf, as well as most major organizations in the field, supported the philosophy (Wikipedia (2010c).

After well over a decade of using total communication, the literacy and academic achievement of most students with hearing impairments remained unsatisfactory. Consequently, a new approach, called the bilingual–bicultural (Bi–Bi) education method, was introduced in the early 1990s. It was thought that the English-based signing used in total communication was responsible for the failure of students with hearing impairments. This is because the English-based sign system called manually coded English (MCE) is not a natural language in its own right. In MCE, ASL signs and some "invented signs," prefixes, suffixes, etc., are used in English language syntax and structure (Rodda & Eleweke, 2000). The proponents of the Bi–Bi approach argued that ASL, or some other sign language, which are complete natural languages, should be the first and primary language of children with hearing impairments. It is considered that ASL has the spatial memory facilities needed to process print English. This, they argued, will lead to reading and writing English successfully by students with hearing impairments who have a good ASL background (LaSasso & Lollis, 2003). Consequently, Bi–Bi philosophies in programs for individuals with hearing impairments have been the vogue since the early 1990s. It began in Sweden and Denmark and continues to spread to other countries (Gibson, Small, & Mason, 1997).

Bi–Bi programs aim to enable students with hearing impairments to acquire competence in two languages (ASL and print English) and two cultures (Deaf and hearing), because they must live and interact with hearing people (Hermans, 2008). A basic foundation for Bi–Bi education is that all children with hearing impairments should develop communicative competency. Sadly, this is a challenge for young individuals with hearing impairments who were born into hearing families and are not exposed to other Deaf people or sign language (Lane et al., 1996). Early exposure to language is vital for language development in children with hearing impairments. Evidence is clear that the later they develop the language, the less proficient their language will be (Baker & Baker, 1997).

Bi–Bi education advocates ASL as the first language of children with hearing impairments because it is easier to acquire than any form of English. Over time, a solid first language (ASL) can lead to better performances in the second language (English). The primary goal for Bi–Bi education is clear and proficient production of ASL and print English (Hermans, 2008; Rodda & Eleweke, 2000). There are several benefits of Bi–Bi education. For starters, it provides early access to a comprehendible language-input that can foster early cognitive development. This in turn can facilitate greater academic achievement resulting in higher self-esteem and confidence (Evans, 2004).

Evidence is strong that students in a Bi–Bi education program, who were skilled signers, were able to make connections between unknown vocabulary words and known signs (Hermans, 2008). According to Hermans (2008), these students were also able to comprehend stories much easier than those who are not skilled signers. Therefore, teaching ASL first could deepen a deaf student's conceptual foundation and provide thinking and problem-solving skills.

Hermans argued that a deaf child with a strong ASL background would have very little trouble developing English literacy skills. In contrast, those who are not exposed to the language could perform considerably lower in both reading and writing skills. Hermans suggested that there is a strong correlation between having a strong first language (ASL) and being proficient with English reading and writing skills. The key point is having a strong first language. Unfortunately, there is a small minority of children with hearing impairments who possess that skill because over 90% of these children have normally hearing families who do not know sign language (National Institute on Deafness and other Communication Disorders, 2010a).

Assessment Issues

The assessment of students who have hearing impairments has been and remains a challenging and complex process (see Anita, 1985; Sisterhen & Rotatori, 1989). This is not surprising, given how these individuals were perceived and treated in the past and at present time in some places due to their inability to use spoken language. It is in view of this that the assessment of students with hearing impairments has been described as one of the most problematic aspects of their teaching and learning (Mayer, Akamatsu, & Stewart, 2003). Nonetheless, reliable assessment data are critically important for students with hearing impairments in that they facilitate appropriate placement, utilization of the mode through which they learn best (auditory, visual, or tactile), curriculum adaptations, supports for amplification and assistive listening devices, and decisions about transition from service to service that families, schools, and individuals with hearing impairments must make (Bochner & Walter, 2005).

Traditional sources of assessment data include observations, recollections, tests, artifacts, extant information, and professional judgment (Schirmer, 2004). It has been argued that in proper assessment of students with hearing impairments, their communication methods, academic, intellectual, medical, behavioral, and audio logical characteristics must be combined to create an interconnected pattern of strengths and needs that parents and teachers must translate into educational goals and objectives (Eccarius, 1997). Nonetheless, given that language acquisition is essential in acquiring the conceptual store or body of knowledge that assessments tap into and that hearing impairment may pose challenges in language development, several questions regarding the assessment of students with hearing impairments have been raised by Moores (1996): "Do children with hearing impairments pass through the same milestones in cognitive development like their hearing peers or do the sequences differ? Are the final levels of abstract abilities achieved by young people and adults with hearing impairments equivalent to those of their hearing peers? Are assessment tools such as IQ tests which are developed and normed on samples of hearing people suitable in assessing individuals with hearing impairments?" (p. 151).

Addressing these questions remains problematic. Although sign language (i.e., ASL) has been proved to be a natural language in its own right (Stokoe, 2005), it remains the case that the vast majority of children with hearing impairments are born to hearing parents who do not know sign language. The implication of this is that the language development of many children with hearing impairments may be delayed (Marschark, 2007). Nonetheless, students with hearing impairments in the United States, for instance, are required to participate in high-stakes standard assessments under the 2001 No Child Left Behind and 2004 Individuals with Disabilities Education Improvement mandates.

Cawthon (2010) reported that although many students with hearing impairments participate in these assessments using testing accommodations, such as extended time, separate setting for test administration, test direction interpreted in sign language, test items interpreted in sign language, test items read aloud, and students signed responses; the teachers have no evidence-based resources to draw upon when making accommodation decisions. Given this dilemma, Mayer et al. (2003) advocated the use of *situated assessment* for learners with hearing impairments. Using excerpts of videotaped classroom dialogue, Mayer and coworkers posited that judgments could be made about the current performance levels of the students, and how curriculum and classroom activities could be modified to best address the needs of learners with hearing impairments. According to these authors, "The challenge is to identify which parts of the 'regular' curriculum need to be modified, and then, from this, to develop goals for the IEP which are truly matched to the needs of each learner and which still hark back to the broader mandated curriculum" (p. 76). However, Mayer and coworkers admitted that doing situated assessment could be more challenging than standardized or conventional assessment because teachers may not have the knowledge and skill of doing it.

It is evident from the foregoing discussion that assessment of learners with hearing impairments remains a challenging issue. Classroom-based studies are needed that will provide useful information to educators of learners with hearing impairments regarding more effective assessment strategies. Further, this author agrees with Mayer et al. (2003) that opportunities for professional development should be provided to teachers on a regular basis so that they will remain up to date on trends in assessment of learners with hearing impairments.

Technology

Changing technological advances have major impacts on many areas of life in the world today for all people including those with hearing impairments. One positive influence of science and technological innovations on hearing impairment was the discovery of a vaccination for rubella, a leading cause of deafness in the past. Before the 1960s, there was a large population of children that contracted rubella which caused deafness, and subsequently the "rubella bulge" of Deaf graduates in the 1980s. After the discovery of this vaccination, there was a noticeable decrease in individuals that were deaf as a result of rubella (Berke, 2009a).

Earlier, an attempt was made to invent a hearing device that would enable those with hearing impairments to hear and use spoken language. Enoch Henry Currier (1849–1917) invented a duplex earpiece devised for instructing students with hearing impairments. The device utilized two bell-shaped tubes for speaking and an earpiece for the person with a hearing impairment. This enabled the user to hear the sound of his/her own voice as well as that of the teacher/speaker. Currier also devised another teaching aid – one bell-shaped mouth piece into which the teacher spoke and several earpiece tubes one for each pupil (Washington University School of Medicine, 2010). However, the first wearable hearing aid made in the United States using vacuum tubes was the *Aurex*, developed by Walter Huth and introduced in May 1938. Other manufacturers of carbon hearing aids, such as Acousticon, Aurophone, Gem, Maico, Radioear, Sonotone, and Western Electric, also switched to the production of vacuum tube hearing aids (Washington University School of Medicine, 2010).

Continuing progress in technology today has significantly improved hearing aids over the decades. Current hearing aids have been greatly improved by the use of digital technology. Digital hearing aids have changed the way consumers interpret sound. With the earlier hearing aids, users received all frequencies and intensities at the same rate. This caused quiet sounds such as an air conditioner humming to be received at the same intensity as speech. This was very frustrating for students with hearing impairments (Kent & Smith, 2006). With digital hearing aids, the brain receives and interprets the sound at various frequencies in its natural manner of working. Also with the advancements in technology, hearing aids are now so portable that they can be virtually unnoticeable on their users.

Developments in loop systems and auditory trainers used in classrooms for students with hearing impairments have been impressive due to technological advancements. In the past, a student with hearing impairment had to wear a bulky hearing aid and a large loop system device connected to the hearing aid. The teacher in turn would have a microphone connected to their shirt as well. Advancements in technology have made the hearing aids and loop systems so portable and virtually wireless that now students use these devices with ease and comfort. In addition, advances in the development of auditory trainers have increased their effectiveness and usage in the classrooms for students with hearing impairments (Alterovitz, 2004).

Efforts to provide a more effective hearing aid resulted in the development of the cochlear implant (CI), which the US Food and Drug Administration approved in 1985. Since 1990, CIs had been implanted into thousands of people with hearing impairments of all ages in the United States and other developed countries (Washington University School of Medicine, 2010). Given that over 90% of children with hearing impairments are born to hearing parents, it is natural for these parents to want their child to be like them, speaking and in the hearing culture (Hurtig & Mueller, 2010). Thus, technological advancements in devices like the CIs have brought a glimmer of hope for hearing parent's wishes and plans for their deaf children. This is because CIs can deliver sound signals more effectively to the brain and therefore, theoretically, can facilitate the development and use of speech in individuals with hearing impairments.

Nonetheless, evidence has been conflicting regarding the benefits of CI devices. In some cases, it's claimed that if implanted before the age of 12 months, deaf children can acquire good spoken language skills and enter kindergarten at the same time as their hearing peers (Bleckly, 2010). However, the Deaf community has some concerns about invasive technological devices like CIs for young children because many doctors, therapists, and teachers recommend against the use of signed language with young CI patients. They often recommend the sole use of spoken language and education in regular classrooms as the ideal setting for those with CIs (Hearing Loss Web, 2010a). Further, it has been argued that some types of technologies such as CIs require extensive therapy and support that are sometimes expected to take place in the classroom. However, it seems to be the case that many regular teachers struggle with knowing how to support the effective use of these types of technologies by students with hearing impairments (Fagan & Pisoni, 2010).

Telecommunication devices for individuals with hearing impairments continue to change and improve with new developments in technology. Robert Weitbrecht, a deaf inventor, invented the acoustic coupler, which made possible a telephone device for individuals with hearing impairments known as the telephone typewriter (TTY). In May 1964, Weitbrecht made the first long-distance call with a TTY (Berke, 2009b). In the United States and Canada, hearing people can call a person with hearing impairment who has a TTY any time on their phone by first dialing the Telephone Relay Service (TRS) number 711. The reverse is true for those with hearing impairments who want to call hearing people. People with hearing impairments who have TTYs can call anybody or agency that also has TTY directly without going through the TRS. TTYs are becoming outdated as many people with hearing impairments who use sign language prefer to see the person at the other end. This brought about the development of video relay services (VRS) and video phones (VPs) (Akamatsu, Farrelly, & Mayer, 2005).

Today, Short Message Service (SMS) texting has become very popular among many individuals with hearing impairments just like for those who hear. This popularity has given the Deaf community freedom and equality in communication because they can use all sorts of mobile communication devices just like people who hear do. These devices can be used not only for e-mailing and instant messaging (IM), but they also have the capability to be used when one is mobile (Power & Power, 2004). Telecommunication technology continues to change all the time and these changes bring new opportunities to people with hearing impairments and to the field of deaf education and services.

Like hearing people, individuals with hearing impairments have been benefitting from advances in computer technology in education and communication. Many different software programs have been specifically developed and are available to facilitate the education of students with hearing impairments. Classrooms for students with hearing impairments in most advanced countries are teeming with amazing computer technological devices and programs. These devices not only benefit students with hearing impairments, but they also provide their teachers and educators the opportunity to be more creative and effective in the classrooms (Reitsma, 2008). In addition, various assistive listing devices that alert people with hearing when the door bell or telephone is ringing, or when the fire alarm goes off are available (Hearing Loss Web, 2010b). Most television broadcasts in the United States and other developed countries are by law captioned for the benefit of individuals with hearing impairments (National Institute on Deafness and other Communication Disorders, 2010b).

Taken together, current technological advancements have created many opportunities for students and individuals with hearing impairments. Although these advancements are revolutionary, the concern remains as to whether educators in regular classrooms have the know-how to utilize them in providing quality education for students with hearing impairments. This is because without appropriate and constant technological support these educators may be unable to keep up with the rate of technological advancements. Today's wonder devices are becoming "outdated" tomorrow, before educators know how to utilize them effectively. Strategies to ensure that educators are supported to keep updating their knowledge on latest technological innovations that impact individuals with hearing impairments must continue to be explored.

FAMILIES OF CHILDREN WITH HEARING IMPAIRMENTS

Any discussion of the history of hearing impairments will be incomplete without mentioning the important roles of families of children with hearing impairments. Evidence is consistent that a significant number of children with hearing impairments lose their hearing prelingually (i.e., before the age of three or prior to complete acquisition of the language spoken around them) and 95% of these children are born to hearing parents who have no previous experience and knowledge of raising a child with a hearing impairment (Holt, Hotto, & Cole, 1994; Mitchell & Karchmer, 2004). The diagnosis of hearing loss in a child can be very devastating emotionally to these parents, given that they have no previous experience of hearing impairment (see e.g., Fitzpatrick, Graham, Durieux-Smith, Angus, & Coyle,

2007; Scheetz, 2001). In addition to their varied emotional reactions to the diagnosis of hearing loss in their children, these parents also worry about whether the children will be able to use speech, speak normally, go to school, obtain employment, and have a family (Marschark, 2007).

With legislative mandates over the decades that promote educating children with hearing impairments and other disabilities in inclusive settings and keeping these children at home (Angelides & Aravi, 2007; Byrnes, Sigafoos, Rickards, & Brown, 2002; Powers, 2002), it has been strongly argued that information about relevant support services must be available to assist family caregivers (Fitzpatrick, Angus, Durieux-Smith, Graham, & Coyle, 2008; McCracken, Young, & Tattersall, 2008). Indeed the importance of incorporating information about support services in the management of children with hearing loss is well documented in the literature (Pendergast, Lartz, & Fiedler, 2002; Yoshinaga-Itano, 2004). Such information could enable families obtain necessary services and other forms of assistance that could enhance their abilities in caring for their children with hearing impairment in the following important areas.

Making Informed Choices and Coping

Providing timely and unbiased information about relevant services to families of children with hearing impairments is crucially important to enable them make informed choices. Given that the majority of them have no previous experience of hearing impairment, they require very timely, clear, and unbiased information that will assist them in obtaining the services that will enable them to cope positively in facing the challenges of raising their children (Sisterhen & Rotatori, 1986). These parents need information that will educate them about childhood hearing loss and its consequences, about the specialized support these children will require to ensure optimum development, and about the options in communication and education available to them and their children (Marschark, 2007). Information about support services for families of children with hearing impairments could assist family members with obtaining services that will enable them to deal in a positive manner with their varied intense and painful emotional reactions when they first learn that their child has a hearing loss (Meadow-Orlans, Mertens, Sass-Lehrer, & Scott-Olson, 1997). If through the information provided, families are assisted to successfully resolve these painful emotions and reactions by accessing relevant support services, they could then move into a position of strength which will enable them to think more clearly and hopefully act more effectively in meeting the developmental needs of their children with hearing impairments (Bemrose, 2003; DesGeorges, 2003).

Participating in Early Intervention Programs

Families of children with hearing impairments also need information and support services to enable them actively participate in early intervention programs for their children. Mandatory Universal Newborn Hearing Screening (UNHS) programs in many developed countries today mean that hearing impairments are now diagnosed in thousands of newborn babies and infants annually. For instance, Cole and Flexer (2007) estimated that between 16,000 and 18,000 babies and toddlers are diagnosed with hearing loss annually in the United States. One to two babies in every 1000 are born with a hearing loss in one or both ears in the United Kingdom (National Health Services, 2008). In Australia, between 9 and 12 children per 10,000 live births are born with a moderate or greater hearing loss in both ears (Australian Hearing, 2008). The implication of this situation is that hearing impairment can be described as one of the most common childhood disabilities. It warrants prompt initiation of early intervention services because it can interfere with the development of language and communication skills on which other aspects of development depend.

Evidence indicates that early identification and prompt initiation of early intervention services could prevent or greatly reduce the communication and developmental barriers posed by hearing impairment (Moeller, 2000; Watkin et al., 2007; Yoshinaga-Itano, 2004). Successful early intervention programs not only focus on the child's needs, but also on the needs of the family system in which the child is nurtured. It is for this reason that early intervention programs are also referred to as parent–infant programs in some literature because of their benefits to parents and young children with hearing impairments (Brown, Abu Bakar, Rickards, & Griffin, 2006; Marschark, 2007; Stryker & Luetke-Stahlman, 2003). These programs focus on language development, parent–child communication, social skills development, and support for the utilization of any residual hearing the children with hearing impairment may have. Further, these programs provide parents with strategies for enhancing their children's educational development (i.e., through instruction to learn sign language, speech training skills, or both depending on the particular program) (Verhaert, Willems, Van Kerschaver, & Desloovere, 2008).

The goal of early intervention must be to foster effective parent–child communication starting soon after the diagnosis of hearing loss. Effective parent–child communication is the best single predictor of success in virtually all areas of development of children with hearing impairment (Marschark, 2007). Clearly, consistent communication interactions with the most appropriate means of communication between caregivers and the child with hearing impairment will provide the child with the opportunity to be involved in most of the normal activities of childhood in both social and academic areas (Baynton, Gannon, & Bergey, 2007; Marschark, 2007).

The involvement of parents and other family members of children with hearing loss is imperative for the success of any early intervention program (Watkin et al., 2007). A child's parents are the ultimate decision-making authority in the management of the child (Brown et al., 2006). Their full cooperation and participation are imperative for the success of early intervention programs. Evidence suggests that the success of early intervention is dependent to a large extent upon the development of relationships between professionals and family members in which family members assume an important role in assessment procedures and in the development and implementation of intervention programs (Watkin et al., 2007). Information about early intervention programs should therefore be readily available to parents of children with hearing impairments through health centers, hearing and speech clinics, and educational programs for children with hearing impairments in the communities. The focus of the information about early intervention provided to parents should be on strategies for enhancing their children's language development (e.g., instruction in sign language, speech training, or both), enhancing parent–child communication, developing appropriate social skills, appropriate support for the use of any residual hearing the children might have, and parent-to-parent support groups or networks.

Supporting Educational Development

The literature indicates that adequate information on support services would enable families to make informed choices and participate actively in the educational development of their children with a hearing impairment (Calderon, 2000; Luckner & Muir, 2001). Evidence indicates that educational outcomes for children with hearing impairments remain problematic (Easterbrooks, 1999; Holden-Pit & Diaz, 1998; United States Department of

Education, 1998). The majority of learners with a hearing impairment graduating from high schools are found to read and write at fourth grade level (Marschark, 2007; Schirmer, 2001). This implies that there is a great need to provide information to parents that will ensure their active participation in educational programs for their children with a hearing impairment and the need for support services which emphasize the importance of early access to comprehensive language input for these children. Although the field has long recognized that parental involvement in education programs is critical for positive educational outcomes for children with a hearing impairment (Mauk & Mauk, 1995), evidence suggests that many parents of children with hearing impairments may have no regular and fruitful contacts with their children's schools (Morton, 2001). He observed that educators in school-based programs for children with hearing impairments often decide on a child's placement, program, curriculum, and services without adequately informing and consulting the parents or caregivers. Nonetheless, the literature has consistently indicated that the educational success of children with hearing impairments is linked to the involvement of well-informed parents who are strongly committed to the development of good communication skills in their children and are actively involved in their children's educational programs (Musselman & Kircaali-Iftar, 1996). It remains the case, however, that due to lack of adequate information, parental involvement may be limited and as a result many children with a hearing impairment do not have a useable language base either in English or in sign language by the time they begin formal education (Paul & Quigley, 1994; Rodda & Eleweke, 2000).

A thorough understanding of families' need for information on issues about their children's education is critically important to ensure their support and participation. The information about the education of children with hearing impairments given to parents should include information that will also facilitate social development, academic achievement, and full access to relevant programs in the community.

Empowerment and Collaboration

The literature indicates that information about support services could make the biggest differences in the lives of families of children with hearing impairment by enhancing their empowerment (Briggs, 1999; Mogharreban & Branscum, 2008). Turnbull, Turnbull, Shank, and Smith (2004) described empowerment as knowing what the family wants for their child, having the motivation to strive to obtain it, and having the knowledge and skills to turn their motivation into effective action. Empowerment is best realized through collaboration with professionals such as the audiologists, speech and language therapists, psychologists, social workers, and teachers of the deaf (Norton, 1998). Collaboration is the process in which the expertise of the family is acknowledged by professionals and used in the selection, implementation, and evaluation of a program of treatment or rehabilitation (Sohlberg, McLaughlin, Todis, Larsen, & Glang, 2001). Collaboration is, therefore, the sharing of resources among individuals working jointly with others and creating a context that enhances collective action. Through empowerment and collaboration, family members strive to take actions to get what they want for the good of the children with hearing impairment (Turnbull et al., 2004).

Collaboration is considered an essential aspect of service provision for families of children with hearing impairment or other special needs in that it enhances a relationship in which family members and professionals work together to provide the best services for the child and family (DeChillo, Koren, & Schultze, 1994; Brown, 2001). Thus, partnership working is critically important for effective collaboration between professionals and families of children with hearing impairment (Department of Education and Skills, 2004). This means that parents and professionals have established arrangements that enable them to work together to achieve set goals for the benefit of the child and family.

The challenge is for professionals in each locality to explore strategies for working as teams to achieve more effective partnership and collaboration with families of children with hearing impairments. Working together with families, key issues and needs of the child and family will be identified. In addition, the relevant sources of information and services will be identified and strategies for utilizing them worked out. In order to achieve these goals, service providers should be committed to finding ways to overcoming historically divergent, strong ideological, and methodological viewpoints that have characterized the field of hearing impairments over the centuries. Further, to ensure the implementation of effective collaboration or partnership working models, it becomes imperative for professionals to be committed to providing unbiased information about the various options available and to alter the traditional service delivery process to include elements that can enable, empower, and strengthen families as well as promote acquisition of competencies necessary to meet the needs of the child and family (Department of Education and Skills, 2007).

AUDISM: GOING BACK TO 1000 BC?

Despite the provisions and protections offered by laws to individuals with hearing impairments and other disabilities, there is currently a hot-button issue facing individuals with hearing impairments in the United States and other countries, termed as *audism*. Tom Humphries defines audism as the notion that one is superior based on one's ability to hear or behave in the manner of one who hears (Silva, 2005). Audism occurs when an individual makes prior judgment on the deaf population as having an inferior intelligence. In other words, audism refers to discrimination that people with hearing impairments encounter simply because of their hearing loss. Audism profoundly affects individuals with hearing impairments in the workplace, schools, healthcare, and other community services. Evidence is consistent in this chapter that since the dawn of time, Deaf individuals have been mistreated and oppressed. Centuries of biases, held by the hearing population, has lowered expectations of Deaf people. This situation continues to this present time and is now known as audism (Bauman, 2004). According to Bauman, audism is caused by defining language as speech. Thus, it may be mistakenly assumed that if an individual with hearing impairment cannot speak, that person has no language and intelligence and therefore cannot think rationally and make independent decisions. Until a couple of decades ago, the term used to describe individuals with hearing impairments was "deaf and dumb." Often the word "dumb" was taken to mean "stupid" or "idiot." For instance, the first school for individuals with hearing impairments in the United States was called the "American Asylum for the Instruction of the Deaf and Dumb."

Despite legislative provisions aimed at ensuring people with hearing impairments or other disabilities are not treated differently, it seems to be the case that this noble goal remains elusive due to audism. For instance, the US Equal Employment Opportunity Commission (EEOC), a federal agency created to enforce the Americans with Disabilities Act, conducted a study between 1992 and 2003 to compare and contrast discrimination experiences of Americans with disabilities. During this period, 8936 allegations of discrimination were brought to the attention of the EEOC. Findings revealed of these 8936 allegations, 25.1% had merit and 74.9% did not. Though nonsubstantiated allegations greatly outnumbered the allegations having merit, 25% of the complaints reported experiencing discrimination based on their hearing loss (McMahon, Bowe, Chang, & Louvi, 2005).

Geyer and Schroede (1999) studied the conditions influencing the availability of accommodations for 232 workers with hearing impairments. They found among other things that seven of 19 accommodations were available to as many as half of the respondents, and none were available to more than 80% of them. These authors suggested that employers probably based the number of accommodations provided on the incorrectly perceived amount of assistance needed for communication in their workplaces. Clearly, there is more than a need for accommodations to be met for Deaf workers to be successful in the workplace. When Deaf employees are denied accommodations, they are being discriminated against. These Deaf and hard-of-hearing employees are unable to work to their best abilities. Without the necessary accommodations, employers will not see the actual capabilities of these workers and the lack of accommodations may prevent these Deaf and hard-of-hearing employees from ever moving up the ladder. In order for employees to be productive, it is necessary that accommodations are made more widely available.

In health and mental care, instances of people with hearing impairments not receiving care because of their hearing status abound (Lewis, 2008; Rosengreen, Saladin, & Hansann, 2009). Health-care providers may refuse to provide interpreters and prefer to depend on hearing family members to communicate for the patient with hearing impairments.

Taken together, it remains the case that audism is a prevalent issue affecting important aspects of Deaf individuals' lives. Though legislation has attempted to override these hurdles, the cycle continues because the problem is with the hearing people. Like the early Civil Rights movement, it took more than the government intervention through legislation for the attitude of many Whites to change and the discrimination against Blacks began to decrease. Things can only change for the better for Deaf people if the majority of hearing people become aware of their own ignorance and cease assuming that because the individual has a hearing impairment, the individual is incapable of performing jobs, thinking rationally, and making independent decisions.

CONCLUSION

The history of hearing impairments seems to be as ancient as humanity. Evidence is consistent for many centuries that people with hearing impairments were not treated fairly. They were not considered as intelligent as hearing people since they could not use speech. Consequently, they were denied rights to education, marriage, and inheritance in some places.

However, as time went on and knowledge continued to grow, there was a better understanding of the nature of people with hearing impairments. Thanks to philosophers, educators, medical professionals, and clergymen who advocated more positive views and treatments of individuals with hearing impairments, their efforts led to the provision of educational programs for individuals with hearing impairments. Earliest programs were established in European countries and then expanded to other countries, such as the United States. There are educational programs for individuals with hearing impairments all over the world today. However, the quantity and quality of these programs vary. Developed countries of the West have better education and other programs for individuals with hearing impairments than developing countries of Africa, Asia, the Middle East, and Latin America.

Continuing technological developments, growth in knowledge, and passing of favorable laws in many countries, especially the developed ones, have brought tremendous benefits in the education of individuals with hearing impairments. In the developed countries, people with hearing impairments can be found in various fields of work and management levels. For example, the current and immediate last two presidents of Gallaudet University are Deaf people. People with hearing impairments can be found at all levels of administration and management. Nonetheless, even in the developing countries, young people with hearing impairments still encounter challenges in education and assessment. Evidence has consistently shown that most students with hearing impairments graduating from high school can only read and write at the fourth grade level. Educators and professionals in the field of hearing impairment must explore ways to improve collaboration in applied research that will produce more insights and outcomes for improving educational performances and assessment practices for students with hearing impairments.

Given that in developed countries most children with hearing impairments live at home due to legislative mandates that promote their education in inclusive settings, it becomes imperative that families of children with hearing impairments be assisted by professionals to learn strategies that will assist them in improving the language, social, cognitive, and educational development of their children. Providing clear, unbiased, and adequate information on the various needs and available resources and options for children with hearing impairment is one means of supporting families of young children with hearing impairments. It remains a challenge to service providers to ensure that parents and other family members have access to all relevant information, which will enable them to decide what is right and best for their children with hearing impairment and themselves.

Actions are required in several areas in order to ensure that parents receive information and support that will adequately equip them to be fully involved in all aspects of their children's development. A team approach by professionals who work with families of children with hearing impairment is an important key to achieving this goal. If these professionals agree that children with hearing impairments are different as will be their special needs, then they would be able to provide unbiased information to parents. Given clear and unbiased information about the needs of their children, parents of children with hearing impairments will be able to obtain the services essential for the children's development. Provided with the right services, children with hearing impairment possess the same potential for optimum development and achievement as their hearing peers.

Despite the progress recorded in the provision of education and other services to individuals with hearing impairments, challenges remain when issues like audism are still rampant. Massive public awareness of the potentials of individuals with hearing impairments is urgently needed in all countries of the world. It seems to be the case that many hearing people may still be unaware about what people with hearing impairments can do. The situation seems like this because many hearing people equated speech with language. Thus, since those with hearing impairments may not have developed the ability to use speech, they may be labeled, misunderstood, denied their rights, and not treated fairly. Although there are laws guaranteeing individuals with hearing impairments or other disabilities equality in most developed countries, massive public awareness campaigns are still needed on an ongoing basis. Professionals involved in the field of hearing impairments need to collaborate with national associations of the Deaf and other such organizations to produce and seek ways to keep disseminating public awareness materials through the use of internet, radio, television, newspapers, magazines, and other such venues. The goal will be educate people everywhere about the nature of hearing impairments, so that, hopefully, they will understand that people with hearing impairments are capable of anything hearing people can do, if they are provided all needed supports.

NOTE

1. The spelling of Deaf with a capital "D" refers to someone who identifies with Deaf culture and who uses ASL or other sign languages as their primary mode of communication.

REFERENCES

Akamatsu, C. T., Farrelly, S., & Mayer, C. (2005). An investigation of two-way text messaging use with deaf students at the secondary level. *Journal of Deaf Studies and Deaf Education,* *11*(1), 121–131.

Alterovitz, G. (2004). Electrical engineering and nontechnical design variables of multiple inductive loop systems for auditoriums. *Journal of Deaf Studies and Deaf Education,* *9*(2), 202–208.

Angelides, P., & Aravi, C. A. (2007). Comparative perspective of the experience of deaf and hearing individuals as students at mainstream and special schools. *American Annals of the Deaf, 151*(5), 476–487.

Anitia, S. (1985). Assessment of hearing-impaired students. In: A. F. Rotatori & R. Fox (Eds), *Assessment of regular and special education teachers* (pp. 383–406). Austin, TX: PRO-ED.

ASLInfo. (2010). Deaf time-line:1000B.C.–1816. Available at http://www.aslinfo.com/trivia. cfm (May 20).

Australian Hearing. (2008). Hearing loss in Australia: It's more common than you might think, July 23. Available at http://www.hearing.com.au

Baker, S., & Baker K. (1997). Educating children who are deaf or hard of hearing: Bilingual-bicultural education, July 13. Available at http://www.cec.sped.org/AM/Template. cfm?Section = Home&TEMPLATE = /CM/ContentDisplay.cfm&CONTENTID = 7889

Bauman, H. D. (2004). Audism: Exploring the metaphysics of oppression. *Journal of Deaf Studies and Deaf Education, 9*(2), 239–246.

Baynton, C. B., Gannon, J. R., & Bergey, J. L. (2007). *Through the deaf eyes.* Washington, DC: Gallaudet University Press.

Bemrose, S. (2003). Giving information to parents – Factors to consider, June 25. Available at http://www.deafnessatbirth.org.uk/content2/support/info/02/index.html

Berke, J. (2009a). Growing up deaf – Rubella: Could it happen again? July 6. Available at http://deafness.about.com/cs/featurescauses/a/rubella.htm

Berke J. (2009b). Robert Weitbrecht-Inventor of the TTY, August 12. Available at http:// deafness.about.com/od/peopleindeafhistory/a/weitbrecht.htm

Bleckly, F. (2010). Benefits of cochlear implants in children, July 5. Available at http:// www.bellaonline.com/articles/art44676.asp

Bochner, J. H., & Walter, G. G. (2005). Evaluating deaf students' reading to meet the English language and literacy demands of post secondary education programs. *Journal of Deaf Studies and Deaf Education, 10*(3), 232–243.

Bragg, L. (1997). Visual-kinetic communication in Europe before 1600: A survey of sign lexicons and finger alphabets prior to the rise of deaf education. *Journal of Deaf Studies and Deaf Education, 2*(1), 1–25.

Briggs, M. H. (1999). Systems for collaboration: Integrating multiple perspectives. *Child and Adolescent Psychiatric Clinicians of North America, 8*(2), 365–377.

Brown, K. T. (2001). *The effectiveness of early childhood inclusion (parents' perspectives).* Special Education Seminar Research Paper. Layola College, MD.

Brown, M., Abu Bakar, Z., Rickards, F. W., & Griffin, P. (2006). Family functioning, early intervention, and spoken language and placement outcomes for children with profound hearing loss. *Deafness and Education International, 8*(4), 207–226.

Byrnes, L. J., Sigafoos, J., Rickards, F. W., & Brown, P. M. (2002). Inclusion of students who are deaf or hard of hearing in government schools in South Wales, Australia: Development and implementation of policy. *Journal of Deaf Studies and Deaf Education*, 7(3), 244–257.

Calderon, R. (2000). Parental involvement in deaf children's education programs as a predictor of child's language, early reading and social-emotional development. *Journal of Deaf Studies and Deaf Education*, 5(2), 140–155.

Cambra, C. (2002). Acceptance of deaf students by hearing students in regular classrooms. *American Annals of the Deaf*, 147, 38–45.

Cawthon, W. C. (2010). Science and evidence of success: Two emerging issues in assessment accommodations for students who are deaf or hard of hearing. *Journal of Deaf Studies and Deaf Education*, 15(2), 185–203.

Cole, E. B., & Flexer, C. (2007). *Children with hearing loss developing listening and talking: Birth to Six*. San Diego, CA: Plural Publishing Inc.

Daniels, M. (1997). *Benedictine roots in the development of deaf education: Listening with the heart*. Westpott, CT: Bergin and Garvey.

Deafhistoryscotland. (2010). Thomas Braidwood, June 30. Available at http://www.deafhistory scotland.org.uk/resources.html

Dechillo, N., Koren, P. E., & Schultze, K. H. (1994). From paternalism to partnership: Family and professional collaboration in children's mental health. *American Journal of Orthopsychiatry*, 64(4), 564–576.

Delgarno, G. (1971). *Didascalocophus*. Menston, England: Scolar Press.

Department of Education and Skills. (2004). Every child matters: Change for children, July 31. Available at http://www.everychildmatters.gov.uk/_files/F9E3F941DC8D4580539EE4-C743E9371D.pdf

Department of Education and Skills. (2007). Aiming high for disabled children: Better Support for families, July 23. Available at http://www.hmtreasury.gov.uk/media/C/2/cyp_disabledchildren180507.pdf

DesGeorges, J. (2003). Family perceptions of early hearing, detection, and intervention systems: Listening to and learning from families. *Mental Retardation and Developmental Disabilities Research Reviews*, 9, 89–93.

Dilka, K. (2006). L'Abbe Charles Michel de l'Epee: Father of deaf education, July 11. Available at Deafed.net Resource: www.deafed.net/PublishedDocs/lepee.ppt

Easterbrooks, S. R. (1999). Improving practices for students with hearing impairments. *Exceptional Children*, 65(4), 537–554.

Eccarius, M. (1997). Educating children who are deaf or hard of hearing: Assessment. ERIC Digest #550. Available at http://www.ericdigests.org/1998-2/hearing.htm

Evans, C. (2004). Literacy development in deaf students: Case studies in bilingual teaching and learning. *American Annals of the Deaf*, 149(1), 17–27.

Fagan, M. K., & Pisoni, D. B. (2010). Hearing experience and receptive vocabulary development in deaf children with cochlear implants. *Journal of Deaf Studies and Deaf Education*, 15(2), 149–161.

Fitzpatrick, E., Angus, D., Durieux-Smith, A., Graham, I. D., & Coyle, D. (2008). Parents' need following identification of hearing loss. *American Journal of Audiology*, 17(1), 38–49.

Fitzpatrick, E., Graham, I. D., Durieux-Smith, A., Angus, D., & Coyle, D. (2007). Parents' perspectives on the impact of early diagnosis of childhood hearing loss. *International Journal of Audiology*, 46(2), 97–106.

Geyer, P., & Schroede, J. (1999). Conditions influencing the availability of accommodations for workers who are deaf of hard-of-hearing. *Journal of Rehabilitation, 65*(2), 42–50.

Gibson, H., Small, A., & Mason, D. (1997). Deaf bilingual education. In: J. Cummins & D. Corson (Eds), *Encyclopedia of language and education* (Vol. 5, pp. 231–240). Dordrecht, The Netherlands: Kluwer Academic Publishers (Bilingual Education).

Hall, W. (2005). Decrease of deaf potential in a mainstreamed environment, June 23. Available at http://www.personalityresearch.org/papers/hall.html

Hearing Loss Web. (2010a). NAD position statements on cochlear implants – Readers responses, July 12. Available at http://www.hearinglossweb.com/tech/ci/ctvs/nad4.htm

Hearing Loss Web. (2010b). Assistive listening devices for people with hearing loss, August 9. Available at http://www.hearinglossweb.com/tech/ald/ald.htm

Hermans, D. (2008). The relationship between the reading and signing skills of deaf children in bilingual education programs. *Journal of Deaf Studies and Deaf Education, 13*(4), 518–530.

Holden-Pit, L., & Diaz, J. (1998). Thirty years of the annual survey of deaf and hard of hearing children and youth. *American Annals of the Deaf, 142*, 72–76.

Holt, J., Hotto, S., & Cole, K. (1994). *Demographic aspects of hearing impairment: Questions and answers*. Washington, DC: Centre for Assessment and Demographic Studies, Gallaudet University.

Hurtig, R., & Mueller, V. (2010). Technology-enhanced shared reading with deaf and hard of hearing children: The role of a fluent signing narrator. *Journal of Deaf Studies and Deaf Education, 15*, 72–101.

Kelman, C., Azulay, B., & Uchôa, A. (2009). Meta-communication strategies in inclusive classrooms for deaf students. *American Annals of the Deaf, 154*(4), 371–381.

Kent, B., & Smith, S. (2006). They only see it when the sun shines in my ears: Exploring perceptions of adolescent hearing aid users. *Journal of Deaf Studies and Deaf Education, 11*(4), 461–476.

Kuntze, M. (1998). Literacy and deaf children: The language question. *Topics in Language Disorders, 18*, 1–5.

Lane, H., Hoffmeister, R., & Bahan, B. (1996). *A journey into the deaf world.* San Diego, CA: DawnSign.

LaSasso, C., & Lollis, J. (2003). Survey of residential and day schools for deaf students in the United States that identify themselves as bilingual-bicultural programs. *Journal of Deaf Studies and Deaf Education, 8*(1), 79–91.

Leigh, G., & Power, D. (2000). Principles and practices of literacy development for deaf learners: A historical overview. *Journal of Deaf Studies and Deaf Education, 5*(1), 3–8.

Lewis, J. (2008). Patient awarded $400K by New Jersey jury for lack of sign language interpreter at medical treatments, July 31. Available at http://www.jacksonlewis.com/legalupdates/article.cfm?aid = 1539

Luckner, J. L., & Muir, S. (2001). Successful students who are deaf in general education settings. *American Annals of the Deaf, 146*(5), 435–445.

Marschark, M. (2007). *Raising and educating a deaf child: A comprehensive guide to the choices, controversies, and decisions faced by parents and educators.* New York: Oxford University Press.

Marschark, M., & Spencer, E. (Eds). (2003). *Oxford handbook of deaf studies, language and education.* New York: Oxford University Press.

Mauk, G. W., & Mauk, P. P. (1995). Seizing the moment, setting the stage, and serving the future: Towards collaborative models of early identification and early intervention services for children born with hearing loss and their families. *Infant–Toddler Intervention: The Transdisciplinary Journal, 5*(4), 367–394.

Mayer, C., Akamatsu, C. T., & Stewart, D. A. (2003). The case for situational assessment and evaluation with students who are deaf. *Deafness & Education International, 2*(2), 75–92.

McCracken, W., Young, A., & Tattersall, H. (2008). Universal newborn hearing screening: Parental reflections on early audiological management. *Ear and Hearing, 29*(1), 54–64.

McMahon, B., Bowe, F., Chang, T., & Louvi, I. (2005). Workplace discrimination, deafness and hearing impairment. *The National EEOC ADA Research Project, 25*(1), 19–25.

Meadow-Orlans, K. P., Mertens, D. M., Sass-Lehrer, M. A., & Scott-Olson, K. (1997). Support services for parents and their children who are deaf or hard of hearing. A national survey. *American Annals of the Deaf, 142,* 278–288.

Mitchell, R. E., & Karchmer, M. A. (2004). Chasing the mythical ten percent: Parental hearing status of deaf and hard of hearing children in the United States. *Sign Language Studies, 4*(2), 138–163.

Moeller, M. P. (2000). Early intervention and language development in children who are deaf and hard of hearing. *Pediatrics, 106*(3), E43. Available at http://pediatrics. aappublications.org/cgi/reprint/106/3/e43. Retrieved on 20 November.

Mogharreban, C., & Branscum, S. (2008). Educare: Community collaboration for school readiness. *Dimensions in Early Childhood, 28*(1), 21–28.

Moores, D. F. (1996). *Educating the deaf: Pyschology, principles and practices.* Boston, MA: Houghton Mifflin.

Moores, D. (2008). Research on bi–bi instruction. *American Annals of the Deaf, 153,* 3–5.

Moores, D. F. (2007). *Educating the deaf: Psychology, principles and practices.* Boston, MA: Houghton Mifflin.

Morton, D. D. (2001). Beyond parent education: The impact of extended family dynamic on deaf education. *American Annals of the Deaf, 145*(4), 359–365.

Musselman, C., & Kircaali-Iftar, G. (1996). The development of spoken language in deaf children: Explaining the unexplained variance. *Journal of Deaf Studies and Deaf Education, 2*(1), 108–121.

National Health Services (2008). NHS newborn hearing screening program, June 30. Available at http://hearing.screening.nhs.uk

National Institute on Deafness and other Communication Disorders (2010a). Communication options for children who are deaf or hard of hearing, July 11. Available at http://www.nidcd.nih.gov/staticresources/health/healthyhearing/tools/pdf/CommOptions Child.pdf

National Institute on Deafness and other Communication Disorders. (2010b). Captions for deaf and hard of hearing viewers, August 11. Available at http://www.nidcd.nih.gov/health/ hearing/caption.asp

New World Encyclopedia. (2010). Thomas Hopkins Gallaudet, June 20. Available at http:// www.newworldencyclopedia.org/entry/Thomas_Hopkins_Gallaudet

Norton, J. L. (1998). Parental perspectives on factors influencing child mental health treatment. *Dissertation Abstracts International, 59*(6-B), 3069.

Nunes, T., Pretzlik, U., & Olsson, J. (2001). Deaf children's social relationships in mainstream schools. *Deafness & Education International, 3,* 123–136.

Patton, R. (2004). *Social skills issues of mainstreaming hearing-impaired children.* Master's thesis, Washington University Department of Speech & Hearing. Available at http://dspace.wustl.edu/bitstream/1838/17/1/Patton

Paul, P. V., & Quigley, S. P. (1994). *Language and deafness.* San Diego, CA: College-Hill.

Pendergast, S. G., Lartz, M. N., & Fiedler, B. C. (2002). Ages of diagnosis, amplification and early intervention of infants and young children with hearing loss: Findings from parent interviews. *American Annals of the Deaf, 147*(1), 24–29.

Power, D., & Power, M. (2004). Everyone here speaks TXT: Deaf people using SMS in Australia and the rest of the world. *Journal of Deaf Studies and Deaf Education, 9*(3), 333–343.

Powers, S. (2002). From concept to practice in deaf education: A United Kingdom perspective on inclusion. *Journal of Deaf Studies and Deaf Education, 7*(3), 30–43.

Reitsma, P. (2008). Computer-based exercises for learning to read and spell by deaf children. *Journal of Deaf Studies and Deaf Education, 14*(2), 178–189.

Reynolds, C. R., & Fletcher-Janzen, E. (Eds). (2007). *Encyclopedia of special education.* New York: Wiley.

Rodda, M., & Eleweke, C. J. (2000). Theories of literacy development in limited English proficiency deaf people. *Deafness and Education International, 2*(2), 101–113.

Rosengreen, K., Saladin, S., & Hansann, S. (2009). Differences in workplace behavior expectations between deaf workers and hearing employers. *Journal of the American Deafness & Rehabilitation Association (JADARA), 42*(3), 152–166.

Scheetz, N. (2001). *Orientations to deafness.* Needham Heights, MA: Allyn & Bacon.

Schirmer, B. R. (2001). *Language and literacy development in children who are deaf.* Boston, MA: Allyn & Bacon.

Schirmer, B. R. (2004). *Psychological, social and educational dimensions of deafness.* Boston, MA: Allyn & Bacon.

Silva, R. (2005). Audism and deaf culture, July 10. Available at http://www.lifeprint.com/asl101/topics/audism.htm

Sisterhen, D., & Rotatori, A. F. (1986). Counseling the hearing-impaired child. In: A. F. Rotatori, P. J. Gerber, F. W. Litton & R. A. Fox (Eds), *Counseling exceptional children* (pp. 99–122). New York: Human Sciences Press Inc.

Sisterhen, D., & Rotatori, A. F. (1989). Individuals with hearing impairments. In: A. F. Rotatori & R. A. Fox (Eds), *Understanding individuals with low incidence handicaps* (pp. 93–1320). Springfield, IL: Charles C. Thomas.

Sohlberg, M. M., McLaughlin, K. A., Todis, B., Larsen, J., & Glang, A. (2001). What does it take to collaborate with families affected by brain injury? A preliminary model. *Journal of Head Trauma Rehabilitation, 16*(5), 498–511.

Stokoe, W. C. (2005). Sign language structure: An outline of the visual communication systems of the American deaf. *Journal of Deaf Studies and Deaf Education, 10*(1), 3–37.

Stryker, D. S., & Luetke-Stahlman, B. (2003). Students with hearing loss. In: F. E. Obiakor, C. A. Utley & A. F. Rotatori (Eds), *Effective education for learners with exceptionalities* (Vol. 15, pp. 235–257). London: Elsevier Science Ltd.

Takushi, R. (2000). Deaf culture and language: Concerns and consideration for Mainstream teachers. Available at http://www.american.edu/tesol/Ruth_Takushi

Turnbull, R., Turnbull, A., Shank, M., & Smith, S. J. (Eds). (2004). *Exceptional lives: Special education in today's schools.* Upper Saddle River, NJ: Pearson-Prentice Hall.

United States Department of Education. (1998). *To ensure the free appropriate education of children with disabilities: Twentieth annual report to Congress on implementation of the Americans with Disabilities Act (IDEA)*. Washington, DC: Author.

Van Cleve, J. V., & Crouch, B. A. (2002). *A place of their own: Creating the deaf community in America*. Washington, DC: Gallaudet University Press.

Verhaert, N., Willems, M., Van Kerschaver, E., & Desloovere, C. (2008). Impact of early hearing screening and treatment on language development and education level: Evaluation of 6 years of universal newborn hearing screening. *International Journal of Paediatric Otorhinolaryngology*, *72*(5), 599–608.

Washington University School of Medicine. (2010). Deafness in disguise: Timeline of hearing devices and early deaf education. Available at http://beckerexhibits.wustl.edu/did/timeline/index.htm

Watkin, P., McCann, D. C., Law, C., Mullee, M., Petrou, S., Stevenson, J., Worsfold, S., Yuen, H. M., & Kennedy, C. (2007). Language ability in children with permanent hearing impairment: The influence of early management and family participation. *Pediatrics*, *120*(3), e694–e701.

Wikipedia. (2010a). Corpus Juris Civilis. Available at http://en.wikipedia.org/wiki/Corpus_Juris_Civilis

Wikipedia. (2010b). Rudolph Agricola. Available at http://en.wikipedia.org/wiki/Rodolphus_Agricola

Wikipedia. (2010c). Total communication. Available at http://en.wikipedia.org/wiki/Total_Communication

Yoshinaga-Itano, C. (2004). Levels of evidence: Universal newborn hearing screening (UNHS) and early hearing detection and intervention systems (EHDI). *Journal of Communication Disorders*, *37*(5), 451–461.

Zapien, C. (1998). Options in deaf education – History, methodologies, and strategies for surviving the system. Available at http://www.listen-up.org/edu/options1.htm

CHAPTER 9

HISTORY OF VISUAL IMPAIRMENTS

Stacy M. Kelly and Christine Clark-Bischke

Blindness has been recognized as a condition that leaves an individual without vision since the beginning of recorded human history. During the ancient times, the term blindness was used to identify people with little or no remaining vision and these individuals were prohibited from participation in many parts of civilization. People who were identified as blind during ancient times or the middle ages were all viewed as being totally blind without considering any amount of remaining vision (i.e., residual vision). Total blindness is a contemporary term but a long-standing concept that refers to the inability to see anything with either eye. The concept of total blindness has been commonly understood (Koestler, 1976), however, the prevalence of total blindness has often been misunderstood (see Heinze & Rotatori, 1986). Although some people who are blind see nothing at all, most people who are blind have some degree of remaining vision. There are many variations and meanings of the term blind that have evolved as people who are blind have become integrated into society.

Various scales were developed in the early part of the 20th century to describe the extent of vision loss and more formally define the wide-ranging degrees of low vision. Legal blindness is a level of vision loss that was defined and adopted in 1934 by the American Medical Association. The definition was incorporated into the Social Security Act of 1935 (P.L. 74-271) to determine the eligibility for government-financed services and benefits during

History of Special Education
Advances in Special Education, Volume 21, 213–236
Copyright © 2011 by Emerald Group Publishing Limited
ISSN: 0270-4013/doi:10.1108/S0270-4013(2011)0000021012

the Great Depression (Corn & Spungin, 2003). This definition became the definition of *legal blindness* that remains in use today:

> Central visual acuity of 20/200 or less in the better eye with corrective glasses or central visual acuity of more than 20/200 if there is a visual field defect in which the peripheral field is contracted to such an extent that the widest diameter of the visual field subtends an angular distance no greater than 20 degrees in the better eye. (Koestler, 1976, p. 45)

Visual acuity is the measure of the eyes' ability to distinguish object details and shape at a given distance. For instance, a visual acuity of 20/200 means that the individual sees at 20 feet what a person with 20/20 vision (i.e., typical or normal vision) sees at 200 feet. This definition implies that a person unable to read print material is considered educationally blind (see Erekson & Rotatori, 1986; Vander Kolk, 1981).

Heinze and Rotatori (1986) have noted that the legal definition of blindness is not as useful to teachers who work with students with visual impairments because it uses rigid numbers as criteria; and it does not require the child's functioning be evaluated on a wide range of tasks, with a wide range of materials, in a wide range of environments. They suggest the following educational definition by Barraga (1976) is more practical and comprehensive in meeting the instructional needs of student with visual impairments: "A visually handicapped child is one whose visual impairment interferes with his optimal learning and achievement, unless adaptations are made in the methods of presenting learning experiences, the nature of the materials used, and/or in the learning environment" (p. 16). Similarly, the original federal (P.L. 94-142) definition of a visual impairment did not include minimal acuity or field measures and defined a child with a visual handicap as one who possess an impairment which, after correction, adversely affects a child's educational performance. According to LaGrow and Ponchillia (1989), the legal definition is often used as a qualifier for certain subsidy benefits whereas the federal and educational definitions are more educationally functional. In essence, the use of a legal or educational definition of visual impairments is more dependent on the child's situation and purpose (i.e., obtaining educational materials from the American Printing House for the Blind (APH) versus writing an Individualized Education Program (IEP) that specifies short-term and long-term objectives in Braille reading).

There are many variations and meanings of blindness that have developed in the past century. The variations of blindness acknowledge the vision that can remain even when an individual loses a portion or significant amount of his/her vision. Several terms were used in the early and middle part of the

20th century to identify people who experienced significant vision loss but were not totally blind. Although no longer the most contemporary expressions, partially blind, partially sighted, short-sighted, high partials, low partials, and "myopes" (a narrow-minded term that identified all partially sighted students as those with myopia or nearsightedness) all referred to people who were somewhat sighted or had some degree of useful vision despite their vision loss.

At the beginning of the 20th century, there was a rapid spread of special provisions in schools for educating students who had what was then identified as partial sight. For the first time in the early 1900s, special attention was paid to the implications of visual limitations of people who were blind with some degree of remaining vision (The Education of Myopes, 1930). Sight-saving classes that resulted from this worldwide movement were special classrooms attended by students who were identified with some degree of partial sight or blindness with remaining vision. The intent of sight-saving classes was to prevent minimal risk of eyestrain and slow the progression of visual impairments by teaching students to save their remaining vision, however, sight-saving classes no longer exist today. The belief that if a student with partial sight were to use his/her remaining vision, he/she would risk losing the remaining vision was disproven by a pioneering study in the 1960s after more than a half century of implementing a fallacious philosophy (Barraga, 1963). A global perspective on the nomenclature of the sight-saving time period is captured in a 1934 issue of the *British Medical Journal*:

> The [Board of Education] committee came to the definite conclusion that the early official term "partially blind" was bad. "Myope class," the common name in England, is considered too limited, since there are pupils who are not myopes. "Sight-saving classes," the usage of the U.S.A., is considered to claim too much. The preference of the committee is for schools for the "partially sighted." (The Education of Partially Sighted, 1934, p. 68)

The present-day concepts of someone having low vision or being visually impaired are major examples of progress in terminology. Currently, there is no legal definition for low vision or visual impairment and there is no single universally accepted way of defining low vision or visual impairment (Corn & Koenig, 2007). However, the well-established common thread among the various definitions and descriptions of low vision and visual impairment is the functional state or status of the vision of a person experiencing the vision loss (Faye, 1984). Functional definitions focus on visual performance with an everyday task. Recent sources may explain that those who are blind and those with low vision can be identified as visually impaired, while others consider the term blindness and the term visual impairment to refer to distinct populations. Both of these perspectives are correct. Thus, it must be noted that finding universal definitions that can clearly distinguish the term low vision from the term visually impaired is not yet possible today. The definitions for low vision can be used interchangeably with definitions for visual impairment when the population of reference is for those with vision better than *legal blindness*. In this chapter, the term visual impairment refers to both individuals who are blind and individuals with low vision. To properly discuss the history of visual impairments, we use low vision or blindness when specifically referring to low vision or blindness.

FUNCTIONAL AND CLINICAL DEFINITIONS OF LOW VISION

Defined functionally, having low vision can mean the inability to read newsprint even with best correction (when wearing conventional eyeglasses or contact lenses) (Maino, 1993). Other functional definitions of low vision refer to a loss of vision that may be severe enough to hinder an individual's ability to complete daily activities such as reading, cooking, or walking outside safely, while still retaining some degree of useable vision. Low vision is decreased visual performance that prevents performance to full capacity compared with a typically sighted person of the same age and gender. It may be a consequence of reduced acuity, abnormal visual field, reduced contrast sensitivity, or other ocular dysfunction (Faye, 1984). This definition includes people who are legally blind and those who have a more significant amount of remaining vision.

Visual acuities are commonly involved in definitions of low vision and have been involved in the definition of legal blindness since it was established in 1934. This measurement is usually given in a fraction and is based upon visible print size. Although visual acuity testing assesses only one aspect of visual function, it is the one test, when administered in a concise and consistent manner, which can measure and detect changes in the integrity of the visual system. Low vision has been defined clinically as a visual acuity of 20/70 to 20/200 in the better eye with best correction, or a total field loss of 140 degrees or worse (Levack, 1991). Visual acuity of 20/70 means that the individual sees at 20 feet what a person with 20/20 vision (or typical vision) sees at 70 feet. As mentioned, visual acuity of 20/200 means that the individual sees at 20 feet what a person with 20/20 vision (or typical vision) sees at 200 feet. The visual acuities for those with low vision can range anywhere between 20/70 and 20/200.

On the whole, the terminology used to describe visual impairment and educational opportunities for those who are visually impaired continues to become increasingly more sophisticated with time. Past, present, and future events in the field of visual impairments are reflected with each additional refined detail.

EARLY PIONEERS IN THE FIELD

"Throughout history, stories have been told about remarkable and talented people who were blind and managed, often with insightful assistance from others, to educate themselves and make significant contributions to their societies" (Holbrook & Koenig, 2000, p. 2). Successful individuals with visual impairments, including Homer, author of the Iliad and the Odyssey who is believed to have been blind, are known as far back as 700 BC. In earnest, the field of visual impairments began in the early 18th century as awareness of the abilities of individuals with visual impairments was finally being recognized by educators and others. During this time, Denis Diderot, a philosopher initiated the foundation for the education of students with visual impairments after being impressed by the abilities of Nicholas Saunderson, mathematics professor at Cambridge, and Maria Theresia von Paradis, Viennese pianist and music teacher, both of whom were blind. Diderot, Saunderson, von Paradis, and others created a legacy that would be followed by individuals with visual impairments and educators in the field. An individual who followed their lead included Johann Wilhelm Klein who, in 1819, saw the possibilities for the use of dogs as guides for individuals who are blind; and Frank Hall who, in 1892, invented the first braille writer providing an easier method for individuals to write in braille (Hatlen, 2000).

Born with sight, Louis Braille became blind at the age of three as a result of an accident with one of his father's tools. Driven by a desire to learn he created a tactile reading method, in 1824 at the age of 15 years, now known as the Literary Braille Code. He continued to develop additional braille symbols with math and music braille added in 1837. While he taught at the Royal National Institute for the Blind for many years after graduating, the braille code was not officially taught until 1868 when individuals in the Royal National Institute for the Blind began working toward public awareness and understanding. This was 16 years after Louis Braille's death (American Foundation for the Blind (AFB), n.d.-b). Braille material was not used in the United States until 1869. At first, all braille material had to be embossed by hand as the first mechanical brailler was developed in 1892. However, it was not until 1920 when the APH (established in 1858, and founded by Congress in 1879) developed a process for making multiple copies of braille materials that it became widely used (Lagrow & Ponchillia, 1989). In the same year, the Chicago Public Schools established the first braille class in a public school (Lagrow & Ponchillia, 1989).

Other individuals with visual impairments continued to be positively impacted through the use of the braille code. Dr. Abraham Nemeth, blind from birth, followed in Louis Braille's footsteps by creating the Nemeth Braille Code for Mathematics and Scientific Notation from 1946 to 1952. The creation of the Nemeth Code allowed him to pursue his dream of being a mathematician. Also born with sight, world-famous speaker and author, Helen Keller, became blind and deaf at the age of 19 months after a short illness. After reading about the education of Laura Bridgeman, an individual who was also deaf and blind, and contacting Dr. J. Julian Chisolm and Alexander Graham Bell, Helen's mother contacted the Perkins School for the Blind in Watertown, Massachusetts seeking an instructor for her daughter (Koestler, 1976; Roberts, 1986). Anne Sullivan, who was also visually impaired, became Helen's instructor and lifelong companion.

Samuel Gridley Howe founded the Perkins School for the Blind in 1829. He held three convictions that were guiding principles for the school including: educating each child according to his individual needs, following the curriculum of public schools to the extent possible, and preparing the student to live an independent life (Hatlen, 2000). William Hadley, a retired high school teacher, lost his sight at the age of 55. Having the desire to continue reading he taught himself braille. Throughout this process, he became frustrated by the limited educational opportunities for individuals who were blind, especially adults. In 1920, the Hadley School for the Blind, a correspondence school for teaching individuals braille, opened to its first student. Edward Hines, Sr., provided land and financial assistance in the building of the Public Health Hospital #76, later renamed the Hines Blind Rehabilitation Center after Edward Hines, Jr. (Miyagawa, 1999). This center was created to assist service men blinded during World War II and evolved into an internationally acclaimed center that has also become known for the development of orientation and mobility. Early pioneers in the field of visual impairments initiated a developing interest in the education of individuals with visual impairments that extended well beyond the classroom.

MAJOR CONTRIBUTORS AND THEIR THEORETICAL IDEAS

In a field that has always been as specialized as visual impairments, the impact of each distinguished leader runs deep into the roots of the profession. It must be noted that the influence of many outstanding leaders not traditionally mentioned in historical reports made each achievement possible and many other remarkable theoretically based changes happen along the way. The field continues to progress with momentum from a community of countless professionals continuously making a difference in significant ways.

Advancements in Braille Reading and Writing

The increased focus on Science, Technology, Education and Mathematics (STEM) education would not be feasible for braille readers without the development of the Nemeth Code. The Nemeth Code is the tactile code for mathematics and scientific notation used today in the United States and other countries around the world. Dr. Abraham Nemeth began his work on his braille math code in the late 1940s while working for the AFB. The Nemeth Code became the official code book for braille math when it was first published in 1952 (Navy, 1991). Dr. Nemeth attended regular public school as a totally blind child. He addressed the lack of braille materials in math and science, both subject areas he had interest of studying at great length (American Printing House for the Blind (APH), 2010). Dr. Nemeth's revolutionary method made this achievement possible for himself, others that worked with him during his career, and all future generations of braille readers.

Once the literary braille code and braille math code were both well established, there was a need to understand the methods students used to read braille and teach the most effective ways of doing so. Research during the 1970s showed that the vast majority of good braille readers use two hands and that very few good braille readers use only one hand (Mangold, 1993). Among Dr. Sally Mangold's (1935–2005) many accomplishments related to braille literacy was her creation of the Mangold Developmental Program of Tactile Perception and Braille Letter Recognition in 1973 (APH, 2010). This instructional tool has been recognized as a landmark program used today around the world to understand and facilitate the teaching of beginning braille skills.

Progress in Educational Programming

Until the mid-1960s, students who were legally blind were taught as if they were totally blind. Students who were legally blind were taught braille to "save their sight." Students who were identified as partially sighted (clinically defined as having a visual acuity of 20/70–20/200) during this time period used large print books and were taught in sight-saving classes. The uniqueness of the impact of each individual's visual impairment on a particular learning medium (any of combination of large print, braille, and/or audio materials) was not recognized in education until after Natalie Barraga (1963) conducted a study that found visual stimulation (or the use of vision) could actually improve visual functioning (or visual performance). Barraga's finding encouraged education to facilitate the use of vision rather than the saving of vision. This marked the end of the "sight-saving" era. Each student's literacy learning needs were considered and assessed based on the individuality of the impact of visual impairment on visual functioning.

During the 1980s, an area of educational programming in need of considerable development was the education of children and infants with visual impairments who had additional disabilities. Dr. Lilli Nielsen, a Danish special education teacher, explained her innovative approach to working with this particular population when she wrote:

> In 1981, an experience with a two-year-old self-mutilating child made me think that the reason for this child's, and many other visually impaired children's difficulties in developing was maybe due to a lack of knowledge about surroundings. I designed the "Little Room" hoping that it would provide the visually impaired child with a frame of reference concerning spatial relations and thus facilitate the child's learning about the outside world. (Nielsen, 1992, p. 1)

The Little Room is an instructional and explorational tool that provides a highly stimulating environment for a child who is visually impaired or has severe disabilities. External stimuli are removed and the child has complete control over the items and activities in the room. Children and infants with visual impairments and additional disabilities showed significantly positive reactions while exploring and playing with the activities in the Little Room (Nielsen, 1991). As noted by a parent of a child with visual impairments after attending a national conference focused on techniques and tools developed by Dr. Nielsen:

> Dr. Nielsen took several traditionally accepted practices and threw them out of the window, much to the dismay of several seasoned teachers of the visually impaired. For example, it is Dr. Nielsen's belief and observance that a child cannot be taught. Rather, a

child must learn for himself how something is done, or it will not register (author's word) for the long term. She is very much against hand-over-hand anything and she told us story after story of instances in which a child learned something himself using her techniques. (Nielsen, 1992, p. 1)

Sacks' (1998) assertion that at least 50% of the children and youth who are visually impaired exhibit additional disabilities along with visual impairment shows that Nielsen's model and the progressive work of many others in this area of education for severely disabled students affect a considerable portion of the population of students who are visually impaired.

CHANGING EDUCATIONAL TREATMENT PRACTICES

Valentine Haüy established the first school for blind children in Paris in 1784. The school, L'Institution National des Jeunes Aveugles (Institute for Blind Youths), had an enrollment of 14 students. However, most children with blindness in the late 1700s and early 1800s were kept in institutions or in homes. The success of the Institute for the Blind and in response to new attitudes toward blindness, residential schools were opened in Europe and the United States to provide educational opportunities that would meet the unique needs of students who are blind or visually impaired (Ajuwon & Oyinlade, 2008). For example, residential schools opened in England (1791), Switzerland (1804), New York (1832), Philadelphia (1833), and Boston (1833) prior to the Perkins School for the Blind (Lowenfield, 1975). Many states followed suit with many operating a school for the blind by 1957 or transporting their students to states providing a residential school. The original focus of the schools was to teach the students to read and write, to perform music, and complete everyday tasks. In addition, there was a desire to eliminate pity and elicit admiration for the student's abilities with a focus on vocational education.

Low-Vision Instructional Delivery Models

Students with low vision during the early 1800s were seen as "misfits" (i.e., a peculiarity of the time period because they required large print instead of traditional braille instruction) within schools for the blind and public schools (Hathaway, 1933). As this concern continued to increase, special classes were created to provide them with facilities specific for their needs.

Sight-saving classes were created in England in 1908, with Europe (1911) and the United States (1913) following close behind (Hathaway, 1933; Hatlen, 2000). The overall goal of these classes was to provide a preferred environment (e.g., appropriate lighting, decorations, and equipment) and a teacher with excellent sight to assist students in saving their vision. Students with low vision (i.e., 20/70–20/200) and students with deteriorating vision (i.e., degenerative eye conditions or diminishing visual abilities) attended sight-saving classes (Hathaway, 1933).

Inclusive Settings

Individuals within the field of visual impairments began an educational shift toward inclusion during the 1940s. The itinerant teaching model was developed during the 1940s to meet the need of students as they were integrated into public schools, moving away from the residential placement (Holbrook & Koenig, 2000). This shift in educational placement for students with visual impairments required residential schools to change their roles to include outreach support for students, professionals, and parents selecting public school placements (Ajuwon & Oyinlade, 2008). In addition, the role of residential schools changed to include services for students with visual impairments and multiple disabilities (i.e., deaf-blindness). This change lead to residential schools providing highly specialized prevocational, vocational, and intense daily living skills rather than traditional academic programs (see Lagrow & Ponchillia, 1989; Miller, 1985). Residential schools were no longer serving students with a visual impairment as their primary and only identified disability. This shift in educational focus, P.L. 94-142, and a more inclusive social attitude lead to a greater emphasis on local school districts to provide an appropriate academic experience for most students with visual impairments (Lagrow & Ponchillia, 1989).

The development of the itinerant model created new challenges for teachers within the field of visual impairments. Within this low-incidence field, itinerant teachers were often required to travel large distances to the schools where students with visual impairments attended to (a) determine the instructional needs and services required for student success, (b) identify time to prepare student materials and instructional plans, and (c) collaborate with other professionals or parents (Hatlen, 2000; Olmstead, 2005). The creation of the consultation model provided an option for the itinerant teachers in decreasing travel when direct services were determined unnecessary for the student. Through this model, the itinerant teacher communicated, at intervals determined by all individuals, to provide general and special education teachers with accommodation and adaptation strategies within the classroom for students with visual impairments (Cook, Klein, & Tessier, 2008).

Working with Families

Parents have encountered many roles throughout history including parents as the cause of the disability or problem, parents as teachers, parents as political advocates, parents as family members, and parents as parents of children with and without disabilities (Alper, Schloss, & Schloss, 1994; Turnbull, Turnbull, Erwin, & Soodak, 2006). As time and public policy have evolved, the roles of parents and families continue to evolve. Support for families, during the child's development, by professionals throughout history has been limited or not existent. During those times when parents were seen as the cause of the disability, children were removed from their homes and contact with parents was limited or not allowed (Alper et al., 1994). Parents have been compelled by professionals to become teachers within their homes (Turnbull et al., 2006), a role that many parents were not comfortable in completing. While the ultimate goal of parents as teachers was to assist in enriching the home environments of children with disabilities, the initial impacts were guilt and stress for parents. Significant changes in the process by professionals are proving beneficial as each individual gains a better understanding of the child, the family, the disability, and outcomes.

Whether a child's visual impairment is identified at birth or occurs later during his/her development, parents more often than not experience the stages of the grief cycle (Cohen et al., 1992). Visual impairments identified at birth, also known as congenital visual impairment, can provide a different experience for the child and family than when the impairment occurs later in life, also known as adventitious visual impairment. Children born with a visual impairment may develop and interact with their environment as many children do when they receive support and encouragement. Through the assistance of professionals knowledgeable in the development of young children with visual impairments, children and their families can gain a better understanding of strategies to develop the skills most commonly impacted by decreased vision (i.e., gross and fine motor skills, mobility skills, and independence skills). The services of an early intervention provider can be invaluable to the family and the child while it is important to remember that the knowledge of the child by the family can be invaluable to the early intervention provider. Ultimately, a family needs the support of professionals and professionals need the support of the family to assure the provision of an appropriate education for the child. By the same token, children for whom the visual impairment occurs later in life need support by their families and professionals for success in the continuation of skills, strategies for accommodating new visual needs, advocating for their needs, and independence. The child and the family have been placed in a new situation, requiring guidance of individuals prepared to support their needs. Prior to the Individuals with Disabilities Education Act (IDEA) in 1997, families were not included in the education of their children. The families were encouraged or forced to place their child in an institution. It was at the institution that individuals "raised" the children with disabilities such as blindness or visual impairment. Around the 1900s more and more families sought to keep their child at home, allowing them to share in the family activities and growth (French, 2007). As parents began developing relationships with their children, they began seeking opportunities and education for their children. For instance, as parents from minority and diverse backgrounds sought educational equality for their children, an excellent opportunity was provided for parents of children with disabilities, including those who were blind or visually impaired.

The Use of Technology

The definition for assistive technology established by the IDEA in 1997 formalized the concept of how technology has been used by people with visual impairments for centuries. The federal law defined assistive technology as "any item, piece of equipment, or product system, whether acquired commercially off the shelf, modified, or customized, that is used to increase, maintain, or improve functional capabilities of individuals with disabilities" (20 U.S.C. § 602, 300.5). At the same time, IDEA defined *assistive technology services* as "any service that directly assists an individual with a disability in the selection, acquisition, or use of an assistive technology device" (20 U.S.C. § 602, 300.6). As shown by the federal definition, assistive technology includes no-tech, low-tech, and high-tech equipment. "No-technology" or "no-tech" refers to any assistive device that is not electronic. No-tech items used by those with visual impairments range from the slate and stylus, dark markers, bold-lined paper, early glasses or magnifiers, and the long cane. Early glasses and magnifiers were used by individuals with visual impairments as early as 1300 AD while the use of a cane, stick, staff, or bamboo pole can be found in the writings of the ancient Hebrews, Greeks, and Chinese (James & Thorpe, 1994; Neustadt-Noy & LaGrow, 1997). The slate and stylus and other writing tools used by those with visual impairments, such as dark markers, bold-lined papers, or signature guides, are commonly used today. Certainly, the long cane is another example of timeless low-tech equipment with historical value and contemporary functionality. "No-tech" items have allowed individuals with visual impairments to access information, travel independently, and participate in a variety of experiences since ancient times.

"Low-technology" or "low-tech" devices may or may not be electronic but do not include highly sophisticated computer components. One of the earliest "low-tech" devices used by people with visual impairments was the braille writer. The braille writer was first produced in 1889 by Howe Memorial Press at the New England Asylum for the Blind (now called the Perkins School for the Blind) located in Watertown, Massachusetts. The design of the braille writer was not refined by the AFB and other individuals until the 1940s when a prototype was created by David Abraham at Perkins that was more durable and significantly quieter than any other braille writers that were available during this time period. Today, the Perkins Brailler is produced in the United States, England, India, and South America to Abraham's exact standards (McGinnity, Seymour-Ford, & Andries, 2004). Other examples of "low-tech" devices, such as an electronic voice-recording device, cassette recorder, talking calculator, and electronic travel aid, were all developed in the past century. On the other hand, "high-technology" or "high-tech" devices utilize complex, multifunction technology and usually include a computer and associated software (Maushak, Kelley, & Blodgett, 2001). Recent decades have shown progression in the advancement of "high-tech" items, such as computer screen reading programs, the Kurzweil Reading Machine, refreshable braille displays, accessible notetakers, and screen-enlargement programs such as the closed-circuit television system (CCTV). Abner and Lahm (2002) summarized the philosophy of individuals with visual impairments toward "high-tech" assistive technology with this statement:

> Over the past decade, advances in technology have provided new opportunities for people who are visually impaired (that is blind or have low vision) to be independent at work, school, and home. These advances allowed them to compete successfully with sighted people and to have equal access to printed information. Optical scanners; closed circuit television systems (CCTVs); optical magnifiers; note-taking devices; and technologies that produce large print, Braille, or speech are examples of technologies that enable individuals who are visually impaired to write and edit papers, conduct research, gain access to information, and develop job skills. (p. 98)

It must be noted that individuals with visual impairments also use a group of assistive technology devices called independent living aids. These devices bridge across the three categories and include tools such as a knife guards, devices with braille labels, large print phones, talking scales, and diabetic insulin monitors. Many of the most basic "no-tech" or "low-tech" independent living aids for people with visual impairments have been used for an entire century. The most advanced or "high-tech" independent living aids became available during the technology revolution of the recent decades.

Furthermore, Lagrow and Ponchillia (1989) noted that advances in medical technology have had a significant impact on the lives of individuals with blindness and visual impairments. For example, improved laser technology allows ophthalmologists to "(a) repair detached retinas of infants less than two months old, (b) dissolve cataracts without surgical intrusion into the eyes, and (c) treat the cancerous tumors of retinal blastoma with the laser, rather than enucleating (removing) the affected eyes" (p. 173). Also, advances in electrodiagnostic testing devices, such as the Visual-Evoked Response (VER) and Electroretinogram (ERG), allow for the examination of pre- and nonverbal persons who have difficulty responding to standard test procedures (Lagrow & Ponchillia). Finally, technological advances in assisting individuals with poor night vision such as the Wide Angle Mobility Light (WAML) and the Night Vision Aid (NVA) allow for increased orientation and mobility (Lagrow & Ponchillia).

Assessment Practices

As students with visual impairments began receiving educational instruction in public or residential schools, educators noted a need for assessments that would assist them in identifying visual functioning, reading mediums (e.g., print, large print, and braille), and accommodations needed within the classroom to support the student's success in the classroom. Ophthalmological and optometric evaluations have been available for several decades and provide valuable information of the unique etiology of students. The clinical low-vision evaluation, beginning in the 1930s, provides a detailed description of the specific low-vision needs and low-vision devices that includes magnification and adaptive devices to support visual functioning within natural environments. The information provided by ophthalmologists and optometrists has been very useful for teachers of students with visual impairments by providing an understanding of the unique etiology of the student. Specific strategies to identify functional vision and student accommodations had yet to be developed. With these specific needs, individuals in the field of visual impairments began the process of creating assessments specifically for use with students with visual impairments.

Initial "functional vision assessments (FVAs)" isolated visual skills. The Corn Model of Visual Functioning, presented in 1989, initiated the process by focusing on visual abilities, environmental cues, and stored/available individuality (Corn, 1989). During the 1980s and 1990s, the FVA evolved to "assess how the individual applies his or her vision in real-life tasks or environments outside of the clinical setting" (Lueck, 2004, p. 14). From these evaluations, professionals are able to provide direction and suggestions for promoting visual functioning within a variety of settings. From the early beginnings of the field of visual impairments, professionals have also sought strategies for the identification of an assessment to determine the primary literacy medium for students who are blind or visually impaired. Prior to the 1980s, professionals used their best judgments to make those determinations. In 1992, Alan Koenig and Cay Holbrook worked to create a framework that would guide professionals in determining the best literacy medium (Koenig & Holbrook, 1995). After receiving comments from other professionals in the field, they published *The Learning Media Assessment* (LMA). *The Oregon Project for Preschool Children who are Blind or Visually Impaired* (Koenig & Holbrook, 1995) is a comprehensive assessment designed to assess the cognitive, language, socialization, visual, compensatory, self-help, fine motor, and gross motor skills of children from birth to six years of age who are blind or visually impaired. These assessments, available from many entities and in a variety of versions, are now used by teachers of students with visual impairments, low-vision specialists, and other professionals in the field of visual impairments throughout the world to identify the individual needs of students with visual impairments (Shaw, Russotti, Strauss-Schwartz, Vail, & Kahn, 2009).

As early as 1891, there was a developing understanding of the additional needs of individuals with visual impairments (AFB, n.d.-a). These additional needs, created when incidental learning was impacted by a visual impairment or blindness, prompted professionals in the field of visual impairments to develop a curriculum to assist in meeting these needs. The expanded core curriculum (ECC) (AFB, n.d.-a) included those areas requiring additional instruction for students who do not have the visual skills to successfully develop independently (Corn, Hatlen, Huebner, Ryan, & Siller, 1995). The addition of the ECC required the development of assessments that look at specific abilities and needs of individual students who are blind or visually impaired (Texas School for the Blind and Visually Impaired, n.d.). Many assessments began appearing in print during the early 1990s with the publication of the *Assessment KIT: Kit of Informal Tools for Academic Students with Visual Impairment* (Sewell, 1997). This instrument provided assessments for many areas of the ECC published in 1997. Prior to this time, teachers of students with visual impairments created their own documents and forms for assessing student skills. Table 1 identifies the specific areas of the ECC, skills within those areas, and the pertinent assessments used today that have been under development for several decades. A comprehensive discussion of the ECC is provided by Sapp (2003).

As early as 1957, teachers and researchers identified difficulties in determining the visual acuity of students with visual and multiple disabilities. In addition to completing the traditional assessments (i.e., the FVA and LMA) with considerations for the student's additional abilities, teachers have access to specialized assessments (see Edris, Rotatori, Kapperman, & Heinze, 1983; Heinze, 1985; Lagrow & Ponchillia, 1989; Longo, Rotatori, Heinze, & Kapperman, 1982; Matson, Heinze, Helzel, Kapperman, & Rotatori, 1986; Rotatori & Kapperman, 1980; Rotatori, Kapperman, & Fox, 1981). These assessments include the following: *Visual Efficiency Scale* (Barraga, 1970), the *Program to Develop Efficiency in Visual Functioning* (Barraga, 1980), the Visual Functioning Assessment Tool (Costello, Pinkney, & Scheffers, 1980), the *Individualized, Systematic Assessment of Visual Efficiency for the Developmentally Young Individual (ISAVE)* (Langley, 1996), *the Peabody Mobility Kit for Infants and Toddlers* (Harley, Long, Merblert, & Wood, 1988), *Braille Assessment Inventory* (Sharpe, McNear, & McGrew, 1996), *the Social Competency Scale for Blind Preschool Children* (Maxfield & Bucholtz, 1958), and the *CVI (Cortical Visual Impairment) Range* Assessment (Roman-Lantzy, 2007). On the whole, significant gains have been made in identifying and meeting the unique needs of individuals who are blind or visually impaired. While the additional assessments take time, the results are necessary in the development of an IEP for each individual student.

Legislative Acts

Legislative acts specific to visual impairment have been situated in the three areas of mobility (such as travel with long canes and dog guides), employment opportunity, and educational programming. For example, in 1879, federal legislation was passed to promote the education of persons with blindness. This act resulted in the payment of an annual sum of money to the APH to cover the cost of printing adaptive books and educational

Table 1. The Expanded Core Curriculum and Corresponding Assessments.

Skill	Description	Sample Assessments	Sample Skills Assessed
Compensatory/ Access/Functional academic	Strategies to increase the understanding of concepts learned through sight	*Assessment KIT: Kit of informal tools for academic students with visual impairments*	Braille reading and writing Concept development Spatial understanding Study and organizational skills Speaking and listening skills
Social interaction	Strategies to increase opportunities to initiate and maintain relationships	*Assessment KIT: Kit of informal tools for academic students with visual impairments*	Social skills Communication Emotions
Career education	Strategies to identify occupational choices and skills	*Assessment KIT: Kit of informal tools for academic students with visual impairments*	Keyboarding skills Career readiness Assistive technology Collaborative skills
Independent living	Skills to independently complete daily living	*Assessment KIT: Kit of informal tools for academic students with visual impairments*	Social competence Self-care and maintenance of personal environment Contributing community member
Recreation and leisure	Skills to increase and maintain a healthy lifestyle	*Independent living: A curriculum with adaptations for students with visual impairments. Volume III: Play and leisure*	Play and leisure Physical activity Socialization
Orientation and mobility	Strategies to increase basic body image and independence in maneuvering and orienting within environments	*TAPS: An orientation and mobility curriculum for students with visual impairments*	Body image Orientation Mobility
Assistive technology	Strategies to access and store information	*Technology assessment checklist for students with visual impairments*	Assistive technology
Sensory efficiency	Strategies to efficiently utilize remaining vision, hearing and other senses	*Learning media assessment combined with assessments from the assessment KIT*	Use of sensory channels Determining types of general learning media Selecting literacy media Making decisions about functional learning and literacy media
Self-determination	Strategies to increase the student's ability to believe in himself while understanding abilities and limitations	*Assessment KIT: Kit of informal tools for academic students with visual impairments*	Social skills Career development Independent living skills

materials for children based on a quota system (Lagrow & Ponchillia, 1989). One of the earliest legislative acts specific to this disability area was the white cane law in 1930. The basic methods of travel for people who are visually impaired include the use of the human guide technique (also commonly referred to as the sighted guide technique), the long cane (also commonly referred to as the white cane), the dog guide, and electronic travel aids (Jacobson, 1993). The long cane and the dog guide methods of travel have specific legislative acts that took place to better facilitate the use of these techniques for people with visual impairments. Mobility aids such as the long cane and dog guide are used by people who are visually impaired to preview objects and changes in their immediate environment immediately before they actually encounter them (Farmer & Smith, 1997). The first white cane ordinance was sponsored by the Peoria Illinois Lions Club and established that the driver of a vehicle must not approach a pedestrian who is carrying a cane or using a dog guide crossing an intersection without taking every necessary precaution to avoid accident or injury to a pedestrian who is blind. The white cane law was passed in every U.S. state in 1931 and remains today (Wiener & Sifferman, 1997). Another legislative act, the Pratt–Smoot Act of 1931 provided funds for the establishment of the National Library Service for the Blind and Physically Handicapped (commonly know as the "Talking Book Program"). This act provides free braille and recorded books for individuals with blindness and physical impairments (Lagrow & Ponchillia, 1989). Another important law for persons with visual impairments is the Americans with Disabilities Act (ADA) that was enacted in 1990. The section of the ADA that significantly impacts travelers who are visually impaired is the public accommodation law. This established that people with disabilities who have service animals, such as dog guides, can be accompanied by the service animals in nearly any public or private venue of any kind (1990, 42 U.S.C. § 36 *et seq.*).

For a significant amount of time, large proportions of the population of adults who have visual impairments have been identified as unemployed or have been identified as not in the labor force (i.e., they were not actively looking for work so they were not identified by the unemployment rate even though they were not working as well). The labor force participation rate among working age adults who are visually impaired has been well established as being too low (Shaw, Gold, & Wolffe, 2007; Wagner, D'Amico, Marder, Newman, & Blackorby, 1992). The Randolph–Sheppard Act (originally named The Blind Vending Stand Act of 1936) made a powerful statement in the mid-1930s about the capacity for Americans who are blind to contribute to society at the highest level. The 1936 federal law mandated a priority to people who are blind to operate vending facilities on Federal property (20 U.S.C. § 107 *et. seq.*). It was intended as an opportunity for people who are blind to maximize their vocational potential through the government sector and intended to impact employment outcomes for adults who have visual impairments. Many years later, the 1997 amendments to the IDEA called for several changes to the IEP development process. The Braille provision (as it is commonly known) was added to IDEA in 1997 and was included in the 2004 reauthorization of IDEA, formally known as Individuals with Disabilities Education Improvement Act or IDEIA. The IDEIA (2004) provision states that:

> The Individualized Education Program (IEP) Team shall — in the case of a child who is blind or visually impaired, provide for instruction in Braille and the use of Braille unless the IEP Team determines, after an evaluation of the child's reading and writing skills, needs, and appropriate reading and writing media (including an evaluation of the child's future needs for instruction in Braille or the use of Braille), that instruction in Braille or the use of Braille is not appropriate for the child. (20 U.S.C. § 614)

Ever since IDEA 1997, federal law has mandated that the IEP team must provide braille instruction for every student who is visually impaired unless the team decides that this is not the appropriate need for that particular student. Braille instruction is a component of the ECC.

Invisible Printing: A Problem for the Partially Sighted

> SIR – I have become increasingly perturbed by the recent tendency for official forms, important announcements, instructions on food packages, etc, to be printed in various colour combinations.
> This is causing great difficulties for partially sighted persons, particularly those who, like myself, have developing lens opacities. One particular PAYE form is printed in pale pink on buff-coloured paper, and this to me is practically invisible. Often, two shades of the same colour are used with similar effect. Victims of this disability are usually elderly and often inarticulate, so that the problem is not widely understood. It would be a great help to many people if those responsible could be informed of this. (Harding, 1981, p. 1060)

For centuries, people with visual impairments have struggled to access printed or complex visual information in a timely manner and there was no regulation to address this vexing problem. Considerable research supports the contention that students who are visually impaired have not received equal access to information in school. The findings of a recent study of students who are visually impaired showed that there is a consistent delay in the delivery of materials for students who use large print or braille materials even though the IDEA mandated equal and timely access to all information presented in school for all students (Smith, Geruschat, & Huebner, 2004). The National Instructional Materials Accessibility Standard (NIMAS), a federally sponsored effort, was recently enacted to address this problem in grade levels kindergarten through twelfth grade. In the NIMAS-related section of the 2004 reauthorization of IDEA, State Education Agencies (SEAs) and/or Local Education Agencies (LEAs) are required to "provide instructional materials to blind persons or other persons with print disabilities in a timely manner" (20 U.S.C. § 612 *et seq.*). This federal legislation mandated textbook publishers to provide materials in a standard electronic format by December 2006 to expedite the distribution of accessible reading materials for students with blindness, low vision, or a print disability. The NIMAS was a major legislative accomplishment for a significant portion of the disability community.

CONCLUSION

As has been demonstrated, technological advancements and federal legislation in the recent century have significantly assisted with access to visual information and opportunities of all kinds for people with visual impairments. Advancements in educational programming, assessment practices, and family-centered services have promoted the well-being of the child. The earliest pioneers paved the way to make this progression possible. Clearly, in a field that has always been specialized, the impact of each contributor runs deep into the roots of the profession. The field of visual impairments continues to develop with momentum from a community of professionals who make a difference in significant ways. More than an entire millennium of progress has contributed to every achievement and all of the possibilities that now exist for people who are visually impaired. It is necessary to keep this momentum going as special education continues to progress.

REFERENCES

Abner, G. H., & Lahm, E. A. (2002). Implementation of assistive technology with students who are visually impaired: Teacher readiness. *Journal of Visual Impairment and Blindness, 96,* 98–105.

Ajuwon, P. M., & Oyinlade, A. O. (2008). Educational placement of children who are blind or have low vision in residential and public schools: A national study of parent perspectives. *Journal of Visual Impairment and Blindness, 102,* 325–339.

Alper, S. K., Schloss, P. J., & Schloss, C. N. (1994). *Families of students with disabilities: Consultation and advocacy.* Boston: Allyn and Bacon.

American Foundation for the Blind. (n.d.-a). Expanded core curriculum. Retreived March 29, 2010, from http://www.afb.org/Section.asp?SectionID = 44&TopicID = 189&SubTopicID = 4

American Foundation for the Blind. (n.d.-b). Louis Braille biography. Retrieved February 26, 2010, from http://www.afb.org/braillebug/louis_braille_bio.asp

American Printing House for the Blind (APH). (2010). Leaders and legends: Inductees in the Hall of Fame. Retrieved on February 5, 2010 from http://www.aph.org/hall_fame/inductees.html

Americans with Disabilities Act of 1990, 42 U.S.C. § 36 *et seq.* (1990).

Barraga, N. (1963). *Effects of experimental teaching on the visual behavior of children educated as though they had no vision.* Unpublished doctoral dissertation. George Peabody College, Nashville, TN.

Barraga, N. (1970). *Teacher's guide for development of visual learning abilities and utilization of low vision.* Louisville, KY: American Printing House for the Blind.

Barraga, N. (1976). *Visual handicaps and learning.* Belmont, CA: Wadsworth.

Barraga, N. (1980). *Program to develop efficiency in visual functioning.* Louisville, KY: American Printing House for the Blind.

Cohen, R. A., Harrell, L., Macon, C. I., Moedjono, S. J., Orrante, L. S., Pogrund, R. L., & Salcedo, P. S. (1992). Family focus: Working with families of young blind and visually impaired children. In: R. L. Pogrund, D. L. Fazzi & J. S. Lampert (Eds), *Early focus: Working with young blind and visually impaired children and their families.* New York: American Foundation for the Blind.

Cook, R. E., Klein, M. D., & Tessier, A. (2008). *Adapting early childhood curricula for children with special needs.* Upper Saddle River, NJ: Pearson Education.

Corn, A. L. (1989). Instruction in the use of vision for children and adults with low vision: A proposed program model. *RE:view, 21*(1), 26–38.

Corn, A. I., Hatlen, P., Huebner, K. M., Ryan, F., & Siller, M. A. (1995). *The national agenda for the education of children and youths with visual impairments, including those with multiple disabilities.* New York: AFB Press.

Corn, A., & Koenig, A. J. (Eds). (2007). *Foundations of low vision: Clinical and functional perspectives.* New York: AFB Press.

Corn, A., & Spungin, S. J. (2003). *Free and appropriate public education and the personnel crisis for students with visual impairments and blindness.* Gainesville, FL: University of Florida, Center on Personnel Studies in Special Education.

Costello, K., Pinkney, P., & Scheffers, W. (1980). *Visual assessment functioning tool.* Chicago: Stoelting Co.

Edris, S., Rotatori, A. F., Kapperman, G., & Heinze, A. (1983). A survey of assessment devices administered to deaf-blind children. *ICEC Quarterly, 32,* 24–28.

Erekson, T. L., & Rotatori, A. F. (1986). *Accessibility to employment training for the physically handicapped.* Springfield, IL: Charles C. Thomas.

Farmer, L., & Smith, D. (1997). Adaptive technology. In: B. B. Blasch, W. R. Wiener & R. L. Welsh (Eds), *Foundations of orientation and mobility* (2nd ed., pp. 231–257). New York: AFB Press.

Faye, E. (1984). *Clinical low vision.* Boston: Little, Brown and Company.

French, S. (2007). Visually impaired people with learning difficulties: Their education from 1900 to 1970 – policy, practice and experience. *British Journal of learning Disabilities, 36,* 48–53.

Harding, W. H. (1981). Invisible printing: A problem for the partially sighted. *The British Medical Journal, 283*, 1060.

Harley, R. K., Long, R. G., Merblert, J. B., & Wood, T. A. (1988). *Peabody mobility kit for infants and toddlers*. Chicago: Stoelting.

Hathaway, W. (1933). Educational opportunities in the United States for partially seeing children. *Journal of Educational Sociology, 6*(6), 331–338.

Hatlen, P. (2000). Historical perspectives. In: M. C. Holbrook & A. J. Koenig (Eds), *Foundations of education: History and theory of teaching children and youths with visual impairments* (pp. 1–54). New York: American Foundation for the Blind.

Heinze, A. (1985). Assessment of visually handicapped students. In: A. F. Rotatori & R. Fox (Eds), *Assessment for regular and special education teachers* (pp. 361–382). Austin, TX: PRO-ED.

Heinze, A., & Rotatori, A. F. (1986). Counseling the visually handicapped child. In: A. F. Rotatori, P. J. Gerber, F. W. Litton & R. A. Fox (Eds), *Counseling exceptional children* (pp. 179–196). New York: Human Sciences Press, Inc.

Holbrook, M. C., & Koenig, A. J. (Eds). (2000). *Foundations of education: History and theory of teaching children and youths with visual impairments*. New York: AFB Press.

Individuals with Disabilities Education Improvement Act of 2004, 20 U.S.C. § 602 *et seq.*, § 612 *et* seq., 614 *et seq.* (2004).

Jacobson, W. (1993). *The art and science of teaching orientation and mobility to persons with visual impairments*. New York: AFB Press.

James, P., & Thorpe, N. (1994). *Ancient inventions*. New York: Ballantine Books.

Koenig, A. J., & Holbrook, M. C. (1995). *Learning media assessment of students with visual impairments: A resource guide for teachers* (2nd ed.). Austin, TX: Texas School for the Blind.

Koestler, F. A. (1976). *The unseen minority: A social history of blindness in the United States*. New York: David McKay.

Lagrow, S., & Ponchillia, S. V. (1989). Children with visual impairments. In: A. F. Rotatori & R. A. Fox (Eds), *Understanding individuals with low incidence handicaps* (pp. 133–186). Springfield, IL: Charles C. Thomas.

Langley, M. B. (1996). *Individualized systematic assessment of visual efficiency for the developmentally young individual (ISAVE)*. New York: American Printing House for the Blind.

Levack, N. (1991). *Low vision: A resource guide with adaptations for students with visual impairments*. Austin, TX: Texas School for the Blind and Visually Impaired.

Longo, J., Rotatori, A. F., Heinze, A., & Kapperman, G. (1982). Technology as an aide in assessing visual activity in severely/profoundly retarded children. *Education of the Visually Handicapped, 14*, 21–27.

Lowenfield, B. (1975). *The changing status of the blind: From separation to integration*. Springfield, IL: Charles C. Thomas.

Lueck, A. H. (2004). Comprehensive low vision care. In: A. H. Lueck (Ed.), *Functional vision: A practitioner's guide to evaluation and intervention*. New York: American Foundation for the Blind.

Maino, J. H. (1993). Geriatric low vision rehabilitation. In: S. Aston & J. Maino (Eds), *Clinical geriatric eye care* (pp. 87–106). Boston: Butterworth and Heinemann.

Mangold, S. S. (1993). *Teaching the Braille slate and stylus: A manual for mastery* (Rev. ed.). Castro Valley, CA: Exceptional Teaching Aids.

Matson, J. L., Heinze, A., Helzel, W. J., Kapperman, G., & Rotatori, A. F. (1986). Assessing social skills in the visually handicapped. *Journal of Clinical Child Psychology, 15*, 78–87.

Maushak, N. J., Kelley, P., & Blodgett, T. (2001). Preparing teachers for the inclusive classrooms: A preliminary study of attitudes and knowledge of assistive technology. *Journal of Technology and Teacher Education, 9,* 419–431.

Maxfield, K. E., & Bucholtz, S. (1958). *A social maturity scale for blind preschool children: A guide to its use.* New York: American Foundation for the Blind.

McGinnity, B. L., Seymour-Ford, J., & Andries, K. J. (2004). *Howe press and the Perkins Brailler.* Watertown, MA: Perkins History Museum, Perkins School for the Blind.

Miller, W. H. (1985). The role of residential schools for the blind in educating visually impaired students. *Journal of Visual Impairment and Blindness, 79,* 160–163.

Miyagawa, S. (1999). *Journey to excellence: Development of the military and VA blind rehabilitation programs in the 20th century.* Lakeville, MN: Galde Press.

Navy, C. (1991). The history of the Nemeth Code: An interview with Dr. Abraham Nemeth. *Raised Dot Computing Newsletter, 9,* 1.

Neustadt-Noy, N., & LaGrow, S. J. (1997). The development of the profession of orientation and mobility around the world. In: B. B. Blasch, W. R. Wiener & R. L. Welsh (Eds), *Foundations of orientation and mobility* (2nd ed., pp. 624–645). New York: AFB Press.

Nielsen, L. (1991). Spatial relations in congenitally blind infants: A study. *Journal of Visual Impairment and Blindness, 85,* 11–16.

Nielsen, L. (1992). Spatial relations and the "Little Room". *Future Reflections, 11,* 1.

Olmstead, J. E. (2005). *Itinerant teaching: Tricks of the trade for teachers of students with visual impairments.* New York: American Foundation for the Blind.

Roberts, F. K. (1986). Education for the visually handicapped: A social and educational history. In: G. T. Scholl (Ed.), *Foundations of education for blind and visually handicapped children and youth: Theory and practice* (pp. 1–18). New York: AFB Press.

Roman-Lantzy, C. (2007). *CVI: Cortical visual impairment range assessment.* New York: American Printing House for the Blind.

Rotatori, A. F., & Kapperman, G. (1980). An instructional interaction observation system for use with low functioning visually impaired students. *Education of the Visually Handicapped, 12,* 47–52.

Rotatori, A. F., Kapperman, G., & Fox, R. (1981). A behavioral analysis approach to the vocational assessment of severely handicapped visually impaired clients. *ICEC Quarterly, 30,* 7–11.

Sacks, S. Z. (1998). Educating students who have visual impairments with other disabilities: An overview. In: S. Z. Sacks & R. Silberman (Eds), *Educating students who have visual impairments with other disabilities* (pp. 3–38). Baltimore: Paul Brookes.

Sapp, W. (2003). Visual impairment. In: F. E. Obiakor, C. A. Utley & A. F. Rotatori (Eds), *Effective education for learners with exceptionalities* (Vol. 15, pp. 259–282). London: Elsevier Science.

Sewell, D. (1997). *The assessment KIT: Kit of informed tools for academic students with visual impairments.* Austin, TX: Texas School for the Blind and Visually Impaired.

Sharpe, M. N., McNear, D., & McGrew, K. S. (1996). *Braille assessment inventory.* Columbia. MO: Hawthorne Educational Services, Inc.

Shaw, A., Gold, D., & Wolffe, K. (2007). Employment-related experiences of youths who are visually impaired: How are these youths fairing? *Journal of Visual Impairment and Blindness, 101,* 7–21.

Shaw, R., Russotti, J., Strauss-Schwartz, J., Vail, H., & Kahn, R. (2009). The need for a uniform method of recording and reporting functional vision assessments. *Journal of Visual Impairment and Blindness, 103*, 367–371.

Smith, A. J., Geruschat, D., & Huebner, K. M. (2004). Policy to practice: Teachers' and administrators' views on curricular access by students with low vision. *Journal of Visual Impairment and Blindness, 98*, 612–628.

Texas School for the Blind and Visually Impaired. (n.d.). The core curriculum for blind and visually impaired children and youths. Retrieved February 26, 2010, from http://www.tsbvi.edu/agenda/corecurric.htm#Core

The Blind Vending Stand Act of 1936, 20 U.S.C. § 107 *et seq.* (1936).

The Education of Myopes. (1930). *The British Medical Journal, 2*, 789.

The Education of Partially Sighted Children. (1934). *The British Medical Journal, 2*, 68–69.

Turnbull, A., Turnbull, R., Erwin, E., & Soodak, L. (2006). *Families, professionals, and exceptionality: Positive outcomes through partnership and trust.* Upper Saddle River, NJ: Pearson Education.

Vander Kolk, C. J. (1981). *Assessment and planning with the visually impaired.* Baltimore: Paul H. Brookes.

Wagner, M., D'Amico, R., Marder, C., Newman, L., & Blackorby, J. (1992). *What happens next? Trends in postschool outcomes of youth with disabilities.* Menlo Park, CA: SRI International.

Wiener, W., & Sifferman, E. (1997). The development of the profession of orientation and mobility. In: B. B. Blasch, W. R. Wiener & R. L. Welsh (Eds), *Foundations of orientation and mobility* (2nd ed., pp. 553–579). New York: AFB Press.

CHAPTER 10

HISTORY OF AUTISM SPECTRUM DISORDERS

Julie A. Deisinger

Autistic disorder, Asperger's disorder, childhood disintegrative disorder (CDD), Rett's disorder, and pervasive developmental disorder not otherwise specified (PDD-NOS) comprise a group of conditions referred to in the *Diagnostic and Statistical Manual of Mental Disorders* (*DSM*) (American Psychiatric Association/APA, 2000) as autism spectrum disorders (ASDs). Several of these pervasive developmental disorders are associated with intellectual deficits, and all of them involve impairments in social functioning and communication, often accompanied by repetitive behaviors, a need for sameness, and strong interests in unusual topics (APA, 2000).

ASDs can be found worldwide (Wilkinson, 2010). Their formal history is less than a century old, yet individuals with ASD probably have existed throughout human existence (Feinstein, 2010), or at least for hundreds of years (Frith, 2008). One of the earliest accounts, contained in a book titled *The Little Flowers of St. Francis*, told about a member of a Franciscan religious order who was known as Brother Juniper (Frith, 2003; Wing, 2005). As described in this 13th century book, Brother Juniper's unusual behaviors suggest that he had an ASD (AWARES, n.d.; Frith, 2003). Famous people from the 15th through the 21st century who have had or been suspected of having an ASD on the basis of their behavior include Michelangelo (Arshad & Fitzgerald, 2004; James, 2006), Isaac Newton (Fitzgerald & O'Brien, 2007; James, 2003; Muir, 2003), the wild boy of Aveyron (Shattuck, 1994; Wolff,

History of Special Education
Advances in Special Education, Volume 21, 237–267
Copyright © 2011 by Emerald Group Publishing Limited
ISSN: 0270-4013/doi:10.1108/S0270-4013(2011)0000021013

2004), Emily Dickinson (Brown, 2010), Albert Einstein (James, 2003; Muir, 2003), and Temple Grandin (Grandin, 1986). This chapter will provide a history of ASDs, with emphasis on autistic disorder and Asperger's disorder.

FORMAL RECOGNITION OF ASDS

Kanner's Predecessors

Child psychiatrist Leo Kanner (pronounced "Konner;" Feinstein, 2010, p. 19) published a ground-breaking paper in 1943 that introduced the world to the present-day concept of autism (Fombonne, 2003; Goldstein & Ozonoff, 2009; Roth, 2010). Prior to Kanner, however, several physicians described the condition of autism without identifying it as such. A textbook published in 1809, titled *Observations on Madness and Melancholy*, contained a description of a boy whose symptoms fit the modern definition of autism (Feinstein, 2010; Vaillant, 1962). The book's author, Dr. John Haslam, wrote about a 5-year-old male who was admitted to the Bethlem Asylum in 1799 with a medical history that included a case of measles when he was 1 year old. The boy's mother claimed that at age 2 years, her son became harder to control. She also indicated that he did not begin to walk until he was 2½ years of age and did not talk until he was 4 years old. Once hospitalized, the boy cried only briefly upon separation from his mother and was "constantly in action" (Vaillant, 1962, p. 376), suggesting that he was hyperactive. Hyperactivity is a characteristic commonly found in children with ASDs (APA, 2000; Wicks-Nelson & Israel, 2009). Although this child watched other boys at play in the hospital, he never joined them and played intently with toy soldiers by himself. The boy could not learn to read and always referred to himself in the third person (Vaillant, 1962). Grammatical errors in speech can be observed among individuals with ASDs (Roth, 2010; Wicks-Nelson & Israel, 2009).

Haslam again examined this boy when the youngster reached the age of 13 years. He still was a loner who was obsessed with toy soldiers and military music. This youth was also preoccupied with attending church services, although it was reported that he did not comprehend their purpose (Wolff, 2004). Prominent psychiatrist George Vaillant (1962) wrote that Haslam came closer than anyone else to anticipating the definition of autism that emerged in the 20th century.

An 1867 book written by Henry Maudsley also predated Kanner's description of modern-day autism. Maudsley's book, called *The Pathology of Mind*, contained a chapter discussing what was termed insanity in childhood (Goldstein & Ozonoff, 2009; Wing & Shah, 2006; Wolff, 2004). It included a case study of a 13-year-old boy whose symptoms would be consistent with the modern definitions of ASDs (Wolff, 2004).

In 1911, a Swiss psychiatrist named Eugen Bleuler coined the term autism, which he derived from Greek words that referred to the state of the self (Feinstein, 2010; Goldstein & Ozonoff, 2009). Bleuler used the word autism to convey the notion of self-absorbed retreat into an idiosyncratic mental state of fantasy, and originally applied this term in connection with schizophrenia (Goldstein & Ozonoff, 2009; Kuhn, 2004). As a consequence, from 1930 until the late 1960s, childhood schizophrenia was the term used in reference to what is now known as autism (Fombonne, 2003; Rutter, 1978; Wicks-Nelson & Israel, 2009).

Leo Kanner

With the publication of his 1943 paper titled "Autistic Disturbances of Affective Content," Dr. Leo Kanner described a clinical syndrome that never before had been identified as a unique disorder of childhood (Fombonne, 2003; Neumarker, 2003; Roth, 2010; Sanders, 2009; Wolff, 2004). Although he adopted Bleuler's term of autism as the name for this syndrome, Kanner clarified the distinction between autism and schizophrenia (Neumarker, 2003; Sanders, 2009). According to Kanner, autism signified a deviation from neurotypical development, rather than a state of regression (Goldstein & Ozonoff, 2009; Volkmar & Klin, 2005; Wicks-Nelson & Israel, 2009).

Kanner's breakthrough article discussed eight boys and three girls ranging in age from 2 to 8 years old. He reported that these children displayed an extreme preference for solitude from birth onward (Neumarker, 2003; Roth, 2010; Sanders, 2009; Wolff, 2004), thereby laying the foundation for the idea that genetic factors played a role in the development of autism (Wolff, 2004). Other features that he described included a marked need for sameness, persistent interests, repetitive behaviors, lack of imagination, and language difficulties such as mutism, echolalia, or pronoun reversal (Neumarker, 2003; Roth, 2010; Sanders, 2009; Schreibman, 2005; Volkmar & Klin, 2005; Wolff, 2004). These symptoms are consistent with current diagnostic criteria for autism.

Several of Kanner's other observations also have stood the test of time. He commented upon the sex ratio of his sample, noting that autism seemed to occur more frequently in boys than in girls (Wolff, 2004). This finding subsequently has been borne out (APA, 2000; Gonzalez, Cassel, & Boutot, 2011; Roth, 2010). He also reported that 5 of the 11 children had enlarged heads (Feinstein, 2010; Wolff, 2004); this characteristic, as well, has been observed in modern-day studies (e.g., Fukumoto et al., 2008).

In addition, Kanner recorded some information about the parents of the children in his sample. He noted that they tended to be intelligent folks who harbored interests in science, literature, or the arts, with somewhat lesser interest in other people (Neumarker, 2003; Wolff, 2004). By doing so, Kanner presaged the eventual recognition of the broader autism phenotype: a set of milder autistic traits sometimes found among the first-degree relatives of individuals with ASDs, which includes features such as social awkwardness, a preference for routine, and the presence of comorbid anxiety (Cassel et al., 2007; Roth, 2010; Schereen & Stauder, 2008).

Hans Asperger

In 1944, only a year after Kanner published his initial description of autism, an Austrian pediatrician named Hans Asperger issued a paper describing what he called autistic psychopathy. Similar to Kanner, Asperger used the term autistic to denote a condition of self-absorbed social isolation; he chose the word psychopathy to indicate a state of disordered personality (Klin, McPartland, & Volkmar, 2005; Roth, 2010). Asperger's daughter, a psychiatrist named Maria Asperger Felder, claims that her father suggested the use of the term "autistic" in a 1934 letter to describe the new diagnostic category; thus, Asperger initiated the use of that term almost a decade before Kanner (Feinstein, 2010).

Asperger's 1944 article included information about four children ranging in age from 6 to 11 years who, rather than displaying deficits in intellect, seemed to be intellectually capable (Klin et al., 2005). However, despite their apparent cognitive ability, these youngsters exhibited poor social and emotional functioning. Although they had no delays in language acquisition, their use of language was rather rigid and adult-like (Sanders, 2009). Additionally, these children were physically clumsy and displayed peculiar interests and repetitive behaviors. According to Asperger, this syndrome was evident from early childhood and persisted throughout life (Wolff, 2004). As is obvious from the above description, the symptoms listed in Asperger's 1944 paper are very similar to those reported by Kanner in 1943.

Nowadays it seems surprising that Kanner and Asperger wrote in such close temporal proximity about similar disorders, each without knowledge of the other's work. In fact, current autism researchers Michael Fitzgerald and Christopher Gillberg both have voiced suspicions that Kanner must have known about Asperger's work (Feinstein, 2010). However, perhaps Kanner and Asperger were truly unaware of each other's writings because the political circumstances of their time (i.e., World War II) prevented the uncensored exchange of information. Furthermore, Kanner wrote his articles in English, which led to tremendous interest in his work following the war. In contrast, Asperger wrote his papers in German; as a result, his work went mostly unacknowledged in countries where German was not spoken (Neumarker, 2003). Recognition of Hans Asperger's contributions did not occur until the 1980s, when an English psychiatrist named Lorna Wing called attention to the similarities between Asperger's and Kanner's papers (Roth, 2010; Sanders, 2009; Wing, 2005). Greater interest in Asperger's work ensued in 1991, when Uta Frith published an English translation of Asperger's original paper (Klin et al., 2005; Sanders, 2009; Wing, 2005).

Theodore Heller

A special educator in Austria by the name of Theodore Heller was the first person to describe an ASD known as childhood disintegrative disorder. Heller identified CDD in 1908, calling it dementia infantilis (Bray, Kehle, Theodore, & Broudy, 2002; Hendry, 2000; Volkmar, Koenig, & State, 2005; Wicks-Nelson & Israel, 2009). Because Leo Kanner's landmark paper was not written until 1943, the history of CDD predates that of autism by 35 years (Hendry, 2000).

Heller studied CDD in 28 children between the years 1905 and 1930. Youngsters with this condition develop in a normal fashion for the first two years of life, followed by the appearance of CDD symptoms, usually by around age 3 or 4 years but no later than 10 years of age. For this diagnosis to be assigned, significant losses of ability must be evident in at least two of the following domains: language, social skills, motor skills, play behavior, or bladder and bowel control (Wicks-Nelson & Israel, 2009). Because CDD did not enter into the *DSM* until 1994, much has yet to be learned about its causes and treatment (Bray et al., 2002); however, suspicion exists that underlying genetic factors contribute to its development (Volkmar et al., 2005; Wicks-Nelson & Israel, 2009).

Andreas Rett

Rett syndrome has the shortest history among the ASDs, having been discovered only in 1965. That year, an Austrian physician named Andreas Rett examined two girls with the same unusual symptom of continual hand-wringing gestures (Sigafoos, 2001; Van Acker, Loncola, & Van Acker, 2005). Both of the girls also had similar developmental histories; they had appeared normal at birth, only to later experience regression in both cognitive and physical abilities (Sigafoos, 2001; Zoghbi, 2002). Rett realized that these girls' symptoms constituted something other than cerebral palsy (Zoghbi, 2002). He and his secretary managed to locate 6 more girls with similar symptoms, eventually identifying 22 patients with the same condition (Sigafoos, 2001; Van Acker et al., 2005).

In 1966, Rett published a paper about the disorder that he had uncovered. Unfortunately, his original paper written in German, as well as a later paper written in English, languished unrecognized for 15 years. It was not until the 1980s that a Swedish physician named Bengt Hagberg independently discovered the same disorder (Sigafoos, 2001; Van Acker et al., 2005; Zoghbi, 2002). Hagberg named it Rett syndrome to honor his predecessor, and alerted the medical community about this condition in a 1983 article (Kerr & Ravine, 2003; Van Acker et al., 2005; Zoghbi, 2002). In 1984, only two English-language articles about Rett syndrome existed; since then, the number of publications has grown to more than 1,000 articles (Sigafoos, 2001).

A team of researchers led by Ruthie Amir identified the cause of Rett syndrome in 1999 as a mutation of a gene called $MECP_2$. Since then, it has been determined that more than 75% of typical cases of Rett syndrome are due to mutations in this gene. Almost 50% of atypical cases, including some in males, also can be traced to mutations in $MECP_2$. An animal model of these mutations has been developed in mice, which may lead the way to ideas for intervention (Kerr & Ravine, 2003).

EVOLUTION OF THE DIAGNOSTIC CRITERIA

DSM-I and DSM-II

Although autism was identified in 1943, the term autism cannot be found in either the first or second editions of the *DSM*, which were published in 1952 and 1968 respectively. Those editions of the diagnostic manual referred to the condition as childhood schizophrenia (Filipek et al., 1999; Goldstein & Ozonoff, 2009; Hincha-Ownby, 2008; Volkmar, 1991; Volkmar, Chawarska, & Klin, 2008a). However, research published by child psychiatrist Israel Kolvin in 1971 showed that the behavior of children with autism differed from the behaviors of children who later developed schizophrenia (Feinstein, 2010; Goldstein & Ozonoff, 2009; Goodyer, 2002; Volkmar et al., 2008a).

In 1972, autism authority Michael Rutter wrote, "We must conclude that the term 'childhood schizophrenia' has outlived its usefulness" (p. 315). According to Rutter (1972), the label of childhood schizophrenia appeared misused as a catch-all name for a group of conditions that included not only autism but also actual schizophrenia, other childhood psychoses, and other developmental disorders such as CDD. He further noted that "Clinicians from different centers use the same term to mean different conditions and different terms to mean the same condition" (p. 315).

DSM-III and DSM-III-R

The third edition of the *DSM*, published in 1980, sought to remedy the confusion described above. It introduced a new group of conditions called pervasive developmental disorders (Filipek et al., 1999; Volkmar, 1991; Volkmar, Bregman, Cohen, & Cicchetti, 1988; Volkmar et al., 2008a). Among these were separate categories for infantile autism, childhood-onset pervasive developmental disorder, residual infantile autism, residual child-hood-onset pervasive developmental disorder, and atypical pervasive developmental disorder (Volkmar et al., 1988; Volkmar & Klin, 2005).

DSM-III listed specific diagnostic criteria for infantile autism, using a modified version of Kanner's original description as an initial basis for the list of symptoms (Volkmar et al., 1988). In *DSM-III*, a diagnosis of infantile autism required the following: onset before 30 months of age and severe deficits in social relationships, accompanied by deficits in language or communication. Additionally, an exclusionary criterion stated that the diagnosis could not be assigned if the person experienced either hallucinations or delusions (Volkmar et al., 1988). An advantage of the new definition was that it provided for the recognition of autism; a flaw was its overemphasis on a very early age of onset.

When a revised version of the third *DSM* (i.e., *DSM-III-R*) was published in 1987, it removed the term "infantile autism" and changed the name of the condition to autistic disorder. By making this modification, *DSM-III-R* acknowledged the reality that most individuals with autism continue to have the condition beyond childhood (Goldstein & Ozonoff, 2009; Hincha-Ownby, 2008; Volkmar et al., 1988). For this same reason, the diagnostic category for residual autism was dropped (Volkmar, 1991). In *DSM-III-R*, the only other diagnostic category for ASDs was PDD-NOS (Feinstein, 2010).

To receive a *DSM-III-R* diagnosis of autistic disorder, an individual needed to meet at least 8 of 16 criteria spanning three different domains of functioning (Volkmar, 1991; Volkmar et al., 1988). This manual inserted a statement indicating that a person diagnosed with autistic disorder could later receive a diagnosis of schizophrenia in rare instances when the person demonstrably suffered from either hallucinations or delusions (Volkmar, 1991). Another change in *DSM-III-R* was the elimination of the category for childhood-onset pervasive developmental disorder. Instead, the label PDD-NOS now classified this condition (Volkmar & Klin, 2005).

A benefit of the *DSM-III-R* definition for autistic disorder was that it enabled a clinician to assign this diagnosis based on a current examination, without a need for information about the client's early developmental background (Volkmar, 1991). However, this approach failed to coincide with research findings which show that autism is in fact a disorder with an early onset (Volkmar & Klin, 2005). Furthermore, *DSM-III-R* created such a broad definition of pervasive developmental disorders that the rate of false positive diagnoses reached almost 40%. In addition, its overemphasis on more severe symptoms tended to hamper the identification of autism in more intellectually capable people (Volkmar & Klin, 2005).

A recent investigation (Bishop, Whitehouse, Watt, & Line, 2008) studied a sample of individuals in the United Kingdom who had been first evaluated in childhood according to the diagnostic criteria in either *DSM-III* or *DSM-III-R*. Using current assessment methods such as the Autism Diagnostic Interview – Revised (Lord, Rutter, & Le Couteur, 1994) and the Autism Diagnostic Observation Schedule (ADOS; Lord, Rutter, DiLavore, & Risi, 1999), the researchers discovered that many of these individuals who originally had been categorized as only language-impaired actually met current criteria for having an ASD. Bishop et al. (2008) noted that the *DSM-III* criteria were more restrictive than the current diagnostic criteria (i.e., *DSM-IV-TR*) and that the earlier criterion sets made it harder to recognize milder autistic symptoms.

DSM-IV and DSM-IV-TR

Noteworthy changes took place with the publication of *DSM-IV* in 1994 (Hincha-Ownby, 2008). Prior to its release, in 1991 Uta Frith published an English-language translation of Hans Asperger's 1944 document. As a result, in 1992 the World Health Organization included the diagnostic category of Asperger's disorder in the 10th edition of the *International Classification of Diseases* (*ICD-10*; Feinstein, 2010). Because *DSM-IV* was designed to closely match *ICD-10* (Volkmar & Klin, 2005), it too included Asperger's disorder, as well as autistic disorder (Hincha-Ownby, 2008; Feinstein, 2010). Other pervasive developmental disorders that were added to *DSM-IV* were CDD, Rett's disorder, and PDD-NOS (Hincha-Ownby, 2008; Towbin, 2005; Van Acker et al., 2005; Volkmar et al., 2005, 2008a; Volkmar & Klin, 2005).

With *DSM-IV*, assigning a diagnosis of autistic disorder required the presence of at least six criteria: two involving social impairment, one pertaining to impaired communication, and one relating to behaviors and interests, as well as an onset before age 3 years, and the exclusion of both Rett's disorder and CDD as possible causes of symptoms (Volkmar & Klin, 2005). A *DSM-IV* diagnosis of Asperger's disorder called for the presence of impaired social interaction and either restricted interests or unusual behaviors, while excluding delays in cognition and language (Klin et al., 2005).

The inclusion of Asperger's disorder in *DSM-IV* proved to be controversial due to considerable disagreement about the most appropriate way to define its symptoms. In addition to the criterion sets listed in *DSM-IV* and *ICD-10*, well-known investigators such as Lorna Wing, Christopher Gillberg, Peter Szatmari, and Digby Tantam have each proposed their own sets of diagnostic criteria for Asperger's disorder (Klin et al., 2005). These other criterion sets differ from the set listed in *DSM-IV*. One bone of contention has been the stipulation in *DSM-IV* that a diagnosis of Asperger's disorder cannot be given if an individual has met the criteria for autistic disorder; this distinction would depend primarily on the age at which the person's symptoms first became evident. Other points of dissension dealt with how language delays are defined, and whether or not unusual interests must be evident in order to receive a diagnosis of Asperger's disorder (Volkmar & Klin, 2005).

Regarding the category of PDD-NOS, *DSM-IV* used the word "or" rather than "and" between diagnostic criteria. As a consequence, what might seem to have been only a tiny mistake had the unfortunate effect of broadening the definition of ASDs (Feinstein, 2010; Volkmar & Klin, 2005). Based on the definition provided in *DSM-IV*, PDD-NOS could be diagnosed if a person showed either social impairment, or communication impairment, or unusual interests and activities. Thus, according to *DSM-IV*, someone could be diagnosed with PDD-NOS even without demonstrating deficits in social functioning, which are a key feature of ASDs. This unintended error in *DSM-IV* was corrected in its 2000 text revision, *DSM-IV-TR* (Feinstein, 2010; Towbin, 2005).

GROWING AWARENESS ABOUT THE CAUSES OF ASDS

The Psychoanalytic View

The search for the etiology of ASDs reveals how explanations about the causes of a disorder can be affected by prevailing beliefs at a given point in historical time (Wolff, 2004). The discovery of autism in the 1940s took place during an era when psychoanalytic theories dominated the field of psychiatry (Cipani, 2008; Feinstein, 2010; Roth, 2010; Sigafoos, Green, Edrisinha, & Lancioni, 2007). According to the psychoanalytic point of view, a child's personality is shaped by early interactions with his or her parents (Roth, 2010). This way of thinking led to a deeply hurtful time for parents of children with ASDs.

One of the most ardent proponents favoring a psychoanalytic explanation of autism was an Austrian therapist named Bruno Bettelheim (Roth, 2010). During World War II, Bettelheim fled from Europe to the United States, where he initially taught art history at Rockford College in Illinois. In 1944, the University of Chicago hired him as the director of its Orthogenic School for children with emotional disturbances, although he had little prior experience in working with such youngsters. As the school's director, Bettelheim was powerfully influenced by Sigmund Freud's and Erik Erikson's theories of personality development, as well as Harry Harlow's studies of infant monkeys who were removed from their birth mothers (Feinstein, 2010).

Bettelheim considered autism to be the result of poor parenting. He believed that "the precipitating factor in infantile autism is the parent's wish that his child should not exist" (Bettelheim, 1967, p. 125). Supposedly due to this wish, parents reacted inappropriately to their children, thereby prompting the children to become withdrawn and unresponsive (Feinstein,

2010). Bettelheim wrote extensively about these notions in a 1967 book called *The Empty Fortress: Infantile Autism and the Birth of the Self*, in which he lay most of the blame on mothers of children with autism. Bettelheim claimed that these mothers were unloving and inattentive, thereby inducing autistic behavior in their children (Cipani, 2008; Feinstein, 2010). He reasoned that the way to therapeutically treat children with autism was to separate them from their parents and to allow them visits with their parents only a few times per year (Roth, 2010).

Bettelheim's assumption about the cause of autism led to feelings of guilt and shame among parents and especially mothers, not only during his lifetime but for several decades afterward (Feinstein, 2010; Roth, 2010). Thankfully, the idea that parenting behaviors are the cause of autism is no longer accepted in the United States (Gonzalez et al., 2011; Wolff, 2004). However, in France the psychoanalytic view of autism still exists, prompting many families there to seek treatment in Belgium instead (Feinstein, 2010).

In the 1960s, parents in the United States and the United Kingdom rejected the notion that they had caused their children's autism due to a lack of nurturance. The year 1965 saw the launching of the Autism Society of America, founded by psychologist Bernard Rimland, himself the father of a son with autism (Parker, 2009; Roth, 2010). That same year, the National Autistic Society began in the United Kingdom (Roth, 2010). These organizations continue today, offering assistance and advocacy for families of persons with ASDs.

Recognition of Biological Factors

Similar to Bettelheim, Leo Kanner initially espoused the belief that the emotionally cold behavior of "refrigerator mothers," as he called them, was responsible for the development of autism in children (Roth, 2010, p. 17). Unlike Bettelheim, Kanner eventually changed his thinking on this issue, stating in 1969, "Parents, I acquit you" (Feinstein, 2010, p. 99).

However, both Kanner and Asperger had reported observing milder autistic-like traits in some parents of children with autism, thereby suggesting the possibility that autism might run in families and might be due to underlying genetic factors (Roth, 2010). To investigate this issue, Susan Folstein and Michael Rutter conducted the first twin study of autism in 1978 (Roth, 2010).

Twin studies capitalize on what is known about the genetics of identical versus fraternal (non-identical) twins. Identical twins emerge from a single fertilized ovum that splits to form two individuals, both of whom have the same genetic makeup. In comparison, fraternal twins derive from two different ova, each of which has been fertilized by a different sperm cell. Thus, although they share the same prenatal environment, fraternal twins are no more genetically similar than any other pairs of siblings; they share approximately 50% of the same genes (Roth, 2010).

Using this research method, Folstein and Rutter located and examined 11 same-sex identical twin pairs and 10 same-sex fraternal twin pairs in which one or both twins had autism. They were interested in determining what percentage of the time both twins in each pair had autism. If genetic factors played a role in the development of autism, then they expected to find that among identical twins, both twins had autism significantly more often in comparison to fraternal twin pairs. This similarity between twins in a twin pair is called the rate of concordance. Folstein and Rutter found that among the identical twins, 4 of the 11 twin pairs were concordant (meaning that both twins had autism), yielding a concordance rate of 36%. In comparison, the rate of concordance for fraternal twins in their study was 0%; in other words, even though one fraternal twin in the pair had autism, the other twin did not. When these two researchers used a less stringent definition of autism with the same sample, they found that the rate of concordance for the identical twins rose to 9 of the 11 pairs, for a concordance rate of 82%. Using this same relaxed definition of autism, only 1 of the 10 fraternal twin pairs was concordant for autism, for a rate of only 10%.

The results of the Folstein and Rutter twin study gave the first indication that genetic factors play an important causal role in autism (Cantwell & Baker, 1984; Roth, 2010). When Anthony Bailey and colleagues replicated and extended this study in 1995, they obtained similar findings and drew similar conclusions (Roth, 2010). Since the 1978 investigation by Folstein and Rutter, many additional studies have supported the finding that genetics contribute to the development of ASDs (Gonzalez et al., 2011; Volkmar, Westphal, Gupta, & Wiesner, 2008b).

In 1998, a study by British physician Andrew Wakefield and colleagues made the claim that use of the measles–mumps–rubella (MMR) vaccine led to the development of autism in children. As a result, some families attempted to prevent ASDs by opting to forego vaccinations for their children. However, numerous other investigations subsequently have demonstrated that the MMR vaccine does not cause autism (Feinstein, 2010; Miller & Reynolds, 2009; Roth, 2010; Smith & Wick, 2008; Volkmar et al., 2008b). In 2004, ten of Wakefield's coauthors retracted their previous claims about the MMR vaccine, and in 2010 the medical journal *Lancet* that published Wakefield's original study issued a full retraction of the 1998 article (DeNoon, 2010). Thimerosol, a mercury compound that was added to some vaccines as a preservative, was similarly suspected as a causal factor for autism; again, later studies have found that this is not the case (Feinstein, 2010; Miller & Reynolds, 2009; Roth, 2010; Smith & Wick, 2008; Volkmar et al., 2008b).

Other biological factors that have been associated with ASDs include abnormal levels of several chemical messengers in the brain such as serotonin, glutamate, and gamma-aminobutyric acid (i.e., GABA). Increases in brain volume, differences in the amount of electrical activity in certain regions of the brain, and problems in the connections between various brain areas have also been implicated (Roth, 2010; Volkmar et al., 2008b).

DEVELOPMENTS IN ASSESSMENT AND TREATMENT

Innovation in Assessment Methods

Polan and Spencer (1959) pioneered the assessment of ASDs by creating a 30-item checklist that allowed a respondent to indicate whether a child displayed symptoms of autism. The items on this questionnaire asked whether a youngster demonstrated problems in family functioning, social relations, activities, disruptive behavior, and obsessiveness (Feinstein, 2010). Psychologist Bernard Rimland created another such measure called the Diagnostic Checklist for Behavior-Disturbed Children (Rimland, 1964), containing 80 questions about a child's developmental history, language abilities, social capacities, and other symptoms. Rimland's purpose in devising this checklist was to provide a method for distinguishing between classic autism and other ASDs (Feinstein, 2010). An American child psychiatrist named Bertram Ruttenberg came up with another assessment device known as the Behavior Rating Instrument for Autistic and Atypical Children (BRIAAC; Ruttenberg, Dratman, Fraknoi, & Wenar, 1966); however, it proved to be incapable of accurately differentiating autism from other types of disability such as mental retardation, language impairment, or psychosis (Feinstein, 2010).

Up to the late 1970s, no objective way to compare symptoms of autism existed. To address this difficulty, physicians Betty Jo Freeman, Ed Ritvo, and colleagues devised the Behavioral Observation Scale (BOS; Freeman, Schroth, Ritvo, Guthrie, & Wake, 1980), which could be used either for diagnostic purposes or to track changes in patients following medical treatment or educational intervention. Also published in 1980 was the Autism Behavior Checklist (ABC; Krug, Arick, & Almond, 1980). This 57-item questionnaire can be used to identify school-aged children with autism. In addition, the year 1980 saw the publication of the Childhood Autism Rating Scale (CARS; Schopler, Reichler, Devellis, & Daly, 1980). This 15-item instrument can be used with children as young as age 2, and is the most widely used standardized measure for the assessment of autism (Feinstein, 2010).

Further advances took place with the development of the Autism Diagnostic Interview (ADI; Le Couteur et al., 1989) and the Autism Diagnostic Observation Schedule (ADOS; Lord et al., 1999). The former instrument underwent revision in 1994 and is now the ADI-R (Lord et al., 1994). Comprised of 93 items, the ADI-R takes from 1½ to 2½ hours to complete. It can be given to parents or caregivers of a person with an ASD to gather information about the person's early developmental history, communication and social skills, activities and interests (Gonzalez et al., 2011). Its companion measure, the ADOS (Lord et al., 1999) is a semistructured behavioral assessment that takes up to 45 minutes to administer. The ADOS consists of four modules, one of which is given on the basis of the client's age and language abilities (Deisinger, 2008a). It allows clinicians to examine a client's capacities for joint attention, adaptive behavior, and social interaction (Gonzalez et al., 2011). These two instruments are considered to be among the best measures for the diagnosis of ASDs (Tomanik, Pearson, Loveland, Lane, & Shaw, 2007).

Progress in Treatment Methods

When Leo Kanner first recognized autism as a new category of disorder, long-term institutionalization of persons with psychiatric and learning disabilities was commonplace (Wolff, 2004). Also during Kanner's lifetime and for approximately the next two decades, psychoanalytic views prevailed about the origins of autism. Thus, the treatment of choice for ASDs was play therapy, which was intended to provide a mechanism by which children with ASDs could express the distress that they felt in response to supposedly having emotionally cold and rejecting parents (Schopler & Mesibov, 1984). While the children were engaged in play therapy, their parents underwent psychotherapy, supposedly to correct parental attitudes and behaviors that were presumed to have induced such conditions in their children (Cipani, 2008; Culbertson, 1977, cited in Cantwell & Baker, 1984; Schopler &

Mesibov, 1984). A 1977 study by Culbertson (cited in Cantwell & Baker, 1984) found that no treatment other than parental psychotherapy was recommended and that when parents inquired about treatments specifically intended for their children, their requests were ignored.

During the 1950s and 1960s, another commonly held assumption about autism was that it was a form of childhood psychosis similar to schizophrenia. Among practitioners who espoused this line of thought, the treatment of autism involved various medical approaches that were used at that time for schizophrenia. These included insulin shock, electroconvulsive therapy, and psychopharmacological treatments using amphetamines, antidepressants, and even LSD. However, similar to psychotherapy for parents, these methods proved to be of no use (Sigafoos et al., 2007).

Charles Ferster and Marian DeMyer (1961) performed the first study investigating the use of positive reinforcement as an intervention for children with autism (Feinstein, 2010). During the 1960s, attention increasingly turned toward applying the principles of behavioral theory to the treatment of autism (Boutot & Dukes, 2011; Foxx, 2008; Granpeesheh, Tarbox, & Dixon, 2009; Wolery, Barton, & Hine, 2005). Behavioral approaches to autism treatment include methods such as applied behavior analysis (ABA; Boutot & Dukes, 2011), early intensive behavioral intervention (EIBI; Foxx, 2008), discrete trial training (DTT; Granpeesheh et al., 2009), pivotal response training (Boutot & Dukes, 2011), and natural environment training (NET; Granpeesheh et al., 2009). These interventions involve observing and measuring the behaviors of an individual with autism (Boutot & Dukes, 2011), and then employing positive reinforcement for desirable behavior while either ignoring or administering undesirable consequences for inappropriate behavior (Foxx, 2008).

O. Ivar Lovaas (1987, cited in Olive, Boutot, & Tarbox, 2011) performed the first controlled study examining the effectiveness of long-term EIBI for children with autism. Lovaas's study involved three groups of children with autism: children who received ABA treatment for 40 hours per week, those who received 10 hours of ABA treatment per week, and those who received 10 hours of other, non-ABA intervention per week. All three groups underwent treatment for a period of 2 years or more. Although the groups did not differ significantly at the start of the study, there were observable differences at its end. In comparison to the other two groups, the children in the intensive ABA group had higher intelligence quotient scores and were able to be placed in general education classrooms in first grade (Olive et al., 2011).

The Lovaas (1987) study (cited in Olive et al., 2011) has been criticized due to flaws in its methodology (Feinstein, 2010). Also, some of Lovaas's early treatment methods (see Lovaas, Freitag, Gold, & Kassorla, 1965; Lovaas, Koegel, Simmons, & Stevens-Long, 1973; Lovaas, Schreibman, & Koegel, 1974) proved controversial because he sometimes used aversive consequences such as shouting, slaps, and even the administration of electric shocks to shape the behavior of children with autism. He justified the use of painful consequences as a means to achieving a greater end, for example, the cessation of self-injurious behavior (Feinstein, 2010). Despite the controversy surrounding Lovaas's work, hundreds of studies conducted over the past 40 years support the use of behavior modification approaches as effective methods for the treatment of autism (Foxx, 2008; Granpeesheh et al., 2009).

Another comprehensive intervention approach for autism is called Treatment and Education of Autistic and related Communication-handicapped Children, or TEACCH (see Lord & Schopler, 1994). A German-born child clinical psychologist named Eric Schopler created this program in North Carolina in 1972, in direct opposition to Bruno Bettelheim's belief that parents should be denied contact with their children with autism. Instead, Schopler and his colleagues sought to empower these parents and involve them in their children's treatment (Feinstein, 2010; Roth, 2010). Other important features of the TEACCH program include considering the whole person, performing regular evaluations to determine each client's needs, providing a structured environment and structured teaching, emphasizing the acquisition of life skills, and working on the generalization of skills from one setting to another. To date there have been no randomized controlled trials or large-scaled studies of the TEACCH method; however, smaller studies have indicated positive outcomes for children enrolled in TEACCH programs (Roth, 2010).

Medications also continue to be used today in the treatment of ASDs, including antipsychotics, antidepressants, anticonvulsants, stimulants, and others (Scahill & Martin, 2005; West, Waldrop, & Brunssen, 2009). Although risperdone is the only medication currently approved by the United States Food and Drug Administration for the management of autism, prescribers may also use other medications to address symptoms associated with ASDs. A comparison of the various drugs found that many of them are moderately useful in treating problems associated with autism, such as inattention, aggression, or repetitive movements; however, they are only minimally effective in addressing the basic deficits of autism, such as impaired social functioning and communication, restricted interests, and a need for routine (West et al., 2009).

NOTEWORTHY LEGISLATION PERTAINING TO ASDS

IDEA

In 1975 Congress passed Public Law 94-142, also known as the Education for All Handicapped Children Act (Zettel, 1977). Under this law, some students with ASDs probably received educational services under the eligibility categories of either mental retardation (Blau, 1985) or emotional disorders (Edmunds et al., 1985). The provisions of Public Law 94-142 were restated and expanded in the Individuals with Disabilities Education Act (IDEA), passed in 1990. At that time, autism was added as a specific category of disability covered by this law (National Association of State Directors of Special Education, 1991); however, IDEA does not stipulate what an appropriate education entails for these youngsters. Because children with ASDs need intensive teaching to achieve genuine gains, an appropriate educational program for them is full-time and year-round, including summers in cases where students with ASDs may regress while away from school for an extended time. Additional in-home or community-based support also may be warranted (Bailey, 2008; Mandlawitz, 2005).

From ages 3 to 21, many children with ASDs will have their special education needs governed by Part B of IDEA. This portion of the law calls for the creation of an Individualized Education Plan (IEP) that tailors each student's educational experience to his or her needs, deficits, and strengths (Boutot & Wahlberg, 2011; Mandlawitz, 2005). An IEP also must document any assistive technology (AT) required by the child, and must cover the provision of services to teach families how to select, obtain, or employ AT devices (West, 2011). Parents should be involved in decisions regarding their child's IEP, and should be concerned if all that is offered is a general "autism program" (Bailey, 2008, p. 314). Parents also should be suspicious if their children with ASDs are automatically placed in mainstream classrooms. According to Bailey (2008), children with ASDs must have certain basic competencies if they are to benefit from interactions with neurotypical classmates in a general classroom setting. These competencies include the ability to communicate and imitate, the capacity to remain on task for at least a short time without direct supervision, and interest in social interaction. Children with ASDs who demonstrate self-injurious, aggressive, destructive, or highly distracting behaviors, or who lack the basic skills mentioned earlier, are better served in a more specialized classroom (Bailey, 2008).

Section 504 of the Vocational Rehabilitation Act of 1973

Children with ASDs who are eligible for public school educational services under IDEA, as well as those who do not qualify for such services, are covered by Section 504 of the Vocational Rehabilitation Act of 1973 (Katsiyannis & Reid, 1999; Turnbull, Wilcox, & Stowe, 2002; VanBiergeijk, Klin, & Volkmar, 2008). Because most individuals with ASDs have milder forms of these conditions as opposed to classic autistic disorder (VanBergeijk et al., 2008), many more children with ASDs may be eligible for academic accommodations through Section 504 rather than IDEA. A Section 504 plan enables them to receive academically related services, such as being administered medications by school personnel (Turnbull et al., 2002). Examples of educational accommodations for children with ASDs that might be listed in a 504 plan are simplified instructions, supplementation of verbal directions with visual directions, modification of class schedules and testing methods, and the use of tape recorders or computer-assisted instruction (CAI), among others (Katsiyannis & Reid, 1999). Another facet of Section 504 deals with extracurricular activities and services such as recess, mealtimes, athletic programs, counseling, and the like. This law demands that students with ASDs must have reasonable access to participation in such activities (Katsiyannis & Reid, 1999).

No Child Left Behind

The year 2001 saw the passage of the No Child Left Behind (NCLB) Act, which pertains to students who are educated in public schools throughout the United States. On the basis of NCLB, schools must offer appropriate accommodations to students with ASDs when they take standardized statewide tests to determine their academic progress. If such students cannot complete standard assessment measures (e.g., due to significant cognitive deficits), then they must be given alternate assessments; an example of an alternate assessment is off-grade-level testing. In addition, parents must be notified about potential consequences related to their children's use of academic accommodations during standardized testing or the use of alternate assessment. In some states, students who take the standard tests with accommodations, or who complete alternate assessments, are ineligible to receive a regular diploma at the time of graduation (Yell, Drasgow, & Lowrey, 2005).

Another aspect of NCLB that pertains to students with ASDs is its insistence that students must be taught using instructional methods that research has shown to be effective (Simpson, 2005; Yell et al., 2005). Such teaching includes a structured learning environment with a curriculum that stresses the development of language and social interaction skills. Furthermore, the instruction must be tailored to students' individual characteristics and must involve families in developing students' educational programs. In addition, punishment-based approaches to the management of problem behaviors are frowned upon; instead, students should be taught desirable skills and behaviors (Yell et al., 2005).

Americans with Disabilities Act

In 1990, Congress reauthorized the Vocational Rehabilitation Act of 1973 and renamed it the Americans with Disabilities Act (ADA). This act governs the way that colleges and universities offer services to adult students with disabilities. College-age students with ASDs are eligible for academic and social supports through ADA because their symptoms may interfere with educational, occupational, and social functioning, all of which comprise life domains covered by the ADA. Additionally, the transition from high school to college may be stressful even for many neurotypical adolescents; therefore, the process of adjustment to college is even more likely to be stressful for young adults with ASDs, because difficulties with transitions are a common symptom of ASDs. Academic accommodations that may be provided to these students might include supports such as note-taking, assistance with organizing assignments and materials, modified assignments, additional time for completing exams, and distraction-reduced settings for taking exams, among others. Colleges and universities may also provide assistance to support social functioning (e.g., role-playing to promote conversational skills; sex education to prevent sexual victimization) and mental health (e.g., directive counseling; VanBergeijk et al., 2008).

The ADA also offers protection and assistance to adults with ASDs regarding discrimination in the workplace. These individuals often struggle to maintain employment because their problems with communication and social functioning may hinder the performance of their duties or may lead to misunderstandings with coworkers or supervisors (Van Wieren, Reid, & McMahon, 2008). A 2008 study by Van Wieren and colleagues concluded that adults with ASDs might not be aware of what constitutes employment discrimination and their rights in this regard. These authors believed that large-scale employers, as well as those in retail and service industries, need to be better educated about the characteristics and needs of adult workers with ASDs. They also stated that adults with ASDs may need more information and education about their rights under the ADA.

Combating Autism Act

Most recently, in December of 2006 then-President George W. Bush signed Public Law 109-416, also known as the Combating Autism Act (U.S. Congress, 2006). This law authorizes almost a billion dollars to be spent over the years 2007–2012 on screening, early intervention, services, and education for ASDs. According to the organization Autism Speaks (2010), the Combating Autism Act is the most comprehensive law ever passed by the United States Congress with regard to a single disorder. The new law is controversial; while many applaud it, some members of the autism community have criticized its perceived goal of eliminating ASDs (Feinstein, 2010).

ASSISTIVE TECHNOLOGY FOR ASDS

Over the years, various forms of AT have been developed for individuals with ASDs (see Nkabinde, 2008). These devices may be used to nurture literacy and communication abilities and to foster interpersonal skills, thus hopefully leading to increased independence (West, 2011). The process of assessing AT needs, obtaining needed equipment, using the equipment, and evaluating its effectiveness should follow the so-called SETT Framework. The acronym SETT refers to Student, Environment, Tasks, and Tools. When making decisions about AT for persons with ASDs, consideration must be given to the needs and skills of the student, the physical environment in which the AT will be implemented, the types of activities in which the AT will be employed, goals for their use, and the types of AT devices that would best serve the student (West, 2011).

One broad category of AT is that of augmentative and alternative communication (AAC). AAC systems range in sophistication from something as simple as a conversation book to something as complex as a computer-based device. When using AAC systems, the focus is on enabling functional communication within natural settings (West, 2011). For example, AAC systems can be used to allow youngsters to indicate preferences at mealtimes, or to help them understand and follow routine sequences at home or in school (Mirenda, 2001). An example of this type of AT is the Picture Exchange Communication System (PECS). Developed by Andrew Bondy and Lori Frost in 1994, PECS allows nonverbal persons with ASDs to express wants and make comments by giving picture cards to another person (Feinstein, 2010; West, 2011). Other types of AAC devices are portable voice output communication aids (VOCA) that create digitized speech (Mirenda, 2001; West, 2011). When used regularly in natural environments, VOCA devices may increase both the expressive and receptive communication abilities of those with ASDs (Mirenda, 2001).

CAI may also be helpful for persons with ASDs. Specialized computer programs such as Boardmaker, Pix-Writer, Picture-It, and Writing with Symbols 2000 can be used to generate pictorial representations of phrases or sentences, construct social stories, or create adapted educational materials (West, 2011).

A newer trend in AT is the use of robots that not only entertain but teach children with ASDs. An example is the Robota project, which began in 1997 using a robot whose head, arms, and legs came from a commercially made plastic doll, and whose body was constructed of Lego pieces and computer hardware. Newer versions of Robota feature robots with simple faces and eyes that move and blink, as well as a moving head, arms, and legs. These robots can imitate the hand or head movements of a user, and can also enact childlike behaviors such as being happy, sad, or tired. They can be used to teach children with ASDs social skills such as imitation and turn taking (Billard, Robins, Nadel, & Dautenhahn, 2007).

WORKING WITH FAMILIES

As mentioned earlier, prior to the 1960s interventions with families of children with ASDs usually consisted of psychodynamic therapy to address a presumed lack of parental warmth which was believed to have induced ASDs in these children (Cantwell & Baker, 1984). However, clinicians' attitudes began to shift away from this outlook in the 1960s and 1970s due to increasing evidence that ASDs were related to biological factors rather than parenting behaviors (Schopler & Mesibov, 1984). Another influence that contributed to this attitudinal shift was the introduction of behavioral treatments for ASDs. During the 1960s, behavior therapists were similar to psychodynamically oriented therapists in that both groups viewed parents as the cause of their children's ASDs. However, while Bruno Bettelheim and other psychodynamic therapists of his time recommended that children with

ASDs should be separated from their parents, the behaviorists believed that parents could help their children with ASDs by learning to use behavior-modification strategies (Schopler & Mesibov, 1984).

The past 25 years have brought increasing recognition of the need to provide support for families of children with ASDs. Research has shown that these families experience levels of stress that exceed the stress associated with raising neurotypical children (Baker-Ericzen, Brookman-Frazee, & Stahmer, 2005; Marcus, Kunce, & Schopler, 2005; Slater & Wikler, 1986; Symon & Boettcher, 2008). Stressors that commonly affect families of children with ASDs include problems obtaining a diagnosis (Marcus et al., 2005; Symon & Boettcher, 2008), uncertain prognosis (Symon & Boettcher, 2008), confusion due to the children's uneven course of development, the children's displays of inappropriate behavior in public (Marcus et al., 2005), and feelings of loss, helplessness, and social isolation, among others (Slater & Wikler, 1986; Symon & Boettcher, 2008). Also, families in racial/ethnic minority communities whose members include children with ASDs have less access to services (Mandell et al., 2009; Theus, 2008; Thomas, Ellis, McLaurin, Daniels, & Morrissey, 2007), which may further elevate their stress levels.

Professionals who work with families of children with ASDs may do so using home-based, clinic-based, school-based, or group-based approaches. The first three approaches differ in the setting in which services are provided, but all three methods involve trainers who coach parents concerning effective techniques for educating and managing their children. These methods may also teach parents to keep records concerning their children's behavior, parents' attempted interventions, and the children's responses to such interventions. In addition, service providers may assist families by directing them to reading materials or educational films that can give them accurate information about child development and the characteristics of ASDs (Marcus et al., 2005).

Support groups for parents of children with ASDs offer parents opportunities to obtain emotional support and share information (Marcus et al., 2005). Parents with experience concerning ASDs may serve as mentors for parents whose children are newly diagnosed with an ASD (Baker-Ericzen et al., 2005; Symon & Boettcher, 2008). Satisfaction with this type of arrangement tends to be greater when the mentors' family characteristics and experiences are similar to those of the parents being mentored (Symon & Boettcher, 2008). Similarly, neurotypical siblings of children with ASDs may benefit from participation in support groups, in which they can talk with peers about experiences and emotions related to having a brother or sister with an ASD (Deisinger, 2008b; Marcus et al., 2005; Symon & Boettcher, 2008).

LOOKING AHEAD

New developments in the history of ASDs surely lie ahead. One possible change concerns the way that these disorders will be defined in the *DSM*, the manual that lists the diagnostic criteria for all psychiatric and developmental disorders. A new edition of this manual, *DSM-V*, is expected for publication in 2013 (Feinstein, 2010). The new manual may contain a markedly different conceptualization of ASDs, with greater emphasis placed on sensory issues associated with these conditions (Feinstein, 2010). Another more startling change may be the elimination of Asperger's disorder from the manual. *DSM-V* most likely will introduce a single category called "autism spectrum disorder," with one set of diagnostic criteria for all ASDs, differentiating them only in terms of severity. The rationale for this change is based on research showing that ASDs exist on a continuum; although their symptoms may range from mild to severe, all of these conditions represent a single type of underlying disorder (Feinstein, 2010; Frances, 2010).

Two potential problems may emerge if these proposed changes in diagnostic criteria are actually implemented. First, it is possible that ASDs may become more rather than less stigmatized because milder ASDs will be grouped together with more serious ones. Second, the definition of autism may expand too far to encompass what now would be considered merely eccentric behavior, thereby leading to an increase in the number of misidentified cases of ASDs. On the other hand, there is an equal possibility that ASDs may become less stigmatized as the general populace learns to associate the concept of ASDs with milder forms of these disorders. Furthermore, the authors of *DSM-V* rightfully should modify the manual according to the findings of research; they cannot be held responsible for the possible future misuse of the new diagnostic criteria (Frances, 2010).

Another phenomenon that is likely to become more noticeable in the future is the so-called neurodiversity movement (Boundy, 2008; Bumiller, 2008; Feinstein, 2010). As mentioned earlier in this chapter, not everyone appreciated the passing of the Combating Autism Act. Members of the neurodiversity movement denounced this law because they do not consider autism as a problem that needs to be fixed or eradicated. These high-functioning individuals with ASDs consider their condition a difference rather than a disorder, and view their ASD symptoms as core components of their personal identities. They resent the notion that they must conform their behavior to the expectations of the neurotypical majority, and instead would prefer for their differences to be looked upon as acceptable alternatives to the usual ways of perceiving the world and interacting with others (Boundy, 2008; Broderick & Ne'eman, 2008).

A distressing idea within the neurodiversity movement is the possibility that someday prenatal screening might be used to identify persons likely to be born with ASDs. As well-known autism researcher Simon Baron-Cohen pointed out, "we would risk screening out talents as well as disabilities; we would be discriminating against those with disabilities; and we would be implying that people with autism are of less value" (Feinstein, 2010, p. 272). Perhaps a preferable goal would be to identify those likely to be born with very disabling forms of ASDs and to provide effective treatment for them as soon as possible (Feinstein, 2010).

As the future of ASDs unfold, much still remains to be learned and done. One necessary but attainable goal is to provide more, and more accurate, information about ASDs in order to counteract the rampant amount of misinformation found among both the general public and treatment professionals. Second, more carefully designed and well-executed research needs to be conducted about which treatments are effective for ASDs and which are not. Finally, let us hope that the future will bring more and better services for adolescents and adults with ASDs (Rapin, 2005).

REFERENCES

All Wales Autism Resource/AWARES. (n.d.). About autism. Retrieved from http://www. awares.org

American Psychiatric Association/APA. (2000). *Diagnostic and statistical manual of mental disorders* (4th ed., text rev.). Washington, DC: Author.

Arshad, M., & Fitzgerald, M. (2004). Did Michelangelo (1475–1564) have high-functioning autism? *Journal of Medical Biography, 12*(2), 115–120.

Autism Speaks. (2010). The Combating Autism Act of 2006. Retrieved from http://www. autismspeaks.org

Bailey, K. (2008). Supporting families. In: K. Chawarska, A. Klin & F. R. Volkmar (Eds), *Autism spectrum disorders in infants and toddlers: Diagnosis, assessment, and treatment* (pp. 300–326). New York: Guilford Press.

Baker-Ericzen, M. J., Brookman-Frazee, L., & Stahmer, A. (2005). Stress levels and adaptability in toddlers with and without autism spectrum disorders. *Research and Practice for Persons with Severe Disabilities, 30*(4), 194–204. Retrieved from http://web. ebscohosts.com

Bettelheim, B. (1967). *The empty fortress: Infantile autism and the birth of the self.* New York: The Free Press.

Billard, A., Robins, B., Nadel, J., & Dautenhahn, K. (2007). Building Robota, a mini-humanoid robot for the rehabilitation of children with autism. *Assistive Technology*, *19*(1), 37–49. Retrieved from http://web.ebscohost.com

Bishop, D. V. M., Whitehouse, A. J. O., Watt, H. J., & Line, E. A. (2008). Autism and diagnostic substitution: Evidence from a study of adults with a history of developmental disorder. *Developmental Medicine and Child Neurology*, *50*, 341–345. doi: 10.1111/j.1469-8749. 2008.02057.x

Blau, G. (1985). Autism – Assessment and placement under the Education for All Handicapped Children Act: A case history. *Journal of Clinical Psychology*, *41*(3), 440–447. Retrieved from http://web.ebscohost.com

Boundy, K. (2008). "Are you sure, sweetheart, that you want to be well?": An exploration of the neurodiversity movement. *Radical Psychology: A Journal of Psychology, Politics, and Radicalism*, *7*(2), 2. Retrieved from http://web.ebscohost.com

Boutot, E. A., & Dukes, C. (2011). Evidence-based practices for educating students with autism spectrum disorders. In: E. A. Boutot & B. S. Myles (Eds), *Autism spectrum disorders: Foundations, characteristics, and effective strategies* (pp. 68–92). Upper Saddle River, NJ: Pearson.

Boutot, E. A., & Wahlberg, J. L. (2011). Working with families of children with autism. In: E. A. Boutot & B. S. Myles (Eds), *Autism spectrum disorders: Foundations, characteristics, and effective strategies* (pp. 93–117). Upper Saddle River, NJ: Pearson.

Bray, M. A., Kehle, T. J., Theodore, L. A., & Broudy, M. S. (2002). Case study of childhood disintegrative disorder – Heller's syndrome. *Psychology in the Schools*, *39*(1), 101–109. Retrieved from http://web.ebscohost.com

Broderick, A. A., & Ne'eman, A. (2008). Autism as metaphor: Narrative and counter-narrative. *International Journal of Inclusive Education*, *12*(5–6), 459–476. doi: 10.1080/ 13603110802377490.

Brown, J. (2010). *Writers on the spectrum: How autism and Asperger syndrome have influenced literary writing*. Philadelphia: Jessica Kingsley Publishers.

Bumiller, K. (2008). Quirky citizens: Autism, gender, and reimagining disability. *Signs: Journal of Women in Culture and Society*, *33*(4), 967–991. Retrieved from http://web. ebscohost.com

Cantwell, D. P., & Baker, L. (1984). Research concerning families of children with autism. In: E. Schopler & G. B. Mesibov (Eds), *The effects of autism on the family* (pp. 41–63). New York: Plenum Press.

Cassel, T. D., Messinger, D. S., Ibanez, L. V., Haltigan, J. D., Acosta, S. I., & Buchman, A. C. (2007). Early social and emotional communication in the infant siblings of children with autism spectrum disorders: An examination of the broad phenotype. *Journal of Autism and Developmental Disorders*, *37*, 122–132.

Cipani, E. (2008). Autism: The early years. In: E. Cipani (Ed.), *Triumphs in early autism treatment* (pp. 141–150). New York: Springer Publishing Company.

Deisinger, J. A. (2008a). Recent developments in the diagnosis and assessment of autism spectrum disorders. In: A. F. Rotatori, F. E. Obiakor & S. Burkhardt (Eds), *Autism and developmental disabilities: Current practices and issues* (Vol. 18, pp. 85–108). Bingley, UK: Emerald Group Publishing Limited.

Deisinger, J. A. (2008b). Issues pertaining to siblings of individuals with autism spectrum disorders. In: A. F. Rotatori, F. E. Obiakor & S. Burkhardt (Eds), *Autism and developmental disabilities: Current practices and issues* (Vol. 18, pp. 135–155). Bingley, UK: Emerald Group Publishing Limited.

DeNoon, D. J. (2010, February 2). Study linking autism to vaccine retracted. *WebMD Health News*. Retrieved from http://children.webmd.com

Edmunds, P., Peterson, S., Nelson, L., Goldberg, M., Goldberg, P., & Leaf, R. (1985). Resource manual on disabilities: A count me in project. Retrieved from http://web.ebscohost.com

Feinstein, A. (2010). *A history of autism: Conversations with the pioneers*. Malden, MA: Wiley-Blackwell.

Ferster, C. B., & DeMyer, M. K. (1961). The development of performances in autistic children in an automatically controlled environment. *Journal of Chronic Diseases, 13*, 312–314.

Filipek, P. A., Accardo, P. J., Baranek, G. T., Cook, E. H., Jr.., Dawson, G., Gordon, B., Gravel, J. S., Johnson, C. P., Kallen, R. J., Levy, S. E., Minshew, N. J., Ozonoff, S., Prizant, B. M., Rapin, I., Rogers, S. J., Stone, W. L., Teplin, S., Tuchman, R. F., & Volkmar, F. R. (1999). The screening and diagnosis of autistic spectrum disorders. *Journal of Autism and Developmental Disorders, 29*(6), 439–484.

Fitzgerald, M., & O'Brien, B. (2007). *Genius genes: How Asperger talents changed the world*. Shawnee Mission, KS: Autism Asperger Publishing Company.

Fombonne, E. (2003). Modern views of autism. *Canadian Journal of Psychiatry, 48*(8), 503–505. Retrieved from http://web.ebscohost.com

Foxx, R. M. (2008). Applied behavior analysis treatment of autism: The state of the art. *Child and Adolescent Psychiatric Clinics of North America, 17*(4), 821–834.

Frances, A. (2010, March 22). Will DSM5 contain or worsen the "epidemic" of autism. *Psychology Today*. Retrieved from http://www.psychologytoday.com

Freeman, B. J., Schroth, P., Ritvo, E., Guthrie, D., & Wake, L. (1980). The Behavior Observation Scale for autism (BOS): Initial results of factor analyses. *Journal of Autism and Developmental Disorders, 10*(3), 343–346.

Frith, U. (2003). *Autism: Explaining the enigma* (2nd ed.). Malden, MA: Blackwell Publishing.

Frith, U. (2008). *Autism: A very short introduction*. New York: Oxford University Press.

Fukumoto, A., Hashimoto, T., Ito, H., Nishimura, M., Tsuda, Y., Miyazaki, M., Mori, K., Arisawa, K., & Kagami, S. (2008). Growth of head circumference in autistic infants during the first year of life. *Journal of Autism and Developmental Disorders, 38*(3), 411–418. doi: 10.1007/s10803-007-0405-1.

Goldstein, S., & Ozonoff, S. (2009). Historical perspective and overview. In: S. Goldstein, J. A. Naglieri & S. Ozonoff (Eds), *Assessment of autism spectrum disorders* (pp. 1–17). New York: Guilford Press.

Gonzalez, K., Cassel, T., & Boutot, E. A. (2011). Overview of autism spectrum disorders. In: E. A. Boutot & B. S. Myles (Eds), *Autism spectrum disorders: Foundations, characteristics, and effective strategies* (pp. 1–33). Upper Saddle River, NJ: Pearson.

Goodyer, I. (2002). Obituaries: Israel Kolvin. *The Psychiatrist, 26*, 396–397. doi: pb.26.10. 396-a.

Grandin, T. (1986). *Emergence: Labeled autistic – A true story*. New York: Warner Books.

Granpeesheh, D., Tarbox, J., & Dixon, D. R. (2009). Applied behavior analytic interventions for children with autism: A description and review of treatment research. *Annals of Clinical Psychiatry, 21*(3), 162–173.

Hendry, C. N. (2000). Childhood disintegrative disorder: Should it be considered a distinct diagnosis? *Clinical Psychology Review, 20*(1), 77–90. doi: 10.1016/S0272-7358(98)00094-4

Hincha-Ownby, M. (2008). History of autism in the DSM: Diagnostic criteria for autism spectrum disorders. Retrieved from http://autismaspergerssyndrome.suite101.com

James, I. (2003). Singular scientists. *Journal of the Royal Society of Medicine, 96*(1), 36–39. doi: 10.1258/jrsm.96.1.36.

James, I. (2006). *Asperger's syndrome and high achievement: Some very remarkable people.* Philadelphia: Jessica Kingsley Publishers.

Katsiyannis, A., & Reid, R. (1999). Autism and Section 504: Rights and responsibilities. *Focus on Autism and Other Developmental Disabilities, 14*(2), 66–72. Retrieved from http://web.ebscohost.com

Kerr, A. M., & Ravine, D. (2003). Review article: Breaking new ground with Rett syndrome. *Journal of Intellectual Disability Research, 47*(8), 580–587. Retrieved from http://web.ebscohost.com

Klin, A., McPartland, J., & Volkmar, F. R. (2005). Asperger syndrome. In: F. R. Volkmar, R. Paul, A. Klin & D. Cohen (Eds), *Handbook of autism and pervasive developmental disorders* (Vol. 1, pp. 88–125). Hoboken, NJ: Wiley.

Krug, D. A., Arick, J., & Almond, P. (1980). Behavior checklist for identifying severely handicapped individuals with high levels of autistic behavior. *Journal of Child Psychology and Psychiatry, 21*(3), 221–229.

Kuhn, R. (2004). Eugen Bleuler's concepts of psychopathology. *History of Psychiatry, 15*(3), 361–366. doi: 10.1177/0957154 x 04044603

Le Couteur, A., Rutter, M., Lord, C., Rios, P., Robertson, S., Holdgrafer, M., & McLennan, J. (1989). Autism Diagnostic Interview: A standardized investigator-based instrument. *Journal of Autism and Developmental Disorders, 19*(3), 363–387. doi: 10.1007/BF02212936.

Lord, C., Rutter, M., & Le Couteur, A. (1994). Autism Diagnostic Interview – Revised: A revised version of a diagnostic interview for caregivers of individuals with possible pervasive developmental disorders. *Journal of Autism and Developmental Disorders, 24*(5), 659–685. Retrieved from http://web.ebscohost.com

Lord, C., Rutter, M., DiLavore, P., & Risi, S. (1999). *Autism diagnostic observation schedule: Manual.* Los Angeles: Western Psychological Services.

Lord, C., & Schopler, E. (1994). TEACCH services for preschool children. In: S. Harris & J. Handleman (Eds), *Preschool education programs for children with autism* (pp. 102–126). Austin, TX: PRO-ED.

Lovaas, O. I., Freitag, G., Gold, V. J., & Kassorla, I. C. (1965). Experimental studies in childhood schizophrenia: An analysis of self-destructive behavior. *Journal of Experimental Child Psychology, 2*, 67–84.

Lovaas, O. I., Koegel, R. L., Simmons, J. Q., & Stevens-Long, J. (1973). Some generalizations and follow-up measures on autistic children in behavior therapy. *Journal of Applied Behavior Analysis, 6*, 131–166.

Lovaas, O. I., Schreibman, L., & Koegel, R. I. (1974). A behavior modification approach to the treatment of autistic children. *Journal of Autism and Childhood Schizophrenia, 4*, 101–129.

Mandell, D. S., Wiggins, L. D., Carpenter, L. A., Daniels, J., DiGuiseppi, C., Durkin, M. S., Giarelli, E., Morrier, M. J., Nicholas, J. S., Pinto-Martin, J. A., Shattuck, P. T., Thomas, K. C., Yeargin-Allsopp, M., & Kirby, R. S. (2009). Racial/ethnic disparities in the identification of children with autism spectrum disorders. *American Journal of Public Health, 99*(3), 493–498. doi: 10.2105/AJPH.2007.131243

Mandlawitz, M. R. (2005). Educating children with autism: Current legal issues. In: F. R. Volkmar, R. Paul, A. Klin & D. Cohen (Eds), *Handbook of autism and pervasive developmental disorders* (Vol. 2, pp. 1161–1173). Hoboken, NJ: Wiley.

Marcus, L. M., Kunce, L. J., & Schopler, E. (2005). Working with families. In: F. R. Volkmar, R. Paul, A. Klin & D. Cohen (Eds), *Handbook of autism and pervasive developmental disorders* (Vol. 2, pp. 1055–1086). Hoboken, NJ: Wiley.

Miller, L., & Reynolds, J. (2009). Autism and vaccination – The current evidence. *Journal for Specialists in Pediatric Nursing, 14*(3), 166–172. Retrieved from http://web.ebscohost.com

Mirenda, P. (2001). Autism, augmentative communication, and assistive technology: What do we really know? *Focus on Autism and Other Developmental Disabilities, 16*(3), 141–151. Retrieved from http://web.ebscohost.com

Muir, H. (2003). Did Einstein and Newton have autism? *New Scientist, 178*(2393), 10. Retrieved from http://web.ebscohost.com

National Association of State Directors of Special Education. (1991). "Side-by-side" profile of changes in new IDEA. *Liaison Bulletin, 17*(1), 1–44. Retrieved from http://www.eric.ed.gov.

Neumarker, K. J. (2003). Leo Kanner: His years in Berlin, 1906–24. The roots of autistic disorder. *History of Psychiatry, 14*(2), 205–218. Retrieved from http://hpy.sagepub.com

Nkabinde, Z. P. (2008). Using assistive technology to educate students with developmental disabilities and autism. In: A. F. Rotatori, F. E. Obiakor & S. Burkhardt (Eds), *Autism and developmental disabilities: Current practices and issues* (vol. 18, pp. 273–285). Bingley, UK: Emerald Group Publishing Limited.

Olive, M., Boutot, E. A., & Tarbox, J. (2011). Teaching students with autism using the principles of applied behavior analysis. In: E. A. Boutot & B. S. Myles (Eds), *Autism spectrum disorders: Foundations, characteristics, and effective strategies* (pp. 141–162). Upper Saddle River, NJ: Pearson.

Parker, P. M. (Ed.) (2009). *Autism spectrum disorders: Webster's timeline history 1965-2007*. San Diego, CA: ICON Group International, Inc.

Polan, C. G., & Spencer, B. L. (1959). A checklist of symptoms of autism of early life. *West Virginia Medical Journal, 55*, 198–204.

Rapin, I. (2005). Autism: Where we have been, where we are going. In: F. R. Volkmar, R. Paul, A. Klin & D. Cohen (Eds), *Handbook of autism and pervasive developmental disorders* (Vol. 2, pp. 1304–1317). Hoboken, NJ: Wiley.

Rimland, B. (1964). *Infantile autism: The syndrome and its implications for a neural theory of behavior*. New York: Appleton-Century-Crofts.

Roth, I. (2010). *The autism spectrum in the 21st century: Exploring psychology, biology and practice*. Philadelphia: Jessica Kingsley Publishers.

Ruttenberg, B. A., Dratman, M. L., Fraknoi, J., & Wenar, C. (1966). An instrument for evaluating autistic children. *Journal of the American Academy of Child Psychiatry, 5*(3), 453–478.

Rutter, M. (1972). Childhood schizophrenia reconsidered. *Journal of Autism and Developmental Disorders, 2*(3), 315–337. Retrieved from http://www.springerlink.com

Rutter, M. (1978). Diagnosis and definition of childhood autism. *Journal of Autism and Developmental Disorders, 8*(2), 139–161. doi: 10.1007/BF01537863

Sanders, J. L. (2009). Qualitative or quantitative differences between Asperger's disorder and autism? Historical considerations. *Journal of Autism and Developmental Disorders, 39*(11), 1560–1567. doi: 10.1007/s10803-009-0798-0.

Scahill, L., & Martin, A. (2005). Psychopharmacology. In: F. R. Volkmar, R. Paul, A. Klin & D. Cohen (Eds), *Handbook of autism and pervasive developmental disorders* (Vol. 2, pp. 1102–1117). Hoboken, NJ: Wiley.

Schereen, A. M., & Stauder, J. E. A. (2008). Broader autism phenotype in parents of autistic children: Reality or myth? *Journal of Autism and Developmental Disorders, 38*(2), 276–287. doi: 10.1007/s10803-007-0389-x

Schopler, E., & Mesibov, G. B. (1984). Professional attitudes towards parents: A forty-year progress report. In: E. Schopler & G. B. Mesibov (Eds), *The effects of autism on the family* (pp. 3–17). New York: Plenum Press.

Schopler, E., Reichler, R. J., Devellis, R. F., & Daly, K. (1980). Toward objective classification of childhood autism: Childhood Autism Rating Scale (CARS). *Journal of Autism and Developmental Disorders, 10*, 91–103.

Schreibman, L. (2005). *The science and fiction of autism.* Cambridge, MA: Harvard University Press.

Shattuck, R. (1994). *The forbidden experiment: The story of the wild boy of Aveyron.* New York: Kodansha America, Inc.

Sigafoos, J. (2001). Editorial: Special edition on Rett syndrome. *Disability and Rehabilitation, 23*(3/4), 97. Retrieved from http://web.ebscohost.com

Sigafoos, J., Green, V. A., Edrisinha, C., & Lancioni, G. E. (2007). Flashback to the 1960s: LSD in the treatment of autism. *Developmental Neurorehabilitation, 10*(1), 75–81. doi: 10.1080/13638490601106277

Simpson, R. L. (2005). Evidence-based practices and students with autism spectrum disorders. *Focus on Autism and Other Developmental Disabilities, 20*(3), 140–149. Retrieved from http://web.ebscohost.com

Slater, M. A., & Wikler, L. (1986). 'Normalized' family resources for families with a developmentally disabled child. *Social Work, 31*(5), 385–390.

Smith, T., & Wick, J. (2008). Controversial treatments. In: K. Chawarska, A. Klin & F. R. Volkmar (Eds), *Autism spectrum disorders in infants and toddlers: Diagnosis, assessment, and treatment* (pp. 243–273). New York: Guilford Press.

Symon, J. B. G., & Boettcher, M. A. (2008). Family participation and support. In: J. K. Luiselli, D. C. Russo, W. P. Christian & S. M. Wilczynski (Eds), *Effective practices for children with autism: Educational and behavioral support interventions that work* (pp. 455–489). New York: Oxford University Press.

Theus, F. C. (2008). Asperger syndrome in the African American community: Barriers to diagnosis. In: A. F. Rotatori, F. E. Obiakor & S. Burkhardt (Eds), *Autism and developmental disabilities: Current practices and issues* (Vol. 18, pp. 109–133). Bingley, UK: Emerald Group Publishing Limited.

Thomas, K. C., Ellis, A. R., McLaurin, C., Daniels, J., & Morrissey, J. P. (2007). Access to care for autism-related services. *Journal of Autism and Developmental Disorders, 37*(10), 1902–1912. doi: 10.1007/s10803-006-0323-7

Tomanik, S. S., Pearson, D. A., Loveland, K. A., Lane, D. M., & Shaw, J. B. (2007). Improving the reliability of autism diagnoses: Examining the utility of adaptive behavior. *Journal of Autism and Developmental Disorders, 37*(5), 921–928. doi: 10.1007/s10803-006-0227-6

Towbin, K. E. (2005). Pervasive developmental disorder not otherwise specified. In: F. R. Volkmar, R. Paul, A. Klin & D. Cohen (Eds), *Handbook of autism and pervasive developmental disorders* (Vol. 1, pp. 165–200). Hoboken, NJ: Wiley.

Turnbull, H. R., III., Wilcox, B. L., & Stowe, M. J. (2002). A brief overview of special education law with focus on autism. *Journal of Autism and Developmental Disorders, 32*(5), 479–493. Retrieved from http://web.ebscohost.com

U.S. Congress. (2006, December 19). Public Law 109-416. Retrieved from http://frwebgate. access.gpo.gov

Vaillant, G. E. (1962). Historical notes: John Haslam on early infantile autism. *American Journal of Psychiatry, 119*, 376. doi: 10.1176/appi.apj.119.4.376

Van Acker, R., Loncola, J. A., & Van Acker, E. (2005). Rett syndrome: A pervasive developmental disorder. In: F. R. Volkmar, R. Paul, A. Klin & D. Cohen (Eds), *Handbook of autism and pervasive developmental disorders* (Vol. 1, pp. 126–164). Hoboken, NJ: Wiley.

VanBiergeijk, E., Klin, A., & Volkmar, F. (2008). Supporting more able students on the autism spectrum: College and beyond. *Journal of Autism and Developmental Disorders, 38*(7), 1359–1370. doi: 10.1007/s10803-007-0524-8

Van Wieren, T. A., Reid, C. A., & McMahon, B. T. (2008). Workplace discrimination and autism spectrum disorders: The national EEOC Americans with Disabilities Act research project. *Work, 31*(3), 299–308. Retrieved from http://web.ebscohost.com

Volkmar, F. R. (1991). DSM-IV in progress: Autism and the pervasive developmental disorders. *Hospital and Community Psychiatry, 42*(1), 33–35.

Volkmar, F. R., Bregman, J., Cohen, D. J., & Cicchetti, D. V. (1988). DSM-III and DSM-III-R diagnoses of autism. *American Journal of Psychiatry, 145*(11), 1404–1408.

Volkmar, F. R., Chawarska, K., & Klin, A. (2008a). Autism spectrum disorders in infants and toddlers: An introduction. In: K. Chawarska, A. Klin & F. R. Volkmar (Eds), *Autism spectrum disorders in infants and toddlers: Diagnosis, assessment, and treatment* (pp. 1–22). New York: Guilford Press.

Volkmar, F. R., & Klin, A. (2005). Issues in the classification of autism and related conditions. In: F. R. Volkmar, R. Paul, A. Klin & D. Cohen (Eds), *Handbook of autism and pervasive developmental disorders* (Vol. 1, pp. 5–41). Hoboken, NJ: Wiley.

Volkmar, F. R., Koenig, K., & State, M. (2005). Childhood disintegrative disorder. In: F. R. Volkmar, R. Paul, A. Klin & D. Cohen (Eds), *Handbook of autism and pervasive developmental disorders* (Vol. 1, pp. 70–87). Hoboken, NJ: Wiley.

Volkmar, F. R., Westphal, A., Gupta, A. R., & Wiesner, L. (2008b). Medical issues. In: K. Chawarska, A. Klin & F. R. Volkmar (Eds), *Autism spectrum disorders in infants and toddlers: Diagnosis, assessment, and treatment* (pp. 274–299). New York: Guilford Press.

West, E. (2011). Assistive technology for students with autism. In: E. A. Boutot & B. S. Myles (Eds), *Autism spectrum disorders: Foundations, characteristics, and effective strategies* (pp. 261–276). Upper Saddle River, NJ: Pearson.

West, L., Waldrop, J., & Brunssen, S. (2009). Pharmacologic treatment for the core deficits and associated symptoms of autism in children. *Journal of Pediatric Health Care, 23*(2), 75–89. doi: 10.1016/j.pedhc.2008.12.001

Wicks-Nelson, R., & Israel, A. C. (2009). *Abnormal child and adolescent psychology* (7th ed.). Upper Saddle River, NJ: Pearson/Prentice Hall.

Wilkinson, L. A. (2010). *A best practice guide to assessment and intervention for autism and Asperger syndrome in schools.* Philadelphia: Jessica Kingsley Publishers.

Wing, L. (2005). Reflections on opening Pandora's box. *Journal of Autism and Developmental Disorders, 35*(2), 197–203. doi: 10.1007/s10803-004-1998-2

Wing, L., & Shah, A. (2006). A systematic examination of catatonia-like clinical pictures in autism spectrum disorders. *International Review of Neurobiology, 72*, 21–39. doi: 10.1016/S0074-7742(05)72002-X

Wolery, M., Barton, E. E., & Hine, J. F. (2005). Evolution of applied behavior analysis in the treatment of individuals with autism. *Exceptionality, 13*(1), 11–23. Retrieved from http://web.ebscohost.com

Wolff, S. (2004). The history of autism. *European Child and Adolescent Psychiatry, 13*(4), 201–208. doi: 10.1007/s00787-004-0363-5

Yell, M. L., Drasgow, E., & Lowrey, K. A. (2005). No Child Left Behind and students with autism spectrum disorders. *Focus on Autism and Other Developmental Disabilities, 20*(3), 130–139. Retrieved from http://web.ebscohost.com

Zettel, J. J. (1977, March 21). Public Law 94-142: The Education for All Handicapped Children Act. An overview of the federal law. Paper presented at the 32nd annual meeting of the Association for Supervision and Curriculum Development, Houston, TX. Retrieved from http://www.eric.ed.gov

Zoghbi, H. Y. (2002). Introduction: Rett syndrome. *Mental Retardation and Developmental Disabilities Research Reviews, 8*(2), 59–60. doi: 10.1002/mrdd.10028.

CHAPTER 11

THE HISTORY OF PHYSICAL AND HEALTH IMPAIRMENTS

Barbara M. Fulk, Emily Watts and
Jeffrey P. Bakken

By 1975, our country's schools enjoyed a rich history with respect to decades of pedagogy in teaching typically developing students. Nonetheless, educators were not prepared to teach students, who could not walk, sit upright, swallow properly, speak without difficulty, or breathe without oxygen. Physicians, school administrators, and well-meaning relatives told countless families routinely to keep their child in an institution, keep them at home, or that their child would be denied services with statements to the effect, "we don't take kids like that." Some explanations that were given for turning students away from school were that seeing a student with a disability could have "a depressing and nauseating effect on the teachers and other students" (*Beattie v. Board of Education of City of Antiago*, 1919) or more recently that the students did not qualify for education due to an inability to benefit (*Timothy W. v. Rochester School District*, 1980).

Prior to the passage of P.L. 94-142, Congress found that the needs of students with disabilities were not being met in public schools. Consider these facts: one million students with disabilities were being excluded from schools and fewer than 50 percent of students with disabilities were being appropriately served in regular classes. In addition, large numbers of students in regular classes had their learning needs and differences ignored. Families with financial means who were turned away from public school doors were

History of Special Education
Advances in Special Education, Volume 21, 269–288
Copyright © 2011 by Emerald Group Publishing Limited
All rights of reproduction in any form reserved
ISSN: 0270-4013/doi:10.1108/S0270-4013(2011)0000021014

forced to seek institutions or private schools, often far removed from their homes and at great expense (Boyle & Weishaar, 2001). State institutions were intended to protect society from the individual rather than to provide appropriate care of individuals, based on their physical, health, and specific educational needs. Institutions were often overcrowded, short of necessary resources, and lacked any type of programs that focused on education.

Now 35 years later after the passage of P.L. 94-142, fewer children receive an education in institution-like settings, hospitals, or nursing homes. The vast majority of students with moderate to significant physical disabilities and health impairments are included in public general education classrooms with fewer living in residential placements or private schools. Special education teachers, general education teachers, paraprofessionals, and related services professionals are now educating students in inclusive or least restrictive environments. This chapter first describes the history and background of education for individuals with physical disabilities (PD) and other health impairments (OHI) followed by sections regarding service delivery, legislative acts, assistive technology, and working with families.

HISTORY AND BACKGROUND

Throughout the ages, caring for an individual with a significant physical disability and/or health impairment has been extremely difficult or perhaps even impossible. Conditions for survival were often hard, requiring all able-bodied family members working from dawn until dark to scratch out even a minimal standard of living. Consequently, little time and resources were available for the care of a loved one with a disability. Safford and Safford's sobering volume (1996) emphasizes that children have always been vulnerable to neglect and children with disabilities were particularly subject to abuse. To illustrate this, children with disabilities were particularly subject to infanticide, abandonment, slavery, sterilization or placed in orphanages, where maiming sometimes occurred to increase the individuals' potential for street corner begging.

Beliefs about disability also had a significant impact on how these individuals were perceived by family members as well as society in general. With the growth of religion in the middle ages, individuals with disabilities were sometimes seen as blessed "children of God" and who needed care and protection. However, also stemming from religious views was the notion that significant physical disabilities were "the mark of the devil" (Safford & Safford, 1996) which led to blame, or fear, ridicule, or ostracism. Individuals with physical "handicaps" have often been particular targets due to fear, prejudice, myth, and/or ignorance about their conditions. Safford and Safford (1996) provide detailed descriptions of the plight of specific subgroups in history including those with epilepsy, tuberculosis (TB), and cerebral palsy (CP). Brief summaries taken from their work are summarized in the next section as representative of the issues.

Epilepsy

The causes of epilepsy have long been misunderstood, attributed at times to emotional disturbance, moral defects, or demonic possession. Parents who believed in the last of these often embarked on difficult pilgrimages to sacred shrines rather than seek medical interventions or surgeries. This was understandable when you consider that one available surgery was "trephination," a brain surgery removing slices of the skull to remove presumed sources of health impairment such as hydrocephaly and epilepsy. Bone slivers once removed were made into amulets to ward off evil spirits.

Cerebral Palsy

CP is a second condition that has long been misunderstood. CP can range from mild to severe. An early belief was that CP always co-occurred with significant cognitive impairment (CI) which prejudged these individuals to be "uneducable." The physical difference made people believe that there was also a cognitive difference. Yes, this can happen in extreme cases, but most often the cognitive aspect of people with CP is not affected like some believe. Due to this belief, however, individuals with CP were not given the opportunity others had.

Tuberculosis

In the 1900s, a drug-resistant strain of TB emerged to make it the most feared contagious disease and in the 19th and 20th centuries "the greatest single medical challenge" (Safford & Safford, 1996). It is interesting to note that many children's hospitals in the 1900s refused to admit children with contagious diseases. Programs were opened for siblings of children with TB as preventative measures. However, some of these programs were forced out of neighborhoods by residents who feared contamination. One educational model that emerged internationally in the early 1900s was the open-air school, designed to address both the health and the educational needs of children with TB. Some of the open-air schools in Europe were located in mountains or forest glades, whereas many of the US schools were in crowded rooftops in urban areas. Once the cause of and effective health measures were discovered, campaigns to eradicate TB were widely instituted. At one time, TB was nearly eradicated in developed countries, which diminished the need for open-air schools. In developed countries, the early focus on TB has paved the way for educational programs for children with "reduced health and vitality" and OHI.

Sadly, a prevalent view in the United States in the early 1900s was that congenital deformity, and diseases such as TB were "unfit" classes. For example, the "American Breeders Association," in 1913, stated that disability subgroups such as these should be "eliminated" in order for our nation to progress. Nonetheless, several institutions and state schools were established in the early 1900s for the care of individuals with epilepsy. The field of medicine became more prominent in epilepsy beginning with the use of bromides in 1857, followed by phenobarbitol and other anticonvulsive medications in 1912. For too many years, however, disabilities such as PD and OHI were viewed from a medical model (as a deficit from normal) that required either rehabilitation or remediation.

Throughout history, successive eras of extermination, ridicule, asylum, and education can be identified, but while the era of education and treatment is commonly said to have begun with Itard and Victor, the "wild boy of Aveyron" extermination, ridicule, and asylum have not disappeared (Safford & Safford, 1996, p. 3). Table 1 presents a sampling of historical events from the Disability Rights Movement of particular salience to individuals with PD and OHI.

Changing Definitions and Language

As far back as in 1975, Gary Best's text entitled "*Individuals with Physical Disabilities: An Introduction for Educators*" discussed the importance of terminology, in this case, specific to PD. First, he reminded readers that students with disabilities are children (and persons) first. He suggests usage of the phrase "individuals with physical disabilities" rather than "physically disabled individuals" or other negative laden terms such as crippled, handicapped, and orthopedically impaired. The use of person first terms is

Table 1. Key Events from the Disability Rights Movement Related to PD and OHI.

Title/Event	Year	Summary
League for Physically Handicapped was established	1935	Held a sit-in to protest job discrimination against the Works Progress Administration in NY against individuals with physical disabilities
American Federation of the Physically Handicapped was formed	1940	First cross-disability national political group formed to end job discrimination and lobby for disability rights
National Employ the Physically Handicapped Week	1948	Presidential commission was formed to publicize and promote hiring of individuals with disabilities
Mary Switzer was appointed as Director of U.S. Office of Vocational Rehabilitation	1950	Began an emphasis on independent living as quality of life issue
The Association for Persons with Physical Handicaps (TASH) established	1975	Founded by special education professionals in response to *PARC v. Pennsylvania* to call for an end to aversive behavior modification and residential institutions for individuals with disabilities
The International Year of Disabled Persons began	1981	Governments were encouraged to sponsor programs bringing people with disabilities into the mainstream
Not Dead Yet formed	1996	Designed to oppose those who supported assisted suicide and rationing health care for individuals with disabilities

Source: Rehabilitation Research & Training Center on Independent Living Management (2002).

not specific to PD and OHI, however. Through the years, schools have become more aware of more positive ways to refer to individuals with disabilities or impairments.

SERVICE DELIVERY FOR STUDENTS WITH PHYSICAL AND HEALTH IMPAIRMENTS

The early model for provision of services for students with physical and health impairments was based on medical services delivered in institutional settings, away from the public's view. Thus discussion of pioneers in PD and OHI must include medical as well as educational leaders. For example, an early medical pioneer in CP was W.J. Little, whose observations about premature as well as difficult births resulted in improved prenatal and postnatal care. Little also recognized that CP was separate from a CI. In the United States, an orthopedic surgeon named Phelps trained numerous teachers and physical therapists to enhance the mobility as well as education of individuals with CP. The work of the Society for Crippled Children was important for beginning nursery school programs for young children as an alternative to residential programs. Another strong advocacy group for individuals with CP was the United Cerebral Palsy Association (UCPA) particularly after World War II (Safford & Safford, 1996).

With the advent of P.L. 94-142, institutions of higher learning began scrambling to develop curricula and certification requirements to prepare teachers to be certified in the area of special education. Orthopedic physicians from a prestigious medical school edited one of the first textbooks available for special education classroom teachers. In their book, *Physically Handicapped Children: A Medical Atlas for Teachers*, Bleck and Nagel (1975) offer "fundamental medical facts" and "practical suggestions for those who teach disabled children in special schools and the regular classroom" (p. ix). This book comprised medical terminology, anatomical illustrations, treatment suggestions, and an explanation of the typical gross motor developmental sequence. In addition, the authors included detailed descriptions of an array of disabling conditions such as spinal muscular atrophy, sickle cell disease, spina bifida, CP, cystic fibrosis, convulsive disorders, asthma, amputations in children, arthrogryposis, and muscular dystrophy. The sections on diagnosis of disabling conditions and the roles of occupational therapist and physical therapist were represented in this groundbreaking medical resource written for teachers. However, it was not meant to be a resource for implementing individualized educational programming.

For specific information on obscure, rare disorders, it was necessary for teachers and school psychologists to consult the latest edition of the *Merck Manual of Diagnosis and Therapy, 13th Edition* (1977), a commonplace tool of physicians that was used as a disease-oriented listing of etiology, symptoms and signs, diagnosis, and treatment options. These and other advances in precise teaching approaches along with policy changes have opened the previously locked schoolhouse doors to welcome students with moderate to significant physical or health impairments.

Campbell, an occupational therapist, contributed significantly to the instructional knowledge base for teachers of students with PD in her chapter "Basic Considerations in Programming for Students with Movement Difficulties" found in the second edition of *Systematic Instruction of the Moderately and Severely Handicapped* (Snell, 1983). Covering the relationship between underlying processes of movement and everyday activities and task performance, Campbell gave instructional staff basic information that set the stage for intervention approaches. Furthermore, here was fundamental information specifically targeting the audience of special education teachers that covered (a) types of equipment and company resources, (b) neurodevelopmental approaches for addressing abnormal tone in children with CP that special education teachers could readily learn and apply in consultation with physical therapists or occupational therapists, and (c) examples of individual educational planning.

With more and more students having PD or OHI coming to school, schools wrestled with how to provide special education programs from a variety of related service personnel in school settings. The early medical model of one-on-one therapy delivered in secluded areas of the school buildings by itinerant related service personnel is most likely still happening in parts of our country today. Nonetheless, for students with PD or OHI, the recommended model of service delivery is one that allows for collaboration among all those who participate in the education of the student, parents or guardians included. The form of the model could be an interdisciplinary approach in which all team members participate in the assessment, instructional planning, and evaluation phases with only a few key members implementing the programming goals and objectives. Another form of the service delivery model could be transdisciplinary in nature. In this model as described by Orelove and Sobsey (1987), related service team members "share and exchange" responsibilities with families and educational staff by communicating general information and teaching suggestions. Conversely, families and educational staff share and exchange general information and teaching suggestions with the related service personnel. It is the premise that we are in this together, sink or swim. Collaboration in any form of teaming is essential.

Perhaps the most dramatic, early event to impact educational programming needs of students with PD and OHI was the beginning of the formation of an organization in 1974, known as The American Association for Education of Severely and Profoundly Handicapped (ASESPH). Major contributors to the formation were Norris Haring, Lou Brown, Marc Gold, Doug Guess, Wayne Sailor, Diane Bricker, Bob York, Francis Anderson, Richard Whelan, Marilyn Cohen, William Dussault, and Laura Dennison (Brown, 1990). After a number of name changes, that same organization, known as TASH today, has evolved into an international advocacy organization focusing on equity issues, more opportunities for people with disabilities, and inclusion in schools and communities. Because students with significant intellectual disabilities shared some of the very same physical and health issues as those without intellectual disabilities, this event had a deep and lasting effect on educational opportunities and instruction for students with PD and OHI.

The professionals who began this organization had a unique vision for making a difference in the lives of children with significant disabilities and their families that were not currently being met in 1975. Looking back, Brown (1990) stated that there was not another entity in our society that was "addressing the ideological, research, financial, and programmatic rights and needs of people with severe disabilities, the most vulnerable, segregated, abused, neglected, and denied people in our society. The people who were quarantined in horrible institution wards; who were excluded and rejected from public schools by too many of the continuum tolerators; who were confined to segregated activity centers and workshops; and who were quarantined in nursing homes and other unnatural living environments that were certified as acceptable by the ruling professionals" (p. 1). Aligned with a small group of dedicated lawyers, these professionals along with devoted, yet outraged, families began legal actions to ensure their children had the right to an education and the necessary, appropriate resources.

Legislative Acts

Following World War II, the large number of disabled veterans with vocational rehabilitative needs began to demand access to jobs and other life activities. As a result, several key pieces of legislation were passed including the Civil Rights Act in 1964 and the 1990 Americans with Disabilities Act (ADA). In 1968, the Architectural Barriers Act was passed followed by the establishment of the Transportation Barriers Compliance Board whose purpose was to set minimal guidelines for physical accessibility. Independent living centers were also established to provide advocacy programs, job training, and attendant care registries to returning veterans (Best, 2010). The Disability Rights movement of the 1970s became a unified voice for services for individuals with disabilities and Section 504 of the Rehabilitation Act passed in 1973 prohibited recipients of federal financial assistance including schools from excluding individuals from participation in any program or activity on the basis of a handicap (Rothstein, 2000).

Soon thereafter in 1975, Congress passed major legislation to facilitate the education of all handicapped children in the United States. Public schools, partly in response to advocacy groups, and court decisions based challenges about the exclusion of these individuals. This law which named 11 disability categories (including orthopedic impairments and OHI) along with

Table 2. Court Cases and Legislation Related to PD and OHI.

Event	Year	Purpose or Outcome
State law passed by Commonwealth of Virginia	1924	Allowed forced sterilization of individuals with epilepsy and other handicaps
Buck v. Bell Supreme Court Decision	1927	Ruled that forced sterilization was not violation of constitutional rights
Social Security amendments passed	1950	Established a federal-state program to aid permanent and total disabilities
Vocational Rehabilitation Amendments passed	1954	Authorized federal grants to expand programs available to people with PD
American National Standards Institute (ANSI)	1961	Published specifications for building accessibility
Vocational Rehabilitation Amendments passed	1965	Authorized federal funds for rehabilitation programs and created National Commission on Architectural Barriers
Urban Mass Transit Act passed	1970	Required new vehicles to be wheelchair accessible
U.S. District Court in District of Columbia	1972	Ruled on *Mills v. Board of Education* that disabled children could not be excluded from school
Rehabilitation Act passed	1973	Sections 501, 503, and 504 prohibited discrimination in programs and services receiving federal funds
The Technology-Related Assistance Act passed	1988	Authorized federal funding for state projects designed to facilitate access to assistive technology
American Disabilities Act (ADA) signed	1990	Provided comprehensive civil rights protection for people with disabilities mandating reasonable accommodation and access to public transportation, communication, and other areas

Source: Rehabilitation Research & Training Center on Independent Living Management (2002).

section 504 of the Rehabilitation Act provided a framework as well as specific legal requirements for special education (Rothstein, 2000). Table 2 presents an outline of selected court decisions and legislation particularly relevant to PD and OHI.

Definitions

IDEA's definition of OHI states that OHI means having limited strength, vitality, or alertness, including a heightened alertness to environmental stimuli, that results in limited alertness with respect to the educational environment, that (a) is due to chronic or acute health problems such as asthma, attention deficit disorder or attention deficit hyperactivity disorder, diabetes, epilepsy, cancer, a heart condition, hemophilia, lead poisoning, leukemia, nephritis, rheumatic fever, sickle cell anemia, and Tourette syndrome and (b) adversely affects a child's educational performance (NICHCY, 2009). Note that this is not an exhaustive list but rather a sample of the acute or chronic health conditions which may make an individual eligible for services under IDEA. Clearly the broad umbrella of OHI consists of a wide range of very different conditions that are further complicated when individuals have combinations of these with other health conditions. Some categories will be explained next.

Attention Deficit Disorder
IDEA does not present ADHD as a distinct category (Yell, 2006). For that reason, children with ADHD who do not qualify for eligibility for special education are served under Section 504 of the Vocational Rehabilitation Act of 1973. IDEA is very specific while the former is broad and subject to interpretation. Consequently, many administrators provide services for ADHD who may not be eligible for special education services under IDEA. Because of the condition of the students with ADHD, they require medication. Students with ADHD fall under the following specification:

• For some students with ADHD, inattention is the primary problem. These students might skip salient information of an assignment, may appear to be day dreaming during the large group instruction, are disorganized, and generally seem forgetful both in school and at home. This variability of disorder is referred to as ADHD – *predominantly inattentive type*.
• For another group of students with ADHD, the salient symptoms are a combination of hyperactivity with a high amount of movement, and impulsivity and a lack of the ability to think before acting. Fidgeting is a common phenomena for students with this type of ADHD. This type of ADHD is called ADHD – *predominantly hyperactive–impulsive type*.
• Some students with ADHD have symptoms suggesting both inattentiveness and hyperactivity. These students are referred to as having ADHD – *combined type*.

As it stands, ADHD is considered neurological, chronic, long-term, and acutely acquired. The primary trait of this condition is an inability to attend beyond what is typical for peers of comparable age. Significant impulsivity may also be a characteristic. ADHD is not situational in that it affects children and adults who have it across all settings. The greatest difficulty often revolves in the production that is in completing their work.

Asthma

The most common chronic illness among children is asthma, a lung disease that causes times of great difficulty in breathing (Gabe, Bury, & Ramsey, 2002). Asthma affects between 5 and 7 percent of all children in the United States. In recent times, the number of cases of asthma has been rising, and the severity of the disease increasing. Experts in the field advise parents to protect their children from known triggers such as tobacco smoke as one means of addressing this problem. For some children, asthma may be fairly benign while for others it can be chronic. For example, one child may have coughing spells when he/she laughs too hard. For another child, the condition can be much more serious. When exposed to certain triggers, these students' airways swell and produce mucus which makes breathing difficult (Lemanek & Hood, 1999) and they may require emergency medical intervention. Asthma is hereditary in nature and in most cases if one of the parents has the disease, the child has a 50 percent chance of inheriting it (see Lemanek & Hood, 1999). However, it is often triggered by allergens, including flowers, grass, pollen, dust, and molds, animal dander, and food allergies such as eggs and seafood as well as by strenuous physical activity (Greiling, Boss, & Wheeler, 2005). However, asthma can be controlled through medication and the avoidance of allergenic environments (Beers, Porter, Jones, Kaplan, & Berkwits, 2006; Taras & Potts-Datema, 2005).

Sickle Cell Anemia

Sickle cell anemia is one form of sickle cell disease that consists of anemia, painful episodes, and complications that can lead to eye disease, spleen dysfunction, or stroke. This is a hereditary disease and mainly affects people of African descent. An abnormal type of hemoglobin (HBS) results in some red cells being shaped like a sickle instead of the normal disc-shaped red cells with pinched-in sides. These poorly formed sickled red cells have a poor shorter life span, and are usually broken down in approximately 20 days instead of the normal 120 days which results in chronic anemia and subsequent fatigue (Jakubik & Thompson, 2000). Teachers should try to prevent the triggers by events of vaso-occlusive crisis and monitor their occurrence. A vaso-occlusive crisis can be triggered by events that cause a decrease in oxygen, such as strenuous exercise, cold weather, dehydration, infection, or high altitude. When a vaso-occlusive crisis begins, some red blood cells change into a sickle shape. These deformed cells can plug the small blood vessels in the body, resulting in localized tissue hypoxia, which leads to further sickling of the blood cells. When blockage occurs in the blood vessel, it results in tissue death (Dorman, 2005). Intense pain ensues after a vaso-occlusive crisis followed by coughing, shortness of breath, and severe abdominal pain. Teachers and service providers should be vigilant and monitor the situation carefully. Treatment for severe crisis may consist of rest, rehydration, pain medication, management of complication, and sometimes blood transfusion (Dorman, 2005).

Physical Impairments

The wide range of health conditions listed above, warrant a wide range of service needs with some students having few restrictions on their activities and learning whereas other students require extensive medical and educational assistance. One student may have multiple disabilities including a severe physical condition that hinders the student's coordination, balance, mobility, and communication and CI in significant ways whereas a second student may be in the above average or gifted range and participate fully in general education classes (http://www.eric.gov).

Physical disability or orthopedic impairment are conditions that seriously impair motor activity and/or mobility including complex conditions such as CP, spina bifida, congenital anomalies, muscular dystrophy, as well as traumas and tumors to name a few. Any of these conditions can also range in severity from mild to moderate to severe, can be congenital or acquired, and may be temporary, intermittent, or chronic and life threatening. Best (2010) describes physical disabilities related to three representative categories of neural tube deficits, traumatic brain injury, and muscular dystrophy as these are typically identifiable to teachers.

Physical disabilities are broadly recognized into neurological and musculoskeletal. Neurological conditions involve damage to the central nervous system. In 1990, traumatic brain injury became a separate category under IDEA. Other major neurological conditions include CP and spinal bifida, a congenital condition in which spinal fluid protrudes through the backbone resulting in partial or total paralysis below the site or nervous damage. Disabilities associated with neurological conditions vary from mild to severe and may involve physical, cognitive, speech-language, or sensory disabilities.

Muscular skeletal conditions include muscular dystrophy, juvenile rheumatoid arthritis, limb deficits or amputations, and a wide variety of other deformities or degeneration of muscle of bones affecting the ability to move, walk, and stand, sit or use hand or feet, a state that largely interferes with functioning. OHI include a wide variety of diseases and chronic problems such as diabetes, epilepsy, cancer, leukemia, cardiovascular complications, and a wide variety of immunodeficiencies (Heller, Forney, Alberto, Best, & Schwartzman, 2009).

ASSESSMENT

When it comes to the assessment of individuals with physical or health impairments professionals working with these individuals must have a broad base of skills in order to adequately measure the functional and cognitive abilities of the students. In addition to the areas traditionally evaluated in the assessment of children with mild handicaps, measures should be included in the areas of fine motor, gross motor, and daily living skills; recreation and leisure skills; augmentative communication; perception; and sensory input. Usually, it will require help from others such as therapists, educators, physicians, nurses, social workers, and others to gather appropriate data and to help develop a functional academic, behavioral, physical, and social plan for the student.

Since the assessment of a student who has physical or health impairment is often time consuming and taxing to both the professional conducting the assessment and the child, the team of professionals should meet before data are gathered to consider: (a) the nature of the data base desired, (b) the potential use of the data, (c) specific measurement techniques or modifications of traditional measures, (d) who should present the items, (e) the method of data collection, (f) appropriate response modes and/or equipment, (g) positioning for testing, (h) stamina and fatigue factors, (i) the order in which professionals will conduct the testing, (j) implications of medications for test performance and for the best time of day to test, (k) how data will be shared when evaluations are completed, and (l) the nature of nontraditional measures that should be incorporated in the assessment (Reynolds & Clark, 1983). Developing a comprehensive preassessment plan ensures that the information necessary for establishing programs and setting priorities for intervention will be available when needed. Since all students are unique as is their physical or health impairment, it will be essential that time and consideration is taken into account to carefully plan the assessments to be given and to evaluate the data that is retrieved. This will be critical in the development of the most beneficial individualized education program (IEP) possible which meets the unique individual needs of the student.

ASSISTIVE TECHNOLOGY

In 1990, assistive technology was added to the list of special education services that must be included in a student's IEP. IDEA defines assistive-technology services as "any service that directly assists a child with a disability in the selection, acquisition, or use of an assistive technology device." IDEA defined an assistive-technology device as "any item, piece of equipment or product system, whether acquired commercially off the shelf, modified, or customized, that is used to increase, maintain, or improve the functional capabilities of children with disabilities."

Although the regulations do not elaborate on how assistive technology must be considered, the law states that the IEP team must be involved in the decision-making process. It further states that outside evaluators must be used when the IEP team lacks the expertise to conduct an evaluation and make an informed decision regarding assistive technology. In addition, it is the responsibility of the school system to secure funding for the device and to provide training to school personnel, family members, and the student as educationally appropriate.

Students with disabilities use a variety of technology tools for their success in academic settings and with organizational skills. For example, students who cannot comprehend printed instructional materials and have difficulty manipulating textbooks physically can use of alternative format, like an audio book. Students with writing difficulties may use pencil grips and adapted paper to write legibly and to complete assignments in a timely fashion. Students with physical or health impairments also require technology to access the classroom curriculum. For example, students who cannot use standard classroom desks may need some type of adaptive seating arrangement. Those who are immobile may require mobility equipments like wheelchairs or walkers. Students who cannot manipulate classroom instructional materials like other students may require adaptive devices to stabilize the materials. Students should also have individual access to computers for completing their assignments. Depending on their level of functioning, they may also need keyboard adaptations, or on-screen keyboards.

When considering assistive technology one must consider hardware and software options for individuals who are physically or health impaired. Often called "accessibility options" when referring to enhancements for using the computer, the entire field of assistive technology is quite vast and even includes ramp and doorway construction in buildings to support wheelchairs (http://www.answers.com/topic/assistive-technology). Enhancements for using the computer include alternative keyboard and mouse devices, replacing beeps with light signals for the deaf, screen magnifiers and text enlargers, and systems that form tactile Braille letters from on-screen text. Personal computers have dramatically changed the way students learn and complete assignments. The average computer, however, may not be accessible to children with physical limitations.

Keyboard Access

Standard keyboards that are inaccessible to students with limited motor skills have many adaptations or alternatives that are available. Keyguards, for example, are hard plastic covers with holes for each key. Children with unsteady fingers can use keyguards to avoid striking unwanted keys. The use of keyguards will increase finger accuracy, maintain correct placement of the hand, and help avoid accidental pressing of keys.

Another option is using an alternative keyboard to meet the specific needs of individual children. An adjustable keyboard has three sections that can be positioned close together or further apart, rotated, and tilted to many angles to meet the comfort level and mobility issues of the student. A miniature keyboard has keys spaced close together to allow children with limited range of motion access to all of the keys. If the student has difficulty spelling words, gets tired, or frustrated easily an option is a programmable keyboard that can be programmed so that letters, numbers, words, or phrases can be entered by pressing custom keys.

For students with more severe disabilities, a pointing or typing aid can be used to press keys on the keyboard. Usually in the form of a wand or a stick, the pointer or typing aid can be worn on the head, strapped to the chin, or held in the mouth or hand. This aid allows the use of a standard or alternative keyboard and in addition can be used with a keyguard. Other wands or sticks are designed for use with a splint on the hand or arm.

Mouse Alternatives

Children who have the inability to control movements often have difficulties positioning the mouse cursor, and they may also have the inability to double click within the time necessary, or click and drag. As a result, assistive technology for children with disabilities includes several options to control the mouse cursor. A common alternative to the mouse is a trackball. Best described as an upside down mouse with the ball exposed; trackballs remain stationary so that only the movement of the ball moves the cursor. Buttons on the trackball can perform single click, double click, and drag-lock functions. The size of the ball on the trackball varies from as large as a cue ball to as small as a marble. A joystick is another input device that can control the cursor. Joysticks offer three types of control: digital, glide, and direct. Digital joysticks allow movement in a limited number of directions. Glide and direct joysticks allow movements in all directions. Direct-control joysticks have the added ability of responding to the distance and speed with which the user moves the stick. In order to choose an appropriate joystick the teacher must investigate the abilities of the student and match that to the needed task. Joysticks can also activate the computer with different parts of the body, such as the head or chin, without the use of hands.

There are obviously thousands of assistive technologies available and all cannot be discussed in this chapter. Some examples were provided to give you an idea of the possibilities available. One must remember that the use of technology can make academic material, physical places, and social activities available to students with physical and health impairments.

WORKING WITH FAMILIES

Public law 94-142 and each subsequent reauthorization of the IDEA has attempted to protect the rights of students as well as parents and to assert parents' rights to participate in the special education decision-making process. In the early years, perhaps because the field of special education was still young, too little emphasis was placed on family participation (Alper, Schloss, & Schloss, 1994). These authors suggest that the primary areas of attention were given to students' social, communication, and academic needs with little attention remaining for families and their roles.

Clearly, the parents of students with disabilities have a number of demanding roles to fill well beyond typical parenting responsibilities such as roles of advocates, teachers, classroom helpers, decision-makers, and service brokers. In 1983, Turnbull wrote that only "in the last decade" had significant attention been paid to parent–professional interactions that focus on mutual respect and decision-making. When considering the views of disability in society throughout the ages, as described above, it is not surprising that families approached school with feelings of fear and mistrust. Parents were sometimes blamed for children's disabilities. Some had been forced into roles of vigilante advocates to attain education and related services for their children; this posture made it difficult to approach the multidisciplinary table with a collaborative attitude. Some professionals would treat parents with little respect, assuming that the parents themselves had CIs and should be treated accordingly. Turnbull wrote about a parent involvement program that used the slogan "Parents are Educable" to suggest the importance of parent training, which parents found to be insulting, regardless of the original intent.

Now, nearly four decades since the 94-142 law was passed, parent–professional interactions are increasingly important and still wrought with difficulties. Teachers and professionals still sometimes speak down to parents or use professional jargon with no explanation of terms or the special education process. Students with disabilities and their families are reflecting increased cultural and linguistic diversity, which further complicate issues of acceptance of disability as well as trust, understanding, and clear communication. Professionals who value parent–professional collaboration will continue to address these issues in the next decade.

Children and Work

Employed parents caring for children with disabilities often find the integration of work and family responsibilities very challenging (Kagan, Lewis, & Heaton, 1998; Rosenzweig, Brennan, & Ogilvie, 2002). Child care arrangements are hard to find and maintain, routine health care appointments must often be scheduled during parents' workdays, children's health or mental health crises can disrupt working hours in unpredictable ways, and special education arrangements must be established and updated. As a result, employers may lose the benefit of these parents' valuable experience, knowledge, and skills when families cannot marshal the supports they need to take care of their children with disabilities while maintaining their employment (Powers, 2003; Rosenzweig & Huffstutter, 2004). This means that employment may be terminated so that the parents can care for their child.

Parents of children with disabilities engage in exceptional caregiving responsibilities, which differ from typical caregiving responsibilities in several dimensions. Children with physical or health impairments can have significantly different needs than other children. Because of these needs family members may spend a significant amount of time arranging care for their children. Care needs of children with physical or health impairments can be ongoing, can persist throughout childhood into young adulthood or beyond, and are more frequent and intense than the care needs of typically developing children (Lewis, Kagan, & Heaton, 2000; Porterfield, 2002; Roundtree & Lynch, 2006).

Families of children with disabilities function more successfully with effective family support. They find it is very difficult to do everything themselves. Family support is a combination of formal and informal services and tangible goods that are defined and determined by families. Each family has different needs and requires different kinds of services. Indeed, family support encompasses "whatever it takes" for a family to care for and live with a child or adolescent who has a physical or health impairment.

CONCLUSION

Although education and treatment of individuals with physical and health impairment and other disabilities has improved significantly from ancient times, "... No one would assert that humanity has left behind cruelty, apathy, ignorance, and fear ..." (Safford & Safford, 1996). Even today, people who would agree in principle that residential group homes are fine, so long as the homes are located in neighborhoods well-removed from their own. We have seen some progress in moving from the medical conception of disability as a "deficit" to conceptualizing disability as one aspect of human diversity, a normal part of life and advanced age (Best, 2010). We must remember that physical or health impairments are limiting only if we allow them to be. Teachers and parents can work with these individuals to help them function with their peers and achieve as well as participate like other students. Assistive technology can give students even more options to fully participate and become independent. Clearly significant advances have been made in the education and treatment of individuals with physical and health impairments and they will only continue to do so in the future.

REFERENCES

Alper, S. K., Schloss, P. J., & Schloss, C. N. (1994). *Families of students with disabilities: Consultation and advocacy*. Needham Heights, MA: Allyn & Bacon.

Beers, M. H., Porter, R. S., Jones, T. V., Kaplan, J. L., & Berkwits, M. (2006). *The Merck manual of diagnosis and therapy* (18th ed.). Whitehouse Station, NJ: Merck & Co.

Best, G. A. (1975). *Individuals with physical disabilities: An introduction for educators*. Saint Louis, MO: The C. V. Mosby Company.

Best, S. J. (2010). Understanding individuals with physical, health, and multiple impairments. In: S. J. Best, K. W. Heller & J. L. Bigge (Eds), *Teaching individuals with physical or multiple disabilities* (6th ed., pp. 3–31). Upper Saddle River, NJ: Pearson.

Bleck, E. G., & Nagel, D. A. (1975). *Physically handicapped children: A medical atlas for teachers*. New York: Gruno & Stratton.

Boyle, J. R., & Weishaar, M. (2001). *Special education law with cases*. Needham Heights, MA: Allyn & Bacon.

Brown, L. (1990). Who are they and what do they want? An essay on TASH. Retrieved October 17, 2010 from the World Wide Web at http://www.tash.org/WWA/WWA_history.html

Dorman, K. (2005). Sickle cell crisis. *Registered Nurses Journal, 68*, 33–36.

Gabe, J., Bury, M., & Ramscy, R. (2002). Living with asthma: Experiences of young people at home and in school. *Social Science and Medicine, 55*, 1619–1633.

Greiling, A. K., Boss, L. P., & Wheeler, I. S. (2005). A preliminary investigation of asthma mortality in schools. *Journal of School Health, 75*, 286–290.

Heller, K. W., Forney, P. E., Alberto, P. A., Best, S. J., & Schwartzman, M. N. (2009). *Understanding physical, health, and multiple disabilities* (2nd ed.). Upper Saddle River, NJ: Merrill.

Jakubik, L. D., & Thompson, M. (2000). Care of the child with sickle cell disease: Acute complications. *Pediatric Nursing, 26*, 373–379.

Kagan, C., Lewis, S., & Heaton, P. (1998). *Caring to work: Accounts of working parents of disabled children*. London: Family Policy Studies Centre/Joseph Rowntree Foundation.

Lemanek, K. L., & Hood, C. (1999). Chronic asthma. In: R. T. Brown (Ed.), *Cognitive aspects of illness in children* (pp. 78–104). New York: Guildford Press.

Lewis, S., Kagan, C., & Heaton, P. (2000). Managing work–family diversity for parents of disabled children: Beyond policy to practice and partnership. *Personnel Review, 29*(3), 417–430.

NICHCY. (2009). *Categories of disability under IDEA*. Wasington, DC: National Dissemination Center for Children with Disabilities. Retrieved September 28, 2010 from www.nichy.org/Disabilties/Specific/pages/healthimpairment.aspx

Orelove, F. P., & Sobsey, D. (1987). *Educating children with multiple disabilities: A transdiciplinary approach*. Baltimore: Brookes Publishing.

Porterfield, S. L. (2002). Work choices of mothers in families with children with disabilities. *Journal of Marriage and Family, 64*, 972–981.

Powers, E. T. (2003). Children's health and maternal work activity: Estimates under alternative disability definitions. *The Journal of Human Resources, 38*(3), 523–556.

Rehabilitation Research & Training Center on Independent Living Management. (2002). *Disability rights timeline (rev.)*. Buffalo, NY: National Institute on Disability and Rehabilitation Research, U.S. Department of Education.

Reynolds, C. R., & Clark, J. H. (1983). *Assessment and programming for young children with low incidence handicaps*. New York: Plenum.

Rothstein, L. F. (2000). *Special education law* (3rd ed.). New York: Addison Wesley Longman, Inc.

Rosenzweig, J. M., & Huffstutter, K. J. (2004). Disclosure and reciprocity: On the job strategies for taking care of business and family. *Focal Point: A National Bulletin on Family Support and Children's Mental Health, 18*(1), 4–7.

Rosenzweig, J. M., Brennan, E. M., & Ogilvie, A. M. (2002). Work–family fit: Voices of parents of children with emotional and behavioral disorders. *Social Work, 47*(4), 415–424.

Roundtree, L., & Lynch, K. (2006). *Exploring the complexities of exceptional caregiving. Executive briefing series.* Boston: Boston College, Center for Work & Family.

Safford, P. L., & Safford, E. J. (1996). *A history of childhood and disability.* New York: Teachers College Press.

Snell, M. (1983). *Systematic instruction of the moderately and severely handicapped* (2nd ed.). Columbus, OH: Merrill.

Taras, H., & Potts-Datema, W. (2005). Chronic health conditions and student performance at school. *Journal of School Health, 75,* 290–353.

Turnbull, A. P. (1983). Parent professional interactions. In: M. Snell (Ed.), *Systematic instruction of the moderately and severely handicapped* (2nd ed., pp. 14–43). Columbus, OH: Merrill.

Yell, M. L. (2006). *The law and special education* (2nd ed.). Upper Saddle River, NJ: Prentice Hall.

CHAPTER 12

THE HISTORY OF GIFTEDNESS AND TALENT DEVELOPMENT

Michelle J. McCollin

OVERVIEW OF THE EVOLUTION OF GIFTED EDUCATION

Societal interest in individuals with high aptitudes, gifts, talents, and extraordinary abilities dates back thousands of years, perhaps as early as 3000 BC. For example, "as early as Biblical times, prophets and learned men were extolled for their wisdom and leadership. Plato likewise accorded positions of supremacy to certain individuals based on their superior endowment of intelligence. Even in the Dark and Middle Ages, generally considered inhibitory of talent and innovation, some members of society were ennobled for their intellectual and religious acumen" (Kaufmann, Castellanos, & Rotatori, 1986, p. 232). Some societies identified children with promise and potential and provided them with special education (Freeman, 1979). This was the case with the Emperor Charlemagne who in 800 AD requested that the state provide and pay for such education for children from the common masses (Schwenn, 1985).

Gifted education was also valued in the early history of the United States. For example, Thomas Jefferson submitted a bill "The Diffusion of Education" in the early 1800s to provide funding for a university education for promising students (Schwenn, 1985). However, it was not until the mid-nineteenth century, that the first large-scale public academic program for the

History of Special Education
Advances in Special Education, Volume 21, 289–313
Copyright © 2011 by Emerald Group Publishing Limited
All rights of reproduction in any form reserved
ISSN: 0270-4013/doi:10.1108/S0270-4013(2011)0000021015

gifted was established in St. Louis in 1868 (Passow, Goldberg, Tannenbaum, & French, 1955). However, in the late 1800s, a number of studies (Lombrosco, 1891; Nisbet, 1891) promoted the connection between genius and abnormality (Kaufmann et al., 1986). Fortunately, these findings were dismissed by researchers (Hollingworth, 1942; Terman, 1925) in the early 1900s.

In Western cultures, interest in gifted and talented has been closely associated with intelligence (Daniels, 2003; McCollin & Daniels, 2010). This theme occurred in the works of Charles Darwin and Sir Francis Galton in the 1800s. In fact, Galton strongly expressed that genius was hereditary in his books, *Hereditary Genius* (1869) and *English Man of Science* (1874). This association became much stronger during the early 1900s when French psychologists Alfred Binét and Theodore Simon (Binet & Simon, 1905) were commissioned to construct a test, Binet–Simon Scales (BSS), for the public schools to determine the educability of students based on intellectual ability. Goddard (1908) published the English translation of the BSS. He viewed the BSS as a useful diagnostic instrument in the assessment of school-aged children with limited abilities for their placement into especially created classroom with specifically trained teachers (Kelley, Sexton, & Surbeck, 1990). Goddard (1920) went on to discuss how intelligence was highly inheritable for both children with mental deficiencies and giftedness. Unfortunately, his intelligence studies (see Goddard, 1913, 1916, 1917) on immigrants and feeblemindedness were found to be highly problematic due to research protocol and control aspects, the bias in the test, and his strong opinion "that testing could create a better society order and that human progress was but a mental test away" (Kelley et al., 1990, p. 16).

Terman (1925) revised and standardized the BSS for use in the United States and published the test, namely, the Stanford-Binet Intelligence Scale (SBIS) in 1916. Terman's major contribution was the concept of intelligence quotient (IQ) which involved a ratio of mental age to chronological age. Using IQ as a basis, Terman stressed that to be considered gifted, a student would need to score an IQ of 140 or better on the SBIC or a similar intelligence scale. Similar to Goddard (1920), Terman viewed cognitive capacity is a genetically fixed entity that manifested itself in a predetermined unfolding of behavioral patterns (Senn, 1975). According to Daniels (2003), this view was too narrow and lead to considerable controversy and studies by researchers that disagreed with this conceptualization. Table 1 provides a sampling of these researchers and their views on intelligence.

While the terms gifted and talented are often used interchangeably throughout the literature, there are some conceptual differences between these two concepts. Gagné (1985, 1991) differentiated the concepts by defining

Table 1. Research on Intelligence that Challenged Terman's Ideas.

Researcher	Concepts
Spearman (1927)	Proposed that intelligence was composed of a general factor and 16 specific factors.
Thurstone (1938)	Proposed that intelligence consisted of a set of primary mental abilities and multiply traits.
Wechsler (1939)	Stressed that intelligence is derived from multifaceted abilities and personality related factors.
Guilford (1967)	Stressed multidimensional aspects (operations, products, content) and 120 independent factors that associated with intelligence and creativity.
Piaget (1954)	Intelligence is a kind of evolving biological adaptation to the outside world that involves an interconnection between maturation and learning.
Cattell (1971)	Two separate types of intelligence (fluid and crystallized). Intelligence is influenced by exposure to a particular culture and formal and informal education.
Sternberg (1985)	Intelligence has three elements – metacomponents, performance components, and knowledge acquisition. It stresses an information-processing approach.
Gardner (1993)	Proposed a multifactor model of intelligence that is composed of seven primary abilities – two of which have interpersonal and intrapersonal dimensions (i.e., emotional intelligence).

"giftedness" as above average competence in natural, untrained, spontaneous, human ability (aptitude, intellectual, or creative abilities) and "talent" as above average competence in an area or field of human activity (e.g., mathematics, music) which manifests itself when the individual engages in systematic learning, training, and practicing.

Early twentieth-century giftedness studies emanated from research on the (a) methods and instructional practices for children who were gifted, (b) inheritance of "mental incompetence," (c) below normal academic achievement among children, (d) development of assessment instruments to measure both the below and above average intelligence, and (e) realization that public schools could not adequately meet the needs of all children who are able to work through the curriculum faster, and whose work is measurably different from that of average students (Coleman & Cross, 2005). Lewis M. Terman and Leta Hollingworth (Hollingworth, 1942; Terman, 1925) noted influential pioneers in the field of gifted education, conducted a comprehensive research study of 1500 gifted individuals in the 1920s that drew attention to the identification, education, and nurturing of students with gifts and talents. They believed that nurturing academically exceptional children was an essential component to our country's success. Their studies dispelled many of the negative ideas that society had about gifted individuals (Bacto, Milan, Litton, Rotatori, & Carlson, 1991).

In spite of these early works, it was the 1957 launch of the Russian space capsule "Sputnik" by the Soviet Union that stimulated momentum in the gifted education movement in the United States. This historical event was viewed as a risk to national security. Not only did it provoke the United States to rethink the quality of American schooling, it also led to the passage of the National Defense Education Act in 1958; the appropriation of federal funding for the establishment of programs for gifted students; the development of ways to identify students with superior abilities and high academic achievement (particularly in math and science); and research to identify effective methods for providing quality educational experiences to gifted students. Bacto et al. (1991) stressed that this momentum lead to more earnest studies on creativity (see Getzels & Jackson, 1961; Torrance, 1960, 1962, 1963) and the development of the Torrance Test of Creative Thinking (Torrance, 1966).

CONCEPTUALIZING GIFTEDNESS AND TALENT

During the late 1960s, emphasis on the education of gifted students shifted and took a back seat to civil rights and antipoverty movement concerns on educational equity and the improvement of schools of at-risk students. However, starting in the 1970s and continuing to the present, National interests in the education of gifted and talented students became important again and led to the commission of several highly publicized reports such as the *Marland Report* (1972), *A Nation at Risk* (Commission on Excellence in Education, 1983), *National Excellence* (1993), and *A Nation Deceived* (Colangelo, Assouline, & Gross, 2004), passage of legislative acts such as The Jacob K. Javits Gifted and Talented Student Education Act (Javits Act) (1988) and the No Child Left Behind Act (NCLB) (2001) and the establishment of a National Center on Gifted and Talented 1990.

The highly acclaimed *Marland Report* (1972), defined giftedness as capacity for high performance, demonstrated achievement and/or potential ability in any of the areas of general intellectual ability, specific academic aptitude, creative or productive thinking, leadership, visual and performing arts, and psychomotor abilities. The report also provided assessments of the needs of gifted students and resulted in direct assistance to gifted education and the establishment of the U.S. Office of the Gifted and Talented. This report's definition of giftedness continues to be the foundation of many gifted programs in most school districts and state departments of education across the country (Karnes & Beane, 2009). The 1983 *A Nation at Risk* report presented startling data that indicated that students in the United States were no longer receiving a superior education, and could not compete globally (Coleman & Cross, 2005). VanTassel-Baska and Brown (2009) indicated that recommendations from the above reports included but were not limited to: standards for identification and servicing of gifted students, increasing services to gifted education programs, improving curriculum enrichment, and creating accelerated instructional approaches.

In 1988, Congress passed the Javits Act. This act provided financial support and resources for (1) the Office of Gifted and Talented Education, (2) a national research center focused on gifted children, and (3) demonstration projects in gifted education. The Jarvis Act had three major components: research on effective methods of assessment; appropriate identification components; and instructional programming that focused on underrepresented populations of gifted students. In 1990, the Jarvis Act provided funding for the National Center on Gifted and Talented (see Daniels & McCollin, 2010; McCollin & Daniels, 2010; Turnbull, Turnbull, Shank, & Smith, 2004). This center was comprised of a consortium of universities. The center's focus was to address research needs in the field.

In 1993, the second national report on the status of educating gifted and talented students was issued by the U.S. Department of Education, Office of Educational Research and Improvement. This report, *National Excellence: The Case for Developing America's Talent*, described the state of gifted education as being a "quite crisis" and identified a number of indicators that pointed to the need for America to change the way it educates gifted and talented youth and those with the potential for high abilities. The report found that gifted education still suffered from a lack of highly qualified teachers, questionable methods for identifying gifted students, weak curriculum standards, limited learning opportunities for economically disadvantaged and culturally and linguistically diverse (CLD) children, and a failure of the educational system to challenge gifted and talented youngsters to work to their full potential. It also questioned the ability of America's youth to compete in a global economy.

In 1994, the Javits Act was reauthorized, but the funding appropriated was significantly reduced as a result of Congressional party changes and the differing political and philosophical views of its constituents. In 2001, the Javits Act was again reauthorized. This reauthorization was contained in the No Child Left Behind Act (NCLB) of 2001 (P.L. 107-110).

NCLB is a historic law that was formerly known as The Elementary and Secondary Act (ESEA). President George W. Bush signed it into law on January 8, 2002. It was enacted to eliminate the achievement gap that exists among students in U.S. schools and ensure that children of all racial, ethnic, cultural and socioeconomic backgrounds, and children with exceptional learning needs (e.g., children with disabilities; children who are gifted and talented) have a fair, equal, and significant opportunity to obtain a high-quality education, and be taught by highly qualified teachers.

In 2004, *A Nation Deceived: How Schools Hold Back America's Brightest Students* described the advantages of accelerated programs for gifted and talented students. This work further highlighted America's inability to effectively address the academic, psychosocial, and emotional needs of its most able students in spite of the overwhelming research supporting accelerated programming and differentiated instructional practice (Callahan, 2005).

The above reports and laws emphasized how gifted and talented concepts have varied over time and throughout different sociocultural contexts. Our present day understanding, description and perception of giftedness and talented has evolved significantly over the last 40 years due to above aspects (Smith, Polloway, Patton, & Dowdy, 2004; VanTassel-Baska & Brown, 2009). Yet even with this more comprehensive conceptualization of gifted and talented, one can find a range of personal beliefs about the word "gifted" by educators that elicits multiple meanings and much nuance. Hopefully, the twenty-first century will provide an opportunity to add to the conceptualization of gifted and talented that enhances the education of children who are gifted and talented.

CHARACTERISTICS OF GIFTED AND TALENTED

The study of giftedness involves the investigation of cognitive, affective, intuitive, and psychomotor attributes. Much of the research on giftedness (e.g., Clark, 2008; Hallahan & Kauffman, 2003; Plucker & Callahan, 2008; Smith et al., 2004) describes gifted and talented children as manifesting a wide range of abilities, including accelerated cognitive and intuitive abilities, a phenomenal memory, excellent recall, visual and performing abilities, and psychomotor intelligence. These children also have the ability to quickly acquire, retain, conceptualize, synthesize, and learn new information; as well as the ability to easily process and manipulate large amounts of information at an accelerated pace.

Gifted and talented children are also highly inquisitive. Not only do they enjoy learning, they also have a strong desire to learn and an intense need for mental stimulation (Robinson & Campbell, 2010). They have the innate ability to learn faster and are more intent and focused on pursuing their interests, a capacity for seeing unusual and diverse relationships, as well as an unusual ability to think abstractly (Gross, 2004). These children also possess superior problem-solving skills, can easily apply and transfer knowledge to new situations, and show an interest in a wide range of topics and disciplines (Eyre, 2009).

Additionally, gifted and talented children are also able to expand their understanding of concepts in a number of ways, including their ability to connect with other ideas (e.g., see the relationship between concepts or through their understanding of the perspectives of others). These children are also persistent and goal directed. They are capable of learning more rapidly than their peers and are knowledgeable about things at a much earlier age. They learn to speak early and can talk in sentences using complex sentence structure before the age of two or three. Consequently, gifted and talented children also have high receptive vocabularies and they come to school reading significantly beyond their chronological age-mates (MacIntyre, 2008). Many possess advance verbal abilities, extensive vocabularies, and vivid imaginations. Because of their unique abilities, they often require accelerated instruction and sophisticated instructional materials (see Robinson, Shore, & Enersen, 2006).

Gifted and talented children are also highly motivated and extremely independent. These children are often recognized by their teachers for their superior achievement in one or more academic domains (e.g., reading, math, science) (Rakow, 2005). These children like to take risks, and have a high tolerance for ambiguity. They have a strong dislike for skill and drill activities; and find conventional instructional practices less motivating, less challenging, and less rewarding. Like students with disabilities, there exist both inter and intraindividual differences in their performance. In addition to their high levels of intelligence, some possess high levels of creativity particularly in the visual and performing arts, while others demonstrate outstanding intuitive, leadership, and psychomotor abilities (Van Tassel-Baska, 2009).

Children who are gifted and talented also display unique social and emotional characteristics (Clark, 2008). They hold high expectations of themselves, possess a keen (sometimes subtle) sense of humor, and have a strong sense of self-awareness. These children strive for perfection, are highly focused, and experience enormous stress from failure (Mendaglio & Peterson, 2007). They possess high morals, have a strong sense of justice, and are sensitive to the feelings and needs of others. They also display high energy levels in their work and play which can sometimes be misinterpreted and misdiagnosed by psychologists and other health professionals as a form of hyperactivity or an emotional or behavioral disorder (see Hershey, 1995; Kaufmann et al., 1986; Mendaglio & Peterson, 2007).

The most common misconception about gifted children is that they lack social and emotional competence (Hershey, 1995). While there are some gifted and talented children who feel different, have low self-esteem, are misunderstood or socially isolated, most are well adjusted, sensitive, healthy, emotionally independent, and stable individuals who are well liked by their peers and who possess emotional traits that are well balanced (Freeman, 2010). It should be noted that the characteristics presented here are only examples of attributes of children with gifts and talents and should not be considered as exhaustive. Not every child identified as gifted or talented will display all of these traits.

GIFTEDNESS AND TALENT: DEFINED

Over the years, many theorists, psychologists, researchers, and practitioners have not only grappled with the concept of giftedness but have also proposed numerous definitions of giftedness. For example, Terman (1925) favored a definition that rested on measured ability alone, whereas other researchers (DeHaan & Havighurst, 1957; Marland, 1972) preferred to identify students who are gifted based on the highest percentages in an ability area (i.e., cognitive functioning, academics, creativity, fine arts). In addition, researchers like Renzullo (1978) delineated a multifaceted and interactive nature of giftedness which included high intelligence, creativity, and task commitment (Kaufmann, 1990). Similar to Renzullo's view, Tannenbaum (1983) addressed the need to include variables such as nomination factors, special ability, environment, and chance (Kaufmann et al., 1990). Lastly, Clark (1983) stressed that the definition of giftedness include biological factors (i.e., brain function and activity). Yet, none have been universally accepted as a standard definitional criterion to describe the extraordinary gifts, remarkable talents, and outstandingly high level of abilities and potentialities of children and youth.

The problems associated with the definition of giftedness stems from multiple sources, including the differing theoretical views on giftedness; the wide range of characteristics associated with children having extraordinary skills, abilities, aptitudes, and talents; the varying definitions of giftedness (e.g., psychometric definitions, trait definitions, educationally oriented definitions); the variance across cultures as to what is considered giftedness; the various terminologies used; and ongoing research in the field (Daniels, 2003).

Although interpretations of the word "gifted" seem limitless, there are a handful of foundational definitions that may be categorized from conservative (related to demonstrated high IQ) to liberal (a broadened conception that includes multiple criteria that might not be measured through an IQ test). The first federal definition of giftedness was introduced in the 1972 *Marland Report*. This report identified six categories of giftedness, encouraged schools to define giftedness broadly (i.e., to extend beyond intellectual ability), and provided the catalyst for the development of a U.S. Office of Gifted and Talented. The report also served as the foundation upon which gifted educational programs are built. According to the *Marland Report*:

> Gifted and talented children are defined as those identified by professionally qualified persons who by virtue of outstanding abilities, are capable of high performance. These are children who require differentiated educational programs and/or services beyond those normally provided by the regular school program in order to realize their contribution to self and society. (p. 2)

The report further enumerates that:

> Children capable of high performance are those who demonstrate any of the following abilities or aptitudes, singly or in combination in any of the following areas: (1) general intellectual ability, (2) specific academic aptitude, (3) creative or productive thinking, (4) leadership ability, (5) visual and performing arts aptitude, and (6) psychomotor ability. (p. 2)

The most current federal definition of giftedness can be found in the No Child Left Behind Act of 2001. Under NCLB:

> The term "gifted and talented", when used with respect to students, children, or youth, means students, children, or youth who give evidence of high achievement capability in areas such as intellectual, creative, artistic, or leadership capacity, or in specific academic fields, and who need services or activities not ordinarily provided by the school in order to fully develop those capabilities. (Title IX, Part A, Section 9101(22), p. 1959)

While federal definitions of giftedness have been criticized over the years (e.g., not providing school districts with the specificity needed to guide professionals in the identification of students with gifts and talents; emphasizing performance as the defining characteristic of giftedness; not placing an emphasis on observable behaviors), many school districts still base their definition of giftedness on federal definitions (Daniels, 2003; McCollin & Daniels, 2010).

Perhaps the most influential contemporary definition of gifted is that proposed by the National Association for Gifted Children (NAGC), an organization composed of parents, teachers, and educators, other professionals, and community leaders. According to the NAGC:

> A gifted person is someone who shows, or has the potential for showing, an exceptional level of performance in one or more areas of expression.
>
> Some of these abilities are very general and can affect a broad spectrum of the person's life, such as leadership skills or the ability to think creatively. Some are very specific talents and are only evident in particular circumstances, such as a special aptitude in mathematics, science, or music. The term *giftedness* provides a general reference to this spectrum of abilities without being specific or dependent on a single measure or index ...

The NAGC further states:

> A person's giftedness should not be confused with the means by which giftedness is observed or assessed. Parent, teacher, or student recommendations, a high mark on an examination, or a high IQ score are not giftedness; they may be a signal that giftedness exists. Some of these indices of giftedness are more sensitive than others to differences in the person's environment. (NAGC, 1990, retrieved June 2, 2010, from http://www.nagc.org)

Thus, definitions of giftedness can reflect a broad array of purposes. They may be used to identify and count children to establish prevalence estimates; diagnose, label, and place students in specially designed accelerated or enrichment programs; enable professionals, parents, and others to communicate effectively about students who have high abilities or talents; serve as a medium to establishing priorities for funding educational or support programs; and facilitate legislative efforts on behalf of gifted and talented individuals (Daniels, 2003; Daniels & McCollin, 2010).

INTELLIGENCE AND GIFTEDNESS

Given what we know about the nature versus nurture argument as it related to human development and intelligence, it is not surprising that giftedness is considered to result from both genetic and environmental influences (Daniels, 2003; Friend, 2005). The correlation between intelligence and gifted education continues to impact our decision-making regarding curriculum models implemented in the school district. Intelligence theories affect the way in which we identify and assess students, our attitudes toward giftedness and gifted students, the curriculum models upon which we base our programs and interventions, and many other aspects of gifted education.

Research in the areas of gifted and talented has been closely linked with intelligence studies (Plucker, 2001). Many scholars concerned with matters of intelligence also focused on manifestations of talent and genius: Terman (1925) initiated long-term studies in giftedness; and Hollingworth (1942) pioneered work with exceptional children and women; Renzulli (1979) concentrated on distinguishing between real world and academic giftedness; Feldman (1980) looked at developmental trajectories unique to each intellectual domain; Gardner (1993) implemented multiple intelligences as a model; Gagné (1985) focused on the differences between giftedness as potential and talent as fulfillment of potential; and Sternberg (1985) examined the types of gifted abilities, as well as the strengths and weaknesses of intelligence, to name just a few. Many of these theories dominate and bridge the chasm between intelligence and gifted education.

INTELLIGENCE AND CURRICULUM MODELS

Connecting intelligence theories to curriculum models requires a juxtapositioning of the theories into a specific curricular model. VanTassel-Baska and Brown (2009) define curricular models as a curriculum design and development framework that provides a systematic approach to developing an appropriate curriculum for the target population. This curricular model must include in its framework the ability to identify curriculum product elements. In order for the model to be effective, it must possess differentiation, flexibility, transferability and usability across content areas, age/grade span, and flexible grouping models. Additionally, it must delineate ways in which it responds to the particular needs of the gifted individual. The models are descriptive and do not validate the most effective method for maximizing student development in a specific time or space. Each of the curricular models discussed below has more than ten years of supportive research, development, and implementation undergirding its pervasive use, endurance, and research attention (Coleman & Cross, 2005; VanTassel-Baska & Brown, 2009).

The Stanley Model of Talent Identification (Stanley, Keating, & Fox, 1974). This model focuses on lifelong education for the individual. Model principles include: (1) utilization of assessment instruments that encourage high-level verbal and mathematical reasoning; (2) diagnostic instructional methodologies; (3) accelerated and fast-paced core content; and (4) flexible curriculum across the school environment. This content-based model is aligned with National standards, is highly sustainable, and demonstrates the benefits of acceleration for advancement.

A Three Stage Model of Gifted Education (Feldhusen & Kolloff, 1978). This model has three levels of instructional activity that can be used intermittently. Stage one activities focus on fundamental divergent and convergent cognitive activities. Stage two uses more complex and creative problem-solving instructional activities, which require increased initiative from the student and less teacher control. Stage three creates the opportunity for students to work on challenging, independent research projects with others or independently.

The Renzuilli Schoolwide Enrichment Triad Model (SEM) (Renzulli, 1986). The major principles of the SEM model are supported by (1) use of interest and learning style inventories to assess inter and extracurricular abilities; (2) provision of curriculum compacting (i.e., the regular curriculum is modified by eliminating mastered content, and substituting alternative work); and (3) accessing of an appropriate triad level based on students' abilities, interest, and task commitment. The SEM has three enrichment levels. *Enrichment level 1* consists of general exploratory experiences (e.g., guest speakers, field trips, interest centers, etc.). *Enrichment level 2* includes instructional strategies designed to promote thinking. *Enrichment level 3* utilizes analytical activities and creative productions that support primary inquiry and thinking.

Gardner's Multiple Intelligences (MI) (Gardner, 1983). The MI uses a core curricula approach employing the multidimensional concept of intelligence (Gardner, 1983). According to Gardner (1983), there are eight types of intelligence, namely, (1) verbal/linguistic, (2) logical/mathematical, (3) visual/spatial, (4) musical/rhythmic, (5) bodily/kinesthetic, (6) interpersonal, (7) intrapersonal, and (8) naturalistic. The MI curricula model has been used as the base curriculum for new schools, identification of individual differences, and evaluation.

The Schlichter Models for Talents Unlimited Inc. and Talents Unlimited to the Secondary Power (TU) (Schlichter, 1981). Talents unlimited was based upon Guilford's (1967) inquiry into the nature of intelligence. Talent Unlimited features four major components which include: (1) a demonstration of talents, productive thinking, decision-making, and academic abilities; (2) instructional materials; (3) in-service professional development for teachers; and (4) assessment of students' thinking skills development (Schlichter, 1986). The model has been noted for developing student's creative and critical thinking.

Sternberg's Triarchic Componential Model (STCM) (Sternberg, 1985). The SCTM is based upon information processing intelligence theory (Sternberg, 1985). This model incorporates three components of the mental processes used in thinking, namely, executive, performance and knowledge acquisition. The *executive process component* is involved in planning, decision-making, and monitoring performance. The *performance component processes* facilitate executive problem-solving strategies. The *knowledge-acquisition component* facilitates the acquisition, retainment, and transference of new information. This model supports the concept that interaction and feedback between the individual and his or her environment within any given context allows cognitive development to occur.

VanTassel-Baska's Integrated Curriculum Model (ICM) (VanTassel-Baska, 1986). The ICM, which was developed for high-ability learners, is based upon three dimensions: (1) *advanced content*; (2) *high-level process and product work*; and (3) *divergent and convergent thought development and understanding*. The ICM uses advanced curricula and accelerated rates of instruction in core subject areas. It is supported by an over 30 years of research that demonstrate the effectiveness of enrichment-oriented models with gifted and talented students (see VanTassel-Baska & Brown, 2009).

Decisions as to which curricular model to implement should be consistent with general premises of general school policy. It is important that the model support students' understanding of reality; recognize curriculum alternatives based on various gifts and talents; and be responsive to the effect of student choices (Coleman & Cross, 2005). Additional research on using differentiated curricular approaches in gifted programs is needed.

DIFFERENTIATING INSTRUCTION AS AN INTEGRATIVE MODEL

The most powerful models of instruction are accelerated, interactive, and differentiated. Differentiation is defined by the individualized learning needs of children who are gifted and talented; the specific content and skill sets of the curriculum; the pedagogy used to convey the content; and the flexible settings needed to effectively implement the curriculum (Kaplan, 2005; VanTassel-Baska & Brown, 2009). Differentiated instruction encourages the learner to construct and produce knowledge in meaningful ways. Within the construct of differentiated instruction, students engage in generating original products, collaborative construction of knowledge, and problem-based learning. Differentiated strategies include but are not limited to:

individual and group summarizing; investigation of divergent perspectives, higher order critical thinking; brainstorming; Socratic dialogue; problem-solving processes; and team teaching.

Differentiated curriculum for gifted students is based on the strengths of the learners and the inability of the core curriculum to meet the needs of this population. The analysis of the skill sets of students who are gifted and talented with respect to the core curriculum traditional content, processes, and product components justifies the rationale for a differentiated curriculum.

Differentiated core curriculum programs for students who are gifted and talented should stimulate the development of students' actual and potential abilities as well as their skills, creativity, and talents. Instructional strategies for students who are gifted and talented, utilize several curriculum modifications to meet the challenges faced by inadequacy of the core curriculum. These modifications include: higher levels of thinking, open-discovery learning, and evidence of reasoning, freedom of choice, group interaction, pacing/acceleration, and variety of processes. By implementing these elements to modify the core curriculum, teachers have an opportunity to present content related to comprehensive, broad-based issues; integrate multiple disciplines; allow for in-depth self-selected learning; develop independent study skills; focus on open-ended tasks; develop research methods; encourage the development of new products and techniques; self-understanding; and self-directedness.

While there are a number of strategies and approaches that can be used to effectively deliver instructional services to students who are gifted and talented, the intent of this section was to share information on some of the strategies and approaches commonly used by school districts. It is important to keep in mind that all programs for students who are gifted and talented, regardless of grade level or how the curriculum model used, must provide for the use of flexible teaching strategies, multiple venues for students to reach their learning and creative potentials, continuous measures to assess progress, collaborative construction of knowledge through peer and teacher interactions, continuity, and highly qualified teachers with specialized training in the areas of gifted and talented teaching strategies.

ASSESSMENT OF GIFTED AND TALENTED

Over the past 100 years, assessment and accountability have played significant roles in the educational reform movement in the United States. In the early 1900s, several assessments instruments were designed solely for the selection of assessment of giftedness and placement in higher education programs (e.g., Terman's 1916 Stanford Binet, the Terman Concept Mastery Test, and the original SAT). After the 1960s, assessments were used to identify students for gifted and talented programs; provide feedback regarding instructional strategies; and determine whether intended goals were achieved (Heward, 2008; Salvia & Ysseldyke, 2001). Identification and classification of students for gifted and talented programs should be based on multifactored, multidimensional, multicultural, and comprehensive methods that access various sources of giftedness and talent. This approach includes but is not limited to data from:

- Individual and group intelligent tests
- Achievement tests
- Portfolios and or demonstrations of student work/talent
- Teacher nomination
- Parent nomination
- Self-nomination
- Peer nomination
- Extracurricular or leisure activities.

Collecting and compiling profile data on each student is necessary for the implementation of an effective differentiated program for the gifted student (see VanTassel-Baska, & Feng, 2004). Hence careful assessment of an individual student's ability, aptitude, interests, and personal values is critical and necessary to that student's success in a gifted program (Hunt & Seney, 2009). These assessments must include but not be limited to data from a student's (a) cumulative records, (b) screening and identification information, (c) intelligence tests, (d) affective instruments (e.g., learning styles inventories, personality types), and (e) portfolios (Coleman & Cross, 2005). And because the use of assessments play such an integral role in the identification and placement process of students with gifts and talents, educators have a responsibility to ensure that all testing is conducted in a fair and ethical manner. The goal of fair and ethical testing can be achieved through the utilization of various assessment vehicles that allow educators to take into account individual variables such as variations in cultural and economic backgrounds, educational experiences, abilities and talents; content knowledge, skill sets, interests, and personalities. Therefore, allowing a student's program to truly be individualized and meet their academic and emotional needs.

Underrepresented Groups in Gifted Programs and Assessments

There has been an historical underrepresentation of socioeconomically disadvantaged students and those from CLD backgrounds in programs for academically talented students (Castellano & Frazier, 2010; Donovan & Cross, 2002; Scott & Delgado, 2005; Van Tassel-Baska, 2009; Yoon & Gentry, 2009). Attempts to address this disparity have been complicated by recurring erroneous beliefs about the (a) nature of academic giftedness and talent; (b) use and analysis of traditional assessments of ability and achievement commonly used in the identification of gifted students, (c) the use of alternative assessments with low-income and CLD gifted students such as nonverbal ability tests, and (d) kinds of the educational programs that have developed to serve gifted students (Gallagher, 2005; Lohman, 2005; Milner & Ford, 2007). Assessments selected for use in the identification of gifted students must be:

• culturally responsive to and appropriate for the characteristics of the students being assessed;
• inclusive of students from CLD and socioeconomic backgrounds;
• psychometrically sound;
• normed accordingly for the population of students and programs; and
• used appropriately (see Lohman, 2005).

It is, however, of utmost importance that educators and policymakers understand that alternatives to traditional assessments are not the universal remedy to the issue of underrepresentation. Each assessment is imbued with its own issues and limitations with regard to reliability and validity – and therefore should by no means be used in isolation to identify children with gifts and talents.

Types of Assessments

The variety of measures used to assess abilities and skill sets vary by dimension assessed such as the:

• standardization (e.g., using national samples, local samples);
• response format (e.g., producing a response, selecting a response from a predetermined set);
• presentation the material (e.g., paper-and-pencil, computerized, oral); and
• subject matter (e.g., mathematics) or construct (e.g., creativity) (see Lohman, 2005; Salvia & Ysseldyke, 2001).

The following assessments are often utilized in identifying and placing students with gifts and talents into specialized academic programs.

1. *Objective-type instruments:* These types of selected-response assessments include nationally norm-referenced standardized paper-and-pencil or computerized tests to locally normed and developed tests (e.g., school-based aptitude and achievement tests, IQ tests).
2. *Performance assessments:* These types of constructed–response/demonstration assessments include performance assessments, authentic assessments, and portfolios (e.g., dance performance, extended response items, write a response to a prompt, artifacts highlighting best work).
3. *Rating scales, interviews:* These types of observational assessments include collections of students' behaviors, characteristics, and useful supplemental data on talents that may not be apparent through conventional aptitude or achievement assessments (see NAGC, 2007).

Protocols for Using Assessments for Identification Purposes

Notwithstanding the type of assessments used for identification and placement of students with gifts and talents, there are several protocols that must be in place for effectiveness in assessment. These include:

- Assessment tools utilized must be aligned with the definition of giftedness determined by the educational entity.
- Identification of gifted and talented students should be based on multiple pieces of psychometrically sound data obtained from a variety of sources rather than a single assessment.
- Testing environment should allow the student the ability to fully demonstrate his or her knowledge, skill sets, and abilities.
- School personnel should be well informed regarding the technical documentation, administration, and scoring of each assessment (NAGC, 2007). Table 2 provides a sample of commonly used assessment devices.

FAMILIES OF THE GIFTED AND TALENTED

Family involvement is an essential component to the academic success of gifted and talented students (see Kaufmann et al., 1986). These family units represent the most important socializing agency in the life of the child and as

Table 2. A Sample of Assessment Devices Used with the Gifted and Talented.

Name of Device	Age Range	Content Area
Creativity assessment packet (CAP) (Williams, 1980)	6–18 years	Cognitive factors (fluency, flexibility, originality, vocabulary, comprehension elaboration).
Gifted and talented evaluation scales (GATES) (Gilliam, Carpenter, & Christensen, 1996)	5–18 years	Characteristics, cognitive skills, and talents.
Profile of creative abilities (PCA) (Ryser, 2007)	5 to 14–11 years	Creative thinking, drawings, naming categories, fluency, flexibility, originality, sensitivity to problems, task motivation.
Screening assessment for gifted elementary and middle students-Second edition (SAGES-2) (Johnsen & Corn, 2001)	5 to 14–11 years	Reasoning, achievement (math, science, language arts, social studies).
Test of mathematical abilities for gifted students (TOMAGS) (Ryser & Johnsen, 1998)	Grades K through 6	Giftedness in math (number-sense, operations, systems, computations, estimation, patterns and relationships) geometry and algebra.

such have a definitive influence on decisions that impact the life trajectory of the student; and even have a significant impact on the family once giftedness has been established. Most gifted children come from backgrounds that encourage the development of giftedness (i.e., opportunity for learning; continuous encouragement and resources). Parents of gifted children (a) know raising them is both a blessing and a challenge; (b) see themselves as responsible for making sure the family functions efficiently; and (c) are accountable for the development of the child's gifts and talents (Coleman & Cross, 2005; NAGC, 2007).

Parents, as the first and most important teacher and advocate, quickly recognize that a child may be gifted and want to foster those gifts and talents. Some of the early examples of giftedness include: (a) an unusual alertness in infancy, (b) recognizing caretakers early, (c) advancement through the developmental milestones, (d) early and extensive language development, and (e) curiosity.

Interestingly, all parents want the best for their children but may be conflicted as to the most suitable course to follow for their gifted and talented child (Coleman & Cross, 2005). And because of the inaccuracies in the early childhood identification process, many parents may experience feelings of dissatisfaction, frustration, and confusion as to (1) what their roles and responsibilities are to the gifted child and (2) how best to present this information to the rest of the family and its impact on their functioning as a whole unit (Hunt & Seney, 2009). Therefore, it is critical that parents gain insights into what giftedness means to them so that they may maintain a practical point of view on both the family unit and individual members.

Gifted students experience asynchronous development (i.e., being out of sync socially, emotionally, physically, and academically) that creates unique experiences that are quite different from the norm. Moreover with increased intellectual capacity the gifted child becomes more asynchronous; hence, developmentally vulnerable, requiring greater parental, instructional, and counseling accommodations (Coleman & Cross, 2005; Hershey, 1995; Hunt & Seney, 2009; Mendaglio & Peterson, 2007; Vondrak & Rotatori, 1995). When parents are aware of the inherent developmental differences of their children they can prepare themselves to act as responsive advocates.

GIFTED IN A DIGITAL ENVIRONMENT

Today's students are living in an ever-changing world of technology and communication, requiring a level of digital literacy that surpasses that of previous generations. Twenty-first century digital literacy demands that students be adept at using technology in an academic and thought provoking manner – thinking critically, creative problem-solving, creating new technologies, and process voluminous amounts of information found in a variety of locations, including the Internet (Burke, 2007; Burkhardt, 2003). Today's students, native in this digital environ, exist in an era of instantaneous communications, infinite information, and continuously changing technologies that results in the need for schools to prepare its students beyond the basic 3Rs of reading, writing, and arithmetic. Twenty-first century literacy demands individuals employ effective communication, inventive thinking, and digital age literacy, creative higher order thinking skills, collaborative work skill sets, and facility with varying technologies. Students with gifts and talents characteristically possess skill sets that are aligned with and improved by current technologies, and it is critical that educators incorporate various technologies within their pedagogy and classroom environments (Porter, 2006; Siegle, 2005).

Technology is constantly changing. Today's student is a native in a digital world to which adults can only hope to gain permission to enter (Porter, 2006; Prensky, 2001; Siegle, 2005). Cell phones are now utilized as cameras, camcorders, computers, music players, televisions, and organizers. Instant messaging, text messaging, and blogging make communication with effortless. The student with gifts and talents gifted is able to seamlessly integrate technology into daily interactions. Therefore providing gifted students with mere access to today's technologies is not enough; educators must apply various learning theories and technologies to be innovative and successful.

Schools have become incompatible with the modern world – many classrooms remain in the nineteenth and twentieth centuries while the outside world is a rapidly evolving matrix of technology and communication. To ignore the presence of technology and the student's interest in technology would be negligent. If we are to successfully prepare, engage, and facilitate gifted students into and beyond the twenty-first century, our pedagogies and methodologies must effectively incorporate the new multimedia technologies and communication vehicles used by these students.

REFERENCES

Bacto, M., Milan, C., Litton, F., Rotatori, A. F., & Carlson, J. (1991). The gifted and the talented. In: J. O. Schwenn, A. F. Rotatori & R. A. Fox (Eds), *Understanding students with high incidence exceptionalities* (pp. 205–234). Charles C. Thomas.

Binet, A., & Simon, T. (1905). New methods for determining the intellectual capacity of people with mental retardation. *L'Annee Psychogique, 11*, 192–244.

Burke, L. (2007). 21st century technology for school administrators. In: F. E. Obiakor, A. F. Rotatori & S. Burkhardt (Eds), *Current perspectives in special education administration* (Vol. 17, pp. 81–200). London: Elsevier Sciences.

Burkhardt, G., Monsour, M., Valdez, G., Gunn, C., Dawson, M., Lemke, C., Coughlin, E., Thadani, V., & Martin, C. (2003). 21st century skills: Literacy in the digital age. Available at http://www.ncrel.org/engauge/skills/engauge21st.pdf. Retrieved on June 10, 2010.

Callahan, C. M. (2005). Identifying gifted students from underrepresented populations. *Theory into Practice, 44*(2), 98–104.

Castellano, J., & Frazier, A. D. (2010). *Special populations in gifted education.* Waco, TX: Prufrock Press.

Cattell, R. B. (1971). *Abilities: Their structure, growth and action.* Boston: Houghton Mifflin.

Clark, B. (1983). *Growing up gifted* (2nd ed.). Columbus, OH: Merrill.

Clark, B. (2008). *Growing up gifted: Developing the potential of children at home and at school* (7th ed.). Upper Saddle River, NJ: Prentice Hall.

Colangelo, N., Assouline, S., & Gross, M. U. M. (2004). *A nation deceived: How schools hold back America's brightest students* (Vol. I). Iowa City, IA: The Connie Belin & Jacqueline N. Blank International Center for Gifted Education and Talent Development.

Coleman, L., & Cross, T. (2005). *Being gifted* (2nd ed.). Waco, TX: Prufrock Press.

Daniels, V. I. (2003). Students with gifts and talents. In: F. E. Obiakor, C. A. Utley & A. F. Rotatori (Eds), *Effective education for learners with exceptionalities* (Vol. 15, pp. 325–348). Oxford: Elsevier Science Ltd.

Daniels, V. I., & McCollin, M. J. (2010). Gifted and exceptional. In: M. Baker, L. McGaw & P. Peterson (Eds), *International encyclopedia of education* (pp. 588–593). London: Elsevier Press.

Dehaan, R., & Havighurst, R. J. (1957). *Educating the gifted.* Chicago: University of Chicago Press.

Donovan, M. S., & Cross, C. T. (Eds). (2002). *Minority students in special and gifted education.* Washington, DC: National Academy Press.

Eyre, D. (2009). *Gifted and talented education.* New York: Routledge.

Feldhusen, J. F., & Kolloff, M. B. (1978). A three stage model for gifted education: Multi-service program. *Journal for the gifted, 6*(4), 230–244.

Feldman, D. H. (1980). *Beyond universals in cognitive development.* Norwood, NJ: Ablex.

Freeman, J. (1979). *Gifted children.* Austin, TX: PRO-ED.

Freeman, J. (2010). *Gifted lives: What happens when gifted children grow up.* New York: Routledge.

Friend, M. (2005). *Special education: Contemporary perspectives for school professionals.* Boston: Pearson.

Gagné, F. (1985). Giftedness and talent: Reexamining a reexamination of the definitions. *Gifted Child Quarterly, 29*(3), 103–112.

Gagné, F. (1991). Toward a differentiated model of giftedness and talent. In: N. Colangelo & G. A. Davis (Eds), *Handbook of gifted education* (pp. 65–80). Boston: Allyn & Bacon.

Gallagher, J. J. (2005). According to Jim Gallagher: The role of race in gifted education. *Roeper Review, 27*(3), 135.

Galton, F. (1869). *Hereditary genius.* London: MacMillan.

Galton, F. (1874). *English man of science.* New York: Appleton.

Gardner, H. (1983). *Frames of mind: The theory of multiply intelligences.* New York: Basic Books.

Gardner, H. (1993). *Multiple intelligences: The theory in practice.* New York: Basic Books.

Getzels, J., & Jackson, F. (1961). Family environment and cognitive style: A study of the sources of intelligent and highly creative adolescents. *American Sociological Review, 26*, 351–359.

Gilliam, J. E., Carpenter, B. O., & Christensen, J. R. (1996). *Gifted and talented evaluation scales (GATES).* Austin, TX: PRO-ED.

Goddard, H. H. (1908). The Binet and Simon tests of intellectual capacity. *Training School, 5*, 3–9.

Goddard, H. H. (1913). The Binet tests in relation to immigration. *Journal of Psych-Aesthetics, 18*, 146–155.

Goddard, H. H. (1916). *Feeblemindedness.* New York: MacMillan.

Goddard, H. H. (1917). Mental tests and the immigrant. *Journal of Delinquency, 2*, 243–277.

Goddard, H. H. (1920). *Human efficiency and levels of intelligence.* Princeton, NJ: Princeton University Press.

Gross, M. (2004). *Exceptionally gifted children.* New York: Routledge.

Guilford, J. (1967). *The nature of human intelligence.* New York: McGraw-Hill.

Hallahan, D., & Kauffman, J. (2003). *Exceptional learners: Introduction to special education* (9th ed.). Boston: Allyn and Bacon.

Hershey, M. (1995). Social emotional needs of youth with gifts and talents. In: A. F. Rotatori, J. O. Schwenn & F. W. Litton (Eds), *Counseling special education populations: Research and practice perspectives* (pp. 167–190). Greenwich, CT: JAI Press Inc.

Heward, W. L. (2008). *Exceptional children: An introduction to special education* (9th ed.). Upper Saddle River, NJ: Prentice Hall.

Hollingworth, L. (1942). *Children above 180 IQ (Stanford Binet): Origin and development.* New York: World Book.

Hunt, B. G., & Seney, R. W. (2009). Planning the learning environment. In: F. A. Karnes & S. M. Beane (Eds), *Methods and materials for teaching the gifted* (pp. 37–74). Waco, TX: Prufrock Press.

Johnsen, S. K., & Corn, A. (2001). *Screening assessment for gifted elementary and middle school students-Second Edition (SAGES-2).* Austin, TX: PRO-ED.

Kaplan, S. (2005). Layering differentiated curricula for the gifted and talented. In: F. A. Karnes & S. M. Bean (Eds), *Methods and materials for teaching the gifted* (pp. 107–135). Waco, TX: Prufrock Press.

Karnes, F. A., & Beane, S. (2009). *Methods and materials for teaching the gifted.* Waco, TX: Prufrock Press, Inc.

Kaufman, A. S. (1990). *Assessing adolescent and adult intelligence.* Needham Heights, MA: Allyn and Bacon.

Kaufmann, F. A., Castellanos, F. X., & Rotatori, A. F. (1986). Counseling the gifted child. In: A. F. Rotatori, P. J. Gerber, F. W. Litton & R. A. Fox (Eds), *Counseling exceptional students* (pp. 232–251). New York: Human Sciences Press Inc.

Kelley, M. F., Sexton, D., & Surbeck, E. (1990). Traditional psychometric assessment approaches. In: A. F. Rotatori, R. A. Fox, D. Sexton & J. Miller (Eds), *Comprehensive assessment in special education* (p. 528). Springfield, IL: Charles C. Thomas.

Lohman, D. F. (2005). The role of nonverbal ability tests in the identification of academically gifted students: An aptitude perspective. *Gifted Child Quarterly, 49,* 111–138.

Lombrosco, C. (1891). *The men of genius.* London: Robert Scott.

MacIntyre, C. (2008). *Gifted and talented children 4-11: Understanding and supporting their development.* New York: Routledge.

Marland, S. P. (1972). *Education of the gifted and talented.* Report to the Congress of the United States by the U.S. Commissioner of Education. U.S. Government Printing Office, Washington, DC.

Mendaglio, S., & Peterson, J. S. (2007). *Models of counseling gifted children, adolescents, and young adults.* Waco, TX: Prufrock Press.

McCollin, M. J., & Daniels, V. I. (2010). Programs and instruction for gifted and talented. In: M. Baker, M. L. McGaw & L. P. Peterson (Eds), *International Encyclopedia of Education* (pp. 829–833). London: Elsevier Press.

Milner, H. R., & Ford, D. Y. (2007). Cultural considerations in the underrepresentation of culturally diverse elementary students in gifted education. *Roeper Review, 29,* 166–173.

National Association for Gifted Students. (1990). Giftedness and the gifted? What's it all about? *ERIC EC Digest #E476*. Reston, VA: ERIC Clearinghouse on Handicapped and Gifted Children.

National Association for Gifted Children and Council of State Directors of Programs for the Gifted. (2007). *State of the states in gifted education 2006–2007*. Washington, DC: Author.

Nisbet, J. (1891). *The insanity of genius*. London: Kegan Paul, Trench, Trubner.

No Child Left Behind Act of 2001 P.L. 107-110, § 115, Stat. 1425 (2002).

Passow, A. H., Goldberg, M., Tannenbaum, A. J., & French, W. (1955). *Planning for talented youth*. New York: Teachers College, Bureau of Publications.

Piaget, J. (1954). *The construction of reality upon the child*. New York: Basic Books.

Plucker, J. (2001). Looking back, looking around, looking forward: The impact of intelligence theories on gifted education. *Roeper Review, 23*, 124–125.

Plucker, J., & Callahan, C. C. (2008). *Critical issues and practices in gifted education*. Waco, TX: Prufrock Press.

Porter, B. (2006). Beyond words: The craftsmanship of digital products. *Learning and Leading with Technology, 33*(8), 28–31.

Prensky, M. (2001). Digital natives, digital immigrants. Available at http://www.marcprensky.com/writing. Retrieved on June 11, 2010.

Rakow, S. (2005). *Educating gifted students in middle school: A practical guide*. Waco, TX: Prufrock Press.

Renzullo, J. S. (1978). What makes giftedness? Reexamining a definition. *Phi Delta Kappan, 60*, 180–184.

Renzulli, J. S. (1979). Some concerns about educational acceleration for intellectually talented youth, or are treadmills really different if we run them at a faster rate? In: W. C. George, S. J. Cohn & J. Stanley (Eds), *Educating the gifted: Acceleration and enrichment* (pp. 190–191). Baltimore, MD: John Hopkins University Press.

Renzulli, J. (1986). The three ring conception of giftedness: A developmental model for creative productivity. In: R. J. Sternberg & J. E. Davidson (Eds), *Conceptions of giftedness* (pp. 53–92). New York: Cambridge University Press.

Robinson, A., Shore, B. M., & Enersen, D. (2006). *Best practices in gifted education*. Waco, TX: Prufrock Press.

Robinson, W., & Campbell, J. (2010). *Effective teaching in gifted education: Using a whole school approach*. Waco, TX: Prufrock Press.

Ryser, G. R. (2007). *Profile of creative abilities (PCA)*. Austin, TX: PRO-ED.

Ryser, G. R., & Johnsen, S. (1998). *Test of mathematical abilities for gifted students (TOMAGS)*. Austin, TX: PRO-ED.

Salvia, J., & Ysseldyke, J. E. (2001). *Assessment* (8th ed.). Boston: Houghton Mifflin.

Schlichter, C. (1981). The multiple talent approach in mainstream and gifted programs. *Exceptional Children, 48*, 144–180.

Schlichter, C. L. (1986). Talents unlimited: Applying the multiple talent approach in mainstream and gifted programs. In: J. S. Renzulli (Ed.), *Systems and models for developing programs for gifted and talented* (pp. 352–390). Mansfield Center, CT: Creative Learning Press.

Schwenn, J. O. (1985). Assessment of giftedness and talented, and creativity. In: A. F. Rotatori & R. Fox (Eds), *Assessment for regular and special education teachers* (pp. 407–428). Austin, TX: PRO-ED.

Scott, M. S., & Delgado, C. F. (2005). Identifying cognitively gifted minority students in preschool. *Gifted Child Quarterly, 49*, 199–210.

Senn, M. J. E. (1975). Insight on the child development movement in the United States. *Monograph of the Society for Research on Child Development, 40*, 161–165.

Siegle, D. (2005). *Using media & technology with gifted learners.* Waco, TX: Prufrock Press.

Smith, T., Polloway, E., Patton, J., & Dowdy, C. (2004). *Teaching students with special needs in inclusive setting* (4th ed.). Boston: Pearson.

Spearman, C. (1927). *The abilities of man.* New York: MacMillan.

Stanley, J. C., Keating, D., & Fox, L. (1974). *Mathematical talent.* Baltimore, MD: Johns Hopkins University Press.

Sternberg, J. (1985). *Beyond IQ: A triarchic theory of human intelligence.* Cambridge, UK: Cambridge University Press.

Tannenbaum, A. (1983). *Gifted children: Psychological and educational perspectives.* New York: MacMillan.

Terman, L. (1925). *Mental and physical traits of a thousand gifted children: Genetic studies of genius* (Vol. 1). Stanford, CA: Stanford University Press.

The Commission on Excellence in Education. (1983). *Nation at risk: The imperative for educational reform.* Washington, DC: Author.

Thurstone, L. L. (1938). *Primary mental abilities.* Chicago: University of Chicago Press.

Torrance, E. P. (1960). *The Minnesota studies of creative thinking in the early years.* University of Minnesota Research Memorandum (No. 59-4). Minneapolis, MN: University of Minnesota Press.

Torrance, E. P. (1962). *Guiding creative talent.* Englewood Cliffs, NJ: Prentice Hall.

Torrance, E. P. (1963). Education and creativity. In: C. W. Taylor (Ed.), *Creativity: Progress and potential* (pp. 40–67). Minneapolis, MN: University of Minnesota Press.

Torrance, E. P. (1966). *Torrance tests of creative thinking: Norms-technical manual.* Princeton, NJ: Personnel Press.

Turnbull, R., Turnbull, A., Shank, M., & Smith, S. (2004). *Exceptional lives: Special education in today's schools* (4th ed.). Boston: Pearson.

U.S. Congress. *National Defense Education Act*, P.L. 85-864. (1958). Washington, DC: Government Printing Office.

U.S. Congress. *Jacob K. Javits Gifted and Talented Children and Youth Education Act*, P. L. 100-297. (1988). Washington, DC: Government Printing Office.

U.S. Department of Education, National Commission on Excellence in Education. (1983). *A nation at risk: An imperative for educational reform.* Washington, DC: Government Printing Office.

U.S. Department of Education, Office of Educational Research and Improvement. (1993). *National excellence: A case for developing America's talent.* Washington, DC: Government Printing Office.

VanTassel-Baska, J. (1986). Effective curriculum and instruction model for talented students. *Gifted Child Quarterly, 30*, 164–169.

Van Tassel-Baska, J. (2009). *Content-based curriculum for high-ability learners* (2nd ed.). Waco, TX: Prufrock Press.

VanTassel-Baska, J., & Brown, E. (2009). An analysis of gifted education curriculum models. In: F. A. Karnes & S. M. Beane (Eds), *Methods and materials for teaching the gifted* (pp. 75–106). Waco, TX: Prufrock Press.

VanTassel-Baska, J., & Feng, A. X. (2004). *Designing and utilizing evaluation for gifted program evaluation.* Waco, TX: Prufrock Press.

Vondrak, R. S., & Rotatori, A. F. (1995). Issues related to counseling gifted females. *ICA Quarterly, 137,* 23–34.

Wechsler, D. (1939). *The measurement of adult intelligence.* Baltimore, MD: Williams & Wilkins.

Williams, F. (1980). *Creativity assessment packet (CAP).* Austin, TX: PTO-ED.

Yoon, S., & Gentry, M. (2009). Racial and ethnic representation in gifted programs: Current status of and implications for gifted Asian American students. *Gifted Child Quarterly, 53*(2), 121–136.

CHAPTER 13

HISTORY OF TRAUMATIC BRAIN INJURY

Anthony F. Rotatori and Sandra Burkhardt

EARLY BEGINNINGS

While traumatic brain injury (TBI) became a special education category within the Individuals with Disabilities Education Act (IDEA) in 1990, societies have dealt with TBI far back in history. According to Granacher (2007), there have been writings about the examination of skulls from battlefields in which a hole was drilled into the skull using a trepanning tool apparently to provide some physical relief for the injured soldier. Interestingly, Levin, Benton, and Grossman (1982) stated that this tool continued to be part of Medieval and Renaissance surgeons' practice. At that time, the surgeons believed that trepanation was a vital procedure to improve the brain pulsations and hence the overall well-being of the person with a TBI; however, the medical effectiveness of this procedure did not materialize and it was replaced by brain surgery in the 20th century (Levin et al., 1982).

As physicians dealt with more individuals with TBI in the Middle Ages, they began to describe physical effects of TBI, such as loss of mobility, sensory capacity, and mental functions (see Sanchez & Burridge, 2007). In addition, the medical profession began classifying TBI symptoms while routinely using the term concussion (Zillmer, Scheider, Tinker, & Kaminaris, 2006). By the 16th century, a system for classifying concussion symptoms in terms of severity was delineated (see Levin et al., 1982). This was followed by

History of Special Education
Advances in Special Education, Volume 21, 315–342
Copyright © 2011 by Emerald Group Publishing Limited
ISSN: 0270-4013/doi:10.1108/S0270-4013(2011)0000021016

the generation of hypotheses for a concussion in the 18th century (McCrory & Berkovic, 2001). In the 19th century, physicians discovered petechial hemorrhagic lesions in patients with severe TBI that led to these being posited as the basis of concussion (Zillmer et al., 2006). Additionally, in that century, the literature reveals the relationship between TBI and the development of psychosis and significant personality changes of injured persons (see Corcoran, McAlister, & Maspina, 2005).

MODERN TIMES

World War I led to improved medical care for returning soldiers who sustained TBI from explosive blasts. With this improvement, TBI patients were admitted to rehabilitation facilities. This created an opportunity for medical personnel to describe the physiological and psychological changes that patients with TBI displayed. Psychological changes that were reported included alterations in social, emotional, cognitive, and personality aspects (see Max et al., 2005; Tyler & Savage, 2003). Since that time, those observed alterations have been substantiated in numerous modern-day studies (Busch, McBribe, Curtiss, & Vanderploeg, 2005; Kim, 2002; Milders, Fuchs, & Crawford, 2003).

An outgrowth of the medical treatment of World War I veterans was psychological efforts to assist these veterans with the following problems: high distractibility, poor ability to attend to relevant cues, mental confusion, and hyperactivity. A pioneer in this work with adults with TBI was Kurt Goldstein who developed a renowned clinic for brain-damaged soldiers called the *Institute for Research in the After Effects of Brain Injury* (see Smith, 2004). Research from Goldstein's (1927, 1939) clinic led to the premise that factors existed that differentiate organically impaired individuals from nonbrained injured individuals, namely the following: loss of abstraction ability, deficits in reasoning ability, and inflexibility in problem-solving tasks (see Cohen & Swerdlik, 2009). Goldstein and his investigators developed a number of devices and tests to identify brain injury, such as the *Goldstein–Scheerer Tests of Abstract and Concrete Thinking* (see Cohen & Swerdlik, 2009). While these tests are out of print, they laid the foundation for present-day neuropsychological assessment devices concerned with measuring recent memory, nonverbal abstraction, flexibility in thinking, and concrete thinking.

In the 1930s and 1940s, Werner and Strauss (1941) expanded on Goldstein's work at the Wayne County Training School in Michigan with pupils diagnosed with educable mental retardation who were thought to be brain injured (see Franklin, 1987). These authors believed that the pupils' brain injury resulted in disturbed, unrestrained, and volatile behavior which prevented them from learning from a traditional curriculum at that time. Based on this premise, Strauss and Kephart (see Franklin, 1987) expanded this work to include children of normal intelligence who were thought to be brain injured. Based on these studies, Strauss and Lechtinen (1947) recommended in their book *Psychopathology and Education of the Brain-Injured Child* that children with TBI be educated using highly structured instructional approaches. In this book, the authors delineated a list of characteristics common to all brain-injured children that remain relevant today.

According to Cohen and Swerdlik (2009), Strauss and Lechtinen's book led to a "better understanding of the behavioral consequences of brain injured children, however, one unfortunate consequence was that a unitary picture of brain injury emerged, namely, that all organic children were presumed to share a similar pattern of behavioral, sensory, and motor deficits regardless of the specific nature or site of their impairment" (p. 449). Another problem with Strauss and Kephart investigations became evident when Kavale and Forness (1985) reanalyzed their original studies on brain-injured children and concluded that the sample size was too small to justify their findings. Furthermore, these studies were criticized because the authors did not provide any evidence of brain damage or other neurological dysfunctions (see Franklin, 1987). Apparently, the brain damage was only inferred from the children's behavior. While the above studies have research weaknesses, Smith (2004) commented that the children described in the Strauss and Lechtinen (1947) study had many characteristics observed in today's children with TBI.

Another pioneering researcher in the field of organic dysfunction was Ward Halstead. He founded a laboratory in 1935 to study the impact of brain function on a diverse continuum of human abilities (Kaplan & Saccuzzo, 2009). Along with his graduate student, Ralph Reitan, numerous laboratory observations and studies were carried out seeking to describe brain function characteristics. Their work examined the usefulness of available assessment devices for the above. Halstead concluded that the assessment of the inadequacy of brain function required a wide battery of tests. From that premise, Halstead and Reitan went on to develop the Halstead–Reitan procedures which led to a comprehensive battery entitled the *Halstead–Reitan Neuropsychological Battery* (*HRNB*) (see Reitan & Wolfson, 1993).

In the 1960s, a number of investigators (see Haynes & Sells, 1963) emphasized that organicity and brain damage should not be considered to be a unitary concept and that children with TBI could exhibit different sets of behavioral characteristics (see Cohen & Swerdlik, 2009). From that period, TBI was viewed as nonunitary in nature and led to a more comprehensive conceptualization of TBI which resulted in more divergent medical and neuropsychological diagnostic procedures to determine the site and the severity of damage (Cohen & Swerdlik, 2009).

Prior to 1990, students with TBI did not have a special education eligibility category but they did receive special education instruction under a category that most closely matched their basic educational needs, such as a student with mild mental retardation or learning disability (Smith, 2004; Tyler & Savage, 2003). Unfortunately, Tyler and Savage (2003) stressed that children with TBI were sometimes misclassified which delayed effective instructional practices for them. Positively, students today who exhibit TBI characteristics briefly after an injury can receive instructional accommodations under Section 504 of the Rehabilitation Act.

DEFINING TBI

When examining the definition of TBI, professionals can focus on the educational definition offered by federal special education law (IDEA, 1990) or medical definitions such as those purposed by the World Health Organization's International Statistical Classification of Diseases and Related Health Problems-Tenth Revision (ICD-10) (see Cassidy et al., 2004), the American Congress of Rehabilitative Medicine (see Comper, Bisschop, Carnide, & Tricco, 2005), or the American Psychiatric Association's (APA) Diagnostic and Statistical Manual of Mental Disorders, Fourth Edition-Revised (see APA, DSM-IV-R, 2004).

The most comprehensive and inclusive educational definition of TBI comes from Public Law 101-476, the Individuals with Disabilities Education Act (IDEA, 1990) which defines TBI as "an acquired injury to the brain caused by an external physical force, resulting in total or partial functional disability or psychological impairment or both, that adversely affects a child's educational performance. The term applies to open or closed head injuries resulting in impairments in one or more areas, such as cognition; language, memory; attention; reasoning; abstract thinking; judgment; problem-solving; sensory; perceptual, and motor abilities; psycho-social behavior; physical functions, information processing; and speech. The term does not apply to brain injuries induced by birth trauma" 34 Code of Federal Regulations* 300.7 (c) (12). According to Tyler and Savage (2003), most state educational associations use the above federal definition; however, some states use a broader definition (see Markowitz & Linehan, 2001).

In general, medical definitions define TBI as "damage to the brain resulting from external mechanical force, such as rapid, acceleration, or deceleration, impact, blast waves, or penetration by a projectile" (Maas, Stocchetti, & Bullock, 2008, p. 728). Furthermore, this external force may result in brain activity that is temporarily or permanently impaired and structural damage (Parikh, Koch, & Narayan, 2007). TBI is sometimes referred to in the medical literature as intracranial injury or head injury (Centers for Disease Control and Prevention) (CDC, 2008). However, head injury is considered a much broader term as it can involve damage to structures other than the brain, such as the scalp and skull (Hardman & Manoukian, 2002).

Brain trauma can be one of three types, namely, *concussion, contusion,* and *laceration* (Burkhardt, 1995). A concussion is a frequently used medical term for TBI (Shaw, 2002); however, many professionals tend to refer to a concussion as a mild traumatic brain injury (MTBI) (see Pearce, 2007). MTBI (concussion) can have temporary effects; however, repeated MTBIs can have a cumulative effect (Kushner, 1998). While many individuals lose consciousness when they sustain a brain trauma, a concussion is not always present in TBI (Ghajar, 2000). TBI may also involve a contusion which is the bruising of brain tissue due to the brain being pounded against the skull (Burkhardt, 1995). Contusions can result in coma and bleeding and cognitive impairment upon waking (Burkhardt, 1995). Lastly, TBI may involve a laceration which is the projection of a foreign object into the brain with subsequent tearing of the brain tissue (Burkhardt, 1995). Lacerations can result in death, permanent significant brain dysfunction, or sometimes no noticeable effects for the individual (Burkhardt, 1995).

Brain damage caused by a stroke, brain tumor, or infection is not considered TBI under the IDEA definition (Burkhardt & Rotatori, 2008). Similarly, brain injury that does not result from a stroke or infection is referred to as *nontraumatic brain* injury by medical professionals. The term does not apply to brain injuries that are congenital or degenerative (Burkhardt & Rotatori, 2008). Brain injury that was not caused by trauma such as near drowning, near suffocation, throat swelling, choking, strangulation, or crush injuries to the chest is referred to as *acquired brain injury* (ABI) and is not considered TBI (Thurman, Sniezek, Johnson, Greenspan, & Smith, 1994). However, the educational and medical rehabilitation necessary to treat ABI is often similar to that of individuals with TBI (Tatzmann, Clancy, & Reagan, 2006). Both the educational and medical definitions recognize that brain injury that leads to TBI may not be visible via medical procedures such as EEGs or brain-imaging techniques (e.g., computed tomography (CT) scans or magnetic resonance imaging (MRI)) (Tyler & Savage, 2003).

The educational and medical literature on TBI classify the brain damage of an individual based on severity, namely, mild, moderate, or severe (see Tyler & Savage, 2003; Valadla, 2004). Generally, the severity of the brain injury rating increases based upon signs of concussion aftereffects and loss of consciousness (Tyler & Savage, 2003). The longer the unconsciousness period, the more severe is the rating. A common scale that is used to assess teenagers and adults is the Glasgow Coma Scale (GCS) (see Tyler & Savage, 2003). Children's severity of TBI is measured using scales similar to the GCS which are adapted for utilization for children, such as the "Children's Coma Scale" and the "Children's Rancho Los Amigos Recovery Scale" (see Cantu, 2001; Tyler & Savage, 2003; Valadla, 2004). Tyler and Savage (2003) caution that medical definitions of severity "may not be the best predictors of outcome or potential for school-related problems ... as children with mild TBI may experience problems months or years after the injury that are just as disabling as problems experienced by students with more severe injuries" (p. 302).

EDUCATING STUDENTS WITH TBI

The education of students with TBI is comprehensive due to the complexity of their educational and medical needs which can change rapidly depending on their recovery process (see Arroyos-Jurado & Savage, 2008; Bowen, 2005; Glang et al., 2008). In fact, it is recommended that a student with TBI has short-term IEP (Individual Education Plan) goals and objectives (e.g., 2 month) and more frequent assessment of their academic progress (Harvey, 2006). Tyler and Savage (2003) developed an education model that integrates special education curriculum concepts, rehabilitation services, and recommended practices that facilitate innovative TBI therapies. In their model, Tyler and Savage delineate procedures to prepare students with TBI for school reentry; specifications for developing a meaningful IEP; and specific instructional interventions for the following: attention/concentration, memory, organization, following directions, and behavioral interventions.

While teachers may find traditional special education instructional strategies effective for students with TBI, other strategies which are more specific to their unique characteristics (e.g., fatigue, short attention, poor concentration, paralysis, thought perseveration, emotional liability, aphasia, agraphia, alexia, dyscalculia, color and movement agnosia, prosopagnosia, vertigo) may need to be incorporated into the curriculum (see Bullock, Gable, & Mohr, 2005; Glang, 1993; Harvey, 2006: Keyser-Marcus et al., 2002; Mayfield & Homack, 2005). In essence, Tyler and Savage (2003) stress that the model of instruction for students with TBI needs to be cohesive and fully integrate best-practice rehabilitation and special education instructional strategies such that students with TBI are "taught not only what to learn (i.e., academic content), but also how to learn it (i.e., information processing)" (p. 310).

Burkhardt and Rotatori (2010) recommend the use of customized programming for students with TBI; however, the effectiveness of the programming is dependent on the special education teachers' familiarity with TBI. Some recommended customized strategies that have been implemented with students with TBI include the following: multimodal instruction, frequent use of review and repetition, task analysis to support skill acquisition, color coding of instructional materials, customized checklists, and breaking down assignments into smaller components (see Bowen, 2005; Keyser-Marcus et al., 2002).

More generalized instructional strategies that have been used for students with TBI to increase academic acquisition and reduce interfering emotional behaviors include continuous positive behavior supports (CPBS) (see Dykeman, 2003) and positive behavior interventions and supports (PBIS) (see Anderson & Warzak, 2000; Todd, Horner, Vanater, & Schneider, 1997; Wheeler & Martin, 2010; Ylvisaker, Jacobs, & Feency, 2003). CPBS is a continuous constructive behavioral management procedure that provides students experiencing behavioral and emotional difficulties with positive reinforcement for appropriate behavior (Burkhardt & Rotatori, 2007). Teachers using CPBS for students with TBI construct a behavioral contract which specifies appropriate behavior that will be reinforced and undesirable behavior that will be punished (Burkhardt & Rotatori, 2010). In essence, CPSB assists educators in reducing undesirable behavior that impedes a student with TBI adjustment while targeting behaviors that will enhance their recovery.

PBIS is a behavioral management procedure for students with challenging behaviors that is endorsed by 1997 IDEA (U.S. Department of Education, 2005). It involves an application of validated research practices to enhance teaching (Wheeler & Martin, 2010). Burkhardt and Rotatori (2008) stress that the purpose of PBIS is to provide a student with TBI proactive behaviors to reduce inappropriate behaviors that may stem from their TBI. It begins with a functional behavioral assessment to identify events that set off and maintain a problem behavior. Based upon this assessment, a positive intervention is constructed to increase the student's appropriate behavior utilizing the following procedures: positive reinforcement (e.g., praise for calm behavior); environmental supports (e.g., reminders prior to an event); and self-control strategies (e.g., self-monitor, self-assessment, self-instruction, self-reinforcement).

Tyler and Savage (2003) delineated other research-supported generalized instructional approaches that have been used with students who have TBI. These include Deshler's *Strategy Instruction* (Deshler, Ellis, & Lenz, 1996), *Directed Instruction*, and *Circle of Friends* (Cooley, Glang, & Voss, 1997; Glang, Singer, Cooley, & Tish, 1992). When using specific and/or generalized instructional strategies with students who have TBI, educators may want to utilize accommodations such as those delineated in Table 1.

WORKING WITH FAMILIES

Working with families of school-aged children with TBI can be divided into the following adjustment periods: *initial incident and stabilization, inpatient rehabilitation and at home recovery*, and *reentry into school*. Families of children with TBI are put into an overwhelming situation when a child sustains a serious head injury. Initially, parents are challenged by the medical treatment (i.e., coma, hospitalization, MRI, surgery) that their children may have to undergo as well as being questioned by police or child welfare social service agencies regarding how the child sustained the head injury (Burkhardt, 1995). Families need professionals to orientate them about the severity of the child's condition, the pros and cons of various medical treatments and procedures, hospitalization aspects, and the overall prognosis (Tyler & Savage, 2003). During the initial incident and stabilization period, families experience an "emotional roller coaster" (see Burkhardt, 1995) as they are uncertain whether the child may live or die and whether a medical procedure will be successful. Relief comes when it is determined that the child will live and medical intervention brings about stabilization (Burkhardt, 1995). Families experience a flood of relief; however, this is replaced by questions concerned with how "normal" the child will be (Burkhardt, 1995).

Once the child's medical condition has been stabilized, inpatient rehabilitation recovery procedures are implemented followed by home care. The inpatient rehabilitation progress of children with TBI varies considerably. Some children with TBI recover with few physical setbacks. In

Table 1. Useful Instructional Strategies and Accommodations for Students with TBI.

Strategy	Purpose
Shorten the school day	Reduces fatigue
Schedule time for physical rest	Reduces fatigue, increases concentration
Have academics first	Increases attention and concentration
Use a buddy system	Provides social support, assists student in keeping track of schedule, refamiliarizes student with school life
Repeat, review, and get frequent feedback	Decreases short-term memory loss
Use both oral and written instructions	Increases information that is lost due to sensory deficits
Use assistive technology – computer talking boards, software	Aids physical agility that has been compromised
Offer accommodations – more time to complete tasks, allow for oral feedback by student, increased use of demonstrations	Allows for better cognitive processing, provides students with another means of communicating, augments grasp of material being taught
Have consistent routines	Reduces emotional liability because student knows what to expect
Reduce distractions	Increases attention to task at hand
Have student kept an assignment book?	Increases organization
Use a tape recorder, sticky notes	Assists in memory
Calendars as self-reminders	
Teach students to categorize or chunk information	Aids retention
Demonstrate techniques, such as mental rehearsal as reminders	Improves memory
Be flexible about expectations	Increases chances for success
Develop coordinated outlines to class lectures	Aids organization
Use written checklists of learning steps for complex tasks	Aids in organization
Rewrite complex directions into simple steps	Aids in following directions
Frequently ask student to repeat instructions to teacher or peer	Aids in following directions
Underline or highlight parts of directions on written assignments	Aids in following directions
Link new academic content to student's relevant prior knowledge	Aids memory

Adapted and modified from NICHY (2006); Tatzmann et al. (2006) Tyler, Blosser, and DePompei (1999); and Tyler and Savage (2003).

contrast, other children with TBI take much longer to recover and have more physical setbacks as well as transitional problems related to weekend home visits (Klomes, 2000). This is a trying time for families and most need considerable support form hospital support staff and medical professionals (Burkhardt, 1995).

Once the child has been approved to go home, families have to put forth a substantial amount of care and vigilance that includes caring for the child's immediate medical needs and daily living aspects, implementing recommended home rehabilitation procedures, and planning reentry into school. During this period, families need to work closely with the child's medical team and outpatient care specialists (psychologists, speech language pathologists, and physical and occupational therapists). To more accurately report the child's progress to medical team and outpatient care specialists, professionals have suggested that families track and log their child's treatment recovery progress (National Dissemination Center for Children with Disabilities, 2006).

According to Burkhardt and Rotatori (2008), treatment recovery rates for children with TBI are difficult to assess and research regarding recovery from TBI is limited in general. Additionally, some populations may be systematically omitted from outcome studies due to economic disadvantage because persons without insurance are often not included in follow-up studies (Burkhardt & Rotatori, 2008). To some extent, success during this period is dependent on the mental health characteristics and financial, cognitive capacity of the family. Unfortunately, family characteristics that put a child at risk for TBI (e.g., poverty, teen pregnancy, substance abuse, poor educational opportunities) become risk factors for recovery (Burkhardt & Rotatori, 2007; Youse, Le, Cannizzarod, & Coehlo, 2002). In addition, recovery can be less than optimal due to the economic resources of the family (Burnett et al., 2003). For example, some families have limited insurance coverage which may limit the amount of funds available to treat TBI aspects (see Burnett et al., 2003). Also, poor families may not have any insurance coverage which makes the child's treatment depend on special education school funding or grants from private foundations or brain injury associations (Burkhardt & Rotatori, 2007; CDC, 2004). Additionally, researchers (Keenan, Runyan, & Nocera, 2006; Schwartz et al., 2003) pointed out that families living in poverty and those who are socially disadvantaged have a high incidence of post-injury behavioral problems. Finally, Burkhardt and Rotatori (2008) stressed that (1) brother–sister relationships for children with TBI were of poorer quality than brother–sister dyads of children with orthopedic injuries and (2) behavior problems following TBI for a family member predict sibling behavior problems.

During the recovery period, parents may notice and be challenged by the changes that their children have due to their TBI. These changes may include the following: aggression, overactivity, temper tantrums, apathy, social disinhibition, fatigue, irritability, passive behavior, depression, forgetfulness, poor organizational skills, difficulty following directions, immature behavior, poor planning and problem-solving, and helplessness (Burkhardt & Rotatori, 2007). During the recovery period, parents can become emotionally drained by the changes in their child. At times, this can lead to grief, guilt, and depression about what has been lost (Tyler & Savage, 2003). Also, it is recommended that parents who experience these emotions contact their local child and family service agencies and ask about counseling (Burkhardt, 1995).

The final period of family adjustment involves the reentry of the child with TBI into school (see Klomes, 2000). It is critical that the family utilizes available resources to make this adjustment successful (Mayfield & Homack, 2005). If a child's TBI necessitates special school services, families need to meet with special education school personnel to devise an IEP that will reflect the best practices to assist a child with TBI to successfully navigate school and graduate (see Arroyos-Jurado & Savage, 2008). The IEP should incorporate specific strategies and necessary accommodations that have been found to be effective with children with TBI (see Bowen, 2005; Tatzmann et al., 2006). These may include the following: adjusted schedules; positive behavioral supports; interventions to compensate for memory loss; customized supports for organization; and social regulation (see Bowen, 2005; Gfroerer, Wade, & Wu, 2008; Todis & Glang, 2008). This is critical because 70% of students with TBI eligibility receive high school diplomas which are the second highest rated among learners with disabilities (Burkhardt & Rotatori, 2008).

Families may seek out other health-care specialists to assist school personnel with educational strategies and best practices for instructing and managing their child (see Klomes, 2000). For example, a state brain injury association can consult with teachers regarding programming or the association may provide a link to medical hospitals and centers that treat children with TBI. Other health-care specialists that can be of assistance include psychologists, speech language pathologists, and occupational therapists. Sometimes, the family is not a viable resource for a child with TBI which necessitates that hospital, social service, court, and school personnel handle the school reentry process (Burkhardt & Rotatori, 2007).

NEUROLOGICAL AND NEUROPSYCHOLOGICAL ASSESSMENT OF TBI

The diagnosis of an individual with TBI requires confirmed neurological and neuropsychological assessment evidence. Since the 1970s, there have been considerable advances in medical and neuropsychological procedures for identifying brain injury (see Cohen & Swerdlik, 2009; Kaplan & Saccuzzo, 2009). TBI produces temporary or permanent injury to the site that is traumatized. Igou (2010) provides a listing of symptoms of brain injury based upon traumatized sites (see Table 2).

Typically, an individual, who is suspected of sustaining a TBI, is brought to a hospital where a standard neurological examination is carried out. Generally, this entails an evaluation of an individual's mental status (e.g., state of consciousness, mood, content of thought, intellectual resources); cranial nerves; motor and sensory system; deep tendon reflexes; gait; coordination and cerebellum; and pupil response to light; and calculation

Table 2. Symptoms of Brain Injury Based on Traumatized Site.

Frontal lobe: forehead
Loss of: simple body part movements, spontaneity in interacting with others, and flexibility in thinking. Thought perseveration: difficulty in problem solving and focusing.
Changes in: personality, mood, social behavior, and planning a sequence of complex movements.
Parietal lobe: near the back and top of head
Inability to: attend or name objects, locate the words for writing, or focus visual attention.
Difficulty in: drawing objects, doing math, distinguishing right from left, and eye–hand coordination. Problems in reading.
Occipital lobes: most posterior, at the back of the head
Difficulty with: reading and writing, locating objects in environment, identifying colors, and recognizing drawn objects. Production of hallucinations. Visual illusions. Word blindness. Inability to recognize the movement of objects. Defects in vision.
Temporal lobes: side of the head
Difficulty in: recognizing faces, understanding spoken words, identifying and verbalizing about objects. Short-term memory loss. Interference with long-term memory. Disturbance in selective attention. Increased aggressive behavior. Inability to categorize objects. Persistent talking.
Brain stem: deep within the brain
Decreased capacity to breath, swallow food and water. Insomnia. Sleep apnea. Dizziness and nausea. Difficulty with: organization/perception of the environment, balance, and movement.
Cerebellum: base of the skull
Loss of: walking and coordinating fine movements. Inability to: reach out and grab objects or make rapid movements. Slurred speech. Dizziness. Tremors.

Adapted and modified from Igou (2010).

of a Glasgow Coma Score (Marion, 1999). A number of medical procedures and techniques (see Table 3) can be used to determine the site, characteristics, and severity of the brain damage.

Neurological tests can be used to assess the presenting structure (e.g., MRI, CT) and function (e.g., EEG, PET Scan) of the brain (Maas et al., 2008). CT is readily available at many emergency rooms and can be administered

Table 3. Medical Procedures and Techniques for Diagnosing TBI.

Computed tomography (CT) provides a computed analysis of a series of cross-sectional scans of the brain that results in a three-dimensional image. CT is quick and easily available.

Magnetic resonance imaging (MRI) is a radiology technique that images the brain structure using magnetized radio waves. MRI is more detailed than CT and can provide information on long-term outcome which CT cannot.

Diffuse tensor imaging (DTI) is a refinement of MRI that uses special software to measure the flow of water molecules and tracks the pathway of white matter in the brain. When there has been damage to the white matter, the molecules display a perpendicular movement. DTI is used to identify structural changes in the brain that cannot be viewed using a normal MRI.

Proton magnetic resonance spectroscopy (1H-MRS) is a noninvasive imagery procedure that can provide information about cellular activity in the brain. 1H-MRS can reveal the relationship of brain chemicals in the brain following trauma. In general, certain compounds change in predictable ways when a brain injury has occurred. In addition, it has the potential for detecting diffuse axonal injury.

Magnetization transfer ratio (MTR) is a technique that reveals the difference in signal intensity transfer when using an MRI of the brain. MTR is a type of MRI that is considered more sensitive in detecting abnormalities in the white matter of the brain following trauma.

Quantitative magnetic resonance (QMR) is a technique used in MRI to assess volume or surface area of a brain scan. QMR data can specify a demonstrable reduction in volume or surface area of a brain after TBI.

Contour plot analysis of an MRI is a graphic analysis that projects a dimensional surface area of the brain. This technique adds to the sensitivity of the imaging in detecting signs of TBI.

Positron emission tomography (PET SCAN) is used to identify abnormal areas of the brain that are underutilizing glucose. PET scans are not widely available because cyclotrons are needed to generate the radioactive gas to tag the glucose molecule.

Electroencephalograph (EEG) is a procedure that captures and plots the electrical activity of the brain. An EEG can be used to identify possible seizure activity after a TBI.

Brain stem auditory evolved potential (BSAEP) is a hearing evaluation technique used for the detection of low-amplitude electrical activity. It can be used to detect possible hearing loss in a person with TBI.

X-rays can provide a picture of the brain using electromagnetic radiation. They are mostly used for detecting head trauma. In general, X-rays are not as useful as a CT or MRI in the diagnosis of TBI.

Angiography is a procedure that allows for the viewing of blood vessels after injecting them with a radio plague dye by outlining them on an X-ray. It is very helpful in detecting blood vessel pathology for penetrating head trauma.

Magnetic resonance angiography allows for the visualization of the carotid and vertebral arterial system in the neck and brain without the need to inject a dye into the bloodstream.

Lumbar puncture is a spinal tap that is used to analyze cerebrospinal fluid to assess whether any bleeding is present in the brain and spinal cord areas.

quickly. CT may be re-administered to assess whether the brain damage has progressed. In general, MRI provides more detailed characteristic information about a TBI than CT. In addition, MRI data provides professionals with added information related to expected long-term outcome which can assist them in future medical treatment and educational planning for an individual with TBI. Today, a number of newer procedures based on the MRI technology, such as IH-MRS, DTI, and QMR, have recently been developed that provide medical personnel with greater details about structural damage to the brain.

Neurological assessment of an individual with TBI via modern imaging procedures (e.g., CT, MRI, DTI) has a limited ability in providing insight into his/her psychological functioning (Silver & Blackburn, 2006). However, neuropsychological assessment can provide a wealth of complex information about an individual's functioning in areas such as cognitive, motor, visuospatial, fine motor, attention, academic performance, language, memory, sensory-perceptual, behavioral/emotional, social, life skills, and executive functioning (see Burkhart, Fox, & Rotatori, 1987; Holmes & Holmes, 1996; Silver & Blackburn, 2006). Traditionally, neuropsychological assessment includes a clinical interview, observations of the child, a developmental history, a review of educational and medical records, and the administration of standard educational tests to determine present intellectual and achievement levels, and specialized tests (i.e., executive functioning, memory, sensation, and perception) that evaluate areas of brain functioning (see Burkhardt, 1995: Cohen & Swerdlik, 2009; Holmes & Holmes, 1996). Information from neurological assessments can lead to the confirmation of a TBI diagnosis; specifics about the area in which the brain has been damaged; how the TBI may impact on learning or behavioral/emotional functioning; and the development of appropriate IEP goals and instructional parameters (see Burkhardt, 1995; Burkhardt & Rotatori, 2007, 2010).

Since TBI was added to IDEA (1990) as a categorical area, there has been a noticeable increase in neuropsychological and educational assessment devices available. This increase relates to the types of brain area functions assessed, the background of the examiners (e.g., school psychologists, neuropsychologists, special educators, speech pathologists), and the age range of the devices. Table 4 provides the reader with a variety of neuropsychological devices for assessing TBI based upon the content area and age range.

A number of neuropsychological batteries have been used to assess children with TBI. The HRNB was the first major battery. It was developed by Ward Halstead and Ralph Reitan (see Kaplan & Saccuzzo, 2009). The HRNB battery was based upon the premise that identifying brain

Table 4. Neuropsychological Devices for Assessing TBI.

Name	Age Range	Content Area
Bender Visual–Motor Gestalt Test, Second Edition (Bender Gestalt II, Brannigan & Decker, 2003)	3.0 to 85 + years	Visual–motor integration
Children's Auditory Verbal Learning Test-2 (CAVLT-2) (Talley, 2002)	6.6 to 17.11 years	Verbal learning, immediate memory and recall, delayed recall, recognition, accuracy
Children's Category Test (CCT) (Boll, 1993)	5.0 to 16.0 years	Higher order cognitive abilities – nonverbal
Children's Color Trails Test (CCTT) (Llorente, Williams, Satz, & D'Elia, 2003)	8.0 to 16.0 years	Executive functioning, sustained attention, sequencing
Cognitive Assessment System (CAS) (Naglieri & Das, 1997)	5.0 to 17.11 years	Cognitive processing (planning, attention, simultaneous, successive)
Comprehensive Trail-Making Test (CTMT) (Reynolds, 2002)	8.0 to 74.11 years	Frontal lobe deficits, psychomotor speed deficits, visual search and sequence, attention deficits in setting
Frenchay Dysarthria Assessment, Second Edition (FDA-2) (Enderby & Palmer, 2008)	12 years to adulthood	Motor speech disorders
Halstead–Reitan Neuropsychological Test Battery, Second Edition (HRNB-2, Reitan & Wolfson, 1993)	5.0 years to adults	Abstraction ability, tactual, rhythm, speech sound perception, finger tapping, time sense, sensory motor
Luria–Nebraska Neuropsychological Battery – Children's Revision (LNNB-CR) (Golden, 1984)	8.0 to 12.0 years	Cognition deficits (lateralization and localization of focal brain impairment)
Luria–Nebraska Neuropsychological Battery (LNNB) (Golden, Purisch, & Hammeke, 1986)	15.0 years and older	Cognition deficits (lateralization and localization of focal brain impairment)
Kaufman Speech Praxis Test for Children (KSPT) (Kaufman, 1995)	2.0 to 5.11 years	Motor-speech proficiency
NESPY, Second Edition (NESPY-II) Korkman et al., 2007)	3 to 16 years	Executive functioning/attention, memory and learning, sensory motor, visuospatial, social perception, language
Quick Neurological Screening Test II (QNST-II) (Mutti, Sterling, Martin, & Spalding, 1998)	5.0 to 18.0 years	Neurological integration (identify soft neurological signs affecting learning)
Rey Complex Figure Test and Recognition Trial (RCFT) (Meyer & Meyer, 1996)	6.0 to 89.0 years	Recognition and recall memory, response bias, processing speed, visual–spatial construction ability
Ross Information Processing Assessment-Primary (RIPA-P) (Ross-Swain, 1999)	5.0 to 12.11 years	Cognitive–linguistic deficits
Screening Test for the Luria–Nebraska Neuropsychological Battery (ST-LNNB) (Golden, 1994)	8.0 years to adults	Cognitive deficits

Table 4. (*Continued*)

Name	Age Range	Content Area
Stroop Color and Word Test (Golden & Freshwater, 2002)	5.0 to 14.0 years	Cognitive processing
Test of Memory and Learning, 2nd Edition (TOMAL-2) (Reynolds & Voress, 2007)	5.0 to 59.11 years	General and specific memory functions
Test of Verbal Conceptualization and Fluency (TVCF) (Reynolds & Horton, 2007)	8.0 to 89.0 years	Executive functioning, verbal ability, language functioning
The Dean–Woodcock Neuropsychological Battery (Dean-Woodcock, 2003)	4.0 years and older	Sensory motor functioning
Tower of London, 2nd Edition (TOL-2nd) (Culbertson & Zillmer, 2000)	7.0 to 15.0 years	Frontal lobe damage, attention, executive functioning
Wide Range Assessment of Memory and Learning, 2nd Edition (WRAML-2) (Sheslow & Adams, 2003)	5.0 to 90.0 years	Memory functioning, immediate and delayed acquisition of new learning
Wisconsin Card Sorting Test (WCST) (Grant & Berg, 1993)	6.6 to 89.0 years	Abstract reasoning, perseveration, maintaining set, conceptualizing

dysfunction necessitates the use of a wide variety of tests that can measure specific abilities and characteristics (Kaplan & Saccuzzo, 2009). Halstead and Reitan carried out many studies (see Reitan, 1994) to demonstrate the effectiveness of their battery in pointing out brain dysfunction. The HRNB is now in its second edition and can be administered to children and adults (see Reitan & Wolfson, 1993).

Another early battery for assessing TBI was the Luria–Nebraska Neuropsychological Battery-Children's Revised (LNNB-CR) (Golden, 1984). The LNNB-CR was based upon Luria's (1966, 1973) approach to assessing brain dysfunction. Luria's approach has the premise that the brain is a functional system that has a number of links. When a link is damaged, then brain dysfunction occurs. This approach differs from Halsted and Reitan's in that no single brain area is solely responsible for a specific behavior (see Kaplan & Saccuzzo, 2009). The LNNB-CR takes about one-third the time to administer than the HRNB. However, the HRNB is more widely used by practicing neuropsychologists (see Cohen & Swerdlik, 2009).

Two recently developed batteries are the NESPY-Second Edition (NESPY-II) (Korkman, Kirk, & Kemp, 2007) and the Cognitive Assessment System (CAS) (Naglieri & Das, 1997). The NESPY and CAS are based upon the Luria (1966, 1973) model of brain development. Each is discussed below.

The NESPY-II provides a tailored single-measure assessment device that is compatible with evaluating impairment areas emphasized in the federal definition of TBI. Its six domain areas include the following: executive functioning/attention; language; memory and learning; sensorimotor functioning; visuospatial processing; and social perception. Administration of the NESPY-II results in the following scores and information: standard scores; process scores for each domain; behavioral observations presented as cumulative percentage or base rates; and contrast/compare scores. The manual reports clinical studies for the following populations: TBI; attention-deficit hyperactivity disorder; language disorder; autistic disorder; Asperger's disorder; emotionally disturbed; mathematics disorder; mild intellectual disability; and deaf and hard of hearing. It has a scoring assistant and assessment planner that facilitates scoring and making decisions about which subtests to administer based on the child's specific situation. Lastly, the NESPY-II, which takes 90–180 minutes to administer depending on the age of the child, includes a comprehensive training CD that walks the examiner through each subtest to administer, score, and interpret results. The age range for the NESPY-II is 3–16 years.

The CAS provides a battery that measures four kinds of cognitive processing, namely, planning, attention, simultaneous, and successive. Planning and attention subtests provide diagnostic information about cognitive deficits in these brain capabilities that may occur due to TBI. An individual's ability to integrate stimuli and understand logical relationships is assessed with the simultaneous processing subtests. Information from the successive processing subtests addresses whether the individual's sequential ordering of stimuli has been affected by a brain injury. Administration of the CAS results in the following scores: standard scores, scaled scores, percentile ranks, and age equivalents. It was standardized on a representational sample of 2,200 children and adults 5.0–17.11 years of age. The CAS norms are reported in four-month age intervals. It comes with an *Interpretive Handbook* that provides the examiner with detailed interpretative strategies and implications for intervention. In addition, it illustrates a number of research-based instructional programs linked to the CAS scales.

TECHNOLOGY AND TBI

Technology assists individuals with TBI to improve the quality of their lives by diagnosing and identifying the severity of their brain injury, guiding medical professionals in rehabilitation endeavors, helping them control activities of daily living in their environment, allowing them increased opportunities to engage with others socially, and enhancing their educational instruction to learn academic content either previously learned or new content. Technology for individuals with TBI can be divided into two types, namely, medical and educational.

Medical technology includes procedures and techniques (i.e., MRI, CT, X-rays) to identify and confirm a diagnosis of TBI. Since the passage of the 1990 IDEA, there has been a tremendous increase in using neuroimaging procedures to determine the diagnosis and prognosis of an individual's TBI (Zink, 2001). In addition, neuroimaging has been extremely helpful for medical professionals in deciding necessary rehabilitation treatments (Kluger, 2009). Table 5 lists some recent advances in the use of technology for individuals with TBI reported by Igou (2010).

The use of educational technology has increased dramatically with the passage of the Technology-Related Assistance for Individuals with Disabilities Act (Tech Act) of 1988 and the 1998 Assistive Technology Act (ATA, 1998) (see Alper & Raharinirina, 2006; NKabinde, 2008). These legislative acts provided the impetus for improving the functional and life needs of individuals with disabilities (Nkabinde, 2008). Primarily, this increase has been in the areas of assistive technology (AT). Typically, AT for students with TBI is divided into three areas, namely, devices for positioning and mobility;

Table 5.   Advances in Using Medical Technology in TBI.

TBI and cerebral atrophy – flare imaging analysis indicated that the more brain white matter damaged found, the greater the brain shrinkage with time.

Diffuse tensor imaging (DTI) – patients with mild TBI have been shown to have structural changes based upon DTI scanning.

SPECT scanning of the brain – more and more validation of this procedure to identify diffuse axonal injury is occurring. This will be helpful in guiding medical professionals in future rehabilitation.

Magnetic fields to reduce depression – firing bursts of magnetic fields across the temporal lobe of depressed clients with TBI can result in a decrease in depressive symptoms.

CT scan in detecting hearing loss – work has progressed on using CT scanning of the bilateral temporal bones to detect hearing loss in patients with severe TBI.

MRI to determine tinnitus – work has been carried out that uses MRI to detect changes in the inner ear that lead to tinnitus in patients with TBI.

Magnetic resonance spectroscopy (MRS) – more and more data has been collected that demonstrates the value of MRS in detecting microscopic brain injury. Also, MRS has been useful in predicting unfavorable outcome from a coma at 1 year from TBI.

Adapted and modified from Igou (2010).

accessing information; and memory and organization (see Project IDEAL, 2010). Positioning and mobility AT devices (i.e., canes, crutches, wheelchairs, specialized chairs, desks, and tables) are incorporated to assist the student in focusing during instructional activities (Project IDEAL, 2010). Access information AT devices (i.e., speech recognition software, screen reading software, tinted overlays for reading and specially designed academic software for students with disabilities) allow the student easier access to academic material (Project IDEAL, 2010). Memory and organization AT devices (i.e., calendar boards, schedule organizers, voice organizers, medication reminders, smartphones, specialized watches, and PDA devices) assist the student in academic functioning that necessitates the efficient use of memory and organizational capacities (Project IDEAL, 2010).

The type of AT devices and programs that can be used with students with TBI is related to the severity of the student's brain injury and to the specific deficits (i.e., memory, reading, math, spelling, mobility and movement, visual processing, speech, cognitive processing) that result from the damage. Because students with TBI have such diverse and at times multiple deficits, AT devices and programs that have benefitted other students with disabilities (i.e., learning disabilities, speech impairments, autism, cognitive impairments) can be incorporated into their school programs. Once special educators have identified a student with TBI-specific deficit(s), they can seek out and match up available AT devices for a particular deficit.

Positively, the literature on impactful AT devices and programs for students with disabilities has grown vastly in the past 10 years (see Alper & Raharinirina, 2006; Bouck, 2010; Parette & Peterson-Karlan, 2010a). In addition, there have been numerous articles that delineate the value, implementation, and program analysis of AT programs for students with disabilities as well as discuss models and frameworks to guide special educators in the consideration of AT for their students with disabilities (see Nkabinde, 2008; Okolo, Englert, Bouck, & Heutsche, 2007; Parette & Peterson-Karlan, 2010b). Furthermore, Bouck (2010) discusses whether present "technology for students with disabilities does what it needs to do?" (p. 100). Also, Parette and Peterson-Karlan (2010a) describe a successful approach that has been used to teach future educators the AT process and making decisions about appropriate AT solutions for students with disabilities. Table 6 provides the reader with a sample of studies on the effective use of AT with students who have disabilities. The table reveals the broadness of AT utilization among students with a variety of disabilities and diverse skill areas.

Table 6. Sample of AT studies with Students with Disabilities Based upon Deficit Area.

Authors	Disability Category	Deficit Area
Anderson and Anderson (2005)	Mild disability	Reading
Banks and Coombs (2005)	Visual impairment	Math and science
DePompei, Gillette, and Goetz (2008)	TBI	Communication/ information access
Dixon (2007)	Developmental disability	Communication
Freitas and Kouroupeteoglou (2008)	Visual impairment	Activities of daily living
Hart (2004)	TBI	Memory and organization
Jeffs, Behrmann, and Bannan-Ritland (2006)	Mild disability	Writing
Peterson-Karlan, Wojcik, and Parette (2006)	Learning disability	Writing
Salend (2005)	Cognitive impairment/ autism	Sensory overload
Schaff, Jerome, Behrmann, and Sprague (2005)	Visual impairment and physical impairment	Science
Skau and Cascella (2006)	Autism	Communication
Stokes (2007)	Autism	Activities of daily living
Strangmann and Dalton (2005)	Learning disability	Reading
Thorp (2007)	Autism	Play skills
Wehmeyer, Smith, and Davies (2005)	Cognitive impairment	Functional living skills

CONCLUDING REMARKS

TBI has been part of society for hundreds of years. Prior to the 1900s, little could be done to change the damage that a student incurred from the original injury. However, during the past 100 years, medical and educational research, intervention, and technology have changed this course for students with TBI and allowed them a greater opportunity to recover and learn, despite the original impairment to mental processes, such as memory, language, and regulation of emotions.

The passage of IDEA (1990) provided students with TBI more specialized, intensive, and individual instruction due to its recognition as a special education category. While students with TBI received some special education service prior to IDEA (1990), their individual educational plans were not as succinct or accurate. The TBI instructional field has grown and the knowledge and research base has improved; however, there exists a lack of research-based instructional and behavioral intervention strategies specifically developed for these students (Tyler & Savage, 2003). In addition, teachers of students with TBI need to be provided increased in-service training on the behavioral and learning characteristics for these students to educate them more efficiently during recovery and reentry situations. Furthermore, educational instruction and related special education services need to be flexible to utilize the student's remaining and emerging strengths (Burkhardt & Rotatori, 2007).

Positive aspects for the future medical and educational interventions for students with TBI include the development of medical and educational technology, more accurate and comprehensive neurological and psycho-neurological diagnosis and assessment devices and techniques and the recognition that families can play a very meaningful part in the recovery of their children. Also, there is some recognition that cultural diversity and poverty issues impact on an understanding of TBI in at least two ways: risk factors and recovery indicators (Burkhardt & Rotatori, 2008). In addition, medical and educational professionals are more persistent in their recommendation that early intervention is beneficial in reducing negative effects of TBI for young children when it is intensive and long term (see Lowenthal, 1998). Lastly, long-term follow-up studies of children with TBI are now reporting the following: the worst the injury, the worst the neurocognitive outcome; time doesn't heal all; most mental processing problems stick; memory and visual–spatial skills appear normal after a few years of the injury; children with severe TBI needed more help and showed robust and significant problems within months on IQ, executive functioning, and verbal memory (see Babikian & Asamow, 2009).

REFERENCES

Alper, S., & Raharinirina, S. (2006). Assistive technology for students with disabilities: A review and synthesis of the literature. *Journal of Special Education Technology*, 21(2), 47–64.

American Psychiatric Association. (2004). *Diagnostic and statistical manual of mental disorders, Fourth Edition- Revised (APA, DSM-IVR)*. Washington, DC: American Psychiatric Association.

Anderson, K. M., & Anderson, C. L. (2005). Integrating technology into standards-based instruction. In: D. Edyburn, K. Higgins & R. Boone (Eds), *Handbook of special education technology research and practice* (pp. 521–544). Whitefish Bay, WI: Knowledge by Design.

Anderson, C. M., & Warzak, W. J. (2000). Using positive behavioral supports to facilitate the classroom adaption of children with brain injuries. *Proven Practices: Prevention and Remediation Solutions for Schools*, 2, 72–82.

Arroyos-Jurado, E., & Savage, T. (2008). Intervention strategies for serving students with traumatic brain injury. *Intervention in School and Clinic*, 43(4), 252–254.

Assistance Technology Act (ATA). (1998). P.L. 105-394. Retrieved from http://www.resna.org/taproject/library/govinfo./laws/htm

Babikian, T., & Asamow, R. (2009). Neurocognitive outcomes and recovery after pediatric TBI: Meta-analytic review of the literature. *Neuropsychology*, *23*(3), 283–295.

Banks, R., & Coombs, N. (2005). Accessible information technology and persons with visual impairments. In: D. Edyburn, K. Higgins & R. Boone (Eds), *Handbook of special education technology research and practice* (pp. 379–391). Whitefish Bay, WI: Knowledge by Design.

Boll, T. (1993). *Children's category test (CCT)*. San Antonio, TX: Psychological Corporation.

Bouck, E. (2010). Technology and students with disabilities: Does it solve all problems? In: F. E. Obiakor, J. P. Bakken & A. F. Rotatori (Eds), *Current issues and trends in special education: Research, technology and teacher preparation* (Vol. 20, pp. 91–104). Bingley, UK: Emerald Group Publishing Limited.

Bowen, J. (2005). Classroom intervention for students with traumatic brain injury. *Preventing School Failure*, *49*, 34–41.

Brannigan, G., & Decker, S. (2003). *Bender visual-motor Gestalt test, second edition (Bender Gestalt II)*. Itasca, IL: Riverside Publishing.

Bullock, L. M., Gable, R. A., & Mohr, J. D. (2005). Traumatic brain injury: A challenge for educators. *Preventing School Failure*, *49*(4), 6–10.

Burkhardt, S. (1995). Counseling issues for children with traumatic brain injury. In: A. F. Rotatori, J. O. Schwenn & F. W. Litton (Eds), *Counseling special education populations: Research and practice perspectives* (Vol. 9, pp. 207–240). Greenwich, CT: JAI Press Inc.

Burkhardt, S., & Rotatori, A. F. (2007). Working with multicultural learners with traumatic brain injury. In: F. E. Obiakor (Ed.), *Multicultural special education: Culturally responsive teaching* (pp. 180–194). Upper Saddle River, NJ: Pearson.

Burkhardt, S., & Rotatori, A. F. (2008, May). Traumatic brain injury. Paper presented at the Annual Young Adult International Convention in New York City.

Burkhardt, S., & Rotatori, A. F. (2010). Educating students with traumatic brain injury. In: E. Baker, P. Peterson & B. McGaw (Eds), *International encyclopedia of education* (pp. 321–345). Oxford: Elsevier Sciences.

Burkhart, J., Fox, R., & Rotatori, A. F. (1987). Neurological assessment of exceptional children: Impact on education. In: A. F. Rotatori, M. B. Banbury & R. A. Fox (Eds), *Issues in special education* (pp. 135–148). Mountain View, CA: Mayfield Publishing Company.

Burnett, D. M., Kolakowsky-Hayner, S. A., Slater, D., Stringer, A., Bushnik, T., Zafonte, R., & Cifu, D. X. (2003). Ethnographic analysis of traumatic brain injury patients in the National Model Systems Database. *Archives of Physical Medicine and Rehabilitation*, *84*, 263–267.

Busch, R. M., McBribe, A., Curtiss, G., & Vanderploeg, R. D. (2005). The components of executive functioning in traumatic brain injury. *Journal of Clinical and Experimental Neuropsychology*, *27*(8), 1022–1032.

Cantu, R. C. (2001). Posttraumatic retrograde and anterograde amnesia: Pathophysiology and implications in grading and safe return to play. *Journal of Athletic Training*, *36*(3), 244–248.

Cassidy, J. D., Carroll, L. T., Peloso, P. M., Borg, J., von Holst, H., & Holm, L. (2004). Incidence, risk factors and prevention of mild traumatic brain injury: Results of the

WHO Collaborating centre task force on mild traumatic brain injury. *Journal of Rehabilitation Medicine, 36*(43), 28–60.

Center for Disease Control and Prevention (CDC). (2004). *Traumatic brain injury.* Retrieved from http://www.cdc.gov/ncipc/factsheets/tbi.htm

Center for Disease Control and Prevention (CDC). (2008). *What is traumatic brain injury?* Retrieved from http://www.cdc.gov/ncipc/tbi/Prevention.htm

Cohen, R. J., & Swerdlik, M. E. (2009). *Psychological testing and assessment: An introduction to tests and measurements* (9th ed.). Boston: McGraw Hill.

Cooley, E. A., Glang, A., & Voss, J. (1997). Making connections: Helping children with ABI build friendships. In: A. Glang, S. Springer & B. Todis (Eds), *Children with acquired brain injury: The school's response* (pp. 255–275). Baltimore: Paul H. Brookes.

Comper, P., Bisschop, S. M., Carnide, N., & Tricco, A. (2005). A systematic review of treatment for mild traumatic brain injury. *Brain Injury, 19*(11), 863–880.

Corcoran, C., McAlister, T. W., & Maspina, D. (2005). Psychotic disorders. In: J. M. Silver, T. W. McAllister & S. C. Yudofsky (Eds), *Textbook of traumatic brain injury* (pp. 213–224). Washington, DC: American Psychiatric Association.

Culbertson, W. C., & Zillmer, E. A. (2000). *Tower of London* (2nd ed.). North Tonawanda, NY: MultiHealth Systems, Inc.

Dean-Woodcock, J. (2003). *The Dean-Woodcock neuropsychological battery.* Itasca, IL: Riverside Publishing.

DePompei, R., Gillette, Y., & Goetz, E. (2008). Practical application for use of PDAs and smartphones with children and adolescents with traumatic brain injury. *Neurorehabilitation, 10,* 30–37.

Deshler, D. D., Ellis, E. S., & Lenz, B. K. (1996). *Teaching adolescents with learning disabilities: Strategies and methods* (2nd ed.). Denver, CO: Love.

Dixon, J. (2007). *ISPEAK at home.* Philadelphia: Jessica Kingsley Publishers.

Dykeman, B. (2003). School-based interventions for treating social adjustment difficulties in children with traumatic brain injury. *Journal of Instructional Psychology, 30,* 225–230.

Enderby, P., & Palmer, R. (2008). *Frenchay dysarthria assessment* (2nd ed.). Austin, TX: PRO-ED.

Franklin, B. M. (1987). From brain injury to learning disability: Alfred Strauss, Heinz Werner, and the historical development of the learning disabilities field. In: B. M. Franklin (Ed.), *Learning disability: Dissenting essays* (pp. 29–46). Philadelphia: The Farmer Press.

Freitas, D., & Kouroupeteoglou, G. (2008). Speech technologies for blind and low vision persons. *Technology and Disability, 20,* 135–156.

Gfroerer, S. D., Wade, S. I., & Wu, M. (2008). Parent perception of school-based supports for children with traumatic brain injury. *Brain Injury, 9,* 649–656.

Ghajar, J. (2000). Traumatic brain injury. *Lancet, 10*(September), 923–929.

Glang, A. (1993). Using direct instruction with brain injured students. *Direct Instruction News, 21*(Fall), 23–28.

Glang, A., Singer, G., Cooley, R., & Tish, N. (1992). Tailoring direct instruction techniques to use with elementary students with traumatic brain injury. *Journal of Head Trauma Rehabilitation, 7*(4), 93–108.

Glang, A., Ylvisaker, M., Stein, M., Ehlhardt, L., Todis, B., & Tyler, J. (2008). Validated instruction practices: Applications to students with traumatic brain injury. *Journal of Head Trauma Rehabilitation, 23*(4), 243–251.

Golden, C. T. (1984). *Luria-Nebraska neuropsychological battery-children's revised (LNNB-CR)*. Los Angeles: Western Psychological Services.

Golden, C. T. (1994). *Screening test for the Luria-Nebraska neuropsychological battery (ST- LNNB)*. Los Angeles: Western Psychological Services.

Golden, C. T., & Freshwater, S. M. (2002). *Stroop color and word test*. Los Angeles: Western Psychological Services.

Golden, C. J., Purisch, A. D., & Hammeke, T. A. (1986). *Luria-Nebraska neuropsychological battery (LNNB)*. Los Angeles: Western Psychological Services.

Goldstein, K. (1927). Die lokalisation in her grosshim rinde. Handb. Norm. Pathol. Psychologie. Berlin: J. Springer.

Goldstein, K. (1939). *The organism*. New York: American Book.

Granacher, R. A. (2007). *Traumatic brain injury: Methods for clinical and forensic neuropsychiatric assessment*. New York: Taylor and Francis.

Grant, D. A., & Berg, E. A. (1993). *Wisconsin card sorting test (WCST)*. Los Angeles: Western Psychological Services.

Hardman, J. M., & Manoukian, A. (2002). Pathology of head trauma. *Neuroimaging Clinics of North America, 12*(2), 175–187.

Hart, T. (2004). Portable electronic devices as memory and organization aids after traumatic brain injury: A consumer study. *Journal of Head Trauma and Rehabilitation, 19*(5), 351–365.

Harvey, J. M. (2006). Best practices in working with students with traumatic brain injuries. In: A. Thomas & L. Grimes (Eds), *Best practices in school psychology* (Vol. 4, pp. 1433–1446). Bethesda, MD: National Association for School Psychologists.

Haynes, J. R., & Sells, S. G. (1963). Assessment of organic brain damage by psychological tests. *Psychological Bulletin, 60*, 316–325.

Holmes, C. B., & Holmes, D. A. (1996). Neuropsychological assessment in special education. In: A. F. Rotatori, J. O. Schwenn & S. Burkhardt (Eds), *Assessment and psychopathology issues in special education* (Vol. 10, pp. 157–176). Greenwich, CT: JAI Press Inc.

Individuals with Disabilities Education Act (IDEA). (1990). Public Law No. 101-476. Section 300.7(b)(12).

Igou, W. (2010). Latest medical research. Available at http://www.braininjury.com

Jeffs, T., Behrmann, M., & Bannan-Ritland, B. (2006). Assistive technology and literacy learning: Reflections of parents and children. *Journal of Special Education Technology, 21*, 37–44.

Kaplan, R. M., & Saccuzzo, D. P. (2009). *Psychological testing: Principles, applications, and issues* (7th ed.). Pacific Grove, CA: Brooks.

Kaufman, N. (1995). *Kaufman speech praxis test for children (KSPT)*. Austin, TX: PRO-ED.

Kavale, K. A., & Forness, S. R. (1985). The historical foundation of learning disabilities: A quantitative synthesis assessing the validity of Strauss and Werner's exogenous versus endogenous distinction of mental retardation. *Remedial and Special Education, 65*, 18–24.

Keenan, H. T., Runyan, D. K., & Nocera, M. (2006). Longitudinal follow-up of families and young children with traumatic brain injury. *Pediatrics, 117*(4), 1291–1297.

Keyser-Marcus, L., Briel, L., Sherron-Targett, P., Yasuda, S., Johnson, S., & Wehman, P. (2002). Enhancing the schooling of students with traumatic brain injury. *Teaching Exceptional Children, 72*(March/April), 62–67.

Kim, E. (2002). Agitation, aggression, and disinhibition syndromes after traumatic brain injury. *NeuroRehabilitation, 17*(4), 297–310.

Klomes, J. M. (2000). The school reentry process for students with traumatic brain injury. In: F. E. Obiakor, S. A. Burckhardt, A. F. Rotatori & T. Wahlberg (Eds), *Intervention techniques for individuals with exceptionalities in inclusive settings* (Vol. 13, pp. 199–216). Stamford, CT: JAI Press Inc.

Kluger, J. (2009, April). *Dealing with brain injuries.* Time Magazine, 57.

Korkman, M., Kirk, U., & Kemp, S. (2007). *NESPY-II.* San Antonio, TX: Psychological Corporation.

Kushner, D. (1998). Mild traumatic brain injury: Toward understanding manifestations and treatment. *Archives of Internal Medicine, 158*(15), 1617–1624.

Levin, H. S., Benton, A. I., & Grossman, R. (1982). *Neurobehavioral consequences of closed head injury.* Oxford: Oxford University Press.

Llorente, A. M., Williams, J., Satz, P., & D'Elia, L. (2003). *Children's color trails test (CCTT).* Lutz, FL: Psychological Assessment Resources.

Lowenthal, B. (1998). Traumatic brain injury in early childhood: Developmental effects and interventions. *Infant-Toddler Interventions, 8*(4), 377–388.

Luria, A. R. (1966). *Higher cortical functions in man.* New York: Basic Books.

Luria, A. R. (1973). *The working brain: An introduction to neuropsychology.* New York: Basic Books.

Maas, A. I., Stocchetti, N., & Bullock, R. (2008). Moderate and severe traumatic brain damage in adults. *Lancet Neurology, 7*(8), 728–741.

Marion, D. W. (1999). *Traumatic brain injury.* New York: Thieme Medical Publisher Inc.

Markowitz, J., & Linehan, P. (2001, January). QTA: Traumatic brain injury. *Project.* Alexandria, VA: National Association of State Directors of Special Education.

Mayfield, J., & Homack, S. (2005). Behavioral considerations associated with traumatic brain injury: Managing the transition from hospital to school. *Preventing School Failure, 49*(4), 17–21.

Max, J. E., Landis, J., Schachar, R., Sauders, A., Ewing-Cobbs, L., Chapman, S. B., & Dennis, M. (2005). Predictors of personality change due to traumatic brain injury in children and adolescents in the first six months after injury. *Journal of the American Academy of Child and Adolescent Psychiatry, 44*(5), 433–442.

McCrory, P. R., & Berkovic, S. F. (2001). Concussion: The history of clinical and pathophysiological concepts and misconceptions. *Neurology, 57*(12), 2283–2289.

Meyer, J. E., & Meyer, K. R. (1996). *Rey complex figure test and recognition trial (RCFT).* Lutz, FL: Psychological Assessment Resources.

Milders, M., Fuchs, S., & Crawford, J. R. (2003). Neuropyschological impairments and changes in emotional and social behavior following severe traumatic brain injury. *Journal of Experimental Neuropsychology, 25*(2), 157–172.

Mutti, M., Sterling, H. M., Martin, N., & Spalding, N. V. (1998). *Quick neurological screening test II (QNST-II).* Los Angeles: Western Psychological Services.

Naglieri, J. A., & Das, J. P. (1997). *Cognitive assessment system (CAS).* Itasca, IL: Riverside Publishing.

National Dissemination Center for Children with Disabilities (NICHCY). (2006). Traumatic brain injury: Fact sheet. Retrieved from http://www.nichcy.org/pubs/fatshe/fs18xt.htm

Nkabinde, Z. (2008). Using assistive technology to educate students with developmental disabilities and autism. In: A. F. Rotatori, F. E. Obiakor & S. Burkhardt (Eds), *Autism and developmental disabilities: Current practices and issues* (Vol. 18, pp. 273–285). Bingley, UK: Emerald Group Publishing Limited.

Okolo, C. M., Englert, C. S., Bouck, E. C., & Heutsche, A. M. (2007). Web-based history learning environments: Helping all students learn and like history. *Interventions in the School, and Clinic*, *43*(1), 3–11.

Parette, H. P., & Peterson-Karlan, G. R. (2010a). Assistive technology for students with disabilities. In: F. O. Obiakor, J. P. Bakken & A. F. Rotatori (Eds), *Current issues and trends in special education: Research, technology and teacher preparation* (Vol. 20, pp. 73–89). Bingley, UK: Emerald Group Publishing Limited.

Parette, H. P., & Peterson-Karlan, G. R. (2010b). Integrating assistive technology into the curriculum. In: P. Peterson, B. McGaw & E. Baker (Eds), *International encyclopedia of education* (pp. 178–198). Oxford: Elsevier Sciences.

Parikh, S., Koch, M., & Narayan, R. K. (2007). Traumatic brain injury. *International Anesthesiology Clinics*, *45*(3), 119–135.

Pearce, J. M. (2007). Observation in concussion: A review. *European Neurology*, *59*, 113–119.

Peterson-Karlan, G. R., Wojcik, B. W., & Parette, H. P. (2006). *The effectiveness of "SOLO" on the writing outcomes of students with learning and academic disabilities.* Final report to the National Center on Technology Innovation, Illinois State University. Special Education Assistive Technology Center, Normal, IL.

Project IDEAL. (2010). *Traumatic brain injury.* Retrieved from http://www.projectidealonline.org/brainInjury.php

Reitan, R. M. (1994). Ward Halstead's contributions to neuropsychological and the Halstead–Reitan neuropsychological test battery. *Journal of Clinical Psychology*, *50*, 47–70.

Reitan, R. M., & Wolfson, D. (1993). *The Halstead–Reitan neuropsychological test battery: Theory and clinical interpretation* (2nd ed.). Tucson, AZ: Neuropsychology Press.

Reynolds, C. R. (2002). *Comprehensive trail-making test (CTMT).* Austin, TX: PRO-ED.

Reynolds, C. R., & Horton, A. M. (2007). *Test of verbal conceptualization and fluency (TVCF).* Austin, TX: PRO-ED.

Reynolds, C. R., & Voress, J. K. (2007). *Test of memory and learning* (2nd ed.). Austin, TX: PRO-ED.

Ross-Swain, D. (1999). *Ross information processing assessment-primary (RIPA-P).* Austin, TX: PRO-ED.

Salend, S. J. (2005). Using technology to teach about individual differences related to disabilities. *Teaching Exceptional Children*, *38*(2), 32–38.

Sanchez, G. M., & Burridge, A. L. (2007). Decision making in head injury management in the Edwin Smith Papyrus. *Neurosurgical/Focus*, *23*(1), 78–88.

Schaff, J. L., Jerome, M. K., Behrmann, M. M., & Sprague, D. (2005). Science in special education: Emerging technologies. In: D. Edyburn, K. Higgins & R. Boone (Eds), *Handbook of special education technology research and practice* (pp. 643–661). Whitefish Bay, WI: Knowledge by Design.

Schwartz, L., Taylor, H., Drotar, D., Yeates, K., Wade, S., & Stancin, T. (2003). Long-term behavior problems following pediatric traumatic brain injury: Prevalence, predictors, and correlates. *Journal of Pediatric Psychology*, *28*, 251–263.

Shaw, N. A. (2002). The neurophysiology of concussion. *Progress in Neurobiology*, *67*(4), 281–344.

Sheslow, D., & Adams, W. (2003). *Wide range assessment of memory and learning* (2nd ed. (WRAML-2)). Lutz, FL: Psychological Assessment Resources.

Silver, C. H., & Blackburn, L. B. (2006). Neurological evaluation. *Archives of Clinical Neuropsychology*, *21*, 741–744.

Skau, L., & Cascella, P. W. (2006). Using assistive technology to foster speech and language skills at home and in preschool. *Teaching Exceptional Children, 38*(6), 12–17.

Smith, D. D. (2004). *Introduction to special education: Teaching in an age of opportunity* (5th ed.). Boston: Allyn and Bacon.

Stokes, S. (2007). *Assistive technology for children with autism.* Retrieved from http://www.cesa7/k.12.wi.us/sped/autism/assist/.assist10.htm

Strangmann, N., & Dalton, B. (2005). Using technology to support struggling readers: A review of the research. In: D. Edyburn, K. Higgins & R. Boone (Eds), *Handbook of special education technology research and practice* (pp. 545–569). Whitefish Bay, WI: Knowledge by Design.

Strauss, A. A., & Lechtinen, L. E. (1947). *Psychopathology and education of the brain injured child.* New York: Grune & Stratton.

Talley, J. L. (2002). *Children's auditory verbal learning test-2 (CAVT-2).* Los Angeles: Western Psychological Services.

Tatzmann, M., Clancy, K. A., & Reagan, J. R. (2006). *Traumatic brain injury impacts education and learning. Focus on Results.* Michigan City, MI: Michigan Department of Education, Office of Special Education and Early Intervention Services.

Technology-Related Assistance for Individuals with Disabilities Act. (1988). Pl 100-407. U.S.C.2201et seq: U.S. Statues at Large, 102, 1044–1065.

Thorp, D. M. (2007). *Computer play as clinical intervention.* Retrieved from http://cesa7/k12.wi.us/sped/autism/assist/assist10htm

Thurman, D. J., Sniezek, J. E., Johnson, D., Greenspan, A., & Smith, S. M. (1994). *Guidelines for surveillance of central nervous system injury.* Atlanta, GA: US Department of Health and Human Services, Public Health Services, CDC.

Todd, A. W., Horner, R., Vanater, S., & Schneider, C. (1997). Make a change: An example of positive behavior support for a student with traumatic brain injury. *Education and Treatment of Children, 20*, 425–440.

Todis, B., & Glang, A. (2008). Redefining success: Results of a qualitative study of postsecondary transition outcomes for youth with traumatic brain injury. *Journal of Head Trauma Rehabilitation, 23*(4), 252–263.

Tyler, J., Blosser, J., & DePompei, R. (1999). *Teaching strategies for students with brain injuries.* Wake Forest, NC: L&A Publishing Training.

Tyler, J. S., & Savage, R. C. (2003). Students with traumatic brain injury. In: F. E. Obiakor, C. A. Utley & A. F. Rotatori (Eds), *Effective education for learners with exceptionalities* (Vol. 15, pp. 299–350). Boston: JAI/Elsevier Sciences.

U.S. Department of Education, Office of Special Education Programs. (2005). *Technical assistance center on positive behavioral interventions and supports.* Final report. Author, Washington, DC.

Valadla, A. B. (2004). Injury to the cranium. In: E. J. Moore, D. V. Feliciano & K. L. Mattox (Eds), *Trauma* (pp. 385–406). New York: McGraw-Hill.

Wehmeyer, M. L., Smith, S. J., & Davies, D. K. (2005). Technology use and students with intellectual disabilities: Universal design for all students. In: D. Edyburn, K. Higgins & R. Boone (Eds), *Handbook of special education technology research and practice* (pp. 309–323). Whitefish Bay, WI: Knowledge for Design.

Werner, H., & Strauss, A. A. (1941). Pathology of figure-background relation in the child. *Journal of Abnormal and Social Psychology, 36*, 236–248.

Wheeler, J. J., & Martin, M. R. (2010). Other innovative techniques: Positive behavior supports and response to intervention. In: F. E. Obiakor, J. P. Bakken & A. F. Rotatori (Eds), *Current issues and trends in special education: Identification, assessment, and instruction* (Vol. 19, pp. 199–212). Bingley, UK: Emerald Group Publishing Limited.

Ylvisaker, M., Jacobs, H. E., & Feeney, T. (2003). Positive supports for people who experience behavioral and cognitive disability after brain injury: A review. *Journal of Head Trauma Rehabilitation, 18*, 7–32.

Youse, K. M., Le, K. N., Cannizzarod, M. S., & Coehlo, C. A. (2002). *Traumatic brain injury: A primer for professionals.* Retrieved from http://www.asha.org/about/publications/leader-online/archive/2002/12/020625a.htm

Zillmer, E. A., Scheider, J., Tinker, J., & Kaminaris, C. I. (2006). A history of sports-related concussion: A neuropsychological perspective. In: R. J. Echemendia (Ed.), *Sports neuropsychology: Assessment and management of traumatic brain injury* (pp. 21–23). New York: The Guilford Press.

Zink, B. J. (2001). Traumatic brain outcome: Concepts for emergency care. *Annals of Emergency Medicine, 37*(3), 318–332.

CHAPTER 14

HISTORY OF BILINGUAL SPECIAL EDUCATION

Fabiola P. Ehlers-Zavala

In the United States, bilingual special education corresponds to the specially designed educational practice meant to ensure that bilingual exceptional learners develop to their fullest potential. In this chapter, bilingual learners with exceptionalities are defined as learners who have "a set of specific abilities or disabilities that are especially valued or that require special accommodation within a given subculture" (Hallahan, Kauffman, & Pullen, 2009, p. 94). In the United States, common to all of these exceptional children is the fact that they speak a language other than English. For this reason, they can also be referred to as English language learners (ELLs) with exceptionalities. Their presence in U.S. classrooms is not a twentieth-century phenomenon. Any individual who is familiar with the history of American education, and its rich multilingual and multicultural landscape even prior to the arrival of Europeans (Baker, 2006; Lessow-Hurley, 2005; Wiley, 2007), can confidently come to terms with the fact that bilingual children with exceptionalities have always been part a of the human make-up of this country.

Unfortunately, however, throughout history, many bilingual children with exceptionalities have not been properly identified or educationally served in U.S. schools. Because of their lack of English proficiency, some bilingual learners with exceptionalities have not been identified, and have been therefore left unattended. Yet other bilingual learners without exceptionalities have been either misplaced in special education classes or referred to special

History of Special Education
Advances in Special Education, Volume 21, 343–361
Copyright © 2011 by Emerald Group Publishing Limited
All rights of reproduction in any form reserved
ISSN: 0270-4013/doi:10.1108/S0270-4013(2011)0000021017

services because their lack of English proficiency has been wrongly misunderstood as a disability, leading to their overrepresentation (Cummins, 1991; Hamayan, Marler, Sanchez-Lopez, & Damico, 2007). While there are many underlying reasons (e.g., ideological, political, and so forth) that explain the lack or misdiagnosis of bilingual learners, in the end, all of them directly connect to the shortage of bilingual special educators in U.S. schools, that is, professionals who hold the proper educational training to carry out more specialized teaching to ensure the overall success of bilingual exceptional children. Given that bilingual special education constitutes a fairly new field (Baca & Cervantes, 2004; Reynolds & Fletcher-Janzen, 2007), the main goal of this chapter is to relate the history of bilingual special education in the United States, a country uniquely and continuously challenged by its multiculturalism. This chapter is organized into two sections. The first section discusses how bilingual special education is positioned in the larger context of multicultural education. And, the second section presents the major historical developments that have affected the education of bilingual exceptional learners in U.S. public schools.

BILINGUAL SPECIAL EDUCATION
AND MULTICULTURAL EDUCATION

Over the course of several decades, the field of bilingual special education has found much support in the reform movement that has become known as multicultural education. Born out of the 1960s civil rights movement (Mclaren & Muñoz, 2000), multicultural education "is a field in education that is dedicated to equal opportunity for all students. Even groups who appear to be monocultural are diverse in regards to class, gender, and language" (Ooka Pang, 2005, p. 213). Multicultural education "assumes that race, ethnicity, culture, and social class are salient parts of U.S. society. It also assumes that ethnic and cultural diversity enriches the nation and increases the ways in which its citizens can perceive and solve personal and public problems" (Banks, 2002, p. 1). Thus, multicultural education supports the call for bilingual special education in teacher preparation and in schools. For special educators, in particular, understanding the link between exceptionalities and cultural diversity is fundamental to their professional role (Hallahan et al., 2009). In the context of a multilingual and multicultural country, such as the United States, bilingual special education is no doubt the best way to ensure that a subgroup of our population (i.e., bilingual exceptional children) has real opportunities to succeed. A major concern for any educator, but especially for bilingual special educators who value and seek to implement multicultural education, is to ensure that bilingual exceptional learners are not placed at a disadvantage because of their linguistic and cultural backgrounds. Here the term culture encompasses all the various aspects (subcultures) that contribute to define an individual. These are race, ethnicity, language, exceptionality, sexual orientation, gender, religion, socioeconomic background, and age.

When educators are attentive to individual differences and adopt an educational framework that celebrates the subcultures that serve to describe and define an individual, then educators have greater chances to help learners succeed. However, the methods that educators may choose to implement may not be free from controversy (Hallahan et al., 2009). This situation is the ongoing challenge for bilingual special educators, who may be confronted with many questions: When is it appropriate to teach an exceptional learner in a first or second language? What is to be done with exceptional learners who have specific disabilities that may challenge the acquisition/learning of a second language, such as English in the United States? Though answers to these questions are varied, there seems to be growing consensus as to the need to ensure that exceptional learners are taught the skills necessary to survive in their local communities, and ideally in the at-large society in this global economy (Hallahan et al., 2009).

It is important to note that, in the United States, English is certainly a priority. Thus, the question for the bilingual special educator who adopts a multicultural approach to the education of exceptional learners is similar to the one that a regular bilingual teacher is often confronted with within the profession: How much of the native language can/should be incorporated in the classroom in light of the programmatic options available in the school? In this chapter, answers to these questions will be addressed in the historical context of federally supported U.S. public education. Answering from methodological and programmatic perspectives is outside the scope of this chapter. However, in understanding the evolutionary historical course of U.S. bilingual education, it is necessary to have a sense for what has been actually programmatically possible in the education of bilingual children with exceptionalities.

HISTORICAL TRENDS IN BILINGUAL EDUCATION

Unlike the present state of special education in the United States, which "has become an expected part of the public education system, a given rather than exception or an experiment" (Hallahan et al., 2009, p. 37), bilingual special education is not. There are no specific U.S. laws that contribute to, support, or regulate bilingual special education per se. Any regulations affecting bilingual learners with exceptionality come from the provisions stipulated in the Individuals with Disabilities Education Improvement Act of 2004, and Title III of the No Child Left Behind (NCLB), which addresses ELLs without exceptionalities. For the past 30 years, any educational protection available to bilingual children with exceptionalities has been the direct result of major legal landmarks in the history of bilingual education and the history of special education. This section first presents the major historical events that have contributed to the history of bilingual special education. Then, it details the major events following the beginnings of bilingual education as a federal mandate.

U.S. Bilingual Education and Its Multilingual Beginnings

To have a sense for the beginnings of bilingual education, the following discussions focus on the happenings from the seventeenth century to the twentieth century.

The Seventeenth Century and Before

U.S. bilingual education finds its roots at the time prior to the arrival of immigrants. During this time, there was a considerable level of linguistic tolerance or diversity (Crawford & Krashen, 2007). Worth singling out is the fact that there were already hundreds of native Indian languages being spoken during and prior to the arrival of immigrants (Baker, 2006; Crawford & Krashen, 2007; Wiley, 2007). Those "indigenous languages were not immediately colonized" (Baker, 2006, p. 189). As Baker (2006) pointed out, "led by Jesuits and Franciscans, the Catholic church sometimes taught through Spanish (also French and English) but often through a native language. Other missionaries (e.g., Dutch Reform and German Moravian) also instrumentally used indigenous languages to secure conversion to Christianity and for teaching" (p. 189). Thus, it is not unreasonable to conclude that this period of perceived linguistic tolerance was the result of both an initial necessity to preserve the immigrants' own heritage, and their need to be strategic in a foreign land where survival was the goal. Linguistic tolerance allowed immigrants to begin their colonization of a new land, and also aided in the promotion of their religious indoctrination of native peoples. To a large degree, immigrant linguistic and cultural heritage preservation certainly resulted in the establishment of bilingual schools in many parts of the country. African slaves brought their own languages (Crawford & Krashen, 2007); other immigrants continued to arrive from countries such as England, Sweden, Norway, the Netherlands, Poland, France, and Ireland, and they spoke their languages in this land. Notably, however, until the middle of the nineteenth century, most immigrants in the United States were primarily from English-speaking countries (Wiley, 2007).

The Eighteenth Century
In the eighteenth century, due to the anti-British sentiment of the era, which was supported by the efforts of the American Revolution (1775–1783), English was never adopted as an official language, despite efforts by some groups (e.g., mission schools that attempted to promote English) (Wiley, 2007). German-English and Scandinavian schools in the midwest (MO, MN, PA, OH) constituted some of the first examples of bilingual schools in the United States (Baker, 2006; Wiley, 2007). Ohio was the first to adopt bilingual education (German/English) in 1839, followed by Louisiana in 1847 (French/English) (Crawford & Krashen, 2007). But, even during the eighteenth century, examples of linguistic intolerance existed (Baker, 2006, Crawford, 2004). For instance, Benjamin Franklin expressed his anti-German position in 1750, and John Adams attempted to persuade the Continental Congress to adopt English in 1780.

The Nineteenth Century
In the nineteenth century, German immigration reached its highest level (Wiley, 2007), and the trend of dual language schools (schools where two languages were used and taught) that had begun in the previous century continued to be popular in the nineteenth century. By this time, about "a dozen states and territories had passed statutes authorizing bilingual schools" (Crawford & Krashen, 2007, p. 65), and "the belief that all children deserve the right to educational opportunity in publicly supported education—let alone an equal opportunity to learn—received broad support gradually" (Wiley, 2007, p. 91). This belief, ratified by the Supreme Court ruling in *Plessy v. Ferguson*, favored the notion of *separate but equal education* (1896–1954). It did not extend to other minorities (children of color) (Wiley, 2007). Furthermore, other examples of concerted intolerance emerged. The most notable one was probably the Civilization Fund Act of 1819, which was "enacted to promote English education and practical skills among Native American peoples" (Wiley, 2007, p. 92). Another example was

legislation in California, which (by 1855) began to mandate instruction in English (Baker, 2006).

The Twentieth Century

The twentieth century witnessed more radical attitudinal changes toward the use of languages other than English, and immigration. The United States started to experience a markedly more restrictive period, characterized by xenophobia, and stronger efforts to engage in the Americanization of its people. Sadly, this period began to observe significant cultural genocide. The unofficial, but significant, English-only movement that had begun toward the end of the nineteenth century continued to gain much support at the turn of the century. Now, there were policies to prohibit the use of indigenous languages on the part of native Americans. This policy was articulated by J. D. C. Atkins, Commissioner of Indian Affairs. He stated that "Teaching an Indian youth in his own barbarous dialect is a positive detriment to him. The first step to be taken toward civilization, toward teaching the Indians the mischief and folly of continuing in their barbarous practices, is to teach them the English language" (cited in Crawford & Krashen, 2007, p. 67).

Moreover, between the period of 1905 and 1923, national origin began to significantly matter to U.S. immigration (Wiley, 2007). In 1906, the Nationality Act, which required that immigrants seeking naturalization needed to demonstrate oral English proficiency, was passed, and some states, such as California, and New Mexico proceeded to establish "English-only" policies (Baker, 2006). The push for instruction in English continued to gain force – with some exceptions (e.g., Polish immigrants in Chicago attending Catholic schools) (Baker, 2006). Thus, a more restrictive scenario became evident in the limitations on bilingual education during the first half of the twentieth century. According to Baker (2006), the reasons that led to this restrictive attitude were several:

1. The number of immigrants increased considerably (e.g., Jewish, and Italian), and it resulted in a call for Americanization supported by many.
2. The Americanization Department of the United States Bureau of Education specifically issued a call to provide education in English, so by "1923, 34 states had decreed that English must be the sole language of instruction in all elementary schools, public and private" (p. 190).
3. The World War I brought with it an anti-German sentiment, which contributed to support the call for English education.

Within this very restrictive period toward linguistic and cultural diversities, there was one exceptional development. In 1923, the U.S. Supreme Court, in *Meyer v. Nebraska*, issued a ruling against the state of Nebraska overturning a law that prohibited the use of a foreign language in an elementary school. The U.S. Supreme Court found this to be unconstitutional under the Fourteenth Amendment. *Meyer v. Nebraska* involved a case against a teacher who was teaching a Bible story in German to a 10-year-old child. Even though this ruling did not mean that the Supreme Court supported bilingualism or bilingual education, it did represent an example of an exception to the many restrictions that emerged during the first two decades of the past century (Baker, 2006). To some extent, during the first half of the twentieth century, despite all the negative sentiments, interest on the part of some in bilingualism began to take shape in the form of research. Tireman (1941) noted this by referring to Cook's bibliography of studies on the education of minority learners from 1923 to 1932, and to Sanchez's critical review of 40 studies that dealt with bilingual intelligence and related topics, among others.

The advent of the second half of the twentieth century brought new important developments. Despite the restrictive scenario that had developed in the first couple of decades of the twentieth century, a change of attitude began to emerge in the United States. In 1954, in a unanimous decision, the landmark U.S. Supreme Court case, *Brown v. Board of Education* of Topeka, Kansas, signified the end of educational segregation era that had been allowed under *Plessy v. Ferguson* up until that point. This ruling meant that separate education was inherently unequal, and it violated the Fourteenth Amendment of the U.S. Constitution (i.e., Equal Protection), thus contributing to support the cause of the Civil Rights Movement. By the mid-1950s, other world events motivated the United States to remain competitive. During this second half, the Russians launched Sputnik, and this fact sparked the desire on the part of Americans to support foreign language teaching (Baker, 2006). With the advent of the Cold War, there was a need to train spies who could aid the U.S. cause in remaining a super power. Thus, in 1958, the National Defense and Education Act was passed – this Act ensured the allocation of monies toward foreign language education. Also, new waves of immigrants, primarily, the exiled Cubans in Florida, contributed to the call for bilingual education. These immigrants set up the first modern bilingual school (dual language) in South Florida: Coral Way Elementary. The purpose of this school was to educate children to become fully bilingual and biliterate (Spanish/English). Undoubtedly, the most significant event that paved the way for federally mandated bilingual education was the Civil Rights

Movement of 1964. The antidiscrimination stance embodied in Title VI of the 1964 Civil Rights Act affirms the prohibition of any act of discrimination against individuals because of their race, color, or national origin in programs that received federal support (Lyons, 1990). Title VI contained provisions "forbidding discrimination on the basis of language" (Ochoa, Pacheco, & Omark, 1983). In 1965, the passing of the Immigration Act "broke new ground in allowing for expediency-oriented educational language policies" (Wiley, 2007, p. 93).

The Official Beginning of U.S. Bilingual Education as a Federal Mandate

To effectively explicate the official beginnings of bilingual education, discussions in the following subsections focus on activities in the 1960s up to the new millennium.

The 1960s
Though the roots of bilingual education date back to the beginnings of this country, the first bilingual education act in the United States was the Bilingual Education Act (BEA) of 1968 (Cordasco, 1969; Lyons, 1990; Moran, 1987; Ovando, 1983; Rossell, 2000). The BEA, also known as Title VII of the Elementary and Secondary Education Act, was the result of S.428 introduced by Democratic Texas Senator Ralph Yarborough and six others in January 1967. Title VII, as originally drafted, sought to acknowledge the importance of building on the cultural piece that each learner contributes (Cordasco, 1969) – though, in the end, the legislation itself did not necessarily support this view (Ovando, 1983). Yarborough (1969) believed that: "When the light of learning is kindled in a child, when that child embraces and masters his [her] own language and then goes on and gains understanding of other tongues, a foundation for understanding is being laid. With each discovery of nuance or shade of meaning, his [her] ability to communicate is strengthened" (p. 79). In its introduction, the bill focused on the Spanish-speaking children who were falling behind in academics due to the lack of English proficiency. Later on, this bill, promoted by Maine's Democratic Senator Muskie, was revised to encompass learners of other languages as well. Signed in to law by the Ninetieth U.S. Congress, S. 428 constituted an amendment to the Elementary and Secondary Act of 1965, and represented the origins of a federally supported bilingual program in the

United States (Cordasco, 1969; Lyons, 1990; Moran, 1988). However, as Davies (2002) noted:

> The bill passed easily, but the Johnson administration was hostile, partly on fiscal grounds, partly because the United States Office of Education (USOE) believed that bilingual programs were already permissible under the original Act. Johnson refused to make any appropriation for bilingual education for what remained of the 1968 fiscal year, and he recommend only $15 million for fiscal year 1969, a move that was denounced by Yarborough as "tokenism" and "an empty gesture" that would "be effectively dashing to the ground all the hopes we have raised." (p. 1407)

According to Baker (2006), the BEA "provided a compensatory 'poverty program'" for the educationally disadvantaged among language minorities. Lyons (1990) noted that this original amendment sought authorization for the appropriation of monies that would fund the following activities:

1. bilingual-education programs;
2. the teaching of Spanish as the native language;
3. the teaching of English as a second language;
4. programs designed to impart to Spanish-speaking students a knowledge of and pride in their ancestral culture and language;
5. efforts to attract and retain as teachers promising individuals of Mexican or Puerto Rican descent; and
6. efforts to establish closer cooperation between the school and the home (p. 67).

However, as Lyons pointed out, despite the Senate's authorization of the previously mentioned activities, and though the bill was signed into law, its focus differed in two main regards from the original concept. First, there were significant changes in the wording of the version initially authorized in the Senate. Specifically, the original reference to "Spanish-speaking children" changed to "children of limited-speaking ability" (p. 68). Second, three of the activities were no longer part of the law: (a) the teaching of Spanish, (b) the teaching of English as a second language, and (c) the recruitment and retention of teachers of Mexican or Puerto Rican origin/ background. Exclusion of these activities would undoubtedly negatively impact the course that bilingual education would follow because there was both a lack of recognition for the necessary type of instruction that children would need as well as a lack of value for the cultural appreciation that comes from the teaching of other languages, and of teachers of diverse backgrounds. Also, as Yarborough (1969) himself noted, the BEA was far from being perfect, and despite all the rhetoric, it was "a quite modest grant-in-aid program" (Moran, 1987, p. 327). Yarborough emphasized the need to work toward amendments that would ensure benefits to other groups who had been ignored up until that point (e.g., Blacks, Native Americans, and adult learners) (Davies, 2002). By 1969, it had become clear that speakers of languages other than English were receiving improper educational treatment. Many of them were sent to classes for the mentally retarded (Davies, 2002). This situation led activists in California to file suit. In *Diana v. Board of Education*, 1970, "the state's school districts were ordered to reexamine in their native languages all non-English speaking children who had been classified as mentally retarded on the basis of English-language tests" (Davies, p. 1417).

The 1970s

The 1970s brought important new developments. The passage of the Vocational Rehabilitation Act of 1973, PL 93-112, Section 504 (Note 3) (Ochoa et al., 1983, p. 417) indirectly contributed to establish the right of bilingual special education services for bilingual students with learning disabilities. This law marked the first official step toward meeting the needs of bilingual learners with disabilities. The 1970s also began to witness the subsequent reauthorizations of the BEA of 1968 (1974, 1978, 1984, 1988, 1994, and 2001) (Baker, 2006; Rossell, 2000). In 1974, it was revised to expand the program by "authorizing new grants for state education-agency technical assistance; training programs; and a national clearinghouse to collect, analyze, and disseminate information about bilingual education programs" (Lyons, 1990, p. 69). By this time, the appropriation had increased to $35 million (Davies, 2002), and it has been argued that its survival was because the Nixon administration wanted to build a "new Republican majority" (p. 1408). Nixon hoped to appeal to and attract the Democratic Spanish-speaking Americans – a strategy that had already proved successful. He had won a third of the Latino support, thus twice as large as in the previous election (see Davies, 2002). Even though the Nixon administration was more concerned with the politics of Title VII than with educational effectiveness (Davies, 2002), in 1973, California Senator Cranston introduced the 1974 amendment. Section 703 of the amendment "narrowed the definition of the eligible population to those who were of 'limited-English-speaking ability,' not just from a non-English-speaking family" (Rossell, 2000, p. 217). Also, as Baker (2006) noted, for the first time, its wording defined the bilingual education program as transitional program. Cranston (1974) stated: "In simple terms, bilingual education involves the use of two languages, one which is English, as mediums of instruction. Both languages are used for the same student population – not as an isolated effort, but as a key component of a program embracing the total curriculum" (p. 58). That is, transitional bilingual education (TBE) was conceived as a program intended to assist the ELLs in making progress in academic subjects. In this revision, the native language of the learner was meant to be used as a support in pedagogical practices. Now students could demonstrate educational progress via the native language or English. This situation generated subsequent debate of how much use of the learners' native language was to be allowed (see Baker, 2006). In addition, there was no proposal to further the development of the learner's native language. Enrollment in this type of program would be voluntary. This amendment also "barred federal support for two-way bilingual-education programs" (Lyons, 1990, p. 69). In other words, programs that aimed at helping learners become fully bilingual did not receive federal support.

Toward the mid–1970s, another important Supreme Court ruling took place. In 1974, in *Lau v. Nichols*, a case originally rejected by the federal district court and court of appeals, was accepted by the U.S. Supreme Court. In this case, the U.S. Supreme Court ruled in favor of the parents of over 1,800 Chinese learners who had filed a class-action suit against the San Francisco public school system (Jarvis, 2006). The Supreme Court determined that schools had the legal responsibility to teach children in a language that they could understand. It also determined that merely providing instructional materials in English, and submersing learners into English, was not enough to ensure equal treatment in offering meaningful education (Baker, 2006; Lyons, 1990). Because the district was not properly educating the learners, the district was found to be in violation of the Fourteenth Amendment and Title VI of the Civil Rights Act of 1964 (Baker, 2006; Jarvis, 2006; Lyons, 1990). Thus, the Court's decision represented the codification of the Equal Educational Opportunity Act (EEOA), and it led to the "*Lau Remedies of 1975*," which highlighted the need to provide ELLs with proper pedagogical assistance and specified guidelines for "(1) identifying and evaluating national-origin-minority students' English language skills; (2) determining appropriate instructional treatments; (3) deciding when limited English proficient (LEP) students were ready for mainstream classes; and (4) determining professional standards to be met by teachers of language-minority children" (Lyons, 1990, p. 72). Though the *Lau Remedies* were important in its symbolic stance, they did not necessarily define the kind of bilingual education that minority learners needed to receive for educational success. What they did was to take a step forward in the establishment of language rights for minorities in the United States (Baker, 2006). Interestingly, in 1975, the passage of Public Law (PL) 94-142 known as the "Education for All Handicapped Children Act" was signed into law by President Ford on November 29. This law was meant to address the need to properly support the public education of children with disabilities in an inclusive environment whenever possible. Clearly, this legislative event marked a crucial point in the history of special education (Baca & Cervantes, 2004). This development also contributed to offer some protections to bilingual learners with special needs.

In 1978, once again the BEA was reauthorized, and expanded: Section 7003 of the 1978 amendment changed the term to refer to bilingual language learners. Now "limited English proficiency" would be the term used, and eligibility for services was extended to American Indians and Alaskan natives (Rossell, 2000, p. 217). This amendment also "added reading and writing to the difficulties children might have in English" (Rossell, 2000, p. 217) that could interfere with their academic progress and achievement. Fiscal support increased, new grants were authorized, and there was a push for collecting and disseminating information related to bilingual education that was very much needed. As Ovando (1983) pointed out, prior to 1978, no committee had been charged with the task of monitoring research on bilingual education, which would be needed for the 1983 reauthorization. Also, a new definition of the learner was introduced. Thus, the term "limited English-speaking" would be used instead of the term "limited English proficient" (Lyons, 1990, p. 69). The ban previously set on programs that aimed at teaching a foreign language was also eliminated (see Lyons, 1990); however, the native language of the learners could only be used for transitional purposes: to achieve English proficiency. Though new grants were authorized, Title VII moneys could not be used for developmental bilingual education (DBE) or maintenance of the native language programs (Baker, 2006). It became clear that bilingual education during the 1970s was very much experimental in nature (see Ovando, 1983). This fact was evident in the lack of clarity as to the needed directions, and also in the lack of systematic research used by both those legislating over its expected course, and those who were in charge of implementing it at the classroom level.

The 1980s
The 1980s continued to witness some events in favor of, and in opposition to, bilingual education. On the positive side, in *Castañeda v. Pickard* (1981), bilingual learners found some protection. Here, an "Appeals court decision established a three-part test to determine whether schools were taking 'appropriate action' under the 1974 Equal Educational Opportunity Act. Programs for LEP students (bilingual or otherwise) must be: (1) based on

sound educational theory, (2) implemented with adequate resources, and (3) evaluated and proven effective" (Baker, 2006, p. 202). Thus, as Crawford and Krashen (2007) noted, this case remained as the "primary tool for enforcing the requirements of *Lau v. Nichols.*" Moreover, *Plyler v. Doe* (1982), another U.S. Supreme Court ruling, established that "schools may not discriminate on the basis of immigration status" (p. 55).

Nevertheless, the 1980s still represented what could be perceived as a step backwards in the progress toward bilingual education, given that resistance against strong forms of bilingual education (i.e., forms that aim at full bilingualism and biliteracy) started to clearly emerge. In 1982, the BEA was amended by a bill introduced by California Senator Hayakawa. The bill would eliminate the requirement of using the native language of the student for pedagogical purposes. Hayakawa, who was the founder of the U.S. English Movement, became known as a fierce proponent of English as the official language of the country by seeking to amend the constitution (Moran, 1987). He succeeded in recruiting followers, some of whom succeeded in this enterprise at the state level (e.g., California), but as of today, there has been no change at the federal level.

The subsequent reauthorizations of the BEA (1984, 1988, and 1994) did not change the definition of LEP learners, and the monies allocated were assigned based on the number of LEPs reported by the schools (Rossell, 2000). In 1984, the BEA was again amended; but this time, it sought to expand the BEA to do what was necessary for children to become proficient in English, allowing for other "special instructional programs" (Rossell, 2000, p. 228) that were neither TBE nor DBE programs. This time, programs for ELLs specifically called for the structured teaching of English. Funds were now also allocated to offer other kinds of programs in support of ELLs, such as "Family English Literacy" programs for adults and out-of-school youths; pre-school, special-education, and gifted and talented programs for LEP students; development of instructional materials for LEP students; and identifying bilingual-education programs of demonstrated academic excellence" (Lyons, 1990). By now, there were two types of bilingual education programs that were authorized: TBE and DBE. As stated earlier, the former focuses on ensuring the transition of ELLs into English, and their native language is used to support this process. The latter aims at helping learners become fully bilingual and biliterate in two languages; therefore, the native language of the learner continues to be supported. The expectations around this period were that, when possible, DBE programs would seek to enroll native English speakers as well. Nevertheless, this legislation met opposition in the Reagan administration "on the grounds that they did not authorize monolingual English instructional programs for LEP students" (p. 76). The legislative compromise that the House sought to put in place resulted then in the "authorization of a third category of general instructional grants, for special alternative instructional programs (SAIP), that is, monolingual English programs" (p. 76). Funding for these SAIP programs was done through formula grants. However, before the implementation of the BEA, Secretary of Education Bell resigned during the Reagan administration, and Secretary Bennett took over, launching a serious attack against bilingual education policy. As Lyons (1990) stated, during "1986 and 1987, Secretary Bennett and other department officials pushed to remove the funding limit on SAIP grants, asserting that English-only instructional programs were as effective for LEP students as bilingual instructional programs" (p. 77). Contradicting this set of beliefs, the 1987 General Accounting Office report titled "Bilingual Education: A New Look at the Research Evidence," previously requested by the House of Education and Labor Committee Chairman Hawkins, showed that monolingual English education was not as effective as claimed.

In 1988, the Reagan administration did not make it a point to seek reauthorization of the BEA, except for insisting "on removing all restrictions on the amount of BEA funds that could be devoted to English-only SAIP programs" (Lyons, 1990, p. 77). The Reagan administration was fairly "hostile to bilingual education" (Baker, 2006, p. 194). The 1988 reauthorization:

> Included further provisions to allow school districts to use different approaches to the education of LEP children. Part A authorized 75 percent of the total grant funds to school districts for transitional bilingual education but increased to 25 percent the amount of grant funds that could go to special alternative instructional programs that did not use the native tongue. In addition, a three-year limit was placed on a student's participation in a transitional bilingual education program or in alternative instructional programs, although under special circumstances, a student could continue in a program for up to two additional years (Rossell, 2000, p. 228).

Another important fact worth noting is that, during the Reagan administration, the *Lau Remedies* were withdrawn, and local governments were expected to develop and implement their own policies in the education of ELLs, resulting in the implementation of weak forms of bilingual education (i.e., transitional bilingual programs) (see Baker, 2006).

The 1990s
Later, the 1994 reauthorization under the Clinton administration allocated "$215 million for fiscal year 1995, gave funding priority to programs that

provide for the development of bilingual proficiency both in English and another language, but kept the 25 maximum allocation for programs that did not use the native tongue" when resources were not identified (shortage of teachers that could teach low-incidence languages for a few students) (Rossell, 2000, pp. 228–229). By 1997, there was a crucially important development for ELLs with exceptionalities. The Individuals with Disabilities Education Act (IDEA) "was amended by Public Law 105-17," and became known as IDEA 97. This amendment marked the need for a different kind of bilingual education. IDEA required "that states include alternate assessment of culturally and linguistically diverse students with special needs" (Rodriguez, 2005, p. 1966). What was now required was bilingual special education teachers that could meet the needs of linguistically diverse students with special needs.

The 1990s, however, witnessed a major change in educational reform with the election of Clinton through the *Goals 2000* legislation, known as the *Educate America Act or Improving America's Schools Act*. This school reform acknowledged the need for ensuring that ELLs reached high standards in academic achievement. As Baker (2006) stated, "such legislation aimed to provide children with an enriched educational program, improving instructional strategies and making the curriculum more challenging" (p. 194). This reform reauthorized Title VII, and there was a push for viewing language as a resource, and now bilingualism was viewed as an asset. While there were more funds available for strong forms of bilingual education (i.e., dual language programs for bilingual and biliteracy development), the authorization of Title VII met criticism and resistance intended to eliminate the law. Though efforts to eliminate the law failed, "Title VII appropriations were reduced by 38% between 1994 and 1996 leading to cuts in bilingual programs, in teacher training and reducing the budgets for research, evaluation and support of bilingual education in the United States" (Baker, 2006, p. 195). On the whole, despite some of the good news for bilingual education in the 1990s, this decade also solidified some of the strongest criticism that bilingual education has received. English-only initiatives succeeded in three states. California passed Proposition 227 in 1998, which sought to dismantle bilingual education – this initiative mandated that ELLs in California schools were taught in English; thus, English-immersion programs have been in place since then (see Baker, 2006).

The New Millennium
Subsequently, the advent of the new century continued to bring disappointing results for bilingual education. Two additional states joined

the English-Only Movement: Arizona (2000) and Massachusetts (2002). Arizona's Proposition 203, also known as "English for the Children," limited the types of programs available for ELLs. Massachusetts' Referendum Ballot Question 2 required English-only for ELLs after the 30 years of TBE. All of these initiatives were successfully supported by a California millionaire, Ron Unz, who has consistently fought against bilingual education. However, his main defeat was in Colorado (Amendment 31), in 2005, where he was unsuccessful in passing the initiative that would have also dismantled bilingual education and instead mandated English-only in public schools. In 2001, during the George W. Bush administration, the BEA was not reauthorized. Instead, it was replaced by the NCLB Act. This time, this piece of legislation met with bipartisan support (381 to 41 votes in the House of Congress). The NCLB Act was signed into law in 2002. The section of the law that addressed the case of ELLs changed from Title VII to Title III. Title III, "Language Instruction for Limited English Proficient and Immigrant Students," of the NCLB Act places a heavy accountability burden on the states. The states are now required to:

- identify languages other than English in the student population;
- develop academic assessments;
- use English language (oral, reading, writing) proficiency assessments with LEP students on an annual basis;
- include LEP Grade 3 to Grade 8 students in the assessment of reading and mathematics with appropriate accommodations; and
- administer reading assessments in English to students who have been in US schools for at least three years; but in 2004 states were allowed to exempt LEP students for one year from reading assessment during their first year of enrollment in a U.S. school and were allowed some flexibility in including former LEP students or adequate yearly progress calculations (Baker, 2006, p. 199).

In Title III, the focus is on English-only instruction for ELLs, and high-stakes assessments in English are the way to account for ELLs' progress. Title III clearly eliminates direct federal support for bilingual education. The competitive nature of Title VII grants were now replaced by formula grants that are administered by state education agencies that, in turn, "make subgrants to eligible local education agencies (i.e., school districts and charter schools" (Wright, 2010). Though "funding for LEP nearly doubled, and for the first time federal funds for LEP students went to nearly all eligible schools," (Wright, 2010, p. 59), the result has been that resources have been stretched even further, and they are still not enough to meet the demand. There is no mention of aiming at bilingualism or biliteracy development in this piece of legislation (Baker, 2006; Wright, 2010). As Wright (2010) noted, "developing and promoting bilingualism is no longer a federal goal. The recognition of the linguistic resources ELL students bring to school and the benefits of bilingualism to society so apparent in the 1994 reauthorization of Title VII have been stripped from the federal law" (p. 65). Also the Office of Bilingual Education and Minority Language Affairs (OBEMLA) established by Congress in 1974 was replaced by the National Clearinghouse for English Language Acquisition and Language Instructional Programs (NCLA). Most recently, in this current administration, President Obama has been critical of the strong emphasis on high-stakes testing of the NCLB, and he has expressed his support for bilingual education. However, there have been no "concrete proposals for legislative changes to the ESEA, which is now due for reauthorization" (Wright, 2010, p. 67). The major education reform of the Obama administration is the American Recovery and Reinvestment Act of 2009 (ARRA), which focuses on the disadvantaged, but it is not clear what the impact on the education of ELLs will be. Despite President Obama's critical stance on high stake testing, the emphasis on this has not been dropped, which continues to be disconcerting to ELL supporters who understand the detrimental effect of this single method of accountability to demonstrate ELL progress and effective practices on the part of teachers of ELLs (see Wright, 2010).

CONCLUSION

This chapter showed how what can be considered the history of bilingual special education has been closely connected to both the rich multilingual/multicultural history, and the laws that govern the U.S. educational system. It has shown how since the official beginning of bilingual education as a federal concern in the United States, many of these developments eventually translated into changes to educational policy. These changes have been the result of a contentious history of litigation, court rulings, and political battles fought across the country to ensure social justice. At present, given that NCLB Act continues to be in place, it is unlikely that Federal Government support will go in the direction of bilingual special education per se in the foreseeable future. NCLB Act eliminated the use of the word "bilingual" from Title III, thus ratifying an ideological and political stance that has remained unchanged, and legally uncontested, since it became law under the George W. Bush administration. In the current context, it should not be surprising to observe the lack of support toward any educational endeavor with the word *bilingual* in it. This situation has a direct detrimental impact on the main historical problem: the gross significant shortage of bilingual special educators. The primary goal of NCLB will only be accomplished when this problem no longer exists.

REFERENCES

Baca, L. M., & Cervantes, H. T. (2004). *The bilingual special education interface* (4th ed.). Columbus, OH: Pearson/Merrill Prentice Hall.

Baker, C. (2006). *Foundations of bilingual education and bilingualism* (4th ed.). Buffalo, NY: Multilingual Matters.

Banks, J. (2002). *An introduction to multicultural education* (3rd ed.). Boston, MA: Allyn and Bacon.

Cranston, A. (1974). Why the bilingual education amendments deserve support. *The Phi Delta Kappan, 56*(1), 58–59. Available at http://www.jstor.org/stable/20297789

Cordasco, F. (1969). The bilingual education act. *The Phi Delta Kappan, 51*(2), 75. Available at http://www.jstor.org/stable/20372531

Crawford, J. (2004). *Educating English learners: Language diversity in the classroom* (5th ed.). Los Angeles, CA: Bilingual Education Services.

Crawford, J., & Krashen, S. (2007). *English learners in American classrooms: 101 questions & 101 answers*. New York: Scholastic.

Cummins, J. (1991). *Bilingualism and special education*. Austin, TX: PRO-ED.

Davies, G. (2002). The great society after Johnson: The case of bilingual education. *The Journal of American History, 88*(4), 1405–1429. Available at http://www.jstor.org/stable/2700603

Hallahan, D. P., Kauffman, J. M., & Pullen, P. C. (2009). *Exceptional learners: An introduction to special education* (11th ed.). Available at http://instructors.coursesmart.com/9780137144853

Hamayan, E., Marler, B., Sanchez-Lopez, C., & Damico, J. (2007). *Special education considerations for English language learners*. Philadelphia, PA: Caslon.

Jarvis, G. L. (2006). A new look at bilingual education. *Hispania, 89*(1), 167–169. Available at http://www.jstor.org/stable/20063268

Lessow-Hurley, J. (2005). *The foundations of dual language instruction* (4th ed.). Boston, MA: Pearson/Allyn and Bacon.

Lyons, J. J. (1990). The past and future directions of federal-bilingual education policy. *Annals of the American Academy of Political and Social Science, 508*, 66–80. Available at http://www.jstor.org/stable/1047619

McLaren, P., & Muñoz, J. S. (2000). Contesting Whiteness: Critical perspective on the struggle for social justice. In: C. J. Ovando & P. Mclaren (Eds), *The politics of multiculturalism and bilingual education* (pp. 23–49). Boston, MA: McGraw Hill.

Moran, R. F. (1987). Bilingual education as a status conflict. *California Law Review, 75*(1), 321–362. Available at http://www.jstor.org/stable/3480582

Moran, R. F. (1988). The politics of discretion: Federal intervention in bilingual education. *California Law Review, 76*(6), 1249–1352. Available at http://www.jstor.org/stable/ 3480675

Ochoa, A. M., Pacheco, R., & Omark, D. R. (1983). Addressing the learning disability needs of limited-English proficient students: Beyond language and race issues. *Learning Disability Quarterly, 6*(4), 416–423. Available at http://www.jstor.orf/stable/1510528

Ooka Pang, V. (2005). *Multicultural education: A caring-centered approach* (2nd ed.). Boston, MA: McGraw Hill.

Ovando, J. C. (1983). Bilingual/bicultural education: Its legacy and its future. *The Phi Delta Kappan, 64*(8), 564–568. Available at http://www.jstor.org/stable/20386806

Reynolds, C. R., & Fletcher-Janzen, E. (Eds). (2007). *Encyclopedia of special education: A reference for education* (3rd cd.). San Francisco, CA: Wiley.

Rodriguez, D. (2005). A conceptual framework of bilingual special education teacher programs. In: J. Cohen, K. T. McAlister, K. Rolstad & J. MacSwan (Eds), *ISB4: Proceedings of the 4th international symposium on bilingualism* (pp. 1960–1969). Somerville, MA: Cascadilla Press.

Rossell, C. H. (2000). The federal bilingual education program. *Brookings Papers on Education Policy, 3*, 215–264. Available at http://www.jstor.org/stable/20067223

Tireman, L. S. (1941). Bilingual children. *Review of Educational Research, 11*(3), 340–352. Available at http://www.jstor.org/stable/1168704

Wiley, T. G. (2007). Accessing language rights in education: A brief history of the U.S. context. In: O. García & C. Baker (Eds), *Bilingual education: An introductory reader* (pp. 120–144). Buffalo, NY: Multilingual Matters.

Wright, W. E. (2010). *Foundations for teaching English language learners: Research, theory, policy and practice.* Philadelphia, PA: Caslon.

Yarborough, R. W. (1969). Bilingual education as a social force. *The Bulletin of the Rocky Mountain Modern Language Association, 23*(2), 69–72. Available at http://www.jstor. org/stable/1346696

CHAPTER 15

HISTORICAL AND CONTEMPORARY CONTEXTS, CHALLENGES, AND PROSPECTS IN THE EDUCATION OF STUDENTS WITH EXCEPTIONALITIES

Festus E. Obiakor

From time immemorial, individuals with exceptionalities have lived in our midst. They have existed, functioned, and participated in our societal functions in one way or another. For instance, the Jewish Talmud, Moslem Koran, and Christian Bible made particular references to persons who were atypical in nature. In fact, all societies have continued to focus on how to take care of their less fortunate, less powerful, disenfranchised, and disadvantaged (Obiakor & Algozzine, 1995). From these historical and contemporary contexts, it appears that efforts have concentrated on how to tolerate and/or be nice to persons with exceptionalities rather than on functional goal-directed efforts to truly educate them with *real pedagogical power*. Hilliard (1992) explained that real pedagogical power means that "all children who may have disabilities receive sophisticated, valid services that cause them to do better than they would have done if they had not received special services at all" (p. 168).

In the late 18th century, Jean Marc Itard, a French physician believed in real pedagogical power when he decided to take on the task of educating

History of Special Education
Advances in Special Education, Volume 21, 363–378
Copyright © 2011 by Emerald Group Publishing Limited
ISSN: 0270-4013/doi:10.1108/S0270-4013(2011)0000021018

Victor, the "wild boy" of Aveyron, France. Even this "wild boy" was able to acquire some skills, an indication that special education works. In the early parts of the 20th century, Dr. Alfred Binet, the brain behind the current Stanford–Binet Intelligence Scale, noted that human knowledge and/or intelligence can be improved. Using his experiences with his special class, Binet (1909) warned against the overreliance on his intelligence quotient tool. As he remarked, "It is parochial sense, the only one accessible to us, that we say that intelligence of these children has been increased. We have increased what constitutes the intelligence of a pupil: the capacity to learn and to assimilate instruction" (p.104). More than two decades ago, Gould (1981) decried the mismeasure of persons with different personal idiosyncrasies and argued that "if Binet's principles had been followed, and his tests consistently used as he intended, we would have been spared a major misuse of science in our century" (p. 155). In addition, he warned against the blind following of the theory of biological determinism (i.e., the belief that human attributes are only genetically based) because it hampers human valuing and the ability to engage in real pedagogical power. Goodlad (1993) corroborated Gould's premise and noted that:

> We appear incapable of getting beyond individuals as the units of assessment with the accompanying allocation of responsibility for success and failure. We must adopt as standard practice the kind of contextual appraisal that tells whether schools have in place the curriculum, materials, pedagogy, and other conditions necessary to the good education of individuals. The absence of these exposes and brings inequities that are the moral responsibility of a caring people in a just society to correct. (p. 20)

I strongly believe students with exceptionalities deserve to be educated. Apparently, measurable efforts have been made and continue to be made in this regard. The broad goal of special education continues to be to provide students with exceptionalities the education that is different from, additional to, and supplementary with those provided in the regular classroom with a systematic modification and adaptation of instructional techniques, materials, and equipment (Blackhurst & Berdine, 1993; Obiakor, Utley, & Rotatori, 2003; Smith & Tyler, 2010). To achieve this broad goal, it is critical to know who these students with exceptionalities are. Not surprisingly, these students fit into broadly or globally recognized categories of exceptionalities, namely, cognitive disabilities, learning disabilities, emotional/behavioral disorders, communication disorders/speech and language impairments, visual impairment/blindness, hearing impairment/deafness, autism, traumatic brain injury, gifted and talented, physical disabilities, and other health impairments. While some of these categories are fewer in some countries, every country wants to demonstrate its interest in helping students with exceptionalities to maximize their potential. Clearly, the questions continue to be: How have these students or those miscategorized to be these students historically maximized their fullest potential? How have our dynamic special education methods and techniques contemporarily mirrored our changing times in our complex world? In other words, have we learned anything from history? This chapter responds to these critical questions.

HISTORICAL CONTEXTS AND REALITIES

It is common knowledge that people like to associate with those who behave, look, speak, and act like themselves. Anyone who does not fall in that norm is traditionally perceived, treated, and educated differently (James, 1958; Obiakor, 2008, 2009). Clearly, students with exceptionalities have been discriminated against, ostracized, labeled, and called demeaning names (e.g., stupid, imbecile, and little dummies). Today, it has become increasingly clear that differences are a part of life. Advocates of students with exceptionalities have pressed for ways to positively respond to their needs in quantifiable ways (Obiakor, Harris, & Beachum, in press). In the United States, it is impossible to divorce the education of these students from the Civil Rights Movement and the subsequent events that followed. To a great extent, the education of these students has been historically influenced by social developments and court decisions in the 1950s and 1960s. For example, the landmark *Brown v. Board of Education of Topeka* (1954) case was a civil rights case that declared separate education as unequal education and unconstitutional (Obiakor, 2009). This was significant because it had the goal of ending racial segregation in schools. Logically, this opened doors of advocacy for students with exceptionalities. The ruling of this case became a catalyst that prompted parents and professionals to lobby for equitable education for their students.

The *Brown* ruling, in the United States, encouraged parent groups to petition the courts to allow students with exceptionalities to be educated in public schools. In addition, it led to more landmark cases that have had historical impacts. For example, the P*ennsylvania Association for Retarded Children v. Commonwealth of Pennsylvania* (1972) (PARC) case held that children could not be denied access to public schools, and entitled them to a free and appropriate public education (FAPE). In the *Mills v. Board of Education* (Mills, 1972) case, a class action lawsuit was filed on behalf of 18,000 children with varied exceptionalities in the Washington,

DC schools. In this case, the court ordered the district to educate all children, including those with special needs and further clarified that specific procedures had to be followed to determine whether a student should receive special services. Generally, these cases and other subsequent cases formed the framework for the laws that currently guide the field of special education (Yell, 2004).

In the United States, many laws have historically impacted the fields of general and special education. For instance, the 1964 Civil Rights Act (PL 88-352) provided legal rights to equality in education and other sectors of human interactions. In 1973, Section 504 of the Vocational Rehabilitation Act (PL 93-112) was passed to provide persons with exceptionalities with (a) free and appropriate public education, (b) civil rights, (c) accessibility of programs, and (d) employability rights. In 1975, the Education of All Handicapped Children's Act (PL-94-142) was passed with the following fundamental ingredients: (a) education for students from 3–21 years, (b) free and appropriate public education, (c) identification of students, (d) nondiscriminatory assessments, (e) placement in the least restrictive environment (LRE), (f) confidentiality of information, (g) procedural safeguards, and (h) development of individualized education plans (IEP). In 1986, PL 94-142 was amended to accommodate young children from birth to three years. Education of All Handicapped Children Act Amendments (1986) (PL 99-457) was enacted to provide not just IEPs for children but also individual family support programs (IFSP) for parents and guardians. In 1990, PL-94-142 was renamed as the Individuals with Disabilities Education Act (IDEA; PL101-476). This Act involved funding for states to provide educational services to students from birth through 21 years, and ensured procedural safeguards for parents that guarantee meaningful participation in the evaluation process (Katisyannis, Yell, & Bradley, 2001). Additionally, IDEA guaranteed improvement in the education of students with exceptionalities through research training and technical support and transitional supports for students when they are 16 years old. To challenge the private sectors, the 1990 Americans with Disabilities Act (ADA; PL101-336) was passed to provide more societal opportunities for persons with special needs. In 1997, IDEA was reauthorized as PL 105-17 to facilitate disciplinary procedures and reduce litigation costs. In 2001, the No Child Left Behind Act (NCLB; PL 107-110) was passed to educate all learners and quantifiably account for their progress at all levels. Later, in 2004, IDEA was again reauthorized as the Individuals with Disabilities Education Improvement Act (IDEIA; PL 108-446). This law mandated that teachers of students with exceptionalities be highly qualified, meaning they must be certified in the content areas that they are teaching (Smith, 2005). No doubt, these governmental efforts would not have been possible without the historical advocacy of the citizenry.

CONTEMPORARY CHALLENGES AND PROSPECTS

The goal of any educational program is to maximize the fullest potential of students. In other words, the goal must be to truly leave no child behind despite his/her ability or disability. The critical question remains: Do we stay the course, resist change, or move forward in the education of students with exceptionalities? Almost two decades ago, Schrag (1993) confirmed that "the proportion of students being served within special education programs today and in the future is changing, which requires closer integration and coordination of services within the educational system and with a broader array of health and social services" (p. 208). The response of the federal government with regard to these imperatives has been "accountability without accountability" (i.e., accountability that focuses narrowly on the exclusion of students via assessment). Sadly, some accountability measures are already hurting the spirit of special education. In his piece titled, "The Death of Special Education," Lieberman (2001) argued that:

Special education has been swallowed by the beast: the school system, with its mandated curriculum, mandated tests, and mandated standards. Now, children with disabilities are entitled – no, are practically required – to have the same education as every other child, regardless of whether or not that education is of high quality or is appropriate for a child with a disability. (p. 39)

While it is iconoclastic to believe special education "has been swallowed by the beast" because of accountability challenges that are forced upon it, it is equally unrealistic to assume that we should just "stay the course" in special education. Any field or profession that does not believe in positive change is dead. Clearly, recent demographic changes in our society have challenged general and special educators and leaders to look for innovative ways to maximize all students' potential in school programs (Obiakor, 2007; Rueda, 2007). As Rueda argued, "given the longstanding but continuing controversy over the issue of overrepresentation of diverse students in special education, the future implications for identification, referral, assessment, and instructions are abundant" (2007, p. 292). To respond to contemporary realities, avoid historical mistakes, and advance the field of special education, efforts must be made to (a) listen to new voices in the field and (b) shift paradigms in professional preparation.

Listening to New Voices in the Field

Of late, there have been some traditional moves to silence new voices and/or critics of the current system of special education that tends to overrepresent culturally diverse students (e.g., African American learners) in programs for children with emotional/behavioral disorders and under-represent them in programs for students with gifts and talents. Kauffman (2002, 2003a, 2003b, 2004), Mostert, Kauffman, and Kavale (2003), and Sasso (2003) agreed that it is wrong to criticize the current system of special education. In fact, in their works, they have been less receptive on the issue of the disproportionate representation of culturally and linguistically diverse students in special education. For instance, Kauffman (2003b) argued that:

> The assumption that special education, which is at its best the fair treatment of disability, *creates* stigma is not just wrong; it is perverse. It confuses treatment with cause, just as if we were to make the assumption that identifying and treating cancer caused the stigma that used to accompany having it. Without willingness to talk about disabilities in a simple and straightforward way, we cannot address the problem of stigma. Euphemisms are cloaks that hide nothing effectively. Always and inevitably, they are stumbling rags that trip up prevention. (p. 196)

There is no doubt that the current special education system works for some children. However, the question is: Do critics of the current system of special education believe in the spirit of special education? Sure, they do! The reality is that special education has become an important educational phenomenon that works well when it does not misidentify, misassess, miscategorize, misplace, and misinstruct students who are racially, culturally, linguistically, and socioeconomically different. It seems unpro-fessional and immoral to hide under the cloak of special education to get rid of students just because they exhibit different behavioral and learning styles. Again, while there is great need for evidence-based practice in special education, I strongly disagree with Kauffman's (2003a) assertion that "if you discount science as a way of finding things out and believe that special education is fundamentally flawed, second rate, ineffective, unfair, and oppressive, then you're not going to use it for prevention" (p. 206). It is my belief that science is necessary; however, the indiscriminate use of a scientifically proven medication to cure all illnesses is dangerous, unethical, and immoral (Obiakor, 2004). The "heart" or respect for humanity must be incorporated into whatever we do as professionals even though one's "heart" or spirituality cannot be measured. Science may not always be the only answer in special education; feelings should matter too! Even in the medical field, the touch of the doctor and the feelings of the patient can facilitate and advance the healing process. Why should the education of students with exceptionalities be any different?

In their study titled, "Do race of student and race of teacher influence ratings of emotional and behavioral problem characteristics of students with emotional disturbance?", Cullinan and Kauffman (2005) concluded that "results did not support the position that, among students with ED [emotional disturbance], overrepresentation of African Americans arises from racial bias in teacher perceptions of emotional and behavioral problems" (p. 393). Coupled with the study's limitations and weaknesses as identified by Cullinan and Kauffman, there is the presumption of innocence of teachers just because of their race or culture. In many urban schools in the United States, there are culturally and linguistically diverse professionals who through their actions have devastated the lives of students and their parents (Obiakor, 2001b, 2003). Also in the United States, historically, there have been some Black policemen or women who have wrongfully arrested, brutalized, shot, and killed fellow Blacks in strange attempts to maintain law and order. Their race or culture must never be an alibi that exonerates them from being criticized or sued for violating the civil rights of others (Prater, 2006). Clearly, on issues of misidentification, misassessment, miscategorization, misplacement, and misinstruction of students, a poorly prepared general and special educator will not advance the education of all students (Obiakor, 1999, 2001b, 2003, 2004, 2007, 2008, 2009; Obiakor & Beachum, 2005; Obiakor & Ford, 2002; Obiakor, Grant, & Dooley, 2002; Utley & Obiakor, 2001).

I am more convinced than before that we must listen to new voices as we advance creative strategies for educating *all* students, their exceptionalities notwithstanding. As it appears, we cannot help *all* students unless we take advantage of the Comprehensive Support Model (CSM), a model that taps on the energies of *all* stakeholders (Obiakor, 2003, 2007, 2008, 2009; Obiakor et al., 2002). Based on the multidimensional nature of the CSM, the contributions of individual students, families, schools, communities, and government agencies are teamed together. While there are no magic solutions, all stakeholders can collaborate and consult for the common good. The individual "self" is important because without personal responsibility or self-improvement, it will be difficult to manage behavior and learning problems. The family is important because it is the cornerstone of the special student and the bridge that connects the student with the school. The school is important because it has general and special education teachers and professionals who have the power to shift their paradigms regarding demographic changes. The community is important because it provides a variety of opportunities and choices for our children and youth who have been labeled as "trouble makers" or "problem students" because of their different styles. Finally, the local, state, and federal governments are important because they generate equitable policies that strengthen the multiple voices of all students. Evidently, a responsible government must be worried about the civil rights of its people, even those of people who have special needs or exhibit nonproductive and antisocial behaviors (Obiakor et al., 2002).

To advance the historical importance of special education, the whole process of special education must be available to those students who have exceptionalities. It is imperative that general and special educators and leaders demonstrate their willingness to listen to new voices by:

- developing and using identification, assessment, and instructional strategies that function within the context of cultural competence;
- creating a collaborative system of community support that focuses on eradicating social stereotyping based on race, ethnicity, national origin, gender, and socioeconomic status;
- developing an awareness and appreciation for the many family forms that value individual differences and strengths;
- thwarting conditions that lead to violence in the home or community and cultivate a sense of safety for children and families;
- advocating economic policies and human services that are pro-family by virtue of proven outcomes;
- promoting culturally competent practices in schools and in the larger society to respect differences in worldviews and learning styles among individuals;
- advocating expanded services that provide for affordable quality child-care to meet the varied needs of all families and children;
- developing collaborative community approaches to problem solving that involve students, parents, schools, and community leaders;
- recognizing that the focus of the problem in at-risk situations is not only in the individual but also in institutional barriers in the environment;
- reconfiguring curricula that incorporate culturally sensitive variables;

- reinstituting rites of passage and service opportunities that cultivate a sense of belonging and resiliency in youth; and
- broadening visions in educational reform that include economic reform and the investment in human capital.

Apparently, by listening to new voices in this age of change, general and special educators can assist all students in school programs. For instance, they can prevent and manage violent behaviors that have created psychological setbacks for students by shifting their own personal paradigms. In contrast to the "get-tough" no-nonsense approaches (e.g., zero tolerance or three-strikes-you-are-out disciplinary models), school personnel can teach prosocial skills and educate children to manage interpersonal conflicts nonviolently (Goldstein, 1999; Long, 1997; Obiakor, 2001a). After a lifetime of experience with youth with emotional/behavioral disorders, Long (1997) simply suggested using "kindness" or what we call the "heart." General and special educators employing caring transitional strategies must focus on a variety of communication skills that enable young people to manage their behaviors and respond to others in ways that do not provoke confrontations. They must revisit the traditional emphasis on intelligence or academic achievement that seems to downplay the emotional intelligence and resiliency needed to survive in a changing society (Gardner, 1993; Goleman, 1995; Obiakor et al., 2004; Obiakor, Mehring, & Schwenn, 1997). As Goleman (1995) remarked, emotional intelligence entails "abilities such as being able to motivate oneself and persist in the face of frustrations; to control impulse and delay gratification; to regulate one's moods and keep distress from swamping the ability to think; to empathize and to hope" (p. 34). He added:

> Academic intelligence offers virtually no preparation for the turmoil – or opportunity – life's vicissitudes bring. Yet even though a high IQ is no guarantee of prosperity, prestige, or happiness in life, our schools and our culture fixate on academic abilities, ignoring emotional intelligence, a set of traits – some might call it character – that also matters immensely for our personal destiny. (p. 36)

Some proactive measures have been found to foster emotional intelligence in all learners, including those with exceptionalities! These measures incorporate partnership programs, prosocial skills instruction programs, and mentorship programs. How can students value differences if differences are not valued in their homes, schools, and communities? How can they work together if adults and communities fail to work together? People who have emotional intelligence skills can help dissipate some of the cultural forms of "heartlessness" that permeate schools, for example, putdowns based upon race, ethnicity, gender, or disability. Students must work together, their families must cooperate with each other, their schools must work collaboratively, and their communities must work together (Obiakor, 2004; Obiakor et al., 2002). These collaborative and consultative behaviors frequently lead to cooperative resolutions of situations at all levels and help students, parents, and professionals to maximize their potential.

Shifting Paradigms in Professional Preparation

Clearly, all students exhibit special and different learning and behavioral patterns. As a consequence, they are intentionally or unintentionally misidentified, misassessed, miscategorized, misplaced, and misinstructed in school programs (Mukuria & Obiakor, 2004; Obiakor, 1999, 2001b, 2003a, 2003b, 2007; Obiakor & Beachum, 2005; Obiakor & Wilder, 2003; Utley & Obiakor, 2001). What then are the roles of professional preparation programs for learners who are different? Even with the best intentions, many colleges and universities have failed to satisfactorily prepare educators for today's classrooms. Years ago, Haberman (1995) asserted that upon completion of traditional teaching programs teachers and service providers are as prepared for today's classrooms as a swimmer who prepared for the English Channel by training in the university swimming pool. It is important that teacher educators and leaders take the bull by its horns! They must be professionally responsible – they must prepare general and special educators and leaders to respond to demographic changes. They must shift their own paradigms to prepare teachers and leaders who can shift their paradigms (Smith, Richards, MacGrawley, & Obiakor, 2004; Winzer & Mazurek, 1998). For those engaged in research, they must broaden their horizons in their understanding of nature versus nurture and other human behaviors and attributes. As scholars, they must go beyond the archaic theory of biological determinism and the myth of socioeconomic dissonance to make sense of their research (Fordham, 1988; Gould, 1981; Weikart, 1977). For instance, Weikart (1977) warned that the deficit model of thinking, when applied to a certain population, "seems to limit potential assistance to that group because it channels thinking in ways that emphasize weaknesses rather than strengths, and it interprets differences from the norm as individual deficits" (p. 175). The logical extension is that:

> We cannot limit ourselves to the identification of trait dimensions or typological classifications across individuals without also considering the characteristics of the environments within which individuals function. Nor can we limit ourselves to an

analysis of the environmental determinants of human differences without also considering the hereditary determinants. Finally, we have to ask ourselves what kind of society is most desirable for the expression of human diversity – for the opportunity for each of us to grow as individuals and at the same time not infringe on the rights of others to develop their own individuality. (Minton & Schneider, 1985, p. 489)

Minton and Schneider's (1985) statements have far-reaching implications for research, policy, and practice in general, and special education and leadership. For instance, first, research that focuses on behavior problems of children and youth needs to address measures that will help us to understand them. When we understand them, we assist them to be functional, goal-directed decision makers in our complex society. Put another way, research that focuses on underlying pathological attributes of students needs to be valued with caution because such a research is deficit-oriented and lacks measurable or observable solution-based attributes. Second, research, policy, and practice ought to go hand-in-glove. Many years ago, Keogh (1990) noted that "from this perspective, policy should follow research, and change should be found in evidence" (p. 186). It is apparent that something is wrong with our intervention strategies for culturally diverse students with exceptionalities. Third, research that divorces itself from the fundamental principles of individualized instructional programming fails to appreciate or value individual differences in people. In the end, we need redirection in research funding and projects to reflect culturally sensitive proactive measures. Research studies with skewed divisive, emotionally loaded, political underpinnings must be discouraged in special education. Any research that does not lend itself to common-sense problem-solving interpretation and practice must be viewed with caution. Fortunately today, most scholarly publications (e.g., *Behavior Disorders, Exceptional Children, Intervention in School and Clinic, Journal of Special Education, Multicultural Learning and Teaching, Multiple Voices, Remedial and Special Education, Teacher Education and Special Education*) are demanding practical implications to works. Consequently, scholars, educators, and leaders must begin to broaden their definitions, theories, and intervention models to reduce illusory conclusions, perceptual assumptions, and prejudicial generalizations (Obiakor, 2007). Special students need specialized training of professionals. Strategies that empower all students must be developed if education is to get its desired respect. For instance, teacher educators and leaders must begin to realign themselves with new ways of thinking that go beyond games and politics.

It has become very apparent that poorly prepared teachers teach poorly. It is important that teacher educators and leaders practice what they preach.

In this age of change, they must use divergent techniques to prepare future educators who will, in turn, use divergent techniques to teach learners who exhibit different styles and exceptionalities. To look for the "magic pill" that can cure educational problems of *all* students is not realistic. However, the key is for teacher educators and leaders to prepare those who value individual differences and exceptionalities (Ford, Obiakor, & Patton, 1995; Obiakor, 2001b, 2003, 2007; Obiakor & Beachum, 2005; Obiakor & Ford, 2002; Obiakor, Harris, Rotatori, & Algozzine, 2010; Obiakor, Schwenn, & Rotatori, 1999; Obiakor et al., 2002; Wilder, Obiakor, & Algozzine, 2003). By so doing, they become aware of emotional first-aids needed to address crises confronting their students (Obiakor et al., 1997). Earlier, Price (1991) explained that it is nonproductive to bemoan new multicultural paradigms that incorporate quality and equity in educational programming. We must avoid any kind of multiculturalism that tends to project "goodness" with underlying negative intentions, and phony sense of community that hampers ways to increase knowledge about the interactions between human behaviors and cultural styles. To this end, teacher educators and leaders must make efforts to recruit and retain culturally sensitive students, faculty, and staff to remain competitive in this age of change (Obiakor, 2001b, 2007; Obiakor & Beachum, 2005; Obiakor & Utley, 1997; Wald, 1996).

CONCLUSION

While the United States and other countries have done a commendable job of instituting historical policies and legal mandates to protect students with exceptionalities and provide them with equal public education, the interpretation and implementation of those laws have many loopholes that need to be sealed. Overrepresentation of students from culturally and linguistically diverse background in special education has caused great concerns. If students have been misplaced, it means that their educational needs cannot be met. Appropriate placement should be in least restrictive environments in which students' cultures and language do not result in misidentification, misassessment, miscategorization, and misplacement. The heart and soul of quality service delivery for students with exceptionalities must include nonrestrictive environments and settings that maximize their potential. Finally, such environments must be culturally, linguistically, and socioeconomically accepting.

REFERENCES

Americans with Disabilities Act (1990). Pub. L. No. 101-336.

Binet, A. (1909). *Les ideas modernes sur les enfants (Modern ideas for children)*. Paris, France: Hammarion.

Blackhurst, A. E., & Berdine, W. H. (1993). *An introduction to special education* (3rd ed.). New York: Harper Collins.

Brown v. Board of Education of Topeka Kansas, 347 U.S. 483, 745-ct-686, 98 L. Ed. 873, 530. 0. 326 (1954).

Civil Rights Act (1964). Pub. L. No. 88-352.

Cullinan, D., & Kauffman, J. M. (2005). Do race of student and race of teacher influence ratings of emotional and behavioral problem characteristics of students with emotional disturbance? *Behavioral Disorders, 30*(August), 393–402.

Education of All Handicapped Children Act (1975). Pub. L. No. 94-142.

Education of All Handicapped Children Act Amendments (1986). Pub. L. No 99-457.

Ford, B. A., Obiakor, F. E., & Patton, J. M. (1995). *Effective education for African American exceptional learners: New perspectives*. Austin, TX: Pro-Ed.

Fordham, S. (1988). Racelessness as a factor in Black student's success. Pragmatic strategy or Pyrrhic victory. *Harvard Educational Review, 58*, 54–84.

Gardner, H. (1993). *Multiple intelligences: The theory of practice*. New York: Basic Books.

Goldstein, A. P. (1999). *The prepare curriculum: Teaching prosocial competencies*. Champaign, IL: Research Press.

Goleman, D. (1995). *Emotional intelligence: Why it matters more than IQ*. New York: Bantam Books.

Goodlad, J. I. (1993). Access to knowledge. In: J. I. Goodlad & T. L. Lovitt (Eds), *Integrating general and special education* (pp. 1–22). New York: Merrill.

Gould, S. J. (1981). *The mismeasure of men*. New York: W. W. Morton.

Haberman, M. (1995). *Star teachers of children in poverty*. West Lafayette, IN: Kappa Delta Pi.

Hilliard, A. G. (1992). The pitfalls and practices of special education practice. *Exceptional Children, 59*(October/November), 168–172.

Individuals with Disabilities Education Act (1990). Pub. L. No. 101-476.

Individuals with Disabilities Education Act (1997). Pub L. No. 105-17.

Individuals with Disabilities Education Improvement Act (2004). Pub. L. No. 108-446.

James, W. (1958). *Talk to teachers on psychology, and to students on life's ideas*. New York: W. W. Norton.

Katisyannis, A., Yell, M. L., & Bradley, R. (2001). Reflections of the 25th anniversary of the Individuals with Exceptionalities Education Act. *Remedial and Special Education, 22*(6), 324–339.

Kauffman, J. M. (2002). *Education deform? Bright people sometimes say stupid things about education*. Lanham, MD: Scarecrow Education.

Kauffman, J. M. (2003a). Reflections on the field. *Behavioral Disorders, 28*(May), 205–208.

Kauffman, J. M. (2003b). Appearances, stigma, and prevention. *Remedial and Special Education, 24*(July/August), 195–198.

Kauffman, J. M. (2004). The President's commission and the devaluation of special education. *Education and Treatment of Children, 27*, 307–324.

Keogh, B. K. (1990). Narrowing the gap between policy and practice. *Exceptional Children*, *57*(2), 186–190.

Lieberman, L. M. (2001). The death of special education. *Education Week*, January 17, 39–41.

Long, N. J. (1997). The therapeutic power of kindness. *Reclaiming Children and Youth*, *5*, 242–246.

Mills v. Board of Education of the District of Columbia (1992). 348 f. Supp. 866 (D.D.C.1972).

Minton, H., & Schneider, F. (1985). *Differential psychology*. Prospect Heights, IL: Waveland Press.

Mostert, M. P., Kauffman, J. M., & Kavale, K. A. (2003). Truth and consequences. *Behavioral Disorders*, *28*(August), 333–347.

Mukuria, G., & Obiakor, F. E. (2004). Special education issues and African diaspora. *Journal of International Special Needs Education*, *7*, 12–17.

No Child Left Behind Act (2001). Pub. L. No. 107-110.

Obiakor, F. E. (1999). Teacher expectations of minority exceptional learners: Impact on "accuracy" of self-concepts. *Exceptional Children*, *66*, 39–53.

Obiakor, F. E. (2001a). Developing emotional intelligence in learners with behavioral problems: Refocusing special education. *Behavior Disorders*, *26*, 321–331.

Obiakor, F. E. (2001b). *It even happens in good schools: Responding to cultural diversity in today's classrooms*. Thousand Oaks, CA: Corwin Press.

Obiakor, F. E. (2003). To asses or not, Is that the question? Who benefits from the No Child Left Behind Act? Invited scholar presentation sponsored by the Institute on Multicultural Relations and the Milwaukee Urban League, University of Wisconsin- Milwaukee, Milwaukee, WI.

Obiakor, F. E. (2004). Impact of changing demographics on public education for culturally diverse learners with behavior problems: Implications for teacher preparation. In: L. M. Bullock & R. A. Gable (Eds), *Quality personnel preparation in emotional/ behavioral disorders: Current perspectives and future directions* (pp. 51–63). Denton, TX: Institute for Behavioral and Learning Differences at the University of North Texas.

Obiakor, F. E. (2007). *Multicultural special education: Culturally responsive teaching*. Upper Saddle River, NJ: Pearson/Merrill Prentice Hall.

Obiakor, F. E. (2008). *The eight-step approach to multicultural learning and teaching* (3rd ed.). Dubuque, IA: Kendall/Hunt.

Obiakor, F. E. (2009). Educating African American urban learners: Brown in context. In: M. C. Brown, II & R. D. Bartee (Eds), *The broken cisterns of African American education* (pp. 61–72). Charlotte, NC: Information Age.

Obiakor, F. E., & Algozzine, B. (1995). Educating learners with problem behaviors: An unresolved issue for general and special educators. In: F. E. Obiakor & B. Algozzine (Eds), *Managing problem behaviors: Perspectives for general and special educators* (pp. 1–19). Dubuque, IA: Kendall/Hunt.

Obiakor, F. E., & Beachum, F. D. (2005). *Urban education for the 21st century: Research, issues, and perspectives*. Springfield, IL: Charles C. Thomas.

Obiakor, F. E., Enwefa, S., Utley, C., Obi, S. O., Gwalla-Ogisi, N., & Enwefa, R. (2004). *Serving culturally and linguistically diverse students with emotional and behavioral disorders*. Arlington, VA: Council for Children with Behavioral Disorders, the Council for Exceptional Children.

Obiakor, F. E., & Ford, B. A. (2002). *Creating successful learning environments for Africa American learners with exceptionalities*. Thousand Oaks, CA: Corwin Press.

Obiakor, F. E., Grant, P. A., & Dooley, E. A. (2002). *Educating all learners: Refocusing the comprehensive support model.* Springfield, IL: Charles C. Thomas.

Obiakor, F. E., Harris, M. K., & Beachum, F. D. (in press). The state of special education for African American learners in Milwaukee. In G. Williams & F. E. Obiakor (Eds.), *The state of education of urban learners and possible solutions: The Milwaukee experience.* Dubuque, IA: Kendall/Hunt.

Obiakor, F. E., Harris, M. K., Rotatori, A. F., & Algozzine, B. (2010). Beyond traditional placement: Making inclusion work in the general education classroom. In: F. E. Obiakor, J. P. Bakken & A. F. Rotatori (Eds), *Current issues and trends in special education: Identification, assessment, and instruction* (Vol. 19, pp. 141–156). Bingley, UK: Emerald Group Publishing Limited.

Obiakor, F. E., Mehring, T. A., & Schwenn, J. O. (1997). *Disruption, disaster, and death: Helping students deal with crises.* Arlington, VA: Council for Exceptional Children.

Obiakor, F. E., Schwenn, J. O., & Rotatori, A. F. (1999). *Multicultural education for learners with exceptionalities* (Vol. 12). Stanford, CT: JAI Press.

Obiakor, F. E., & Utley, C. A. (1997). Rethinking preservice preparation for teachers in the learning disabilities field: Workable multicultural strategies. *Learning Disabilities Research and Practice, 12,* 100–106.

Obiakor, F. E., Utley, C. A., & Rotatori, A. F. (2003). *Effective education for learners with exceptionalities* (Vol. 15). Oxford, England: Elsevier Science/JAI Press.

Obiakor, F. E., & Wilder, L. K. (2003). Disproportionate representation in special education: What principals can do. *Principal Leadership, 4*(October), 17–21.

Pennsylvania Association for Retarded Children v. Commonwealth of Pennsylvania, 343 F. Supp. 279 (D. C. Pa 1972).

Prater, L. P. (2006). Institutionalized terror: A social system's analysis of police brutality. Paper presented at the Annual Professional Development Conference of the National Social Science Association, San Francisco, CA, October

Price, H. B. (1991). Multicultural education: The debate. *Humanities in the South, Fall,* 1–8.

Rueda, R. (2007). Multicultural special education: Future perspectives. In: F. E. Obiakor (Ed.), *Multicultural special education: Culturally responsive teaching* (pp. 290–297). Upper Saddle River, NJ: Pearson/Merrill Prentice Hall.

Sasso, G. M. (2003). An examined life: A response to James Kauffman's reflections on the field. *Behavioral Disorders, 28*(May), 209–211.

Schrag, J. A. (1993). Restructuring schools for better alignment of general and special education. In: J. I. Goodlad & T. C. Lovitt (Eds), *Integrating general and special education* (pp. 203–227). New York: Merrill.

Smith, D. D., & Tyler, N. C. (2010). *Introduction to special education: Making a difference* (7th ed.). Upper Saddle River, NJ: Merrill.

Smith, T. B., Richards, P. S., MacGrawley, H., & Obiakor, F. E. (2004). Practicing multiculturalism: An introduction. In: T. B. Smith (Ed.), *Practicing multiculturalism: Affirming diversity in counseling and psychology* (pp. 3–16). Boston, MA: Allyn & Bacon.

Smith, T. E. (2005). IDEA 2004: Another round in the reauthorization process. *Remedial and Special Education, 26*(6), 314–323.

Utley, C. A., & Obiakor, F. E. (2001). *Special education, multicultural education, and school reform: Components of quality education for learners with mild disabilities.* Springfield, IL: Charles C. Thomas.

Vocational Rehabilitation Act (1973). Pub. L. No. 93-112.

Wald, J. L. (1996). Diversity in the special education training force. *NCPSE News*, 1, 1 & 6.
Weikart, D. P. (1977). Preschool intervention for the disadvantaged child: A challenge for special education. In: H. H. Spicker, K. J. Anastasiow & W. L. Hodges (Eds), *Children with special needs: Early development and education* (pp. 73–89). Minneapolis, MN: Leadership Training Institute/Special Education, University of Minnesota.
Wilder, L. K., Obiakor, F. E., & Algozzine, B. (2003). Homeless students in special education: Beyond the myth of socioeconomic dissonance. *The Journal of At-Risk Issues*, 9(Summer), 9–16.
Winzer, M. A., & Mazurek, K. (1998). *Special education in multicultural contexts*. Upper Saddle River, NJ: Merrill/Prentice Hall.
Yell, M. L. (2004). *The law and special education* (2nd ed.). Upper Saddle River, NJ: Prentice Hall.